# STORYTELLER

# A LIFE OF ERSKINE CALDWELL

## C. J. Stevens

JOHN WADE, *PUBLISHER*
*Phillips, Maine 04966*

Published by John Wade, Publisher
P.O. Box 303
Phillips, Maine 04966

All acknowledgments for permission to use previously published or unpublished material will be found following the "Asides" section in the Appendix.

includes index

Storyteller: A Life of Erskine Caldwell
1. Caldwell, Erskine, 1903-1987—Biography
2. 20th Century—American novelist and short story writer
3. United States—20th Century Literary Scene and Response to his Work

Library of Congress Control Number:
00-133004

ISBN # 1-882425-11-1 cloth

Manufactured in the United States of America

FIRST EDITION

Books by C. J. Stevens

*Poetry*
Beginnings and Other Poems
Circling at the Chain's Length
Hang-Ups
Selected Poems

*Biography*
Lawrence at Tregerthen (D. H. Lawrence in Cornwall)
The Cornish Nightmare (D. H. Lawrence)
Storyteller: A Life of Erskine Caldwell

*History and Adventure*
The Next Bend in the River (Gold Mining in Maine)
Maine Mining Adventures
The Buried Treasures of Maine

*Translations*
Poems from Holland and Belgium

*Animal Behavior*
One Day With a Goat Herd

*Fiction*
The Folks From Greeley's Mill
Confessions

# CONTENTS

"I don't think I've ever written a line for any other purpose than to tell a story."

ERSKINE CALDWELL

from *The Rocky Mountain News*
January 20, 1947

*STORYTELLER*

*A LIFE OF ERSKINE CALDWELL*

# OPENINGS

Erskine Caldwell had little control over the things he was writing; he never allowed himself the luxury of interfering when a character in his story misbehaved. If a person stole, swore, or committed incest, there was just no helping it. He, the author, had no right to shackle this fictional offender with virtues. Every tale he wrote was a discovery as one sentence sparked another until the conclusion—Caldwell had to wait and see the unveiling of words much in the way a bystander witnesses an accident.

An early practitioner of black humor, his naturalism, combined with emotion and irrationality, often caught critics off guard and gave his fiction a uniqueness that captured both the frequent and casual reader. He was difficult to pigeonhole, and as a consequence, Caldwell has been labeled realist, social critic, naturalist, symbolist, romanticist, and humorist. Probably, he stood in all corners of this hexagon at times in his writing career, but to himself he was a worker of words.

Blessed with a colloquial authenticity, he gave his fictional characters a rugged durability by keeping the diction simple—he sidestepped the rhetorical with a factual prose that sharpened dialogue. Slapstick bubbled from his pages in combinations rarely exhibited by contemporaries. Caldwell possessed the true burlesque touch: vulgarity mixed with rural humor and folklore, neurotic situations passed off as ordinary occurrences, and tragedy which began with laughter and ended without remorse.

To a multitude of readers, his robust style peeled away the veneer of civilization and revealed a country peopled with victims and degenerates. So many of his stories spoke in the vernacular of the common folk, and the characters he created were strong and unforgettable as they strutted their foibles—syphilis, miscegenation, and adultery were ordinary occurrences. There existed a mob of customers who turned the pages of his novels in search of explicit scenes to match what was promised on garish book covers. He had, however, a loyal and solid following: those admirers who came to him for the telling of a tale much in the same way as they picked up a book by Hemingway to be swept along on a tide of love and adventure.

In this country, during the mid-forties and early fifties, inexpensive editions of Caldwell's books on circular "Spin-It" racks in drugstores and corner groceries became a distribution sensation. His paperback publisher, New American Library, proclaimed him to be "The World's Best-Selling Author!" It was more than a buzzword gathering to decorate the eye-teasing jackets—only the Bible was ahead in sales. Overseas, in dozens of countries, his popularity grew. Today, his books have sold more than 80 million copies in forty-three languages, and this does not include pirated editions which probably have appeared in the hundreds of thousands.

After the publication of *Tobacco Road* and *God's Little Acre* in the early thirties, William Faulkner ranked him among America's five most promising novelists. Thomas Wolfe was given the lead, followed by Faulkner, John Dos Passos, Caldwell, and Hemingway. His reputation soared from 1934 to 1944 and then nose-dived. By the end of World War II, the literary establishment shunned him, though he had a huge following for several more years.

Caldwell became better known to the general public through Jack Kirkland's stage adaptation of *Tobacco Road*. The drama ran for seven and a half years on Broadway and there were three road companies that crisscrossed America—the production closed in New York after a record-breaking 3,180th performance. Controversy chased *Road*, and whenever city fathers closed it there were longer lines at ticket booths. Over a five-year period, Caldwell and his associates defended the play thirty-six times in court.

Theatergoers who saw the production read Caldwell's books, and many were jolted by his style: a frank, plain, open delivery—there wasn't a writer around quite like him. In many ways his creations epitomized the 1930s as he roamed the country in search of its essential Americanness, spurred by his fascination with the lives of ordinary people and his outrage when social injustice overtook them. This was an author who was aware of the conflict between new and old ideas while looking forward rather than back. "Caldwell," declared Malcolm Cowley in *And I Worked at the Writer's Trade*, "presents to the world, and to himself, the writing man as an ideal....His only aim is to set down, in the simplest words, a true unplotted record of people without yesterdays. Past literature does not exist for him, and he is scarcely aware of having rivals in the present. As with Adam in the Garden, every statement he makes is news."

He had no desire to praise his Georgia heritage, and from the beginning he felt compelled to expose Southern flaws. Agrarians labeled him a scalawag; he was the traitor who found more inspiration from literary naturalists and Marxists than from his region's past. "I'm not read very much in the South," admitted Caldwell, "because they are very touchy about what they regard as unkind criticism." He was read more in Communist countries than in his native Georgia, he once told a reporter, and explained: "Russians and Europeans get a less erroneous image of America from my books than they do from American films about a mink-penthouse-Cadillac society."

There were 25 novels, 150 short stories, 12 nonfiction collections, and even 2 books for young readers. The novels *Tobacco Road* and *God's Little Acre* endured (they often can be found in bookstores), and a number of Caldwell's short stories were consummate achievements. Among the 150, at least a dozen rank with the best work produced in the twentieth century. Readers have only to experience "Kneel to the Rising Sun," "A Knife to Cut the Corn Bread With," "Daughter," "The People vs Abe Lathan, Colored," "A Country Full of Swedes," and "Candy-Man Beechum" to gauge the range of his originality.

There did exist an unevenness in his work from the beginning of his career which became more noticeable in the late forties when critics abruptly turned away to welcome a new generation of writers. Caldwell plunged on with a book a year to appease the insatiable appetite of inexpensive paperback editions. Then came slippage. The flat, direct style was now unfashionable, and after the decline of his publishing base, New American Library, most of his books fell out of print. "Erskine Caldwell?" too many readers would ask: "Was he the guy who wrote *Tobacco Road*?"

In recent years, a revival has been initiated by the University of Georgia Press. Though they reprinted several attractive paperback and hardcover editions of his work, the residue of neglect lingers. When an anthology publisher collected short stories for a Southern literature volume, Caldwell was excluded. This omission was protested by family and supporters, and an editor of the publishing house defended the oversight by saying that "Kneel to the Rising Sun" was too long for inclusion—there were a number of shorter stories that could have been considered.

This book is an attempt to better understand an American storyteller. In our rush to embrace that which is current, we sometimes ignore past practitioners. Caldwell, however, was not forgotten entirely—a number of writers who first became visible in the late forties and fifties acknowledged him as an elder brother. His bold and dramatic renderings of downtrodden sharecroppers and rural misfits during the Depression era of the thirties influenced these younger siblings: they admired his courage, respected his lack of timidity, and saw in him a surer way of seeing themselves.

# LONELY BEGINNINGS

The flickering of kerosene lamps and sputtering flames in the central wood fireplace did little to bring cheer to the manse's five rooms. The woman on the bed felt the first waves of labor as gusts of icy wind slipped through the cracks of the thin exterior walls of weathered boards; it had been a difficult pregnancy and for the moment both husband and wife were clearly worried. It wasn't until late that night, December 17, 1903, that the baby was born, a sturdy man-child with his mother's red hair and blue eyes. He was named, not after the Associated Reformed Church leader, Ebenezer Erskine, but for Erskine College where the young couple met in Due West, South Carolina.

The church community of White Oak, Georgia, three miles from Moreland and about thirty-five southwest of Atlanta, had less than two hundred inhabitants. It was a farming district where cotton was grown on limited scale; a place where people planted gardens and kept a few chickens. The farmer who owned a milk cow and had land enough to raise a cash crop was considered fortunate. Since the new arrival's father, Ira, gave spiritual comfort to parishioners who had barely enough money to look after themselves—the minister's salary was only $300 a year—it is little wonder that the manse was a bleak and uncomfortable living arrangement. There were no screens on the windows to keep out mosquitoes, no running water, the well was under the back porch with a trapdoor covering, and an outhouse was in the backyard.

Ira was too preoccupied with visiting his congregation of thirty and trying to establish a local school with a full academic schedule to notice the poverty of his surroundings. The nearest classroom was twelve miles away in the town of Newnan, and many students had stopped attending. His role as spiritual counselor for these poor farmers wasn't his only concern. Some of them were nearly destitute, and often he visited their shanties to distribute badly needed food and clothing. Ira seemed possessed by a restless eagerness to help everybody: he frequently went to Newnan to deliver sermons for convicts on the chain gang, and when there was spare time he stopped in Moreland where he was organizing an orphanage.

The wife of this newly appointed minister was very aware of her environment. The unpainted house with its small barren yard depressed Caroline and she felt marooned. In former days she had luxuriated in the comfort of rooms she kept while teaching at Due West, South Carolina before marrying Ira. Often the drafty quarters of the manse caused her to look back wistfully to the conveniences she had taken for granted in the sprawling plantation home of her childhood in Staunton, Virginia. Carrie missed the companionship of fellow teachers, and she soon decided that the people of White Oak were too coarse and unsophisticated to share her intellectual interests.

The members of Ira's congregation did not warm to this woman whose aloofness they resented, and Carrie had more than her attitude that the natives found troubling. She was, after all, not an ardent Associated Reformed Presbyterian, and such secular miscegenation was viewed as a threat. When she did go to church, Carrie was often late, and her march down the aisle to the reserved pew was performed with no sign of repentance. Ira was oblivious to this arrival midway through his sermon, nor did he pressure his wife to adopt his faith. He loved and respected Carrie and tolerated her behavior in full sight of his nettled flock.

Within a year, and with relentless perseverance, Ira had built a schoolhouse across the road from the church, and both the young minister and his wife began teaching full-time. Carrie, a lifelong and dedicated educator, no longer felt completely cornered. There remained the cramped quarters called home and tongue-clicking parishioners, but standing before a class again gave her a sense of fulfillment

Ira Sylvester Caldwell was an unusual minister of the A.R.P. Church. Later, as Secretary of Home Missions, he traveled throughout the South in order to settle disputes among various quarreling congregations. One ruckus was over church carpeting—the membership had quibbled for weeks, and Ira was irked by their illogical stubbornness. He felt that teachers and welfare workers were more needed than preachers. The pettiness he frequently encountered made him steadfast in his role as a minister of the downtrodden. On one occasion, he coaxed a girl who was disfigured by a harelip to the hospital, and paid for the operation himself. Yet such humanitarian activities and criticism of social wrongs were sometimes met with resistance. Many thought him meddlesome, and once when he tongue-lashed a white landowner for abusing a black sharecropper, the recipient of Caldwell's wrath asked the Ku Klux Klan to run this preacher out of town. Ira's reaction was fearless— "there has not been a new idea to penetrate the skull of these broken-down aristocrats since Sherman's march through here sixty years ago."

Ira Caldwell was born in the middle of North Carolina cotton country in 1875. The eldest of seven children on a farm where each member was expected to work, he soon learned that a good book and the nearby schoolhouse got him away from the harvest field and the hubbub of siblings. An interest in the Bible overjoyed his mother, Rose Hunter Caldwell, a staunch Associated Reformed Presbyterian. But his father, John Harvey Caldwell, had very little patience for the strictness of this sect; it was more logical and profitable to work hard than endure the drudgery of such a pious life: no card games, no nips of anything alcoholic, dances were taboo; reading newspapers, getting together with friends—such activities on the Sabbath were forbidden.

The A.R.P. Church had jurisdiction over the local school, and Rose Caldwell insisted that Ira attend classes there. Although the father was embarrassingly critical of the church and felt his son should be more useful on the farm, he finally relented, and, to the family's surprise, did so again after Ira had completed high school. This time it was Erskine College in Due West, South Carolina.

Ira glittered academically and was superior in nearly every sport: he was one of the most talked about athletes in the school's history. President of a literary society, straight-A student, champion debater—in spite of a slight stammer—Ira Caldwell was known for his frankness, no matter how sensitive the subject. It was at this time that the sociologist in him found roots, and he became increasingly disturbed by the A.R.P.'s unwritten mandate of avoiding social problems beyond the confines of the steeple. After graduating with highest honors, he was accepted as a student in the Erskine Divinity College, though the elders found his modest regard for theological matters worrisome. They felt his attention was too much focussed on helping the poor and saving the environment.

Caroline Preston Bell was very aware of being a tenth generation Virginian. One of her ancestors had served in the Revolutionary War under Lafayette, a detail that she often pointed out with pride. She was born in 1872. Carrie's father, Richard Henry Bell, was an accountant for the railroad. There were eight children in the family, and though they still owned their commodious Victorian house, most of the land had been lost due to poor management and the Civil War.

Since they were unable to educate all their children, it was fortunate that Carrie won a scholarship to Mary Baldwin College, then called Augusta Seminary. Upon her graduation in 1893, she was awarded the school's Star Medal for exceptional scholarship. Carrie was now ready to embark upon a career she had dreamed of ever since childhood—teaching.

It is not clear why she taught at three different schools the first three years—in Atoka, Mississippi; Pocohontas, Virginia; and Chatham, North Carolina—but it may have been because the curricula were inadequate for her high standards. Caroline Bell was a perfectionist and quick to show displeasure if there was laxity or rules were broken.

She met Ira on a train when returning for classes at her fourth school, Due West Women's College. Three years younger, he was still at Erskine College, a complication which would have scandalized the conservative A.R.P. citizens of Due West had this student-teacher courtship been discovered. Instead of hand-holding, they were limited to quickly-passed notes and letters posted at the local post office. The two shared so many common interests: both were fond of reciting poetry and reading the British Romantic poets as well as Virgil and Shakespeare; they didn't drink, dance, or swear; both pursued hobbies: she was teaching herself Greek, and he was often out in the Low Country woods looking for Indian artifacts. But there were personality differences, more obvious to parishioners who knew them after their marriage than to the participants of the secret courtship. Ira enjoyed the company of farmers and factory workers; she preferred socializing with fellow teachers. Because she defended her feelings of separateness with a standoffish manner, people who didn't know Carrie well thought her snobbish. Ira was easy to be with, and even when dressed in his best suit he gave the appearance of a country bumpkin visiting Atlanta.

Notes and letters continued to be exchanged while Ira attended divinity college. They both felt it best to postpone their wedding until he was ordained or had his own parish. Then came surprise: Ira left school and joined the military to fight in the Spanish-American War. This decision troubled Carrie, though she enjoyed teaching and had definite reservations about having children and the responsibility of running a household—how could marriage not terminate her career?

Ira returned from Cuba without seeing combat and recommenced his religious studies with the same high marks. (He did battle a tent mate and thrash him soundly for making fun of Ira's nightly Bible readings.) In the spring of 1900, he was ordained, but again their wedding was postponed. This time it was Caroline: she loved Ira dearly, but the thought of leaving her Due West job, cultural interests, friends and following him to the isolated parish of White Oak was almost unthinkable. She couldn't bear it just then; more time was needed; he must be there without her for now. Her decision disturbed Ira and worried the Bell family—all her younger sisters were married. Would she be an old maid?

For more than a year letters were posted at Due West and White Oak until Carrie's surrender. The wedding finally took place at the

Bell home in Staunton. It was October 1901, and after a few more months of teaching the bride joined her groom in Georgia.

The new mother clutched Erskine and refused when anyone asked to hold him. She repeatedly combed his hair and adorned him with delicate baby clothes. Yet, at times, Carrie resented his presence—he was taking her away from the world of books. She often escaped by taking trips into Newnan and leaving Erskine with neighbors. More than once, Carrie was in such a rush she forgot the baby's diapers and sitters had to substitute by using flour sacks. Too often, the parishioners saw the child crawling under pews during Ira's sermons, while Carrie apparently had forgotten her son's existence. Gossip intensified when the child was seen playing outside in a cold winter rain without shoes and hat. Probably his mother's moods of indifference alternating with her sudden rush to smother him scarred Erskine: his mistrust of women and certainty that they would in the end betray him led to three divorces.

Caldwell's under-the-pew excursions were tolerated by some members of the congregation and criticized by others—the freedom to wander at will was no doubt aided and abetted by permissive parents. Ira believed that constraining a small child was a denial of freedom of action and a danger to the growth of independence. Carrie's acquiescence may have had unmotherly reasons: one being that she easily tired of restraining her restless charge.

Whether it was the mother's inability to contain her child or her lapses into apathy, young Erskine was prone to mishaps. At one he drank a near-fatal quantity of kerosene, and a few months later he badly sliced his hand on his father's straight razor. But the most frightening disaster came when the child began to walk. Supper was being cooked, and Carrie had left a large bowl of boiling grease on the sideboard to congeal. Erskine, wandering about the kitchen, reached up and pulled the container down on himself. A woman who lived nearby heard Carrie and Erskine screaming. Before the doctor's arrival, she was able to quiet a hysterical mother and to examine the child who was writhing in pain on the kitchen floor. The grease had melted pajama buttons into his skin and there were severe burns crisscrossing down the front from neck to waist. While Carrie sat in a chair and sobbed, the neighbor rubbed chimney soot and lard into the blistering skin. It was a near call, and one which left lifelong scars to match that other searing—those psychological wounds from the mother-son relationship.

Parish affairs, the orphanage, and five years of teaching at the new school consumed all of Ira's time, but it didn't ease his restlessness. In 1906, when he was offered an A.R.P. parish in Prosperity, South Carolina, he quickly accepted, much to the surprise and sorrow of his congregation. For Carrie, it was a move she had wanted from the moment she saw the uncomfortable White Oak manse. In addition, she was quite aware of generating gossip and shunning sociability. Leaving might smooth another complication: Carrie still had health problems from her pregnancy and Erskine's birth—physicians had suggested a hysterectomy but there were no nearby facilities capable of handling such a surgical procedure.

The leave-taking was rushed. They were given a farewell dinner in the church, and there were hurried good-byes as the family left with their entire belongings packed into three suitcases and two trunks.

In his autobiography, *With All My Might*, Caldwell gives a descriptive account of the train trip to South Carolina—an elaborate travel tale beyond the recall of a child not yet three. Caldwell stated that he was six when they moved. A photograph of Carrie with her son on the porch of their Prosperity home leaves one to guess that Erskine was in error. The barefoot boy in the picture isn't six or seven—he's four or nearly five.

Since this is the case, Caldwell's only childhood friend in White Oak, a "chubby-faced mulatto boy," had to be an imaginary playmate. It also would change categorically his 1965 semi-autobiographical book, *In Search of Bisco*, to a work of fiction.

According to Caldwell, the two met when they both were three. "Bisco," he was called, and the youngsters were inseparable. For two years they had friendly rough-and-tumble wrestling matches, and Erskine enjoyed "the hot collard pot likker and sliced chitterling bread" Bisco's mother gave him when he stayed one night for supper. She was an ample-fleshed woman with a warm smile and glowing mulatto coloring. Caldwell recalls her singing to them and holding both boys on the soft pillows of her bosom.

Then Erskine was told by his parents they were going to live in South Carolina. His unhappiness had nothing to do with leaving White Oak, his birthplace—it was the fear that he and Bisco would be parted forever.

The manse in Prosperity didn't differ much from the one they had left in White Oak; it was a weathered house of four rooms with a fireplace and a battered flue for the kitchen stove. However, the structure did have front and back porches, vegetable plot, and there was a peach orchard on the two-acre lot.

The town's name was a misnomer. There were few prosperous farmers and many hungry black sharecroppers in rundown cabins. Across the railroad tracks, on the other side of Prosperity, was a squalid settlement that housed the poorly-paid mill workers. Ira, with his usual crusading spirit, slanted his sermons to matters of conscience and told church members that local working conditions must be improved. His outspokenness jarred several parishioners, and soon there were rumblings about the new parson who was fond of "the goddam niggers."

Carrie riled the female members of the church when she complained about the cramped living conditions in the manse and how little Erskine had to sleep on a cot in his father's study. Her cool demeanor provoked one of the ladies to say that a good Christian minister and wife should practice restraint and not allow themselves to have large families.

But there was little time to complain. Barely a month after their arrival, late at night, Ira woke and found the house in flames. Sparks from the stove had smoldered in plaster around the defective flue. The Caldwells managed to escape by the front door as roof and exterior pine boards ignited. The three were in their night-clothes, and by the time the fire department arrived the building was nearly leveled. Most of their belongings were lost in the flames—Ira's leather suitcase and Carrie's gold watch were saved, but gone were their paintings, books, and family photographs. The Caldwells were taken in by a widow who had a large house, Ira continued his parish duties, and Carrie, who enjoyed drawing and painting, began sketching floor plans for a new and larger manse which would be built by members of the congregation.

Ira had little time at home; his trips around the parish were endless. For Carrie, it was a less lonely time, not at all like White Oak. Her sisters visited frequently, and there were spirited con-versations and merriment. Ira, when he was around, was disturbed by their shrill laughter and "incessant gabbing." Carrie now made arrangements to undergo the postponed hysterectomy in nearby Columbia. This operation was a blessing for her; it would bring to an end the discomfort she had endured since Erskine's birth, and more important, there would be no more children.

Carrie continued to smother or neglect her son, depending on her mood. Now that he was entering a boyish, naughty stage, she would punish Erskine by not speaking to him for two or three days. Probably more painful than the silent treatment was the clothing she made him wear, which consisted of a white linen blouse that hung halfway to his knees, a slack leather belt ornamented with a brass buckle, and loose trousers that were knee-length. Ira didn't interfere with his wife's eccentric costume creation, but he did at times gaze wonderingly at the unmanly togs.

Needless to say, the boy was teased whenever he came into con-tact with other children. Also painfully striking were the long red-dish curls that hung to his shoulders. When Ira finally objected to his son's hair, Carrie was adamant—the locks would remain.

Her sister, Emma, a registered nurse from Richmond, was shocked by Erskine's appearance when she came to stay with her sister for a week. Soon after her arrival she and Ira went on a walk. The next day, according to Caldwell, his aunt coaxed his mother to take a pill—it would help soothe the nervous tension Carrie was experiencing after the excitement of seeing her sister again. While the mother calmed down and napped peacefully, the three slipped out of the house and Erskine was rushed to a barbershop. Then he was herded to the nearest clothing store where his Russian-style blouse and short pants were replaced with long pants and a shirt.

When his mother woke at noon and asked for a glass of water, the boy was taken into her room. Immediately, there was a cry of anguish as the water spilled on the bed. Why should a strange child be allowed in her bedroom? "Where's Erskine?" she called. When told this was truly her son, the mother shouted: "Don't you come near me!" Then, overcome with tears, she meekly accepted another pill from her sister and closed her eyes to avoid the painful sight of this shocking transformation.

It was decided early that Erskine would be tutored at home; Carrie insisted that her son be isolated from ruffians at the local school; he wasn't going to learn coarse language, and when he did cuss at home she cleansed his mouth with water and ashes. Though Ira taught school in the area and felt his son needed more contact with children, the mother's wishes ruled. The boy did learn to write, read, and solve simple arithmetic problems, but Carrie's frequent moods of indifference slowed his progress.

More and more, Ira was away from the house, while Erskine, isolated at home with visiting aunts and a mother whose attitudes ran cold and hot, responded predictably. He thought his father a saint and resented his mother. Women were not to be trusted, he learned early, and it was an opinion he held to doggedly until his fourth marriage. He and his father were together sometimes: there were rides to nearby Newberry for cinnamon buns, and once Carrie allowed Ira to take their son to a carnival. But it was a lonely time for this child as he watched the trains slide in and out of town and his father's Ford coupe disappear down the road.

Living in Prosperity came to a close when Ira was appointed

Secretary of Home Missions. Since the job required a flexible life-style and frequent changes of address, Erskine saw even less of his father. Ira enjoyed the challenges of his post: there were disputes to be settled, pastors selected, and salaries established. This new position of troubleshooter at times required tact and discretion: in one church, divided family members sat on opposite sides of the aisle and refused to speak to one another. In three years, Ira visited more than a hundred parishes throughout the South. Erskine once heard his mother say to his father in a moment of banter that if Ira hadn't become a minister he would have been content as a traveling salesman peddling shoes.

He had kept his long pants and ordinary shirts—the Russian-style blouses were things of the past—however, Erskine was still being home taught. An only child with no playmates, this isolation had its effects on him. He mumbled his replies and had difficulty carrying on conversations.

When Ira was away on trips, Carrie and Erskine stayed at the Bell home in Staunton. Being with her family in Virginia brightened Carrie's disposition; she became more high-spirited and talkative, though she did miss her husband when his stays were prolonged. When Ira had to settle in one place for several months, his wife and son joined him. For the next three years, after leaving Prosperity, the Caldwells lived in Timber Ridge, Virginia; Charlotte, North Carolina; and Bradley, South Carolina.

Timber Ridge, midway between Lexington and Staunton, Virginia, was in apple orchard country of the Shenandoah Valley. The local school was only a quarter of a mile away, within easy walking distance, but Carrie still insisted that her son learn at home. She didn't want him to be handicapped by lack of ambition and vision. Anybody could cut trees and dig ditches: he must strive for the best.

The lonesome boy soon found a granite quarry not far from his home, and whenever Erskine had spare time from his studies he would sit on the edge of the pit to watch the workmen drill and blast rock. He went there every day when it didn't rain and stayed for two or three hours. But these excursions came to an abrupt end when he told his mother what he had just seen. Two workmen were tamping dynamite into a deep hole and there was an explosion. Both men were killed, and a shoeless foot fell near Erskine.

The move to Charlotte, North Carolina did little to change his predicament. When a truant officer descended, Carrie told the man that her son was gravely ill and must be taught at home. She did let her son attended a local school in Staunton for a brief time, but when the Caldwells moved to Bradley, South Carolina, he became housebound again.

There was little that a boy of twelve could find to do in Bradley, and Erskine soon became depressed by the lack of activity. There were no playgrounds or parks, and all the children his age were in school from early morning to late afternoon. Doubtlessly, even on holidays Carrie restricted his contact with playmates. The smothering continued, and when he complained bitterly of always being alone, his mother sometimes responded with her silent treatment.

He did get permission to earn money doing odd jobs, and one summer he collected old automobile tires for a scrap merchant. Erskine also prowled the street for cigarette packages, collecting the aluminum linings, and for a time had a *Grit* paper route of twenty-two customers. His most enterprising effort was a laundry bluing business. He ordered by mail five-cent packages of bluing powder and sold them for ten cents to black washwomen.

His paper route and bluing customers gave him some contact with other people, but the time in Bradley was soon over. Ira had been sent to Atoka, a small community in Western Tennessee, to settle a church dispute. The congregation was in an uproar, and the stay there would be longer than anticipated. Carrie and Erskine soon followed—this would be the Caldwells fifth move in four years.

Ira became temporary pastor of the Salem A.R.P. Church just outside Atoka. The Caldwells lived in several rented rooms on the second floor of a farmhouse with the church nearby. A squabbling congregation took up most of Ira's time, and Carrie began teaching in the local school. Erskine, eager to earn money, picked cotton, drove a team of mules for a neighboring farmer, and spent a month at Millington Army Base as a driver for the YMCA. Since he was a chauffeur for officers, Erskine lived on the base, took his meals in the enlisted men's mess, and was on call around the clock. His parents were reluctant to have their son away from home, but it was 1917 and patriotism was in ascent. The job proved to be more worldly than the minister and his wife could imagine: the thirteen-year-old spent much of his time driving officers to brothels in Memphis. When the YMCA chief was transferred to another war-time location, Erskine was abruptly relieved of his duties.

Back home, the gangling teenager was restless and moody. He found no interest in familiar surroundings after having experienced the excitement of a strange outside world. He wanted to keep his personal life private, but the need to express himself was surfacing. He would make his own world—alone and without anybody looking over his shoulder.

He took up pencil and paper and began to write a novel. He had no idea what the requirements of storytelling were, for he had never read a full-length piece of fiction. His mother had spoken of certain classical writings when tutoring him, but there was a period when he thought that novels were only written by Sir Walter Scott or Victor Hugo. He had read short stories—Carrie subscribed to *The Saturday Evening Post*, *Redbook*, and *Cosmopolitan*—but most of his reading had been limited to baseball news.

Behind the locked door of his room, he wrote on blue-ruled tablet paper, haltingly but as rapidly as he could, the tale of a boy who ran away from home to escape the cruelty of a harsh mother and father. Erskine did not consider that he was presenting unfair reflections of his upbringing. What was written came with the feeling that the gift of imagination became alive through exaggeration—his mother had told him that the use of fantasy was one of the basic elements of fiction. The novel was called "A Boy's Own Story of City Life"—a slender first book of seven chapters, twenty-two pages scrawled in pencil.

When this first work of fiction was shown to Ira and Carrie—though there is some doubt that he shared his work: many of Caldwell's autobiographical renderings are from the land of his imagination—their reaction was discouraging. He was soon to hear that his handwriting needed drastic improvement. True or not, Erskine's parents did have reason to worry over the results of his housebound education. In a 1915 letter to his Aunt Sallie, he depicted a dark night without a "latern" when he and a friend "camped out dors as far as from the top of the hill down there."

Carrie may have had other reasons for concern: adolescent hardons were preoccupations; they were thrilling and unexpected for the smothered youth on the fringes of manhood. He now had reached beyond her, no longer the sheltered child she could clutch to her bosom. Erskine's horizon was beginning to stretch as he distanced himself from her. The teaching position at the Atoka public school was a godsend: it gave Carrie space and a balm for her self-esteem which was threatened by Ira's preoccupation with congregational affairs and Erskine's rejection of her mothering. Whatever the reason, she finally relented, and the son who had been denied public school lessons was now enrolled.

The principal of the Robison School in Atoka decided that Erskine would start in the seventh grade, probably at Carrie's urging that her son had been extensively tutored at home. There were three teachers for grades six through twelve, and students were expected to be orderly and apply themselves. It was no easy time for Erskine, and his passing grades were largely due to his mother's help, though he did win an elimination quiz in geography. The prize was a copy of Edward Gibbon's *The Rise and Fall of the Roman Empire*, a book that he proudly kept on the table in his room.

Erskine was the proverbial young colt let loose to pasture for the first time as he entered the social swirl with his peers at recess time. He was good enough to play on Robison's basketball team, and there were Boy Scout camping trips along the Mississippi. His innate mechanical abilities also strengthened his ties with others: he stripped the engine of Ira's Ford, cleaned the cylinder heads and spark plugs, and as a reward was given permission to use the car for an hour or more—Erskine and his friends roared down the back roads with foot-heavy acceleration.

There was, however, a social bumbling as he tried to impress his schoolmates so they would accept him. The lonely years at home left scars: often, he was withdrawn, a silent spectator on the sidelines, listening, watching. When he tried to show off his cusswords, he was faulted for his English—it was too proper, too good. The best friend was James Boyce; they went fishing, played catch, and smoked cigarettes on the sly. A case of puppy love captured Erskine. Elise Strong was fifteen and pretty, and his wooing once led him to wire the steering wheel of his father's Ford. He drove the vehicle back and forth in front of her house, blowing the horn while crouching out of sight on the floor of the car.

But there was mischief making that couldn't be overlooked as pranks. Erskine tipped over outhouses (as Ira had done before him), slashed bags of grain, broke windows, drove his father's car recklessly—once smashing into a mule cart. The most serious act was firing a .22 rifle over the head of a boy who ran screaming to his mother. During another deliberate show of rough behavior that ignited gossip he drank a huge quantity of moonshine and passed out stone drunk on a neighbor's porch. He didn't care anymore and seemed to find pleasure in being caught.

Erskine's behavior worried his parents at a time when Ira's feuding congregation exploded into A.R.P. open warfare. Nearly a third of the members were threatening to leave and form a new church. Ira was blamed for spending far too much time in establishing a new country school and organizing food drives for hungry sharecroppers. He was accused of being rigid when conducting parish affairs and meddling in things that didn't concern him. This led to other difficulties: the school board was reluctant to renew Carrie's teaching appointment, and the Robison School was having trouble finding room for Erskine—they now claimed to be overcrowded.

Local resentment kept building daily, and a rock shattered one of the windows where the Caldwells were living. Then Erskine was found unconscious by the road—he had been waylaid. After four years of church bickering, Ira had more than enough. He would take up a parsonage in Georgia. Years later, Carrie Caldwell wrote her son that his father's life was a struggle. "If the story of his sacrifice, privations, hardships, heart-bruises and wounds of the spirit were written, it would read like a page from the book of martyrs."

The Caldwells' new home in Wrens had five rooms, a detached woodshed and chicken house, and was situated on a narrow lot under high sprawling weeping willows. Behind the one-story manse was a small vegetable plot, and trellises of morning glories brightened the surroundings. There was no running water, but each room had a coal fireplace, and the bathroom had a built-in tub. It was by far the most comfortable accommodation the A.R.P. Church had provided them. The Caldwells' arrival was carried in the July 25, 1919 issue of *The Jefferson County Reporter*, and for all three, this small eastern Georgia community must have seemed a sanctuary after feuding Atoka.

Located thirty-five miles southwest of Augusta on a railroad line, Wrens was a bustling town of more than a thousand inhabitants. There were a cottonseed-oil mill, a small ironworks, sawmill, and an ice factory. The several stores along Main Street, with post office and jail, doubtlessly made a cosmopolitan impression on the fifteen-year-old Erskine as he wandered about town for the first time.

The economy was thriving—cotton prices had risen to nearly sixty dollars a bail—and close to the town were some of the best stands of timber in Georgia. Owners of sharecropping plantations, forest lands, and mills were getting wealthier by the year, but there were obvious disparities. Near Wrens, on the barren sand hills and depleted tobacco lands lived the impoverished people whose only source of income and food came from begging. They frequently could be seen going door-to-door, dirty and hungry, and usually carrying one or more crying and sickly-looking babies. The residents of Wrens called them "the Weepers." Carrie, and particularly

Ira, gave generously, sometimes depriving themselves. Shortly after their arrival in Wrens, Erskine's mother became so provoked that she jabbed the straw end of her broom at several Weepers who lingered on their porch and continued moaning long after Ira had given them a bag of sweet potatoes and several cans of pork-and-beans. Carrie knew they were deserving and hungry, but there had to be a compromise. "We need food ourselves, too," she reminded Ira, "and there's not always enough of it. From now on, there's going to be a limit to how kindhearted we can be at this house."

Instead of being enrolled as a freshman at Wrens High School, Erskine joined the senior class because of his age and size—he was a nearly six-foot, broad-shouldered teenager who might have disrupted classroom studies had he been placed in a lower grade. The school, built the previous spring, had twelve classrooms, library, two laboratories, music room, woodworking shop, and auditorium. Ira assured the school superintendent that his son would apply himself and get passable grades. But Erskine was never an exceptional student, and his first report card must have caused his parents concern. There was a C in quadratic equations, plane geometry C, and in his mother's class, Latin, he was given a C- with the admonishment that he hadn't completed required readings of Cicero. Erskine's poor spelling and grammar brought his English grade down to a C+, and his best showing was a B in world history. Caldwell had an explanation: "I suppose one reason for my indifference to formal schooling was because in my early years I had not been subjected to the discipline of required study and attendance."

A different environment didn't end his social transgressions which had flared in Atoka. He sought the company of a wild group at school and soon had the reputation of being a mean hell-raiser. It was typical of Erskine to throw a stone through his math teacher's window and then stand calmly in front of the house waiting for the police. He still enjoyed being caught; there was satisfaction in parading maliciousness. Erskine continued to drive his father's Ford recklessly and found the ringing of a belfry bell late at night the easiest way of getting a policeman's attention. However, with all this boisterousness and crude behavior, he still was the moody, often sullen, bystander who said little and found it difficult to place trust in others.

Soon, a new Elise Strong captivated Erskine in Wrens. Sara Farmer was blond and shapely—a girl who was fiercely chaperoned by worried parents. The two had met at a school dance and were often seen together. In their A.R.P. circle, it is doubtful whether the wooing got past hand-holding and a furtive kiss in the shadows of a porch swing. Demanding as he was, and accustomed to getting his own way at home—when Carrie was in a smothering mood—Erskine quarreled with Sara. Once, during a sour exchange of words, he climbed out on the roof of a portico at school and re-fused to come down until she asked forgiveness.

Erskine learned more about the Weepers when he took a part-time job as a driver for Dr. Pilcher, a local physician. Inside the one- and two-room cabins there would be as many as four or five people living in squalor. Many of the ragged children were from incestuous relationships and all were suffering from malnutrition. The young doctor did what he could for these patients and without charge. Erskine also accompanied his father along the abandoned flat roads where hogsheads of cured tobacco were rolled to the Savannah River for shipping. "Those folks are like toads in a post hole!" Ira told his son bitterly. "They just have no fair chance at all." Food from the Caldwell larder was always stacked on the seat of the vehicle—whatever scraps they could spare—and though Carrie cautioned her husband not to be overly generous, she fre-quently stuffed candy in his sack for the children and elderly.

Young Caldwell was never lazy, and even while struggling to keep up with his studies at high school he was eager to work. During the middle of his school year at Wrens he took a night job at the cottonseed-oil mill, and this was done without his parents' knowledge. Several nights a week he shoveled cottonseed into conveyor troughs. This earned him a dollar a night and entrance to an unfamiliar world. For the first time in his life he was exposed to the underground society of black houseboys and yardmen who needed the extra work—their wages: fifty cents a night. Erskine prized this interracial experience and called it "the only completely democratic institution in town." There were no racial distinctions, and he enjoyed the "lighthearted banter" that was both profane and obscene. Such contact excited the sixteen-year-old after the serene and puritanical surroundings of a parsonage. But his new worldly exposure came to an end abruptly. He fell asleep one morning at the breakfast table after having worked a full midnight shift. "That was when I had to confess to my parents and tell them what I had been doing the past month while they slept soundly through the night." Carrie immediately put a stop to her son's moonlighting. "Shortly afterward, my father said that perhaps no great harm had been done but that it would have been better for me to be older before being exposed to anything like playing the dozens."

It came as no surprise to Erskine when he was told by the principal that he had not earned enough credits to graduate. Though he would be allowed to participate in the graduation ceremonies, his diploma would be a blank certificate.

Carrie seemed unruffled when Erskine rose before an audience of two hundred to receive the bogus scroll, but there were a few in the crowd who exchanged glances as they applauded. Ira, as usual, kept his calm demeanor, but both parents must have been disturbed by Erskine's plunging grades and frequent days away from classes throughout the school year. "Being in the midst of my classmates and in full view of the onlookers," admitted Caldwell, "I did have moments of feeling out of place, but nevertheless I was not to be shamed into a state of regret and remorse for my predicament."

Wrens, which had played an important part in his young life, suddenly was less glamorous now that his fellow students were perusing college catalogs and planning their futures. He felt marooned, and the town began to irritate him; an attitude that worried Carrie and Ira—with no job to keep their son occupied, they feared more bell ringing and broken windows.

An uncle and aunt in northern Georgia came to the rescue. Erskine could stay with them in Calhoun and work as an assistant for a local stonemason. (In both *With All My Might* and *Call It Experience* Caldwell placed this summer job as following his freshman year of college.)

The work was both rigorous and muscle-building. For two long months he carried heavy loads of mortar and blocks up a ladder as the walls of a small church were raised.

In letters to his mother, Erskine was proud of his $22.00 a week salary. "If I save $100. this summer do you think that my vacation will be well spent?" He still solicited Carrie's approval, yet when she suggested a visit in late July, Erskine quickly responded: "You are not to come here till the last of August, because you are not needed out here and it will be better for you to stay away as long as possible." Perhaps "not needed" but there was soon a cry from the wage-earning son: "Send me some underwear *post haste*, pronto, quick, am out, totally."

The granite walls of the church were completed earlier than expected—by mid-August—and Erskine returned to Wrens. It wasn't a homecoming etched with enthusiasm: so many of his school friends were joining the military forces or preparing to go off to college. Carrie had wanted her son to become a student at the University of Virginia, but the out-of-state tuition was much too high. Ira favored Erskine College for sentimental reasons and because the tuition was reduced for the sons of A.R.P. ministers. Longing to escape the parental nest and Wrens, and with few options since he had no high school certificate, Erskine agreed. It was one way, at least, to be himself.

## DUE WEST, WRENS, AND BOGALUSA

Erskine College was named in honor of Ebenezer Erskine, a Scottish theologian, who founded the A.R.P. Church in Scotland and moved its ministry to Due West, South Carolina. The school, established in 1839, was designed for the training of ministers. Over the years, its academic requirements had changed little, and at the time of Caldwell's enrollment there remained the same scholastic strictness. After the daily chapel service at eight, students had courses in Bible study, English, and mathematics; Latin, German, or Greek; and one elective in classes of science, English history, or American literature.

Due West was a community that revolved around the activities of Erskine College and Due West Women's College. The town is located in the western part of South Carolina, about thirty miles from the Georgia border, and the farms at that time were spotted with less than thriving cotton fields—a recent decline in prices had paralyzed the area commercially. The few stores, huddled along an unpaved street, were dependent on the students and faculty. When the two colleges recessed for summer, Christmas and spring breaks, the shops closed their doors.

Caldwell was delighted to escape Wrens and enter any college, though what he found in Due West was not to his liking. The campus was littered with trash, he complained, and the one main street of town was either dusty or muddy.

Erskine was carrying his father's two battered suitcases when he stepped off the train—a six-foot, redheaded boy dressed in his Sunday suit and with hair parted in the center. It had been an all-day journey from home with the changing of trains in Augusta, Greenwood and Donalds, South Carolina. "Due west of nowhere," the students were fond of saying, and Erskine soon felt the accuracy of this description. He had expected more worldliness, and had not envisioned attending a college where the enrollment was less than that of Wrens High School.

One of the first decisions he made upon entering college was to join the football squad; the bright scarlet E on a white woolen sweater of a player seemed to him the school's beckoning flag of approval. After a week of rough practice it became obvious that he would not be in the starting lineup. Since the team had few players, he was designated as a backup linebacker on defense and a center on offense. But there was no denying his ferocity in scrimmaging—he competed with teammates who outweighed him by twenty or thirty pounds. Day after day, from four to six, he was battered about with never a complaint, and he kept pushing himself with punishing results. When a first-stringer was injured on one of the final games of the season, the coach allowed Erskine to play in his first college game. There were hoots of derision when this bench-warming freshman ran on the field, but an older player recalled Erskine making "tackles from end to end and threw 'em for losses damn near every play."

Behind the scenes at Erskine College a subculture of rebellious students defied school regulations. This may have been an institute established to educate the sons of A.R.P. ministers, but out of sight, in dormitories, the cruel sport of sophomores hazing the lowly freshmen was taking place. "Rats" these first-year students were called, and they were ordered to attend weekly "rat meetings" where sophomores subjected them to pain and degradation. Dashing without trousers through the paddle line or bending over to be stung on the rump with a heavy textbook was an anticipated ritual. Poker games went on at all hours, and freshmen were ordered to raid the dormitory larder, shine shoes, and carry messages between rooms.

Caldwell boasted years later that from the beginning he decided not to be a freshman who would cowardly submit to abusive hazing. He claimed his six feet of height and deep voice partly discouraged the hazers. Instead of being humiliated with paddlings, Caldwell said he was given the role of smuggler. His job was to steal food from the dining room and to creep into the kitchen pantry after midnight.

However, Erskine's height and the swagger he perfected to command some respect, along with a hat he donned jauntily while smoking a cigar didn't deter his upperclassmen—it marked him as a likely candidate for extra punishment. During one incident he was ordered to copulate with a tackling dummy while sophomores stood by and hooted encouragement.

His closest companion was fellow freshman Andrew Murphy—a surprising friendship since the two were so different. "Murph" was talkative, bubbling with champagne humor, witty, and forever the clown. In appearance, they were opposites: Erskine with his red hair and six-foot height, Murphy with his dark complexion and short stature. They prowled the campus together and soon were involved in college pranks. The two found collaborators, and Caldwell was a natural and experienced leader: cows were milked after midnight, chickens stolen for outdoor roasts, windows nailed shut, and the clapper of the chapel bell disappeared. Predictably, Erskine was unable to keep these high jinks to himself, and he wrote his parents: "We have been having *some* time the past weeks. Thursday morning his (Professor McCain's) buggy was up in his class room and his horse spent the night in the Chapel Hall." One can picture Carrie's worried frown and Ira's resigned sigh.

Erskine did enjoy these shenanigans with fellow pranksters in what was called the "Night Hawkers Club"—a fraternity of chicken stealers whose password was "poultry" and purpose was to "borrow the feathery dames." But he still distanced himself from the others—a gap that even the spirited Murphy couldn't narrow.

His behavior was often unexpected and bewildering. One night a "Hawker" bet Erskine a dollar that he couldn't smash the tip of the room's only lightbulb with a baseball bat. Caldwell slammed his dollar on a table, picked up the bat, swung, and plunged the room into darkness. When light was restored, Erskine with a stone expression calmly and silently pocketed his winnings.

The hazing continued, and in order to escape the brunt of it, he and Murphy began taking weekend rides on freight trains. They would slip unseen from the campus, walk to the nearby rail yard, and wait for the 11:00 p.m. freight to Greenwood. When the cars were being shunted and coupled, the pair would jump into a boxcar. Caldwell never dared to ride on a passenger train without a ticket. During his first trip, a friendly hobo had warned him that such cars often carried United States mail. If caught, there was the likelihood of being arrested and jailed.

After the journey to Greenwood, he and Murphy would walk the empty streets and spend hours in the all-night Busy Bee Cafe near the station before hopping a freight back to Due West. They sat in a booth sipping mugs of coffee, chain-smoked cigarettes, and listened to the conversation of drunks and misfits.

They soon expanded these weekend adventures and became frequent visitors to Anderson, Spartanburg, and Columbia. Only once did Caldwell get as far as Charleston and return at the end of a weekend. Expense money for these excursions was realized by skipping meals in the college dining hall.

There was much that sparked the argumentative side of Caldwell's religious independence in Bible class. Ira and Carrie always had given their son free reign in deciding for himself the boundaries of his faith. Most A.R.P. ministers and educators violently opposed Darwin's theory of evolution, and Erskine's Bible professor, John Irenaeus McCain, was no exception. The student from Wrens and McCain soon clashed, since this professor had no patience for a fledgling who rejected the Garden of Eden and the Bible's explanation of mankind's origin. If a freshman disagreed he was dismissed from class for the day.

Caldwell further distanced himself from the spirit of the college and often shocked his classmates with his incessant foul language. "Cussin Erskine" he was nicknamed. His exaggerated exploits of sexual conquests and scatological fascinations were paraded daily to increase his campus notoriety.

His first semester grades at Due West matched the dismal ones he had received at Wrens High School. Caldwell's frequent cutting of classes and inattentiveness became a way of life as he teetered scholastically. His best marks were in American literature, history, and surprisingly, Bible—in each he was given a D; he "conditionally failed"—meaning he would have to make up the courses later—

English composition and algebra; and received a D- in German.

Erskine's Christmas visit home was not all festivity. Carrie scolded him for his laziness and plunging grades: it was embarrassing for the family, and his poor showing was blemishing his father's position as an A.R.P. minister. He mustered contriteness—perhaps to avoid another of his mother's prolonged punishing silences—and promised to improve.

Second semester results, however, were even more discouraging: his D- in German became another "conditional" grade; D in English history slipped to a D-; marks in algebra were so low that he was dropped from class with a zero; yet somehow "Cussin Erskine" surprised his fellow students with a D+ for Bible studies.

Although he had little use for Professor McCain who taught both Bible and English composition, Erskine had some success in the writing class. The emphasis was on grammar, but more important for that surprising literary career ahead, he was assigned essays focusing on "the study of life." Caldwell turned in every writing assignment, earned a C, and his letters home, though still faulty, showed definite improvement.

His favorite class was American literature. It was an informal gathering of students tutored by Edgar Long, who had recently graduated from the University of North Carolina. Long's easy demeanor and enthusiasm as he introduced a wide array of classic American material ignited Caldwell; it was a new and fresh exposure to fiction; "the best sport here" he labelled the young professor. The first semester grade was a D, but applying himself, Erskine achieved an 82, a C+—the highest mark he would get at Erskine College. This was just enough to lift his yearly average to a passing 73 and assure him the status of a sophomore.

June finally arrived, and Erskine returned to Wrens for the summer. He was relieved that the freshman year with all its hazing was behind him. Again, his few friends were bewildered when he made no attempt to say good-bye. "One moment Caldwell was here," recalled a classmate, "the next, he had just up and left."

Back in Wrens, and through much of the heat of the summer, Erskine was caught up in a social swirl. His high school girlfriend, Sara Farmer, had graduated and would be enrolled at Wesleyan College in Macon, Georgia. The two were regulars at local weekend dances, church concerts, and box-lunch auctions where Erskine and local swains would bid for the refreshments prepared by the girls of their choice. There were also poker games, moonshine whiskey, and tall tales of adventure with ladies of the evening in Avery, Georgia. Ira's car frequently spun from the yard and Erskine with former high school cronies roared recklessly up and down the dusty back roads. Sometimes, he joined his father's pickup baseball team on Saturdays and played well at first base, though his performance at the plate was poor.

Erskine had difficulty finding a summer job. He did work for *The Jefferson County Reporter* for a brief time as a typesetter, errand boy, and solicitor of advertising, but many of his friends remembered how he would stroll listlessly about town and was often seen with his feet on the editorial desk and a cigarette in his mouth.

According to Caldwell, in both *Call It Experience* and *With All My Might*, during his first summer in Wrens he got a job turning a handpress at the paper. (Dan B. Miller, who interviewed several residents of that Georgia town for his 1995 biography, *Erskine Caldwell: The Journey From Tobacco Road*, gives the date as 1921, the summer *after* the first year at Erskine College. Such differences are not unusual: Caldwell's fondness for a good story and careless disregard of dates often taint his autobiographical renderings. To fuel this confusion is his statement that he started as a junior in high school; Miller, rightfully, claims the senior class—there is a yearbook confirming it. Probably this discrepancy is furthered by Caldwell giving the date of his arrival in Wrens as 1918 instead of 1919.)

Erskine's version of the job had him setting type, and soon he was permitted to write notes about engagements and marriages for the society page. When Charles Stephens, the owner and editor, decided to go on a lengthy fishing trip, the recently hired apprentice was left in charge of production and distribution. After the vacationer returned, his young helper felt that he should be paid for his labors. "Now look here, Erskine," Stephens told him. "You came in here of your own free will and said you wanted to work on the paper. Not a single, solitary word was said about paying you to learn newspapering. That's the honest truth, isn't it?" When Caldwell reminded his employer that he had been paid a dollar a night at the cottonseed-oil mill, the newspaperman replied: "You'd better hurry back down there to that mill and try to get your old job back again if money's the only thing in life you're after." This was Caldwell's recall of his first newspaper experience, and after some deliberation, he had quit. The owner's son, Ralph Stephens, in an interview with Miller, had a different version: Erskine was fired.

Ira's frequent letters to editors and his newspaper articles on the plight of hungry sharecroppers amid their tragic surroundings did much to nudge Erskine into journalism. After *The Jefferson County Reporter* fiasco, young Caldwell began sending dozens of dispatches to newspapers in Atlanta, Macon, and Augusta. Any local newsworthy event or calamity was painfully pecked into shape on a secondhand typewriter he had purchased with money earned from doing odd jobs. But these pieces suffered the usual fate of a beginner's work: they were all rejected. He did, after a time, manage to contribute squibs on local baseball games to the *Augusta Chronicle*. But this success as a reporter was limited and made no impact locally—he had no byline. In truth, his entrance into the field of journalism was clearly less illustrious than the fictionalized accounts found in both of his autobiographies.

Unable to find work near home, Erskine went with his father on humanitarian rounds throughout the parish where sharecroppers faced starvation and their hopeless, hapless futures. In addition to the devastating drop in cotton prices, from sixty cents a bale to thirteen, 1921 was also the summer of a boll weevil plague. Field after field lay desolate, and as plant life withered so did the spirit of those who once tended crops. Out of desperation, many hungry cotton planters, now reduced to Weepers, surrounded Wrens like a noose.

Ira and Erskine traveled the dusty back roads in their old Ford, from one ramshackle hovel to another, delivering food. On Sundays, Ira continued preaching to the county chain gang as they sat shackled, and later, on the ride back, father and son had long talks about the wrongs of the Georgia penal system. Slowly and indelibly, Ira's lectures crystallized into lifelong social convictions for Erskine.

There were other exposures on their travels into the Georgia countryside that summer. Ira's fascination with the extreme splinter groups of fundamentalist religion had its impact on Erskine. There were clay-eating rituals in a church near Wrens, and on a remote road near Augusta, a foot-washing ceremony. Once the two witnessed a ritualistic snake handling. Then there was the determined preacher who wanted to get closer to God—his method disgusted both father and son. The performance was self-inflicted theater: this man in the pulpit kept banging his head with a mallet. One Holy Rollers service was also on their tour of fundamental oddities. This shrieking, writhing, slobbering ritual with its orgasmic overtones appalled Erskine, and he stared coldly at the epileptic ceremony. Within him, a social scaffold was being erected, a framework that would support some of the trenchant scenes in his short stories and novels.

Young Caldwell was reaching out in other directions as he impatiently waited for the long summer to end its oven heat so football season could begin—he had gained weight, was now one hundred and seventy pounds: maybe this would be enough to get him on the varsity squad. Erskine spent hours loitering at the train station and listening to gossip in the pool hall and barbershop. He even spent time at the cottonseed-oil mill with his black friends. There seemed to be a need to strengthen and personalize what he and his father had experienced that summer.

When he returned to Due West, the coach selected him for the varsity team at the conclusion of the first week of practice. His coach and teammates liked his determination and fierceness on the gridiron and Caldwell did get to play in every game that season. Though he still was a backup, the right to sport the crimson E on his white sweater nearly made up for frequent bench-warming sessions.

Erskine College that year played the best game in its school's history—they defeated the Clemson College Tigers 13 to 0 and did it with their thirteen-player squad. It was a David-versus-Goliath victory for this small religious college, and a feat that is still being talked about in Due West. The team was met by the entire faculty and student body and astonished townspeople. After speeches and ovations, the victorious thirteen were escorted down Main Street and around the campus in a torchlight procession.

During the fall term his grades improved and he enthusiastically attended classes and completed every assignment. But once back into the daily grind of college without football, he soon found himself in scholastic difficulty. Though he asked one of his professors to advise him on planning a schedule of study to overcome his deficiencies, everything remained anticlimactic as he wandered from one class to the next. Then one morning Erskine woke with the realization that he had reverted to his previous tendency of complete dissatisfaction with everything around him; he was now overwhelmed with renewed hostility.

It all seemed so meaningless as grades plummeted and attendance slipped. By the Christmas holiday he was in danger of being expelled. Erskine's best efforts were in European history and English literature with shaky C's, there were D's in trigonometry and physics, the failure in Bible was conditional, and he flunked German with a mark so low he cut the class entirely.

The somber God-fearing atmosphere with its religious emphasis tinting the curriculum at Due West irritated Erskine. He found the daily prayer meeting at chapel and the mandatory Bible course insufferable. At sixteen, he considered himself an agnostic, and when the Caldwells moved to Wrens, Erskine either spent his Sundays driving Dr. Pilcher on rounds or accompanying his father when Ira preached to chain gangs.

Young Caldwell's religious stance made him the outsider; many of his classmates in Wrens were churchgoers, and nearly everybody in Due West, on and off campus, adhered to A.R.P. disciplines in public. There was also behavioral surveillance at Erskine College. Dating was not permitted and any unchaperoned event unthinkable. At dances, male and female were quickly separated when the music stopped. The Junior-Senior Dance was the season's most liberal gathering. On this night sweethearts were given fifteen minutes of unchaperoned conviviality before the bugle ordered a change of partners.

Feelings of hopelessness and suffocation gave way to indifference. Erskine no longer cared how he looked—the crimson E had lost its luster. He still wore his sweater, but it was smudged, and his trousers had a moldy appearance. The moonshine he had enjoyed sharing with friends was now quaffed in solitude. One night he became so drunk on a mix of liquor and lemon extract that a friend had to keep him hidden for fear that Erskine would be expelled.

Soon, that indifference soured into rebellion, and he became intentionally obnoxious and destructive. Erskine and Murphy printed huge letters of thick tar on the steps of the administration building shortly after the Clemson game: ERSKINE BEAT HELL OUT OF CLEMSON? SHE MUST OF DID. SHE DIDN'T LOSE. Then on a train with the basketball team, he went down the aisle gathering all the coffee mugs and threw them out the window. One prank could have had serious consequences: Erskine uncoupled a baggage car from a train before its departure. The car slipped free on a steep rise, rolled backwards, and stopped just short of being derailed. He was caught stealing food from the kitchen, college officials ousted him from the dormitory, and he moved to a boardinghouse. Here, he soon offended the landlady, who came to clean his room and found him reading in bed with muddy boots. After she complained, Erskine ordered her to leave, and later the woman found a note pinned to the door: "Stay out unless you are invited in!"

Though he tried to escape some of the hazing during his own freshman year, as a sophomore Erskine was relentless in making life miserable for the new batch of first-year students. "Go get me a pack of cigarettes," he would roar at a trembling freshman, and seconds later came the growl: "you're not back yet?" His brand of hazing frequently dismayed his classmates. When he took part in some of the traditional initiations—rituals which were carried out with lightheartedness and humor—Erskine spoiled them by behaving badly. If he could hurt, make the ceremony more painful, he could be counted upon to do so. But his obnoxious behavior would sometimes backfire into gleeful campus teasing. When a second cousin in the freshman class was embarrassed by Caldwell's incessant foul language, this ardent young A.R.P. student entreated: "Please, Cousin Erskine, stop swearing so much!" The nickname "Cousin Erskine" became a substitute for the previous "Cussin Erskine."

After Christmas vacation Caldwell returned to Due West with the realization that he was at a precipice. His grades were so low that even he felt twinges of guilt as he avoided classes and failed to complete assignments. With his unhappiness on the increase, Caldwell claimed that he tried to find ways of antagonizing the college administration to the point of expelling him.

This was partly bravado. Expulsion would have embarrassed Ira who had somehow managed a scholarship for his son at Erskine College, and Carrie's anticipated treatment under such circumstances surely caused Erskine some anxiety. By now, his dilemma had snarled a shawl of depression about him.

To postpone the inevitable, he planned a trip and somehow induced a doubtful Murphy to accompany him on the adventure. In mid-January, the two withdrew their combined savings of eighty dollars, then fled unseen to Donalds and took a Pullman for New Orleans. The fictional side of Caldwell was in full play years later when he spoke of their arrival in New Orleans. He and Murphy immediately passed muster and were hired as gunrunners. There were whistling bullets to dodge and cutthroat pirates out to slit their gullets. Both got on well with the hardened crew as the vessel prowled the dangerous South American waters. What really happened was the opposite. When these greenhorns, without passports, asked for work, members of the crew laughed at them.

No statement about himself can be taken as an absolute, and he has confounded biographers with his inventiveness. Even in notes prepared for *Twentieth Century Authors* he left a trail of color, such as the often-used chestnut of going to sea on a boat that was running guns for a revolt in South America. An early publicity release had him as an innocent passenger on a banana boat which was smuggling gold from Honduras. When the crew discovered he knew too much, they took him to a New Orleans hotel to insure his silence. He hung from a windowsill while the outlaws shot each other in the darkened room.

They found no employment in New Orleans, and decided to take their chances in Bogalusa, a city seventy miles to the north. They were routed there because a wealthy local businessman was getting married and free train transportation was accommodated all who claimed to be wedding guests. In a romantic mood, Erskine shipped a box of pralines to his sweetheart, Sara Farmer, at her college in Macon before he and Murphy boarded the luxurious passenger car and took full advantage of the complimentary cocktails.

They stopped at a rundown boardinghouse near the train station and soon found their room noisy and crawling with bedbugs. All night long they heard a Victrola play "Tuck Me To Sleep In My Ol' Kentucky Home." As uncomfortable as their lodgings were, Erskine was exhilarated by his newfound freedom and the adventure of travel; Murphy less so—he already was homesick for college and had regrets.

The two thought of working in an oil field, but a man at the train station told them that his entire pay for a week on a rig was only good enough to buy a pair of boots. At the time, Bogalusa was the last place in Louisiana to be looking for employment: the city was crippled by strikes and labor violence, as local lumber and wood-working mills were waging open warfare to keep the IWW from unionizing. Several labor organizers had been shot, and the local police force was out in full strength.

For more than a week, Erskine and Murphy stood in line outside a lumber mill gate in hopes of finding one of the scarce day jobs. But the few openings available went to older and more experienced workers. With their funds dangerously low and no work in sight, Murphy telegraphed his parents for money and returned to Due West.

Shrugging off the many days of unemployment in Louisiana, and still clinging to his colorful occupations, Caldwell would later write about his jobs as a stable boy at a racetrack and as a deck hand on a cargo ship. Then he was hired as a magazine-subscription salesman.

The sales crew was divided into pairs and each team peddled a hunting and fishing magazine to workers inside the lumber and woodworking mills. They were told that from each dollar collected the crew manager would receive twenty-five cents, the magazine publisher fifty cents, and the salesman the remaining amount. But it wasn't to be. At the end of the third day, Erskine's crew manager disappeared with all the money.

With his rent at the boardinghouse a week behind, he was now unemployed and nearly penniless. Erskine was searching for work when he was approached by two police detectives on the street and arrested. After a few hurried questions at the booking desk of the precinct, he was thrown into jail without counsel of attorney, and accused of "maliciously and willfully loitering around suspicious places without being able to give a satisfactory reason theretofore." The charge wasn't clear-cut vagrancy; it was more suggestive of a suspected association with Bogalusa's IWW organizers—the revealing "suspicious places" placed him squarely in the middle of a labor dispute.

Caldwell's stay in the Bogalusa jail had several fictional twists and turns over the years. In *Call It Experience*, he writes of a "middle-aged Negro trusty" who understands the plight of being behind bars: "I sure know how you feel, though, because I feel like

I've been locked up in here all my life my own self." *With All My Might* has its own unexpected decorations: There is now a cell mate, an "elderly black man who had white hair and an upper row of bright gold teeth." Perhaps there were a black fellow prisoner called Bojo *and* a black trusty, but these members of his auto-biographical cast, real or imagined, would be useful in later years when he discussed Southern race relations.

Erskine had no way of knowing how long he would be kept in jail—Bojo had told him it could be months. But his short incarceration gave the young man a better understanding of injustice; these were the familiar themes he and his father had discussed at length while handing out spare morsels of food to downtrodden sharecroppers.

Caldwell claimed that he begged an envelope and sheet of paper from the jailer and immediately wrote a letter to his father informing him of his difficulties. In *With All My Might*, he had only a quarter in his pocket, and just a nickel in *Call It Experience*. (One wonders why the earlier autobiography wasn't read to refresh his memory of that memorable time.) "Climbing to the top of the cell where there was a small iron-barred window," he wrote, "I waited hopefully for many hours to see somebody on the outside whom I thought I could trust to mail the letter for me." A barefooted ten year old with tan skin stopped near the jail window, and Erskine coaxed him closer. After assuring the boy that he meant no harm, the letter and nickel-quarter were dropped from the window and the messenger skipped out of sight.

Erskine College officials had alerted the parents of their son's disappearance, and Ira telephoned Sara Farmer in Macon to ask if she knew what had happened. The pralines posted from New Orleans gave the Caldwells a compass direction, and it also soured the romance with Sara—Erskine never forgave her for telling his father. Murphy was next interrogated, and he admitted having left Erskine in Bogalusa.

They had finally found him: Ira contacted the jailor and wired train money to the local YMCA for the journey home. After a free dinner and a much-needed shower, Erskine was on his way back to Wrens. His father was at the depot when the train arrived. The two shook hands, and Ira, with his usual calmness, showed no trace of displeasure. "What did you think of Louisiana, Son?" he asked. "It's a much different part of the world, isn't it?"

Betrayed by Sara, and with few friends left in town, Erskine again felt stifled and depressed. The spring and summer passed with tortoise passage, and there was no work to be found. His desire to become a string correspondent for morning newspapers in Augusta, Macon, and Atlanta was back in full bloom, but his best chance of seeing himself in print was reporting the outcome of games played by the local baseball team. Erskine's attendance at the park was frequent enough for the coach to take him on as their scorekeeper. Throughout the steaming months of July and August, he sat in the dugout recording hits and errors and later shaping them into presentable newspaper submissions on his typewriter. He also made claims of more exciting coverage. Wrens wasn't the sort of locality where a freelancer could provide columns of copy, but Erskine was making some noticeable headway as his grammar improved and his work habits became more diligent.

September threatened a more familiar jail than the one endured in Bogalusa. The thought of returning to the campus at Due West plunged Erskine into despair, but Ira insisted that he attend. Carrie sent several letters to the University of Virginia requesting a last-minute transfer but these were all rejected. In September of 1922, he returned with a sentence of three more years.

Football, which had provided an oasis for Erskine in the previous season, no longer held a lifesaving appeal. Since some of the first-string players had graduated and vacant positions on the squad were filled by newcomers, he had more of a chance to play. But it was a disastrous year for the team—they didn't win a game all season. There were no cheering crowds or triumphant parades down Main Street.

His academic performance remained at a low level, and he still was the renegade when strict A.R.P. codes of discipline interfered with personal plans or follies. Again, his best grade was a C in English, though his attendance was sketchy and he studied little. More often than not, he seemed to be elsewhere as he wandered about campus. "His spirit was still Bogalusa bound," said some of his classmates as they noticed his remote smile while he stood in the middle of a fun-loving crowd.

Conservative Erskine College founded on paternalism, and the willful, unhappy son of a highly-respected minister who tested the school's authority with prankish behavior and open contempt, were opposing forces about to collide. Trouble began after the first baseball game of the season. The manager of the visiting team complained that their lockers had been ransacked and several items were missing. The school was outraged that this could happen on campus and appointed two members of the student council to keep watch on the visiting team's belongings during the next home game. They stationed themselves in a room above the lockers where a crack in the floorboards gave them a clear view. After the game was underway, Erskine and a fellow Night Hawker entered and began to empty pockets. A number of wallets, watches, and fountain pens were in their possession when the council members confronted them.

Normally, an act of this magnitude would result in immediate expulsion, but out of respect for Ira, both the school administration and student council agreed that Erskine could finish his year but he would not be permitted to return for the fall semester.

For him, it was an oxymoron: humiliation gilded with great relief. He would miss Murphy and several cronies in the Night Hawkers Club, but it would have been impossible for him to bear another year at Due West. There had to be another way, some other college, a place where he could project himself towards a meaningful future. He left Erskine College showing his back and with no sentimental last looks. Over the years, in his recollections of that time, he never had praise to offer the school, and usually tended to ignore it. In a June 27, 1934 article in *The New Republic*, Caldwell did criticize "the dishonesty of the South Carolina college which taught by suppression and censorship." His own lack of honesty in the locker room was never mentioned in any of his writings, and at the time of the incident he and his accomplice preferred to think of it as a prank: they were only "switching the players' belongings from one locker to the next."

Ira and Carrie insisted that their son somehow finish college. His mother wanted him to attend the University of Virginia at Charlottesville—"Mr. Jefferson's University." But the out-of-state tuition and boarding costs were beyond their means; his father had already taken a cut in his minister's salary because of the drop in cotton prices. Including tuition and living costs, the expense of attending the University of Virginia at that time was at least twelve hundred dollars a year. Ira sadly explained that the limit he would be able to raise was only a third of the sum.

Erskine continued to earn spare change as a string correspondent for Georgia newspapers that summer, but he was more preoccupied with the task of getting back into some school and out of Wrens. During July and August, he and Carrie spent their evenings perusing university brochures and catalogues for scholarship awards. Acceptance based on his academic record was out of the question, and the abysmal showing at Erskine College limited the possibilities. They were delighted when they discovered a grant given by the United Daughters of the Confederacy to descendants of Civil War veterans—one so obscure it hadn't been awarded in years. The Bell family's bravery on the battlefield, and slack entrance standards at the university in the early 1920s gave Erskine an unexpected advantage. He regarded his acceptance with amusement. The admission committee of the university must have been surprised when it discovered that a student with such a poor transcript had been accepted in any institute of higher learning. The only explanation would be that the transcript dropped to the floor during a meeting, which was held on a blustery day, and somebody with muddy shoes trampled on it.

Erskine was on his way.

Erskine had been through Charlottesville a number of times on trips to the Bell family home in Staunton, and he and his mother were well acquainted with both the university's luxurious setting and Monticello gracefully poised on a hillside near the campus. Upon his arrival, he was struck by the contrast of a small, isolated religious college and this worldly university that promised what Jefferson had ordered inscribed on the entrance of the school: "Enter this Gateway and Seek the Way of Honor, the Light of Truth and the Will To Work for Man."

The boardinghouse he found at the edge of the campus was a dilapidated, three-story building with a neglected lawn. However, the location was excellent: it was near campus bookshops, stores, and lunch counters. There was also a streetcar that took one to downtown Charlottesville, a beehive of more than ten thousand and with every known diversion. Erskine was fortunate to find a room—so many World War I veterans were returning to school. What he liked best of all was the freedom to come and go as he pleased. The place didn't have the shackles of Due West; the fifteen hundred University of Virginia undergraduates had the same liberties as faculty.

Caldwell was too private a person to gladly share a room, but he liked Louis Ballou, his roommate at Miss Yeager's boardinghouse. Ballou was a student of architecture who hovered over his sketchbooks and regarded himself as a killer with the ladies. Appearance was important, and he took great pride in his evening clothes. Erskine, whose hallmark had been sloppiness, now did his best to become more of a clotheshorse. He soon was bragging that neckties hung from his collar from the time he dressed in the morning until he retired at night.

There was barely enough money set aside for Erskine to survive the expense of a university education. The United Daughters of the Confederacy Scholarship did pay full tuition, but Ira and Carrie had little extra to give him. As soon as he had settled in his room at Miss Yeager's, he began looking for work, and after only a few days he got a job at Johnny LaRowe's Poolroom near the campus. LaRowe, who had been a champion boxer before being wounded in battle, was now paralyzed and in a wheelchair. Erskine swept floors, racked balls, emptied trash cans, and repaired broken cue tips. He was paid a dollar for six hours' work, every night but Sunday—from six to midnight—and there were a few tips, enough to bring his total monthly earnings to thirty dollars. He felt grateful to have the work, in spite of one disadvantage: he was there to wait on pool players who were students, and this gave him the feeling of being excluded from campus life.

Erskine could not afford white-tie functions and dances in the gym where big-band orchestras played far into the night for well-heeled fraternity boys. Even simple dinner dates were beyond his means. He had to stand back and watch, in the same way he had done voluntarily at Erskine College, but now—it was ironic—he felt a need to belong and to take part in social activities. The one friend, his roommate, unintentionally was distancing himself from Caldwell—there were too many things on campus to snag Ballou's attention.

Fraternity members who belonged to the F.F.V.—"First Families of Virginia"—dominated campus society, and although his mother claimed such a heritage, he was cast as an outsider: the son of a minister whose unpretentious parish was situated in one of the remoter settings of Georgia. Caldwell had no background to elevate him to the upper echelons; there was no sheepskin from a prestigious prep school; he was probably the only student on campus who hadn't graduated from high school.

Erskine did his utmost to hide his feelings of inadequacy and claimed to be fully at ease with the lifestyle of the university. But he soon was telling fellow students that he was born in worldly Atlanta, not in rural White Oak, Georgia. Then, at a golf outing, he boasted of recent escapades in Europe, on "the Continent" he said breezily to impress his companions. There was dire need to improve what he felt lacking in social credentials: his father was listed as a "newspaper editor" instead of minister on a registration form, and Erskine gave himself the middle name "Preston" in order to substantiate a Virginia "First Family" heritage.

Poor grades continued to chase him and tax the patience of his parents. The long hours in the poolroom, his lackluster attempts to complete assignments, and Caldwell's disregard for priorities—he only worked hard when he was seriously involved—were enough to duplicate the dismal Erskine College showing.

His courses at Charlottesville were English literature, geology, psychology, Spanish, and physical training. The yearly average in psychology was 55, 70 in Spanish, and a shocking 38 in physical training. He did manage a C in geology, probably because of his and Ira's fondness for artifact hunting at the Cherokee Indian burial grounds near Wrens. His best grade was in the English literature class, with a 76 average for the year. In this course he read several Shakespearean plays and selections of eighteenth-century essayists, such as Addison, Johnson, Swift, and Burke. More appealing to Erskine were the fiction assignments featuring Kipling and Stevenson. This course was taught by an imaginative professor of literature, John Calvin Metcalf, who later established the highly-respected *Virginia Quarterly Review*.

As the year wore down, every effort was made to intercept the inevitable report card before it was mailed home, but Erskine was informed by the registrar that a student had to be twenty-one before achieving this privilege. Ira, the former star athlete and part-time coach, must have been perplexed when he saw his son's grade in physical training. An outright failure in three courses out of five left Erskine a number of credits behind, and when a fellow student told him that the University of Pennsylvania offered an excellent make-up program during the summer, Carrie and Ira were quickly informed. He sweetened the idea of living in distant Philadelphia and getting a part-time job by telling them he might take a course in economics, a subject that fascinated Ira, and for Carrie such a class could lead her son into a business career. It was one chance for Erskine to see more of the world—another escape from Wrens. In early June, Ira and son drove their old Ford to Virginia where the train to Philadelphia was waiting at Richmond Station.

Erskine enrolled at the Wharton School of the university with make-up classes and an economics course. He was convinced that economics and sociology were necessary studies if one wished to achieve reality in imaginative and interpretive storytelling. But Erskine soon found school less interesting than the streets of Philadelphia and the distraction had predictable consequences. His semester averages were no different than earlier college grades. Trying to cast the results in a softer light, he informed his parents: "Passed 2 courses and failed 1....That gives me two units for the summer. So it wasn't wasted entirely."

It didn't take him long to find employment at Nedick's Lunch on lower Market Street, a hash house where he worked from six to midnight as a counterman and grill cook. The pay was more than he had earned racking pool balls in Charlottesville, and there was the added feature of being able to consume an unlimited number of hot dogs and glasses of orange soda. Most of the customers who came into this cubbyhole of a place were men going to the Trocadero, a burlesque house located just down the street.

Life in 1924 Philadelphia was an enormous contrast to an easier style of living in Wrens; often too much of a difference as he felt the first pangs of homesickness. "I was always fevered by the thirst for knowing what men and women would do on earth when I was dead," he wrote in his experimental prose poem, *The Sacrilege of Alan Kent*. "Just before daybreak each morning but while there was still no light, I forgot about the people who would be alive and thought of my own self in that everlasting silence of darkness."

His present way of life in a urban setting may have struck Caldwell as a sort of drifting about in a noisy, crowded limbo, but for the first time he was questioning his own identity—the former "Night Hawker" was no longer forcing a cold and rebellious smile on that mask of freckles. There were feelings of nostalgia as he thought of the farm country where he had grown tall. Then came the rush of distrust for the city setting where "men bathed themselves every day and the women sometimes bathed three or four times" but somehow they never "smelled as nice to me as the young colt or even the oldest horse."

In late June, Erskine became acquainted with Wu Hsi-shan, a Chinese student in one of his classes. The son of a wealthy Shanghai merchant, this young man—Caldwell's age—was shy and unfamiliar with American customs. He needed a part-time companion, bodyguard, and tour guide, and when his generous offer was made, Erskine quickly accepted it as an afternoon job.

They frequently attended movies featuring such screen cowboys as William Hart and Tom Mix—the excited Asian riveted to his chair as he followed a favorite gunslinging scene. Then the two often strolled down to Wanamaker's department store where Wu Hsi-shan splurged on clothing he didn't need. On several occasions they treated themselves to performances at the Trocadero where they were entertained by "hootchy-kootchy" dancers and methane-blowing comedians.

In a way, the Trocadero compensated Erskine for all the carnivals in Wrens that he had missed because of Carrie's rigidity, and it exhilarated him that he could now choose smut if he so pleased. Such a freedom easily replaced rebellion, and as the summer closed around him and autumn threatened, he realized there was no more longing for home. When was he coming back? His parents were asking this in their letters, and there were sometimes two mailings a day.

"Have decided the best thing to do this year is to stay here and work," Erskine wrote his parents in early September. He was encountering so many things about life that a return to Virginia just then would be a mistake. He intended to send them a "big-city" newspaper; they soon would realize all the things they were missing by staying in Georgia. "If either one of you see anything in the ads you want—tear the ad out and send it back and I'll get it."

One reason for Erskine's reluctance to start the fall semester at Charlottesville was his father. Ira's heavy workload, often more than eighteen hours a day, had been too much: the stress of trying to find enough money to pay for his son's tuition had made him ill. The scholarship that kept Erskine in college had been rescinded because of his poor grades. This was not the time to place extra financial burdens on his parents. "Don't overwork now because there's no need of it," he wrote his father. "Better to slow up a little than have to slow up altogether." He just couldn't "go back to Virginia and take the money you both need."

Carrie and Ira were not at all assured that life in the streets of Philadelphia was a suitable educational substitute. Experience and observation in the college of hard knocks would one day lead him to a high-paying job, he assured them. By carefully observing local Jewish businessmen—"and you know how they are about work and money"—Erskine thought such a route would be profitable, and he had learned to "keep up with anyone."

His course in economics had led him to stray from textbook solutions of commodity futures, due bills, and demurrage to the need to enhance his knowledge with practical experience—or so he believed as he perused newspaper help-wanted ads and found that a part-time position as an assistant stock manager was open in a Kresge's department store in Wilkes-Barre, Pennsylvania. Hurriedly, he quit his three jobs: at Nedick's, with Wu Hsi-shan, and at the Trocadero where he often swept floors after the late show. Carrying Ira's old suitcase that bulged with rumpled clothes, he boarded the train for the coal-mining city.

Erskine found himself a five-dollar-a-week apartment in a dismal building near Kresge's and spent his afternoons in a drafty basement of the store cataloging barrels of cotton goods, glassware, and toys before delivering them to the salesclerks upstairs. It was grueling work and not the sort of practical experience in economics he had anticipated. To appease his mother, Erskine registered for two morning classes at Lehigh University in Bethlehem.

One of the assistant managers at the store suggested that Erskine learn window dressing after closing hours at six. But already the idea of being a business success had soured; he had no wish for

increased involvement. Caldwell now had a more important challenge in mind: It was his intention to learn the craft of writing. He
had known for some time that other activities were secondary, and
their real usefulness was to help him reach the ultimate goal of being an accomplished storyteller.

Three weeks in the drafty basement and the first Arctic nibbles
of autumn were having their effects on Erskine. He had a sore
throat and a bad cold that lingered. His salary of twenty-two dollars
a week, after the rent was paid, left him very little for food—he
had lost ten pounds and sometimes went to bed hungry. When a
job opened at the Wilkes-Barre train station restaurant, Erskine
quickly gave notice at Kresge's. The salary was no better, but he
could eat as much as he pleased from the menu: sausage, ham,
eggs, Danish pastry, glazed doughnuts, and best of all, chocolate
pies. Another bonus was being able to observe the street people
who slumped over steaming cups of coffee to escape the late-night
chill.

He needed a weekend job to supplement his restaurant salary, and
instead of seeking some innocuous clerical or service form of employment, Erskine tried out for a spot on the local semipro football
team, the Wilkes-Barre Panthers. His bushy-haired coach with
bulging muscles was unimpressed with Erskine's spindly appearance—most players on the squad weighed two hundred pounds or
better. The team laughed when he said his position in college had
been as a ball-snapping center; he had never played any other
position. "Not on this team you won't," the coach told him. "Maybe
you can play end and catch passes." But he was no match against
the sturdy coal miners and three former University of Pennsylvania football stars on the squad. Severe batterings in scrimmage
and a broken nose brought to a merciful end his career on the
gridiron within two weeks. But Caldwell and his publicists would
find this limited experience useful years later: one of the more than
a dozen occupations on his literary résumé was "professional football player."

By early November, Erskine's boastful letters of self-sufficiency had turned into whining complaints: winter threatened, he owed money on a suit and overcoat, and another bad cold had hit him. Both Ira and Carrie knew their son was homesick and weren't surprised when he wrote them that he wanted to return to Wrens before Christmas. Erskine estimated the train fare would be about thirty-five dollars and practically begged for the money. Finally, by early December, he had saved just enough to reach home where his parents were thinking of financial ways to get him back in school at Charlottesville.

# A GIRL CALLED HELEN

Erskine's return to Charlottesville in January of 1925 wasn't what he expected. The Jazz Age now gripped the campus with its roaring roadsters and bathtub gin parties. Women had been permitted to enroll the previous year, and their presence soon transformed the gentlemanliness of "Mr. Jefferson's University" into a lavish carnival of bright colors. The students seemed so young and frivolous to Erskine as he stood back and watched; they hadn't struggled to survive in the real world the way he had in Philadelphia and Wilkes-Barre. He was a man now, twenty-two, broad-shouldered, muscular, and with ramrod posture. His sandy-red hair was brushed back and parted in the middle like a surgeon's incision. When he stared at one, his blazing blue eyes were cold and reptilian, but his mouth sometimes would collapse into a curl of amusement. Some of his college acquaintances sensed a cruelness waiting behind his wooden-Indian mask of freckles.

With the scholarship gone and barely enough money to pay tuition, Erskine found work again in the poolroom and lodged with his friend, Louis Ballou.

Predictably, Caldwell continued to cut classes and flunk simple assignments, but he did find satisfying a graduate course in English composition taught by Atcheson Hench. "Atch," as he wanted his students to call him, conducted his course in creative writing with informal discussions at a large round table. There were twelve in the class, and Erskine couldn't help but notice the girl with blond hair who sat opposite him. Helen was her name, daughter of Henry Haden Lannigan, the school's popular track coach. There were no Southern teams that could match the ones "Pop" Lannigan turned out, and his athletes frequently competed with Ivy League colleges in the North.

Helen was a first year graduate student at the university with a major in English and a minor in both German and French. She had just returned from the Middlebury College summer school and was only a few credits away from her master's degree in French literature. "Pop" Lannigan's precocious daughter had entered high school at eleven and graduated with honors at the College of William and Mary shortly before her eighteenth birthday. Helen liked English poetry and classical music, and at spare moments would try her hand at writing and painting. At the time she met Erskine, she was playing the lead role in a campus production of Molière's *Cercle d'Odéon.*

Louis Ballou studied his crowded date book in hopes of finding a companion for the lonely roommate. But his efforts went unappreciated—Erskine seemed indifferent to coeds and student nurses that Ballou brought by for inspection. When there was a date, the young man from Wrens was an ungracious escort: he reacted coldly to any conviviality, kept his distance, and was sometimes rude. On one occasion, when he called on a young lady, his breath was heavily spiced with corn liquor.

Ballou had dated Helen several times, and though there had been no mutual attraction, he guessed that she and Erskine might take to each other. It was an immediate matchmaking success. "From the moment I introduced them," recalled Ballou, "I was past history." Caldwell had a different memory of that first meeting. He was leaving Atch's class one afternoon, his mind elsewhere, and the two collided. (This was more dramatic than being introduced by a worrying friend, and an excellent example of embellished reminiscences.)

They attended a concert on their first date, and looking back on that evening, Helen preferred to say that she was "raped by Rachmaninoff," not by Erskine's crude farewell on her doorstep: "I'd like to knock you on the head with a rock and fuck you."

Helen Lannigan stood out on campus, and the building she lived in was a landmark within the confines of the university. "The Chateau" was a dark Gothic structure with a moat and drawbridge. Behind the house were two abandoned ice pits which served as an area where "petting parties" went on at all hours. But this passionate daughter of the track coach had nothing but contempt for the erotic goings-on in sight of her bedroom window; she had no patience for the slim-figured flappers who flaunted their sexual wares promiscuously.

Helen knew she was attractive: her medium height, those features that were soft and oval, and there was a hint of plumpness in her figure as she walked with a slight sway. One friend recalled that she was "extremely proud of her bosom." She would brag about being "completely liberated" and spoke of losing her virginity to an older man when she was sixteen.

Erskine's coarse parting words on the doorstep hadn't changed Helen's opinion of him. She was deeply impressed with his almost brutal physique and good looks, and his intensity ignited her. Most of the young men on campus were boring and childishly incomplete; they had no inner core, no rough, worldly edges or sense of adventure. With a helplessness that was uncharacteristic of her usual response to men, Helen was moved by Erskine's energy, hunger for adventure, and probably, without being aware of it, his interest in the obscene.

"I fell on my knees and cried with joy because she had been made as she was," wrote Caldwell in *The Sacrilege of Alan Kent*. "We both knew now why God had made her with such passion and me a man." His confidence in himself soared as the relationship quickly ripened into a passionate affair. He now had the strength of a giant and displayed a new swagger. Eating lunch with a friend one day, Erskine pointedly ordered a helping of raw oysters to fortify his boastful tale of conquest. In Helen he had found "all the eagerness he had ever hoped to find" in a woman.

In *Sacrilege*, Erskine recalls the loneliness of his college years. "I had no place to go and nothing to do," he admitted. "Almost everybody else I saw had someone who loved him and they were happy together." But this had been more Caldwell's fault than the intentional superciliousness of the opposite sex—he easily could have snared quick glances from passing coeds.

Erskine was known to be more of an onlooker than a participant. In his second year at Due West, he visited a bordello in Augusta with several older students, and while the others were upstairs, Caldwell sat in the lobby alone, feeding coins into a player piano and watching the prostitutes and their clients—his companions scoffed and were convinced that here was someone "too afraid to try."

The innocent adolescent relationships he had with Elise and Sara were long over and forgotten; he now preferred women who were the opposite of his mother's Victorian idea of a suitable mate. The lascivious tales he heard when visiting former fellow workers at the cottonseed-oil mill and sordid stories told by traveling salesmen who stopped at the poolroom fascinated him.

"I do believe," said Helen, in one of several interviews with this author, "that Erskine's aversion to 'good women' was rooted in the smothering attention he received growing up from his mother and her sisters." That moralistic viewpoint they tried so hard to instill in him left him defiant. "Grandma Bell," said Helen, "often washed Erskine's mouth out with ashes and water when he used foul language." Unwittingly, they created "Cussin Erskine"—a young man who delighted in the vulgar dances and smutty vaudeville acts he saw over and over at the Trocadero.

In *Sacrilege*, Caldwell recollects a number of prostitutes who satisfied his lust before disappearing with the coming of dawn, though these revelations, including an incident in Bogalusa where he claimed to have met "a brown-limbed girl" who "warmed" him and "helped me lick my wounds," are suspect. Erskine may have found the courage to move beyond voyeurism into an acceptable range of normalcy, but he still hadn't got over being the onlooker. Playboy clubs were favorite nightspots.

Several accounts of sexual adventures can be found in the autobiographical *With All My Might*. Without doubt, the inclusion of this material taints the veracity of the more believable incidents in his life. He meets Rosie, a prostitute, on a Philadelphia street— probably one of the dancers at the Trocadero. She is tired, rain-soaked, and is in desperate need of shelter for the night. Erskine takes her to his room, gives her his bed, and camps out on the floor with blanket and pillow. When he wakes the next morning, Rosie is gone. She has stolen his one-dollar pocket watch and nearly three dollars in change that he had placed on his study table.

He seemed to find satisfaction in the idea of being victimized by bad girls, and one is left with the impression that writing this scene was an act of rebellion—an intentional time-out to be boyishly naughty and to shock Mama and the Bell aunties. Of course, they were no longer around when the book was published—had they been, he might have deleted the incident.

Erskine's physical relationship with Helen became more intense with each passing day—they constantly were in search of hide-aways where they could be alone—but in this fierce closeness there were formal demands: he insisted that they become one; she must be made "an honest woman." Helen thought he was in too much of a hurry. "Christ Almighty," she said, raising her voice, "I didn't want to get married, but he kept at me! In fact, he didn't use any-thing, and I was so afraid of getting pregnant." But there was no denying him or herself—they were too much in love.

Erskine borrowed a clean shirt from Ballou and met Helen at the Charlottesville railroad station for the ride to Washington, D.C. It was March 3, 1925, the day of Calvin Coolidge's inauguration. Helen told her mother that she was going to see the presidential parade down Constitution Avenue and this was the reason she was wearing her best dress. Upon their arrival in the bedecked capital, Erskine and Helen found a romantic taxi driver, Jerry, who took them to the home of his pastor. In a dark back parlor, with their grinning cabby and a weeping minister's wife, the two exchanged vows.

The wedding night was definitely a disappointment for Helen, though she did her best to suppress any signs of prudishness at his unconventional conduct. In his second autobiography, Caldwell renders a colorful two-page version of their return to Charlottesville on a slow-moving train. Not satisfied with handholding and kisses in front of amused passengers, the two consummated their hurried wedding ceremony in the swaying and cramped compartment of a ladies' toilet. In reality, the couple honeymooned in Baltimore that night where Erskine took Helen to five burlesque shows in the red-light district. She tried to tell herself that she was enjoying the crude spectacle of the strippers but was hurt by Erskine's behavior. "I really had to blush and was shocked when he tried to get me to go down the runway and do a striptease with the other dancers." No explanation was given when Helen asked him why he wanted her to do such a thing, but debasing her by such coaxing may well have been in order to emphasize his own sexual expertise and virility.

"Pop" Lannigan and his wife were noticeably unhappy when Helen and Erskine returned to Charlottesville. Their daughter's education had been very important to them, and they were proud of her academic record. The Lannigans knew little about this minister's son from Georgia, but enough to lament his solemn presence, lack of money, and poor academic showing. He smoked too much, drank heavily on occasion, and when he did have something to say to his in-laws there was seldom eye contact.

Ira and Carrie also were unhappy with the sudden news, and hurt because Erskine had not given his studies priority as promised. They did send a small check and politely welcomed Helen to the family. Ira did his best to accustom himself to his son's new situation in life but Carrie remained upset for days.

It was decided after several awkward talks in the Lannigan's parlor that the young couple would stay at "The Chateau" to save money on rent so Helen could continue her studies. Erskine kept his job at the poolroom and made a pretense of attending classes in geology, English, and two in economics. Again, his grades were abysmal: he flunked all four and received no marks in two of the courses due to poor attendance. According to Helen, their bedtime hours were much more gratifying: "We made love every night," she boasted. "Never missed!"

Tempers flared throughout the spring semester but eased when the family traveled to the Lannigans' summer home in Mount Vernon, Maine. This rambling structure was roomy enough to give the young couple some privacy: there were trails to hike, Parker Pond to swim in, and their second-floor bedroom was several partitions from disapproving Lannigans. But Erskine still felt uncomfortable; he had no independence; everything he needed had to come from in-laws, and there was the additional embarrassment of his suspension from the university. Then, in early July, Helen discovered that she was pregnant. He now realized it was time for him to face responsibilities with a full-time job.

Helen begged him to seek employment in Charlottesville—this way she could complete her master's degree. It was a plan her parents fully endorsed, but Erskine had had enough quibbling with in-laws; they must sever all ties for the sake of the marriage.

Caldwell appealed to his father, and Ira contacted Hunter Bell, City Editor of the *Atlanta Journal*. Would he "give the young man a chance" on the paper? Bell, who respected Ira's freelance contributions to the *Journal*, agreed to an interview.

Erskine provided his own rendition of the hiring in both autobiographies: He nervously entered the large newsroom and told Bell that he was an English major who had studied sociology and economics and once wrote jokes that were published in *College Humor*. Bell sighed wearily. "Listen to me," he told the young man. "Forget about those college-boy jokes of yours." A newspaper wasn't a joke book. The applicant was sent to see the business manager, and when Erskine returned a half hour later the job was his. "I'm taking you on," Bell told him. He was to write obituaries, and the pay was twenty dollars a week. "That's your station, Caldwell," said the editor, pointing. "And you can start right away." But Erskine said he wanted to return to Charlottesville; he had books to pack. "Books! Books!" Hunter Bell yelled. "If I'd known you think more of your bologna-stuffed books than you do about a newspaper job, I'd never have hired you. I want a hard-assed reporter—not a soft-assed bookworm." Erskine quickly relented—so went the story. "My wife can pack the books for me and bring them down when she comes," he told Bell. "Wife!" shouted the editor. The hard-nosed journalist suddenly softened and admitted that a similar thing had happened to him when he was young and newly married—maybe not exactly that way.

In early August, Helen and Erskine began their new life together. They rented an unfurnished flat at 43 Currier Street, a rundown neighborhood on the outskirts of Atlanta.

# ON FIRE IN ATLANTA AND CHARLOTTESVILLE

"Now get busy and wind up that typewriter and phone all the undertakers in the city and take in fresh obits," Hunter Bell growled at the novice. "I don't care how short your obit sticks are just so you fill up two columns of space every day." There were to be no excuses, the city editor reminded him. "People are dying day and night all over town—and complaining like hell about not getting their names in the paper."

Erskine faced his upright Underwood and began typing a disjointed obituary flowered with adjectives describing a funeral with grief-stricken relatives. Bell put an end to this kind of reporting with his soft-lead pencil. Faced with three hundred words about a holdup or accident, he slashed until there were a mere dozen lines left. A story or obit would only be used if it were written in half as many lines.

On one of his first assignments as a police reporter, Erskine was sent to get details about a man who had died in a cheap hotel. When the desk clerk told him that more suicides occurred on Monday mornings when drunks woke up sober and broke, he rushed back to his desk and wrote a two-page report honoring the downtrodden: this lonely middle-aged man who believed life had treated him unfairly; a person who no longer wished to live in an unsympathetic world. Bell trashed it after a breezy reading. "What are you doing—writing his five-dollar-a-copy biography?....No name. No home address. No story." He wanted a half stick for a final about the police discovering the body. "When I want a sob story," said Hunter Bell drily, "I'll send Peggy Mitchell."

Margaret Mitchell was a feature writer for the *Journal's Sunday Magazine*, and Erskine had been told that she was going to leave newspaper work to write a novel. He admired her for having the confidence, then wondered if he would be able to make such a decision for himself. "I said nothing to Hunter about my ambition to write books," wrote Caldwell in *Call It Experience*, "because I knew what his reaction would be, but nevertheless I was thinking about it more and more all the time. Anyway, Peggy Mitchell had resigned and, after ten years of work, *Gone With The Wind* was published in 1936."

Hunter Bell gave Erskine his first shove into what would become eventually a crisp prose style. Bell's emphasis on the economy of words was painful to Caldwell as he struggled with padded creations that the city editor was sure to cut in order to fit a stick of type. There was too much of the stringer correspondent in Erskine's outpourings; he had to write and rewrite in order to fill the role of a competent reporter. He remembered the job as being a realistic course in writing—completely different from any college English class. Caldwell felt fortunate to have had such tutelage and the experience of working on a newspaper.

In 1925, Atlanta was one of the better cities in the country in which to learn the craft of reporting. There were three competitive newspapers—the afternoon *Journal* and *Atlanta Georgian* and the morning *Constitution*. The city was known as "The Big Hustle" and those in search of stories were busy trying to outdo each other— anything to capture banner headlines. In ten years, this metropolis had doubled its population to 235,000, going from horse-drawn carriages to endless snarls of automobile traffic. New buildings seemed to lift skyward overnight, and there were a staggering number of plush stores to accommodate the rush of customers. Atlanta was fast becoming a convention center and idling place for the multitudes on their way to invest in Florida real estate.

After several weeks of undertaker chasing, Erskine was assigned to cover banquets and luncheons sponsored by the social and business clubs. Newsmen called it the "chicken à la king and strawberry shortcake circuit." It was a quick way of getting a free meal, and to an underpaid reporter comparable to a small raise in salary. But Erskine was no handshaker and easy talker as he circulated at these functions for news nibbles. His brown tweed coat with frayed cuffs and baggy gray trousers embarrassed him. He and Helen had little money to spare for clothes, but at her urging, he bought a derby hat and a walking stick—he felt this purchase would give him more confidence than any new three-piece suit.

Erskine proved to be less effective as a reporter when he moved to the police beat. Atlanta, with all its development, was caught in a number of mill labor strikes that had turned bloody. Predictably, his sympathy was with the workers; he would always be influenced by the time spent driving Dr. Pilcher on his rounds in Wrens and talks with Ira on trips into the sand hills. But his sentiments were in opposition to the editorials paraded in the *Atlanta Journal*. The paper sided with management in the controversies and labeled all opponents "outside agitators." The "Colored" and "Whites Only" signs in public places and Ku Klux Klan revivals in Atlanta further alienated him, but he was forced to conform his opinions to those of the paper's largely white audience, namely that "nigger murder wasn't news."

Erskine's salary of twenty dollars was barely enough to meet food and rent expenses, and with a child expected shortly, the couple felt apprehensive. Frank Daniel, a fellow reporter on the *Journal* who had become friendly with Erskine, suggested book reviewing. There was no payment, but the reviewer was allowed to keep the books, and these could be resold to local bookstores for a quarter apiece. Better than the peddling of books was the guarantee of a byline with each review, a dream that most string reporters entertain while submitting anonymous squibs of local news to big city publications.

After the heady experience of seeing his name in print, Erskine began to wonder if there was a possibility of syndicated exposure. He wrote several letters to book editors offering his services. Only one answered, Cora Harris of the *Charlotte Observer*, and she responded at once. She was "delighted to send books for review, and in fact was mailing half a dozen that same day."

The Caldwells' tiny apartment soon was lined with new books along the baseboards, and Erskine was prowling the secondhand bookshops in search of first editions to upgrade his growing collection. Not knowing which books to sell or keep, he wrote May Becker, book editor at the *Saturday Review*: "We are building up a library," he began. "Could you recommend some ten or a dozen recent publications suitable for a young man and his wife (both college graduates)...dealing with books of interest to collectors?"

As his confidence began to increase, Caldwell asked Medora Field Perkerson, book editor of the *Atlanta Journal's Sunday Magazine*, if he could review books for her. She searched for a volume that would be easy for an unskilled reviewer and chanced upon a thin one that seemed appropriate. He returned it quickly, saying it wasn't good enough to be noticed, and Perkerson consigned it to the discard heap. Several weeks later, when the book was hailed a sensation, she realized that Caldwell had rejected Anita Loos's *Gentlemen Prefer Blondes*.

Erskine's book reviews were done in a rush, and he spent little time revising and proofreading. The time for his dependence on Helen to mend his grammatical errors had not yet come—he was only feeling his way into words during the Atlanta months, just beginning to be on fire as a writer—and these reviews did leave an indelible record of literary shortcomings. In H. G. Wells's *Christina Albert's Father*, Erskine tried to reveal the plot while stumbling badly: "The father, we find is not the parental relative, which at first glance seems paradoxical; but the husband acquires a daughter, much to his apparent satisfaction."

These reviews began appearing in the *Journal* and *Charlotte Observer* in November of 1925 and ran every week or two for more than six months. Erskine's workload was now horrendous: Up every morning at dawn, bleary-eyed, he would gulp his breakfast before the mad rush to the newspaper office; then throughout the evening hours at home, and past midnight, he would be reading and writing under pressure to meet review deadlines. Few beginning writers had Caldwell's dedication and endurance: he refused to slacken pace; if he got exhausted, it was time to make more of an effort. Somehow, he found room to write short pieces and stories about wrongful labor practices and racial violence. They were crude, clumsy attempts, but they throbbed with a raw energy that was softened by empathy as he groped for a better choice of words. These outpouring were submitted regularly to magazine editors who rejected them without comment.

The birth of Erskine, Jr., in February 1926, further complicated their lives. Money was so short that the Lannigans had to step in and pay Helen's hospital expenses. The new mother hated Atlanta and longed to return home to Charlottesville to be with friends and finish her degree. The cramped conditions of their apartment, with a howling infant, and the huge collie, Borzoi, that she had given Erskine for Christmas, were taxing her patience. She knew her husband was feeling the same strain and wondered how long it would be before he fell apart. It was Erskine who finally relented, but not because of his low salary and endless hours. Charlottesville now seemed the ideal place; there he would have time to fulfill an obsession; he knew now that more than anything he wanted to become a writer of fiction.

In both autobiographies Erskine disregarded his third enrollment at the University of Virginia—from the fall of 1926 to the spring of 1927 when the Caldwells left Charlottesville for Mount Vernon, Maine—he continued to be a year behind in his recall, as if he had been born in 1902 instead of the following year. This session on the campus was his most successful venture academically, and he attended more classes than he cut. The hope of writing fiction gave him an additional nudge toward becoming involved in classroom activities.

Upon returning to LaRowe's Poolroom, late at night after most of the students had left, he usually found time to do some writing. His efforts were no grand flights—most of the material he produced was college humor, jokes that he continued to slip under the door of the university humor magazine, *Virginia Reel*. A few were published, but they were beginner's exercises. Still, in an unexpected way, this gave him a chance to be imaginative—they were better than the squibs he had shaped as a string correspondent from Wrens. More important was the discovery he made at the college library in an out-of-the-way alcove: on a table were publications featuring experimental fiction and poetry. The little magazines, some of which were only a dozen or so pages, were as strange to him as the names of the writers contributing. A new world had opened before him; the view so breathtaking that he knew this was something he must seize for himself. Instead of the well-known magazines his mother subscribed to were curious names, such as *transition, This Quarter,* and *Dial.*

It was the keen interest in the work published by little magazines that led him to discover, in book form, Theodore Dreiser's *Sister Carrie,* Ernest Hemingway's *In Our Time,* and Sherwood Anderson's *Winesburg, Ohio.* After that, he felt assured that the writing of stories was to be the work of his lifetime.

A sociology course called "Poverty and Dependency," offered by Associate Professor William Bean, had the right slant to capture Erskine's full attention. Bean took his class to visit hospitals, homes for the aging, and the county's insane asylum in order to better evaluate societal ills. These trips were reminiscent of those taken in Wrens with Ira and were a confirmation of the many things they had discussed on their long drives back to the manse. Erskine stuck with the factual when submitting his homework—that hard-boiled journalistic approach learned so painfully from Hunter Bell—and Professor Bean was impressed with the analysis. Erskine achieved his first A.

His class in the nineteenth-century British novel, taught by A. K. Davis, was far less successful, and it wasn't long before Erskine floundered in the familiar quagmire of disinterest. Instead of sitting with the other students at a table up front, he sprawled in a far-corner chair, morose, and ignored most of the assignments. Years later, Erskine recalled Davis with disgust: The professor had a "cold, objective, Oxfordian manner," one who prominently displayed a Phi Beta Kappa key and flaunted his Virginia heritage— the kind of Southern aristocrat that Carrie and her Bell sisters would have found praiseworthy. But the way the course was presented irritated Erskine even more. He had no patience for written assignments on "Humanity as Exemplified by the Lake Poets" and "What Wordsworth Means to Me" and couldn't understand why such topics were relevant to the British novel. Davis was equally unimpressed with his student, and when it came time to grade this backroom lounger, he flunked him without comment.

Professor Atcheson Hench's second English composition course was perfectly suited for a student of Erskine's intensity and need for finding his own way of expression. The class met weekly at Atch's round table, and most of the two-hour session was spent in discussing weekly essays. Erskine, who hated evaluations of any kind, and who was particularly vulnerable to criticism, felt at ease with Hench. He was helpful, remembered Caldwell, understanding, and more patient with a student's bumbling attempts to learn how to write than anybody. What Erskine liked best about Atch's informal approach was the freedom to express oneself on any subject; Hench recalled those stories about dispossessed people of lower-class origins and Ku Klux Klan lambastings—pieces unlikely to be accepted by any publication. Most of these writings originated from field trips with Professor Bean in remote regions of Albemarle County. Poverty and unfair labor practices were scrambled into essays with painful liberal conviction: "The Stench of Civilization," "God's Children," and "The Promised Land"—these were some of the titles that led Atch to later comment that they were: "overwhelmingly lacking in anything remotely resembling a social conscience." And yet here was, as Hench put it, a student "with the world upon his shoulders."

As much as Erskine enjoyed the informality of the round-table discussions, he realized that Hench wasn't lax when it came to voicing criticism. He didn't like the tone and sparseness that seemed to be building in Caldwell's work; the "staccato style" and "intentional drabness of the English" bothered him. A story entitled "Florence" was given a C by Hench with the comment: "Sex too crude, it seems to me."

Erskine's most notable success in English composition was his "Georgia Cracker," a four-page essay which was accepted for publication by *The Haldeman-Julius Monthly,* known as the "Little Blue Books" series. The essay was a response to an *Atlanta Jour-*

*nal* editorial by Harlee Branch. "No state in the Union (Georgia) has a purer strain of Anglo Saxon blood running through the veins," boasted Branch. "No state in the Union has produced a longer list of distinguished men and women."

This was too much for the preacher's son who had become acquainted with extreme fundamentalist practices while traveling with Ira into the remote countryside beyond his father's parish.

"Georgia suckles more Holy Rollers, Snake Charmers and the like, than any other state in the Union," Erskine countered. This is followed by a description of a young woman at a revival, and the material is presented in a way that readers of his work in later years would easily identify as Caldwellian:

> There she was, clothed only in a scanty piece of underwear, using her stomach and hips to great advantage, but the bowed worshippers continued for more than fifteen minutes, during which she sported herself like a hoochy-coochy teaser, a contortionist, and an epileptic recovering from a fit. At last she ran out of the church into the arms of one of the male preachers who quickly carried her off into the darkness.

The piece becomes slapstick when a buxom woman weighing three hundred pounds is told by one of the clergymen to get down on the floor and roll her sins away. Unable to make a complete revolution, she is given a hand, and once started, she doesn't stop rolling. Two preachers, up front with their backs turned, are struck by the rolling woman, and they fall backwards, their heads hitting the uncarpeted floor. "Those two men of God were familiar with more oaths than any laymen I ever heard," Caldwell added, "but possibly that was because they knew more of the words."

Then the essay drifts to an account of the crucifixion of "unruly convicts" and the lynching of a feebleminded black man. Erskine's aim is to shock, even at the risk of losing credibility through exaggeration. He closes with a regional summation:

> So this is Georgia—whose inhabitants do cruel and uncivilized things; whose land is overrun with bogus religionists, boosters, and dema-

gogues; whose politics are in the hands of Klan-spirited Baptists; and yet whose largest city boasts of being the "greatest city in the greatest state of the world."

The publication of "Georgia Cracker" encouraged Erskine and half- or quarter-promised some measure of success as a writer. But the struggle to succeed had only begun: he still had to overcome an awkward style, faulty spelling, and excessive imagery. More and more, he reached out to Helen and she worked hard to help mend his grammar and spelling. "It was a long march over eggshells because of that stubbornness," she told this author, "and it didn't take much to bruise his ego—I had to be careful."

Although he taught Shakespeare, John Calvin Metcalf, who was head of the university's English department, had a predilection for modern American fiction. His English-major students and aspirant authors were benefited by Metcalf's ability in raising funds to pay well-known writers for guest appearances. There were several literary celebrities on campus during the autumn of 1926, including Sherwood Anderson and Carl Sandburg. Erskine was impressed with both men and particularly liked Sandburg because of the poet's nonchalance and sloppy dress.

Anderson's short stories and *Winesburg Ohio* were heady influences when Caldwell was geared to becoming a writer. It was this established author's approach that appealed to Erskine—the stories had fluidity. "He didn't have that stiffness a New England writer would have," said Caldwell. "I had a feeling of more activity and more life than I would find anywhere in, say, Theodore Dreiser." (Both Caldwell and Sherwood Anderson sought to express the power of sex on men and women who dwell in rural surroundings and how it affected their lives. A difference in the two writers was one of technique; Caldwell slashed into the canvas of his stories wielding a palette knife. Instead of Anderson's solemn approach, Erskine found a noisy and grotesque way of expanding humor and violence.)

His first scraps of poetry, written on campus before he and Helen moved to Atlanta, were a painful mangling of doggerel. "Streams are slow, they always flow," was a typical couplet, and snarling back at the elite students who shunned him, he strained into triteness:

> They suck my blood and sap my life,
> My heart they cut as with a knife.
>
> O! Christ! They spit upon my face,
> And laughing still, increase their pace.

It would be several years before he mustered enough courage to mail a batch of poems to Louis Untermeyer for professional assessment. Untermeyer, performing a kindness, told him to stick with fiction. Perhaps the closest Erskine came to capturing his flighty and flirtatious muse was in the prose poem rendering of *The Sacrilege of Alan Kent,* and in his best poem "Face Beneath the Sky."

> A gust of wind evoked a sigh
> From leaded willow branches hour on hour;
> A figure hung beneath the sky
> Its neck was crumpled like a faded flower.
> With glassy eyes he looked at me
> And asked the color of my skin and face,
> I told him White—he laughed with glee
> And loudly cursed his God-forsaken race.
> The man then told me how he died,
> They fought, he said, in anger for his ears;
> His blood they drew with gruesome pride,
> And took his hands away for souvenirs.
> His arm I grasped, and turned away
> From dusky death that hung from drooping limb;
> A fleeting glance at break of day
> Saw weeping willows sadly guarding him.

Erskine wanted more of a role in the university's humor magazine *Virginia Reel* and the student publication *Virginia Magazine,* but again campus elitism barred him from active participation. Yet

he wasn't excluded entirely from social circles. The New Dominion Bookstore in downtown Charlottesville was a literary beehive
where a gang of hopeful writers congregated to discuss how they
were progressing with their work and the latest issues of little
magazines. Gordon Lewis, the proprietor, only a few years older
than the students, often persuaded established writers to talk at his
shop. Caldwell was remembered as the rusty-haired student who sat
on the floor in the back of the store reading everything he could
get his hands on. Among the students, Charles Wertenbaker was
ahead in development, and nearly had completed his controversial
and widely-acclaimed novel, *Boojan,* a story about a Virginia
aristocrat's love affair with a beautiful black girl. Erskine rarely
took part in the heated debates, but accompanied the others when
liberal doses of corn liquor were served. Once he did have something to say and the incident was remembered by several members
of the group. Caldwell had been listening to a prolonged bookish
debate about writing and stunned everyone when he jumped to his
feet. "We can sit around here talking about it all day," he told them
"but there is only one way to get to the top and that is to give up
*everything* but writing." With this long speech behind him, Erskine
marched out of the shop and into the street.

Helen finally persuaded her husband to use the dictionary while
working, and it seemed to give him better word choices and mended his atrocious spelling. Writing was such agony for him: he
would sit frozen in his chair before the typewriter, his back ramrod
straight, and his eyes painfully staring at a blank curl of paper in
the carriage of the machine. Then he would type haltingly until the
words began to flow. "He was possessed by an overwhelming obsession to write," said Helen, and everything he wrote "was like the
delivery of a child."

Helen delayed telling him that she was pregnant again. They had
little money, and his writing often was interrupted by his infant
son's crying. She feared that he would want her to have an abortion
and was relieved when he grudgingly accepted the news. Neither
realized how difficult their lives would become with the birth of

Dabney: now there were two howling infants in a crowded home with in-laws. "When Erskine got angry he was a lot like his mother," remembered Helen. "I would get the same silent treatment he often got from her." His writing "mattered more to him than human beings by far."

Finally, there was a family conference, and the Lannigans tactfully suggested that he, Helen, and the two boys would be happier living in the Mount Vernon house. Summer was coming, he could raise vegetables up there, cut his own firewood, it would be easier on Helen and the babies, and he could have a place to write. The idea of a quiet writing room, more space, and privacy appealed to Erskine and he accepted the offer immediately. He now saw that one-way chance of getting to the top; he would write, write, write.

Greentrees, the Lannigans' summer home, also was used as a training camp for athletes on the university's track team, though Mrs. Lannigan in 1917 had visions of transforming the roomy colonial structure and grounds into a tourist attraction. "Why not spend the summer at Virginia Inn in Mount Vernon, Maine," her brochure began, "located in the beautiful mountains of Kennebec County, seventy miles northeast from Portland?" (Mrs. Lannigan's sense of direction was faulty—Mount Vernon is more north, not a coastal town.) Built in 1742, the place was for many years the home of Noah Greeley, a Revolutionary War veteran. It had been a showplace, but was considerably run down when the Caldwells took up residency. Long winters and unheated rooms had warped the floorboards and cracked the massive fireplace in the living room. The roof leaked in several places, and the plastered ceilings were scaling. Once a hundred-acre farm, the land now was mostly woods, and only a glimpse of Parker Pond could be seen from a second-floor window.

Helen and her younger sister, Virginia, had loved going to Greentrees on holidays, and had made friends with many of the young people in town. But now the summer homecoming was different: there were two little boys to look after, endless chores, and a husband who had no interest in getting acquainted locally. When friends did stop by to see Helen, Caldwell refused to break from his writing, and most of these visits were held in the front yard so he wouldn't be disturbed by the sound of voices. "Erskine was more or less antisocial up here," recalled Helen years later, and added: "It was mutual." One had to live in Maine for a long time before winning acceptance. "They have an expression for it—goes something like this: 'You have to summer 'em and winter 'em before you give 'em a town office.' "

Caldwell's writing day began early in the morning, he would stop briefly for lunch, and then return to his desk for the entire afternoon. Helen was expected to keep Pix (Erskine, Jr.) and Dabney quiet while their father was working—an impossible task since both were under the age of two. If they cried in the morning, Erskine would express his displeasure by not speaking to Helen during lunch, and an afternoon howling might bring about the silent treatment for an entire evening. When the boys were old enough to understand that their father was in the house writing, they spoke in whispers.

Erskine insisted that his sons behave like grownups, and there was to be no baby talk. Crawling about on the floor was not allowed, and the boys were punished for laughing loudly or shouting. He was to be called "Erskine" or "Skinny," never "Dad,"—until Caldwell was twelve he had addressed his mother as "Tarrie" and his father as "I.R." or "Ira." When the two boys were with their father, usually at mealtimes, there was noticeable tension. Dabney Caldwell remembered vomiting at the table after being told to finish his turnips—a vegetable in abundant supply and one he hated— and Erskine demanded that he clean his plate and remain seated until the others were through eating.

Virginia Lannigan, while on a short visit in Mount Vernon, was appalled by the "violent, brutal" way Erskine disciplined her nephews, and Helen admitted that "he beat the hell out of the boys." Sometimes, the punishment was administered with a switch they had to cut themselves, although their father's favorite was the razor strop. Dabney recalled that he and his brother were beaten once with a canoe paddle, and Clayton Dolloff, who lived just up the road, often heard Pix's cries of "No Skinny! Please don't Skinny!" when Erskine felt his son needed a spanking.

Finally, the library at Greentrees proved too noisy for Caldwell, and he retreated to a small guest cottage the Lannigans owned on the shore of Parker Pond. "He does not like to have anyone around him at all," Helen told her parents. "He stays in the cottage all day and writes." Throughout the long, hot summer, into early autumn, he kept working at a plank table in the small cabin with the windows closed. No one was allowed near—this particularly applied to the children—and when he fell ill with a summer flu, Erskine ignored Helen when she tried to get him into the house for some much needed medicine.

Time was often a problem for him when he was writing—once involved in a story Caldwell wanted to forget the framework of passing hours. In Maine there was only a single clock, and often he would hide it in a closet or forget to wind it. There was daylight and darkness: he had no interest in measured intricacies. "But didn't this sort of thing make it tough on your wife?" a reporter asked him years later. "You know how women want to establish a routine in a house." Caldwell's reply was etched behind a grin. "I know," he quipped. "I lost two wives that way." (Helen and June Johnson)

Clayton Dolloff and his father, Arthur, were among the few in town who had a passing acquaintance with Caldwell. Clayton remembers riding to Lewiston in Erskine's Ford to see the boxing matches. But most Mount Vernonites considered the redheaded newcomer from the South distant and "damn peculiar." One man who still lives in the neighborhood of Greentrees bristles whenever he hears the name Caldwell. He feels that his Swedish family had been derisively treated in Erskine's short story "A Country Full of Swedes," and "that miserable bastard wasn't good to Helen and those kids."

Erskine asked Arthur Dolloff how much wood he needed to cut for an entire winter. "Maybe eighteen-twenty cords," Arthur then said. "Unless the Old Boy has a mind to bring down upon us a cold winter. If that's to be, I'd want five-six more for tolerable comfort." When Caldwell's autobiography was opened to where this exchange occurred, Clayton Dolloff glanced at the page. "Yes," he said, "I've read it, and I can assure you that my father didn't speak that way. So many things Skinny wrote about during his time in Mount Vernon just didn't happen. Perhaps he was a little too good at telling stories."

September is the month when native Mainers split their dry wood and store it under cover. Erskine's long summer struggle with short stories and several book reviews a week for the *Charlotte Observer* and the *Houston Post* delayed the wood operation. Instead of oak and maple he cut pine and birch, which brought about another encounter with his next-door neighbor. It looked like a great amount of wood to Caldwell, but Arthur Dolloff shook his head and said: "Cussed birch won't make heat when it's green and won't do nothing but make ashes when it's dry."

The birch and pine he had so proudly stacked in the yard disappeared with alarming speed. The house was uninsulated, and cold air seeped in around the rattling windowpanes. Only three rooms—an upstairs bedroom, the kitchen, and Erskine's study—were heated. Then the water pipes froze, and their only convenience now was a drafty outdoor privy a number of yards from the house. It soon became too chilly for the field rats wintering at Greentrees. They fled, according to Caldwell, to Arthur Dolloff's cellar, and the outraged neighbor could be heard shooting at them—"not the cellar," said Clayton, "in the barn was where father kept the grain." One of Erskine's neighbors quipped that he "would rather sleep in the apple orchard on a cold winter night" than at the Caldwells'. "We are buried in snow and ice," Erskine wrote his parents. "We shall have a rather lonely Thanksgiving—not even a football game or a chicken dinner." The potatoes and turnips were running low and there was only a short supply of kerosene for lights. Even more worrisome was the lack of proper winter clothing. By February, the wood was almost gone, and there was no choice: they packed their few belongings in Erskine's old Ford and hurriedly left Maine to avoid another snowstorm.

Caldwell needed to get away by himself, he told Helen, there never was enough privacy, and insisted that she deposit him in New York City. It wasn't an unusual request, and during their marriage he frequently escaped Helen and the children by renting some cheap room where he could devote all his waking hours to writing. Even on a cross-country bus trip he wrote, finding the motion of the vehicle conducive to productivity. His urge to write was so intense that he would deprive himself of food in order to stretch rent money. Sixteen hours was not an uncommon workday for Erskine during times of total commitment, and his need to get away wasn't limited to Helen and the children: he had to distance himself from everybody. On their visits to Wrens, Ira understood Erskine's need for privacy and rented a fishing shack where his son could be alone.

Caldwell kept to himself long enough to avoid visiting the Lannigans in Charlottesville and joined Helen and the children at his parents' home. He still was preoccupied with his stories and felt closer to the goal of seeing one of them in print.

More and more Erskine relied on Helen to correct his flawed grammar and spelling. She reworked paragraphs for him and dared to tell him what should be deleted. But there was the same unevenness present in his work, and in spite of the rigorous schedule he imposed on himself, progress was disappointingly slow. Helen had to be on continuous call as his editor. "When you read it again," he commanded from New York, "write me the same hour and tell me what feeling it gave you."

Erskine was relentless in submitting his stories to magazine editors, and though he kept at least ten different manuscripts circulating in the mails, they all were rejected without comment. His work was too graphic and ungainly for publication, and he seemed incapable of sustaining a tale longer than a few pages. His stories had no plots—they were more anecdotal sketches than story lines that would catch reader attention.

What Caldwell wanted to bring forth "was a revelation of the human spirit in the agony of stress or the throb of ecstasy." He felt this could be realized when situations and characters were invented by him and were not interpretations and imitations of life—it was imperative for fiction to be more real than life to achieve authenticity for his readers.

Upon their return to Mount Vernon in the spring of 1928, Caldwell again retreated to the small cottage on Parker Pond where he could be alone. There was some effort made for a garden—Arthur Dolloff sent Clayton down to plow and harrow a plot—and Erskine began cutting a stand of hardwood for the cookstove and fireplace. But most of his attention was given to stories, and there were the usual cold rejection slips from magazine editors—a daily ritual was the long wait for the delivery of mail at their roadside mailbox.

As the summer came all too hurriedly to a close, and the first stubborn chill descended on Greentrees, Caldwell had to take stock of their circumstances. The macaroni-and-cheese diet, greens from the garden, and steaming dishes of turnips were not in bountiful supply; their clothes were still inadequate; the boys were often ill. Both the Caldwells in Wrens and the Lannigans sent small checks when they were able, but now it was obvious to Erskine that he must find a job to survive the winter.

It was Carrie who came to the rescue which led them to an unforeseen course of action. She offered to lend Erskine some of the inheritance from her mother's estate, but only if he promised not to spend it as living expenses while writing stories. She insisted that the money be used to start some business. When Helen suggested that they open a bookshop and sell their nearly three thousand accumulated review copies for full cover price, amounts ranging from two to ten dollars a copy, Erskine jumped at the idea. He also felt it was time to stop reviewing books for Cora Harris—there were too many hours of reading involved in their preparation, and the work was taking him away from his fiction.

Caldwell had never forgotten the many hours spent in the New Dominion Bookstore in Charlottesville, and he wanted his shop to be a similar place where hopeful writers and artists could meet and be inspired. With his mother's money and a loan from a bank, he rented a vacant store in Portland, Maine. Early in 1929, the Longfellow Square Bookshop opened its doors for business.

He had grandiose ideas from the beginning, and it was almost inevitable that this struggling author with no marketing experience would fail as a businessman. To begin with, his writing time came first, and he begrudged the hour or two in the shop that kept him away from his stories. It really was Helen's business; she was the one who unlocked and locked the door. The review copies did form a substantial part of the store's initial inventory, but Caldwell had an idea of profiting even more from his supply of books. He would offer them to libraries at a twenty-five percent discount, thus undercutting the wholesale book dealers; this plan immediately jeopardized his limited inventory.

Within several weeks it became obvious that Helen needed assistance in running the bookshop; she had the boys to look after, customers to serve, with very little help from Erskine—he had found a new writer's sanctuary at the small house they were renting in nearby Cape Elizabeth. Caldwell hired Mary Moore (not her real name), an attractive, blonde girl who was a graduate from Smith College. She and Helen got along well, and for a time the store seemed a promising venture, though Caldwell often found fault with the operation. Unexpectedly, he would appear with a barrage of complaints: Helen was faulty in her bookkeeping, she didn't sweep the floor carefully, and Mary used too much paper when wrapping books. "I'm not paying you for that," he told the girl when he saw her with an open book. After berating them both, he would leave in disgust. On one noisy entrance and exit, Helen said to herself, aloud: "I wonder why all laughter ends when that man enters a room."

In a letter to his father, Erskine noted that the business wasn't flourishing. Book customers disappeared proportionally with the dwindling inventory, and Caldwell complained "that New Englanders are hard as the dickens" to persuade that they should change their buying habits. The fifteen-percent profit margin he set for himself was unrealistic; he had to admit that 1929 wasn't the best of years for opening a shop.

Helen had her own burdens—in addition to managing the shop and looking after two young children. Erskine suddenly had fewer complaints when dealing with their lovely blonde clerk. He flirted brazenly with Mary, and as the weeks went by his romantic intentions became embarrassingly obvious. Mary Moore was soon caught in a conflict of loyalties. Fond as she was of Helen, she found herself drawn ever closer to Erskine. When she did succumb, he took pleasure in describing their encounters to Helen in great detail.

There was a sort of burlesque dinginess as he drifted into other affairs. Again, Helen was regaled with an account of his seduction of a schoolteacher on a Portland ferryboat, and not finding enough satisfaction in the telling, he allowed himself to be caught. Helen recalled returning one day to Mount Vernon and finding Erskine and a Portland woman sprawling naked on the swimming deck at Parker Pond.

Caldwell's attitude towards extramarital sex during the writing of his unpublished novel, "The Bogus Ones," is illustrated when the wife of an artist finds her husband in bed with a female friend. Instead of being angered, the wife agrees to share her husband and helps the woman put on her clothes. Helen revealed to this author that such an incident had indeed occurred while she and Erskine were living in Portland.

"He was told in no uncertain terms that I believed in open relationships," said Helen, "and don't ask me why I said it—maybe it was my pride. I had to say something because everything was wrong." On several occasions when he was blatantly aggressive in hurting her, Helen took the boys and fled to Charlottesville. On one of these trips to her parents, she was unfaithful, and triumphantly wrote him and shared her news. Erskine faulted her in a scramble of confused syntax and self-pity:

> If you are going to keep that up like you did last winter, I may as well through the whole thing overboard now. I can't do a damn thing while I know that you doing something I wouldn't want you to do.... If I can't trust a person behind my back, I shall certainly balk at trusting him in front of me. Capone attributed his success, you know, to the fact that he always put double-crossers on the spot. If you want to get out, go ahead; I myself do not. If I had not loved you I wouldn't have married you. I wouldn't live with anyone else. It's either you or *nobody*.

The bookshop gave Helen a chance to be more gregarious than had the dooryard visitations from her Mount Vernon acquaintances. There were a number of struggling writers, painters, and musicians living in the area and they frequently dropped in to browse and talk about their work. "They helped to make my life less lonely," said Helen, "and I was terribly isolated in Mount Vernon—it was like living in the woods." Francis O'Brien, a well-known Portland bookseller and part of this artistic group, recalled the frequent teas and poetry readings that Helen would arrange in the shop's back room. "There were lively discussions, and Caldwell—we all called him Skinny—came several times, though he wasn't part of the regular crowd."

Caldwell's close friendship—and a lasting one—was with Alfred Morang. It was reminiscent of the one Erskine had with college pal Andrew Murphy. Morang's flamboyant style amused him, and they were often seen drinking together in Portland saloons. Another diversion they shared, and one that made a convenient getaway from Portland, was attending boxing matches in Augusta and Lewiston.

Morang, a Maine native, left school early to play violin on classical concert tours before settling in Portland with his wife, Dorothy. They both had a passion for modern painting, and though he gave violin lessons to meet living expenses his dream was to become another Pablo Picasso. Morang was also a talented writer of fiction: during the early- and mid-thirties he produced about sixty short stories of sufficient quality to have one of them included in Edward J. O'Brien's *Best Short Stories of 1935*, while nineteen others were cited in the publication's "Roll of Honor." "He would say the most outrageous things," Helen remembered, "and always to the wrong people. Alfred was death on Herbert Hoover because he was so extremely left-wing in politics. Erskine and I liked the Morangs so much that we were frequently together."

Caldwell's unexpected speech to aspirant writers at the New Dominion Bookstore in Charlottesville had crystallized into a firm belief that talking about art was a sure way of sidestepping the responsibility of getting work done—sheer laziness which tested his patience. He did like the eccentric company of regulars who drifted in and out of Morang's shabby studio apartment and the jugs of cheap red wine, but he felt the participants were mired in fruitless discussion. In "The Bogus Ones," Caldwell indirectly blames himself by having his autobiographical central character admit:

> They aren't artists, they are fools passing away the time—all of them!
> They were even making him one. The hell with them! He looked at
> himself in the mirror. What a damn fool I am! I thought I was getting
> ahead, and I come to my senses and find that I've been doing nothing.
> They act like artists and look like artists—that's as far as they can go.
> None of them has anything inside that makes an artist.

It was a familiar complaint, and one that gnawed at Caldwell as he fought to rise above his clumsy swirl of words. He somehow couldn't clear what shrouded his fictional characters—a dense fog blanketed many of his short stories and brutal outpourings. Erskine was increasingly pessimistic of his chances of ever being published. "If I could get only one piece accepted by an important magazine or publisher it would be easier to have hopes," he wrote Ira. And he had his protagonist of "The Bogus Ones" mirror his own worry: "He should get a good job somewhere, stick to it and save money....He was almost thirty years old. Could he ever shake off this damnable desire to create men and women on paper and make them living, breathing creatures?"

Caldwell retreated to Mount Vernon when the late spring days turned warm, and he wrote endlessly, too busy to notice the time of day or night or the ashtray that overflowed with cigarette butts. Helen remained in Portland, and only on weekends did she leave the bookshop and bring the boys back to that same tense atmosphere where they were expected to whisper when their father was writing.

Then one day as he ambled to the mailbox, Erskine found his story "July" printed in *transition*, an English-language literary magazine published in France. Furthermore, the ecstatic author was invited to submit more work in the future. The breakthrough had finally happened.

There was no payment for "July," later called "Midsummer Passion" in collections and anthologies. It had been written only a few months after he had moved to Mount Vernon and dealt with Maine characters in a local setting.

A celebration on the shore of Parker Pond took place shortly after this unexpected acceptance. With Helen and the boys huddled by a bonfire, Erskine began by burning all the rejection slips he had saved over the years. This was followed with the torching of dozens of short stories and poems that no longer had his confidence; there were to be no reminders of clumsy beginnings.

"Fritz read the letter a dozen times before he fully realized just what had happened," wrote Caldwell in "The Bogus Ones" when trying to describe those special moments of gratification. "He was being accepted among the modern writers!" Clayton Dolloff remembered how astonished a passing neighbor was who heard and saw the usually dour Southerner shouting and cavorting back and forth on the front lawn.

Caldwell barely had time to recover from his first acceptance when word came that *The New American Caravan*, a yearbook of fiction edited by Alfred Kreymborg, Lewis Mumford, and Paul Rosenfeld, had accepted the short story "Midsummer Passion" and a prose-poem piece called "Tracing Life with a Finger." But his jubilation at being included in such a prestigious journal was deflated when he realized that "July" and "Midsummer Passion" were the same story—Erskine had sent the manuscript in two different directions. Fortunately, the editors of both publications excused the double submission and the *Caravan* included it in their October 1929 issue.

Among the twenty-nine contributors to that issue of *Caravan* were John Gould Fletcher, E. E. Cummings, and Ivor Winters. Caldwell was one of only three newcomers, and reactions to his two pieces were positive: F. Scott Fitzgerald thought Erskine showed definite promise, and John Gould Fletcher was taken with the prose poem.

*Caravan's* reputation of publishing the best and most promising writers propelled Erskine's first steps from obscurity to recognition. Little magazines that had rejected his stories without comment now were reacting favorably. Charles Henri Ford, editor of *Blues*, accepted "Joe Craddock's Old Woman," a sketch of a poor farmer's death, and sent Caldwell the names of other editors who might favor him, among them Richard Johns of *Pagany*, a new fiction magazine in Boston.

Caldwell introduced himself to Johns with bluntness: "You don't know me and neither does anybody else. I've been working for seven or eight years unsuccessfully, though several of my pieces are coming out this fall." Johns wasn't disturbed by Erskine's introduction and immediately accepted a submission. So did the editors of *Hound & Horn, Front, Nativity*, and *This Quarter*.

Critics who were impressed with Caldwell's straightforward and sometimes brutal renderings—he was an original—feared that his style of writing might be softened by publications that had literary agendas and were "highbrow." They also believed that Caldwell's sympathies for hungry sharecroppers and deprived mill workers might make him an adopted son of Communist intellectuals. But he had labored too long in a limbo to submit to labeling: "I do not write for a cause like Communism,—or propaganda for Single-Tax, the Pope, more sewers, bigger Buicks, or fewer babies," he wrote one editor, and in a letter to Richard Johns, Erskine reasoned that the ideal magazine "shouldn't be the mouthpiece of a group or a collection of groups." He would go on listening to himself and appearing in any journal that would accept him.

Pleased to have his days as a book reviewer behind him and soon to make an appearance in *The New American Caravan*, Caldwell packed his suitcase full of manuscripts and took the night bus to New York City. He rented a cheap room and began visiting a number of publishing houses with the hope that someone would show interest in his work. Among his manuscripts were two novellas he had completed between 1927 and 1929.

Unable to contact Alfred Kreymborg at the *Caravan* editorial office, Erskine left his name and telephone number. Instead of Kreymborg, an Erich Posselt returned the call. His small publishing house, The Heron Press, was interested in viewing manuscripts.

Overwhelmed that someone should be asking, Caldwell suggested one of the novellas. The interview with the young dark-haired Posselt was conducted in a taxicab—according to Caldwell in both of his autobiographies—and after Posselt had perused the work for an hour, the two signed a contract. As Erskine was leaving the taxi, Erich said the manuscript would require a title and for that he had decided the book should be called *The Bastard*. Caldwell had reservations but was too overcome with the acceptance to argue with the man.

*The Bastard* and the second novella, *Poor Fool*, are companion pieces in the sense that they both were rooted in the tough-guy approach of detective fiction popular in the 1920s. "I'm busted on you, kid," Caldwell has Gene Morgan, the bad-guy hero in *The Bastard* tell his inamorata, "and I'll work like hell for you and keep you like a queen....Jesus, kid, I never thought I'd fall like this for a she, but God knows I'm busted on you. You're the sweetest little kid these old lookers ever looked at. Jesus, kid! I'm plain nuts about you."

A reader can see that Morgan is socially flawed, not the crème de la crème, but appropriately characterized for the sadistic way Caldwell lashes out at women and motherhood. "When Gene Morgan had last heard of the woman who was his mother," the book opens, she "was young no more, nor was she now beautiful as she once had been. But she was experienced in the ways of men and of money, and she possessed a formula for increasing the fee which men were always eager to pay for her knowledge." The mother, a whore in the "hoochie-coochie tent" of a traveling carnival, had murder in her heart at the time she gave birth to Gene. "She cursed all the time she was in labor," wrote Caldwell, and "would have killed him sooner or later if an old negro woman had not offered to raise the child."

He seldom mentioned these two books, though he would list them whenever asked to provide information, and willingly helped to promote a French edition of *The Bastard*. The main character of each title is an unappealing nonentity who can be found readily in a Hemingway tale. *Poor Fool* is a crime story with scenes of necrophilia in big-city surroundings; it deals with boxers in fixed fights and a hero who tries to outwit the system. Both books have the mother figure, fat and testy broads; women who exhibit offensive sexuality and are domineering.

When Morgan comes across his mother again, she is working in a burlesque house—much like the Trocadero that Caldwell frequented in Philadelphia. He pays for her services without telling her who he is, and after the incestuous act he is upset because "she did not know he was her son, or if she did know" the harlot just "didn't care."

A stranger tells Morgan that this woman—known as "Norfork Gertie—Denver Sal—Rose of Scranton—Big Butt Bessie" was in a pit with a "stunted pony" and "had twenty-seven men the Sunday night before." Then the man shows Gene a pornographic card, not unlike the ones Caldwell flourished when attending Wrens High School. "There were the red and blue scars sinking into her hips, the long knife-slash furrowing her belly like a drain ditch cut through the Louisiana swamp, and there too was her left breast nippleless where some drunken horseman had severed it with his teeth."

F. Scott Fitzgerald, who later became an admirer of Caldwell, was not impressed with the blunt dialogue found in *The Bastard*. Fitzgerald's passing commentary was "more crimes committed in Hemingway's name." Much of the dialogue in this first book put off critics who would defend the later novels. There was banality that could not be condoned:

> "Kitty wasn't nothing but a slut."
> "That's what most women are, aren't they?"
> "Kitty was a dirty slut."
> "All of them are either dirty or clean."
> "I like 'em clean."
> "No, there ain't much difference."
> "But that damn Kitty—"
> "I hope she's smoking now."

"And stinking."

James Devlin in his doctoral dissertation on *Erskine Caldwell*, (State University of New York at Binghamton, 1976) stated that *The Bastard* and *Poor Fool* showed hints of a disturbed state of mind. But Erskine defended these two fictional attempts by explaining that he was trying to "create a different world;" he "had to *imagine*—I was not photographing life."

He did at times stray beyond the landscape of his experience: there were pages of guesswork as he developed the characters in *The Bastard* and *Poor Fool*. The same can be said for a number of short stories, such as "Martha Jean" and "Dorothy," where he simulated sophistication in matters of female psychology and urban living.

Caldwell stated that *The Bastard* was written to reveal an "untouched phase of American *mores*" and in bringing front and center the characters in his story he created hypothetical ones not present in the book—such as a girl who loses her job in a cotton mill and becomes a whore. "I have intense sympathy for these people," declared Caldwell as he allowed his imagination to stampede: "I have slept with them in jails, I have eaten with them in freight cars. I have sung with them in convict camps, I have helped the women give birth to the living. I have helped the men cover up the dead."

Caldwell wasn't naive; he realized that this grotesque and pornographic debasement of women and motherhood wouldn't be greeted with warmth in some circles: "The Bastard is coming out November 1st," he wrote a friend. "I still have time to stay away from a certain Presbyterian manse or parsonage." But he wasn't prepared for the vehement reception *The Bastard* was given when he displayed the book at his Longfellow Square Bookstore. The Cumberland County District Attorney, Ralph Inglass, charged that the work was "obscene, lewd, and immoral." Helen looked back at this legal rumpus with amusement and disgust: "They threatened to arrest me for selling the book—'One more copy sold and you will be jailed,' I was told—and we were ordered to ship all the books back to the publisher. If we didn't, we would be prosecuted for selling pornography. That district attorney had it against us from the beginning. Only a week before the book was banned we were ordered to take down a window display of another book they called 'obscene.' This one was by Christian Scientist Mary Baker Eddy!"

There was no money to hire a lawyer to defend the book, and both the Portland police and legal officials looked upon the disheveled artistic youths who gathered at Helen's literary teas with suspicion. These "degenerates" were part of the "unwashed gang" who loitered in waterfront saloons and were unemployed.

Caldwell was outraged by the loss of his book "which is like a first love to me," and feeling that he had been "denied his first amendment rights," responded by printing and circulating a pamphlet entitled "In Defense of Myself." The banning of his book was a "comedy of justice"—he had been deprived a "trial before a judge, or before a jury," and had not been informed what words were "impure and obscene." He insisted that there was a link between poverty and sexual degeneracy, a central theme that he would be better able to handle in later books.

"In Defense of Myself" was only a preliminary salvo at officialdom. In his unpublished "The Bogus Ones," Ted, a brilliant painter, is compelled to destroy his masterpiece because the local district attorney proclaims it obscene. This "little Mussolini" and his crew of "rabid neo-puritans, who think he or she is God himself" were typically regional. "New England isn't mountains and lakes and seashores," Ted proclaims, "but an inhibited and repressed old witch who is a witch if there ever was one."

Erich Posselt had asked Caldwell to send the second novella, and it was accepted by Alex Hillman who took over The Heron Press, calling his new publishing vehicle The Rariora Press. *Poor Fool* met with the same criticism as *The Bastard*: faulty characterization, clichés and hackneyed phrases. Blondy Niles, a seedy boxer, is trapped in an abortion clinic by an obese woman called Mrs. Boxx: her specialty in this establishment consists of killing both mother and child. Mrs. Boxx is also a threat to masculinity; she enjoys castrating virile men, and in Blondy's case the deed is to be done with sharp shears. Why the boxer is powerless to resist the infamous Mrs. Boxx isn't explained, though Caldwell does offer these sentences: "She could make him do anything she wanted him to do. If she had decided she was going to make him submit to that kind of operation she could make him want to have it performed. Blondy suddenly realized the extent of her domination over him and he was frightened. But he could do nothing about it."

Mrs. Boxx's daughter rescues Blondy Niles just before surgery is performed, but the boxer can't come to terms with his loathing and feelings of guilt. "What's it about your mother that she can make me do anything she wants?" Blondy asks the girl. "I want to try and forget that God damn witch. I know she's your mother, but I can't help hating her like hell."

Maurice Coindreau, in the preface to his 1945 French translation of *Poor Fool*, labeled the story as "a chromo illustration of the Oedipus complex and of the castration complex." The book could not be digested completely without using Freudian ingredients. "Psychiatrists," wrote Coindreau, "will be grateful to Erskine Caldwell for having offered them a savory dish that, for good measure, he has seasoned with a pinch of sadism and necrophilia."

In an interview with Coindreau, Caldwell explained that what came in *Poor Fool* was something like those diabolical dreams that rise out of opium. He had allowed his thoughts to gallop without restraint. "I believe if the story has any interest, the reason is the contrast between the madness of the subject and a style that is cold, concise, and perfectly reasonable in the strict objectivity."

Caldwell's only recollection of his book contract for *The Bastard* was that Posselt handed him a check for two hundred and fifty dollars. It was the first money Erskine had ever received for his writings and was such a large sum that all he could do was stare with glazed eyes at the check. But this recall contradicts what Caldwell wrote Milton Abernethy, editor at *Contempo*, months later when the subject was Erich Posselt and The Heron Press: "The bastards who published it vamoosed with all the copies and the money—a clever combination of Hungarian and Jew." What actually happened had lifelong effects: Caldwell never trusted book contracts and was shrewd when dealing with editors and agents.

"I was much impressed by your stories in the *Caravan*," wrote Maxwell Perkins, the fiction editor at Charles Scribner's Sons, "and I thought it possible you might be willing to send something to *Scribner's Magazine*." Caldwell was elated that Perkins should be interested, for he was well aware that Scribner's had stabled some of America's exciting talents—names like Thomas Wolfe, F. Scott Fitzgerald, and Ernest Hemingway. Erskine submitted a humorous Maine piece which was returned promptly and diplomatically. "The story impressed me in the way it was told, and in the quality of authenticity about it," Perkins reported, though "in the superficial sense, which we do have to consider, it would seem too much an anecdote." Could he submit more?

Caldwell, never one to back away from an opportunity, selected several manuscripts, and he and Helen were on the next bus to New York City. In the lobby of the imposing building where Scribner's had their offices, Caldwell told his wife to wait while he went upstairs: she was too shabbily dressed and wouldn't make a good impression. But when he entered the portals of Scribner's he was too nervous to ask for Perkins. Instead, he quickly surrendered his manuscripts to a secretary and fled.

Upon his return to Maine, Caldwell waited anxiously for Perkins's reaction, though inwardly convinced that all his stories would be rejected. Then the telephone rang and he heard that "The Mating of Marjory," had been accepted—a tale about a lonely New England woman in search of a husband. A few days later, there came another call, and Perkins was accepting a second story, "A Very Late Spring," this one about a Maine farmer's infidelity and his forgiving wife.

In *Call It Experience,* Caldwell gives an imaginary spin to the conversation he had with Perkins:

Perkins: Now about these two stories. As I said, we want to buy them both. How much do you want for the two together? We always have to talk about money sooner or later. There's no way of getting around that, is there?

Caldwell: Well, I don't know exactly. I mean, about the money. I hadn't thought much about it.

Perkins: Would two-fifty be all right? For both of them.

Caldwell: Two-fifty? I don't know. I thought maybe I'd receive a little more than that.

Perkins: You did? Well, what would you say to three-fifty then? That's about as much as we can pay for both of them. In these times magazine circulation is not climbing the way it was, and we have to watch our costs. I don't think times will get any better soon, and maybe worse yet. Economic life isn't very healthy now. That's why we have to figure our costs closely at a time like this.

Caldwell: I guess that'll be all right. I'd thought I'd get a little more than three dollars and a half, though, for both of them.

Perkins: Three dollars and fifty cents? Oh, no! I must have given you the wrong impression, Caldwell. Not three dollars and a half. No. I meant three hundred and fifty dollars.

Caldwell: You did! Well, that's sure different. It sure is. Three hundred and fifty dollars is just fine. I didn't expect that much.

A "cool cat" was the way John Hall Wheelock of Scribner's described Caldwell when it came to financial matters—he knew how to negotiate; here was someone who "played it close to the vest." This was no hick in the backwoods of Maine, but a man who knew full well that landing two stories in such a prestigious publication wasn't a three-and-a-half-dollar transaction.

Encouraged by the acceptance, Caldwell began a three-month

crusade by allowing one story to chase another—a productivity he never again would equal—and each manuscript was immediately sent to Perkins. They were all rejected, but gently: this one "did not quite come over" or "I should think you are bound to come out well in the end."

Then in May of 1930 came a resounding endorsement from Scribner's: they would publish a volume of his short fiction the following year. Perkins was now convinced that Caldwell could deliver such a book; it only would be a matter of rounding out the collection with a few new stories.

A $300 advance for the book and $350 for the two stories would buy Caldwell more writing time. No longer interested in the faltering Portland bookshop and the requirements of his family, he decided to get as far away from Maine as a Greyhound bus could take him. Why not write in warm California and avoid a Greentrees or Portland winter? "I begged him not to go," said Helen, "but he wouldn't listen. My God, the shelves in the shop had that empty look, and we barely had enough to eat."

Erskine stopped in New York, and this time had the courage to face Perkins. When he entered the office, the editor was wearing a gray felt hat, his bright tan shoes looked too small, and his brown suit was baggy at the knees. With the typed manuscript, *American Earth*, before them—about two hundred and seventy-five pages in length—the two discussed publication details. There would be some revisions necessary, but Caldwell's literary future also was on the editor's mind. Well aware why Scribner's had rejected *The Bastard*, *Poor Fool*, and "The Bogus Ones," Perkins now suggested a different track. Instead of a New England setting, Caldwell was urged to concentrate on the part of the country he knew best: rural Georgia. After a stand-up meal, at a lunch counter, of cream cheese and nut sandwiches and two glasses of milk, Erskine boarded the bus for California.

With his cigarette-rolling machine, a stack of yellow sheets, and portable typewriter, all the way to Los Angeles he sat cramped and worked on stories. Upon his arrival, he got a cheap room at the

Warwick Hotel in Hollywood and ignored his surroundings. Caldwell didn't "think much of the ungodly country—mostly desert, no trees, no grass—nothing but sand and sage brush."

*American Earth* had a beginning section called "Far South" and a second entitled "Farthest East." "Ten-thousand Blueberry Crates," "John the Indian and George Hopkins," and "The Corduroy Pants" were stories that cut unkind cartoons of his Mount Vernon neighbors; here were small-town characters displaying their stinginess, narrow-mindedness, and buffoonery. Perkins believed that Caldwell overdid himself in depicting these New Englanders and the stories should be tempered. "The Mating of Marjory" type of rendering better displayed his range and talent—John Hall Wheelock had the same assessment. Both realized that the New England stories were not as convincing as those rooted in the South. Told in the first person, his "Far South" stories were more direct and less detached, though the editors expressed concern with the violence in some of the selections. "I think you perhaps bear down too heavily on the beastliness and brutality," Perkins suggested. "The impression of such exaggeration" threatened his credibility and "verged on burlesque."

The third section would be *The Sacrilege of Alan Kent*, his semi-autobiographical prose poem. Coated with elaborate yarns, the *Kent* section was a scattershot rendering of narrative paragraphs and fanciful images. What worried Perkins and Wheelock was the sexual explicitness—book banning was a common occurrence in 1930, and the editors had their firm's reputation to protect. They knew how sensitive their boss, Arthur Scribner, was in preserving respectability. Caldwell deleted the objectionable material with little resistance. "I appreciate the things you said," he wrote Wheelock, "and after forty-eight hours, I am fully convinced that my wisest course is down your stream."

Nearly twenty years after the April 1931 publication of *American Earth*, when the book was reissued by Duell, Sloan and Pearce in 1950, Caldwell had this to say about his first collection of short stories: "I believe I achieved what I set out to do at the time, which was to prove to myself that it was possible to find the materials of fiction in the everyday life around me."

Several New York reviewers approached Caldwell's stories as though they were downwind of an unpleasant odor. The collection sold fewer than 1,000 copies though the author did not go unnoticed.

"Caldwell makes everything interesting," wrote W. A. Swanders in the St. Paul *Minnesota News*. "Yarn after yarn he spins with great simplicity and great scorn for plot." Gorham Munson prophesied that Caldwell might well become America's Henry Fielding. "Directly, simply," wrote Munson in the *New York Sun*, "he relates the scandals of the neighborhood, and with a sunny humor spins some tall yarns."

Several critics were reminded of an early Hemingway. "Mr. Caldwell has something to say," Vincent Wall announced to readers of the *Saturday Review of Literature*, "although he is not always quite articulate....The work on the whole, however, has strength and vigor, and the characters are full-blooded and convincing. Those who keep an ear to the ground for the new voices in literature will be interested in reading his next volume."

*American Earth* had priority as Caldwell wrote new stories, made repairs on the manuscript, and was simultaneously preoccupied with his impending novel. Hour after hour, he sat before the portable typewriter trying to get past an opening chapter. He knew the book had to be about tenant farmers and sharecropping families outside Wrens, but seemed incapable of achieving any narrative sense—memories of those outings with Ira and the doctor he chauffeured evaded him.

He rarely left his room at the Warwick for more than an hour at a time. "When I did leave it," wrote Caldwell, "I usually went to a drugstore on the corner for a fifteen-cent breakfast or for a twenty-cent lunch, and in the late afternoon or early evening I went two blocks up the street to a restaurant on Hollywood Boulevard where a platter of T-bone steak and hash-browned potatoes cost only twenty cents." He was living within his budget of twelve dollars a week and had enough left over to buy tobacco for his rolling machine and to pay postage for the daily submission of stories to magazines. But with the novel there seemed to be a bankruptcy of words.

To Frank Daniel, his friend on the *Atlanta Journal* who asked about the new book, Caldwell replied: "Can't tell you the name of the novel because it isn't written yet." And he guiltily admitted to a curious Wheelock, after telling the editor that the novel had more quality than the short stories, "at least in my mind it is better." However, with Christmas nearing came the realization that he was committed to get the work done but was in the wrong place to do it. California and Georgia were two different worlds; he had to go back to roots; reacquaint himself with what he had known.

Helen and the children met Erskine in Wrens during the holidays but he spent little time with them. Day after day, he and his father were on missions of mercy in Ira's Ford jalopy delivering food and medicine to desperate farm families. "Within a few miles from town," wrote Caldwell in *Call It Experience*, "families on tenant farms were huddled around fireplaces in drafty hovels." Food was scarce, there were no jobs, and no money could be raised to buy seed. Equally disheartening was the futility of their existence: they were cornered in their poverty, trapped and dispirited.

When Erskine wasn't out with his father during the Christmas stay, he tried to write but found his parents' home too noisy and crowded. In an effort to get the novel underway, he moved into a boardinghouse in Augusta, but to no avail. Yet another change of address resulted in the same dry spell, and finally a concerned Ira took his son to the fishing shack that Erskine had used on previous visits home. The more he traveled through Burke, Richmond, and Jefferson Counties, the less satisfied he was with his story. This tale had to be told the way people were living it. Again, he needed a new perspective, and the only solution was to get out of Wrens and isolate himself in New York.

Caldwell rented a hall bedroom on the fourth floor of a brownstone between Fifth and Sixth Avenue, now the site of Rockefeller Center. The modest lodging had only enough space for a cot, table and chair. Rent for the accommodation was three dollars and a half per week, and he was able to live on "fifty cents a day for food, chiefly by buying a loaf of rye bread and a pound of daisy cheese and eating it in my room." (Such dedication in the battle for words to express the fierce need within can rarely be equaled in American literature—here was a man whose obsession totally seized him: he had no need for family, friends or contacts while engulfed in his war with the relentless blank page.) He became so engrossed with the story he wanted to tell that he wouldn't read what had been written the day before. In the rush, he forgot himself: there was only the urge to begin another chapter, and when the second-sheet supply of cheap paper began to dwindle, Erskine used the reverse side to cut expenses.

For two and a half months, from noon to midnight, he wrote and revised and saw only a few people. Erskine did spend an evening with Raymond Everett and Charles A. Pearce, editors at the publishing house of Harcourt, Brace and Company. Then in March, lured by refreshments, he attended a cocktail party arranged by The Macaulay Company, publishers of *The New American Caravan*. Mae West was present to decorate the festivities, and Erskine mingled with Lewis Mumford, Edmund Wilson, Georgia O'Keeffe, and several *Caravan* contributors.

He also met Maxim Lieber at the party. Lieber had been an editor at the publishing house of Brentano's and now was forming his own literary agency. Would Caldwell be interested in becoming a client? The invitation came as a surprise and wasn't taken seriously, but a few months later Lieber wrote asking him if he had made a decision. Delighted to have a professional take over his hit-and-miss submissions, Erskine quickly accepted.

Helen didn't agree with Caldwell's recall of where *Tobacco Road* was written. She told William Sutton in a 1970 interview that only a small part of the book was completed in New York. She re-affirmed it to this author. "I know," she said, "because I helped him—he never felt right doing a thing by himself. He was always so uncertain."

Caldwell left New York in early April and took the bus to Maine. Helen and the children had been staying with the Lannigans in Charlottesville, where Helen came down with the flu and was slow in recovering. Erskine insisted that she return to Mount Vernon immediately. She replied, explaining that she had a hacking cough and pleurisy and the house up north would be damp and cold. But he was stubborn: the novel must be sent to Scribner's as soon as possible and he needed her editing. Dutifully, she came home and the two were hard at work before Greentrees was comfortably warm. "I hope to have my new novel in shape for you to read in about a month," he informed Perkins. "I'll send it to you as soon as I can pull myself away from it."

The book did require Helen's sure touch, but structurally it was sounder than anything Caldwell had done. This work wasn't the murky disorganized puddle of words that had weakened *The Bastard*, *Poor Fool*, or "The Bogus Ones," and when Jeeter Lester and his family spoke, the language they used was strikingly authentic. A reader could depend on how the characters responded—there was no wavering. *Tobacco Road* had benefited from Erskine's long sessions with his short stories; there now was cohesiveness. Helen corrected the spelling, mended grammar, and suggested certain revisions. Then she typed the manuscript on white paper, not her husband's usual water-stained sheets of yellow.

*Tobacco Road* was now a reality. But his claim that the book was completed in a white heat was a fabrication. Some pages of the work had been started in California, and parts were realized during the difficult holiday visit at his parents. Erskine was proud to have such an accomplishment behind him and felt confident that Scribner's would want to publish it. "I have finished the novel I was working on and it was sent to Scribner's Saturday," he wrote Ira and Carrie. "The title is *Tobacco Road*. That should sound familiar to you. The story is about some people not far from Augusta."

After he had mailed the manuscript his optimism dwindled. He knew the editors were "anxious to get a novel," Erskine informed his parents, but "I do not know if this is the one they have been waiting for." And there was another worry, though not an unfamiliar one: they were nearly penniless. The money he had received for *American Earth* had been spent in California, Georgia, and New York, and his recently published short story collection had sold few copies in spite of favorable reactions.

In an effort to keep food on the table, Caldwell frantically wrote more short stories and tried to get editors to pay him for pieces that had been accepted. "Could it be possible (bluntly) to send me a payment for the story in Winter no. 5," he appealed to Richard Johns, publisher of *Pagany*. In desperation, Erskine began doubling and tripling his submissions to magazines with embarrassing results; at times, several manuscripts were accepted by two different editors. "I have allowed my short stories to get into a mix-up," he admitted to Johns, "and I don't know where most of them are now."

Caldwell hoped that Perkins would take a story for *Scribner's Magazine*, but his submission, "A Country Full of Swedes," was rejected. "I think it is one of those stories you have very much overdone, so that it has become burlesque." Perkins was sending it back; he had little patience for Erskine's comic New England tales.

Several senior members at Scribner's were uncomfortable with the explicit language in *Tobacco Road*, and the company's vice president in charge of the education department recalled how Thomas Wolfe's *Look Homeward, Angel* had alienated Southern book customers. If Wolfe's rather benign treatment of the South could hurt sales, what sort of damage would *Tobacco Road* do? Another skeptic was Charles Scribner. While discussing the firm's conservative tendency with biographer William Sutton, John Hall Wheelock joked that "Charles Scribner would no sooner allow profanity in one of his books than he would invite a friend to use his parlor as a toilet room."

It wasn't entirely the question of content that created sharp exchanges between editors—a worrisome belief was that the book wouldn't sell. By mid-June, Perkins informed Caldwell that the outlook wasn't encouraging: "I tell you plainly that I think myself it is well-nigh perfect within its limits. The difficulty on the sales account, however, is very great, and that side of the argument has gained great force on account of the Depression."

Actually, Perkins was sidestepping the main reason why there was reluctance to take on Erskine's novel, though several of the firm's editors wanted it. Caldwell, in negotiating with Heron and Rariora for *The Bastard* and *Poor Fool*, had allowed these two small firms to sell options to Harcourt, Brace & Company for publication rights to his future novels. What now further complicated matters and caused some of the editors to distrust Erskine was that he had accepted a $150 advance from Harcourt for refusal rights, and had neglected to mention this arrangement when dealing with Scribner's. This caused concern—particularly to Arthur Scribner who felt an author's character and work should form a wholesome entity.

"It was such a maddening time," Helen remembered. "Maxwell Perkins kept saying how marvelous the book was, but we were kept waiting. If our parents hadn't sent us money, I don't know what we would have done." The family's survival now depended on a publication advance. "If you had said the book was rotten," Caldwell wrote Perkins, "it would be a different matter; but since I know what of it was written, and the trueness of its people and story, I cannot bring myself to believe that it should be thrown away unread with the published trash of yesterday."

Perkins and Wheelock finally convinced their colleagues that the book should be printed, and Perkins announced that plans were being made to publish it in the spring of 1932. "Within your intentions and the limits set by the nature of the subject, I think the book is extraordinarily fine." But he clouded his news with a reminder that Caldwell could expect little profit. The problem still was "this frightful depression."

What was left unsaid but troubled the publisher became apparent in promotion. Only fifteen hundred copies were printed, the cover displayed an almost socially acceptable Jeeter Lester, while the book's blurb declared the work was "most definitely not a shocker" but a "piece of genuine literature." The dedication also helped to soothe the nervous editors at Scribner's—"For My Father and Mother," Erskine had inserted. But the firm had one stipulation when giving Caldwell his advance on the book: Half of the $300 front money had to be turned over to Harcourt, Brace & Company. Scribner's was taking no chances.

The genesis of *Tobacco Road* can be found in the long drives Ira and Erskine took outside Wrens. The father would lecture his young son, and later when the boy had reached manhood and the two could talk as equals, there was a sociological bonding. There existed curious parallels in their lives and many of their interests were the same. Erskine studied sociology at the University of Virginia, and after his son left school, Ira attended a summer session at Charlottesville and enrolled in a similar course. When he got the young man a job at the *Atlanta Journal*, Ira began contributing a column to the *Augusta Chronicle*. Though Carrie had misgivings about her son's career choice, the other parent so wholeheartedly endorsed it that the churchgoers of Wrens found their preacher tiresome when he proudly expounded about "his boy with the six-cylinder mind." Not to be cast into the shadows, when *American Earth* was accepted, Ira had a work of his own to offer: "I am the father of Erskine Caldwell," he wrote Perkins, "whose book you are about to publish." Would the firm be interested in featuring another author with the same last name?

In 1926, Ira began a weekly column called "Let's Think This Over," which courageously lambasted a variety of societal ills. His "degrading influence of lynching" article angered reading rednecks when he described the scene of "several thousand people watching a cringing, screaming man as his blood was licked up by the raging fire," and lumber mill owners were agitated with his scorn for their random cutting of trees. Highway contractors were not spared and became enraged when Ira mentioned an "eighteen year old boy with shackles on his legs who died of sunstroke on a Greenwood

County chain gang."

Sharecroppers and poor tenant farmers preoccupied Ira as he roamed the outskirts of Wrens and beyond. His war against illiteracy, malnutrition, and incest was too often the struggle of a solitary soldier about to be overwhelmed. Readers of his column and members of the congregation were complacent and had little interest in coming to the aid of "po white trash." At times, when his pleas went unheeded, he would try to persuade readers and parishioners with derision—a favorite shaft was his commiseration with the tragic suffering of landowners as they toiled over the barbecuing of their fancy steaks—too busy to rescue their starving tenants.

Finally, after most efforts failed, Reverend Caldwell decided to conduct an experiment based on the premise that by assisting the poorest in a depressed area one made the first move towards repairing the whole. His choice was a Burke County family that had all the symptoms: incest, hookworm, poverty, illiteracy, pellagra, feeblemindedness. Ira moved them to Wrens, in a modest home, found the father a job in the local cottonseed-oil mill (no easy feat in depressed 1929), put the children in school, clothed the entire family, and made certain they all had a proper diet.

It didn't take long for his experiment to boomerang. The children had Erskine's proclivity for skipping classes and soon left school entirely, the father quit his job, and the entire family went back to their squalid shack in Burke County. These beneficiaries had no feelings of guilt over abandoning the pastor's social experiment; in fact, they blamed Ira for meddling in their lives. It was a bitter blow for this saint of a man who so desperately wanted to help destitute families of rural Georgia, and though he continued to give food and medicine to the needy this failure left him discouraged. In a 1930 article entitled "The Bunglers," published in a New York magazine, *Eugenics: A Journal of Race Betterment*, Ira summarized his endeavor with the reluctant conclusion that sterilization was the only solution for his "like toads in a post hole" poor. He prophesied that an "army of delinquents" would destroy the nation. But he still viewed the overall problem with sympathy and felt that the pathology brought on by desperate poverty was passed from parent to child. "It is not at all pleasing to our vanity; it is not in keeping with our smug complacency to have these people paraded before the world," Ira suggested. "Hence we keep the Bunglers and their type hidden away in the cellar of subconsciousness." He proclaimed there was nothing magnificent in ignorance. "There is no glamour about these tragedies that are dragging themselves across the stage of life in Georgia today."

(Ira was never content to let an opportunity go by in his struggle to help those in need. After seeing a Broadway performance of *Tobacco Road*, he went backstage and solicited contributions from the actors for the people who were living on Georgia's Tobacco Road. His obituary accurately depicts this lifelong dedication: "His was a hand of conscience tearing away the veil of pretense and forcing men to see themselves as they are. Deeply conscious of the injustices and inequalities of our social and economic system, he gave himself to the task of awakening public conscience.")

*Tobacco Road* and Ira's Bunglers article are strikingly similar because Erskine internalized much of his father's thinking. Both Caldwells admired the way these hapless squatters clung to the same plot of earth that had forsaken them—their unshakable belief that somehow cotton would rise from the seedless ground. It was relentless poverty that engendered the amoral climate within the family structure, made bearable by impossible dreams that one day all would be fresh and right with the world. Resigned to their existence, they were still capable of mustering courage and sudden exuberance.

"Make 'em laugh, make 'em cry, make 'em wait!"—this is a stage adage old as the theater, and one that Caldwell used successfully in developing *Tobacco Road*. He never quite paraded a fulfilled sexual encounter before his readers, but they thought one was about to cascade from the pages as they turned them.

Jeeter Lester was brutal, dishonest, and lecherous, but with all his flaws one endearing trait gave some balance to his character: this was the complete trust he had in the soil that brought forth cotton. Every spring he hoped to have enough money to buy seed and fertilizer. It never worked out that way, and soon the reader's pity is transformed into grudging admiration for this downtrodden scoundrel.

The Lesters live in a dilapidated shack on a neglected farm. Most of the day Jeeter, the father, sits around grumbling over his hunger and inability to raise a crop of cotton, while his wife, Ada, yearns for more snuff and a silk dress for her burial. There were seventeen Lester children, but fifteen of them have left the farm. The two remaining siblings are Dude, who is sixteen and has never gone to school—he spends most of his time bouncing a ball against the wall of the shack—and Ellie May, an eighteen year old with a harelip. Grandmother Lester wanders about the place, and everyone wishes her dead so there will be more on the meager dinner plates.

It is a warm February day, and Lov Bensey, Jeeter Lester's son-in-law, is walking up Tobacco Road carrying a gunnysack of turnips. It has been nearly a year since Jeeter sold his twelve-year-old daughter, Pearl, to Lov for seven dollars. Lov enters the yard and complains that he hasn't been getting the benefits of a wife—Pearl spreads a pallet on the floor at night instead of getting into bed with her husband. Jeeter, who has his eyes fixed on the gunnysack, promises to speak to the girl in exchange for turnips but Lov declines. Ellie May, hungry for a man, rubs her bottom along the sandy yard, distracting Bensey. Jeeter lunges, grabs the sack, and runs off into the woods to devour the first good-eating turnips he has had in ages.

Sister Bessie, a noseless, middle-aged, self-appointed preacher of amorous disposition makes her entrance. She fondles Dude and promises him a shiny new automobile with a horn if he will marry her and take up preaching. Bessie's deceased husband had left her eight hundred dollars, and the car salesman sells Bessie a Ford for exactly that amount. With Dude behind the wheel and constantly blowing the horn, there are misadventures: a Negro is killed ("Niggers will get killed. Looks like there ain't no way to stop it."), the grandmother is run over, and all too soon the battered Ford is worthless junk because of Dude's recklessness.

Every spring Jeeter burns over the land in hope of raising a crop of cotton, but one night a spark ignites the dry timbers of the shack and Jeeter and Ada perish in the flames. Dude, surveying the land, says to his preacher wife: "I reckon I'll get a mule somewhere and some seed cotton and guano, and grow me a crop of cotton this year. It feels to me like it's going to be a good year for cotton. Maybe I could grow me a bale to the acre, like Pa always talked about doing."

The early sales of *Tobacco Road*, published in February 1932, were only slightly better than *American Earth*. There were a few serious reviews, and several evaluators objected to the book, particularly his fellow Georgians who believed their state had been defamed. Within the literary community, Caldwell's new work was given encouraging grades: *Tobacco Road* was praised for the memorable characters, humor, and realism.

The general public didn't notice the novel until the play made it popular, though readers were more accepting to its approach than some reviewers—there were critics who couldn't see the connection between reality and the distortions of reality in the book.

"Mr. Caldwell is dealing with important material," Horace Gregory assured his readers in *The New York Times*. The humor was like Mark Twain's and had at its source an imagination to stir emotions. "The adolescent, almost idiotic gravity of Mr. Caldwell's characters produces instantaneous laughter and their sexual adventures are treated with an irreverence that verges upon the robust ribaldry of a burlesque show."

"Mark Twain would have enjoyed writing *Tobacco Road*," William Soskin began his February 12, 1932 review of the novel in the *New York Post*. Like Gregory, he noticed similarities. "But Mrs. Clemens would never have permitted it. She had her husband's most moral interests at heart." Reading the "behavioristic story" finally convinced Soskin that the Georgia author was closer to

Faulkner than Clemens. "*Tobacco Road* is conclusive evidence of Caldwell's ability. What is more, its writing has that reserve power about it, that fertility which gives promise of good things to come."

*Tobacco Road* wastes no time on sympathy, doesn't verge on moral preachments, and is straightforward: these were attributes given in Harry Emerson Wildes' assessment of the book in the *Philadelphia Public Ledger*. "Erskine Caldwell, in his first full-length novel, still shows evidence of short-story technique, but there are few contemporaries with a brighter future. This man has a genius for writing the lowly."

"Caldwell's greatest vice is unquestionably repetitiousness," wrote Kenneth Burke in a major review published by *The New Republic* on April 10, 1935. "He seems as contented as a savage to say the same thing again and again." In analyzing the first four chapters, Burke found that it was a rearrangement of the same topics in different sequences: "Jeeter wants Lov's turnips, Lov wants Jeeter to make Pearl sleep with him, Jeeter's own turnips all have 'damn-blasted green-gutted turnip worms,' hare-lipped Ellie May is sidling up to Lov, Dude won't stop 'chungking' a ball against the loose clapboard, Jeeter hopes to sell a load of wood in Augusta—about ten more details, regiven in changing order, make the content of forty pages. Sometimes when reading Caldwell I feel as though I were playing with my toes."

"I think I have never been so depressed by a book," James Gray concluded in his *St. Paul Dispatch* review, "nor so filled with a desire to do something about all this." Americans were unconscious of the squalor that existed in unseen corners. "*Tobacco Road* should be read aloud to everyone who has ever made glib ignorant generalization about the high standard of life in the United States."

"In some of the Scandinavian countries or in Russia," observed Edward Dahlburg in the March 23, 1932 issue of *The New Republic*, "I believe *Tobacco Road* would be hailed as something of a literary event." But in America, the reviewer predicted, the book would be entombed with *The Enormous Room* by E. E. Cummings. "Not until Mr. Caldwell has learned to make poverty, hunger and sex something that can be nostalgically mistaken for art rather than truth will his writings be widely praised—at least that is one reader's guess." Caldwell was a "much easier writer" than the currently fashionable Elizabeth Madox Roberts or William Faulkner.

The citizens of Wrens, and particularly Ira's congregation, were incensed by the explicit sexuality and language of *Tobacco Road.* Jeeter Lester's habit of beginning a sentence with "By God and by Jesus" riled parishioners. However, the book had an avid following among teenage boys who gloated over the racier pages and kept their worn copies hidden. What local readers found most despicable was the way Caldwell ridiculed his hometown and native state. Even the police chief of Wrens threatened that he would run the author out of town "on a rail if given the chance."

Carrie and Ira were deeply shocked by some of the prurient moments in the book, though they refused to be rattled publicly. "I can take you to the scene and show you the facts!" Ira fired back when confronted. And Carrie defended her son as a "missionary of the truth" and bragged to her high school students that her son's prose "was the most beautiful ever written." But criticism wasn't limited to outraged parish members and neighbors. Carrie's sisters were upset with the book and felt Erskine had disgraced the Bell family.

*Tobacco Road* was a financial failure, just as Perkins had predicted, and though it was reviewed favorably by a number of respected critics, Scribner's did little to promote the book below the Mason Dixon line in fear of jeopardizing their reputation as publishers.

Royalty checks for *Tobacco Road* dribbled sluggishly into the Mount Vernon mailbox—obviously not enough to support a family of four. Caldwell had only one option as winter approached: they must retreat to Wrens in order to avoid starvation. Another complication, and one that had been lingering in the background for many months: "The book shop went sky high in Portland," Erskine announced to his Charlottesville friend, Gordon Lewis. "Did you hear the bang? Jesus, we came out with our clothes, and several (many) hundreds hanging over our heads." The store's demise was not directly caused by the Depression; Caldwell's reputation as a "writer of dirty books" discouraged timid readers. There were other strikes against the Longfellow Square Bookshop: the banning of *The Bastard* and the reaction from adverse newspaper publicity.

Caldwell's mood at home during this lean time plummeted. His behavior became increasingly unpredictable and vicious as the family waited out the gloom for some cheerful news. Too often, Erskine drank heavily to forget his shortcomings, though he demanded his wife maintain puritanical denials. "I think he would have killed me," Helen speculated, "if he caught me once with a drink in my hand." The use of foul language was another taboo. (Cusswords were permitted in his fiction but never at home.) Dabney Caldwell recalled that his father once spanked him because the word "hockey" was used as a synonym for excrement.

Pix, the elder son, rebelled by becoming increasingly difficult with his Mount Vernon playmates. Even today his name will unleash a furious response: elderly men lifting their voices in rage when remembering distant school-day incidents. One of Pix's favorite recess games was demanding a penny from the other children for the make-believe sale of a newspaper. "Pay up or else!" Dabney was more withdrawn; he favored a hurried retreat to avoid his father's wrath.

Caldwell was doggedly riding it out. He was crestfallen and terribly upset—enough to nearly destroy his marriage with Helen—but there still was an ability to overcome defeat. The family left Wrens in the spring of 1932; Helen and the two boys stayed in Charlottesville, a sanctuary from a troubled husband and father, and even more important, where they could get enough to eat. Erskine strayed to New York before taking a bus to Mount Vernon. There were plans to plant a vegetable garden at Greentrees but the new novel was more on his mind. A story which would be called *God's Little Acre.*

Caldwell was ill at ease in the company of other writers, but desperate for funding, he applied for admission to Yaddo, the writers' colony in upstate New York. John Hall Wheelock gladly recommended him, but Yaddo's executive director, Lois Ames, felt uneasy about the application and questioned whether Caldwell could "adept himself to a group of ten or twelve persons living under one roof."

Conforming to this streak of adversity, his proposal to produce another novel about life in a Georgia mill town was turned down by the Guggenheim Foundation because their policy gave prime consideration to authors who were travelling abroad. Caldwell's disappointment had a ring of bitterness: "How about asking all the Guggenheim Fellows in creative writing for the past six or seven years what they have written and published since getting the money?" This was a question he raised in a letter to Milton Abernethy, editor of *Contempo*. Thomas Wolfe hadn't written a book with his grant, nor had Katherine Anne Porter or Jonathan Daniels. Hart Crane had gone "off the deep end" with his money, Caldwell reminded Abernethy.

Nathanael West, author of *Miss Lonelyhearts*, came to the rescue for a short time. He was then manager of the Sutton Hotel on East 56th Street in New York City, and during the Depression the establishment had many empty rooms. The more lights in the windows at night, West reasoned, the better chance of snagging a paying transient. He began offering writers bargain rates when they came to the city to see their publishers: to qualify, an author must keep a light burning until midnight. It was the eccentric manager's habit to rush along the sidewalk, checking on the lights, and one of his customers—Caldwell—sometimes forgot his duty and went to bed early. West would chastise him in the morning and lunch with him at noon.

Max Lieber encouraged Caldwell to accept such hospitality, but there were difficulties: the Tobacco Road outsider from Maine had no patience with the writers sprawled in the lobby and browsing up and down corridors. There was too much talk and little creativity. Caldwell also felt uncomfortable with his modest payments for such sumptuous accommodations. In several letters he prevailed upon Helen, much to her embarrassment, to get extra rent money from her mother.

Eventually, he could bear it no longer. Eating bread and cheese in such lush surroundings was offensive. No matter how much water he drank, he still had difficulty swallowing his meager fare. West urged him to stay, offering Caldwell the room for a dollar a week—or for nothing. But such charity was too painful; it was a reminder to Erskine of his financial plight. Thanking West, he packed his suitcase and found lodgings in a hall bedroom of a brownstone near Central Park.

In a desperate effort to get money from literary journals for his stories, Erskine soon fell again into the habit of doubling and tripling submissions with the same embarrassing results. "If you will let me have it back, I promise never to do such a thing again," he wrote Richard Johns at *Pagany*, "—it was the first time, and it shall be the last." Such a plea must have been irritating for Johns since he had suffered with this inconvenience before.

It was impossible for Caldwell to come up with a prescription story. There were no clever twists of contemporary storytelling— he lacked the breeziness of conforming to popular appeal or, more important, demand. Most of his pieces were vignettes, not plotted tales with a dozen pages or more.

What he needed, Caldwell reasoned, was a special-edition pamphlet to promote his work and to realize some much-needed cash. With this in mind, he got Alfred Morang and Richard Bradford of Bradford Press in Portland, Maine to oversee the project. Morang would supply illustrations for Caldwell's two stories, "A Message for Genevieve" and "Mama's Little Girl." But there were problems from the outset when Bradford was reluctant to bring out "Mama's Little Girl"—it was presently being considered by Nathanael West and William Carlos Williams at *Contact*. "If he won't print them," Caldwell wrote Morang, "bid him good-day, sir, and walk out." It wasn't a question of being loyal to editors or publishers. A story was his property until he signed away its rights.

If Morang and Bradford had been allowed the freedom to act on their skills, the project might have had a better chance of success.

But Caldwell kept intervening and both men became increasingly frustrated. "I am enclosing the drawing I should use if I were you," he wrote Morang. Bradford had wide experience in all aspects of layout, printing and distributing, but Caldwell kept pestering until the printer lost his temper and threatened to quit.

Finally the pamphlet made its appearance: a poorly assembled publication without charm. Though Bradford had warned Caldwell that $1.50 was an unrealistic price in the throes of Depression, the author insisted. Only six copies of Erskine's "reap a little coin" scheme were sold the first month, and sales were no better when the price was cut in half. Even at fifty cents a copy there were few takers. Eventually, he was obliged to send the pamphlet to friends and editors for whatever they could give him.

"Writing is the only source of income I have," Erskine wrote Perkins, "and I must keep everlastingly at it." But the manuscript, "Autumn Hill," that Caldwell had his new agent, Maxim Lieber, submit to Scribner's was so poorly realized that both Perkins and Wheelock knew it would never be brought out by their firm. "In a good many ways it seems to me magnificent," Perkins attempted to soften the blow of impending rejection. "But in other ways we feel doubtful about it." The novel called "for a great deal more development."

The material in "Autumn Hill" had been recast from several unfinished short stories, and the quality of the work was marred by the same hurried writing found in *The Bastard* and *Poor Fool*. The urgent need to extricate his family from their desperate financial plight impaired Caldwell's artistic integrity. This short novel was about "present-day people in the cut-over pulpwood section of West-Central Maine." Since Erskine never visited or took time to befriend his Greentrees neighbors, the patched work from abandoned stories disappointed everyone exposed to the manuscript.

Caldwell felt that he was unable to begin another work until some decision had been reached at Scribner's. A steady bombardment of communications was leveled in the direction of New York. "Is there a prospect of a word about 'Autumn Hill' in the near future?"

In early June 1932 came the rejection that essentially had been decided upon when the manuscript was first read. Perkins tried to soothe Erskine. "The fact is that the depression compels a scrutiny of manuscripts from the practical point of view such as never was before required." It was very difficult to ignore practical realities. "I can't tell you how sorry I am."

By rejecting "Autumn Hill," Scribner's had released Caldwell from his commitment, and Maxim Lieber immediately started looking for another publisher. Lieber was not the sort of person easily discouraged and had the reputation of being an extremely skillful negotiator for struggling authors. Among his clients were Richard Wright and Langston Hughes, and it also was believed that Lieber was instrumental in selling the work of Leon Trotsky to American publications—the agent did have a penchant for leftist causes.

But first there was the confrontation with Perkins at Scribner's. Caldwell was well aware that this kindly and understanding man had stood behind him and was the first to make generous advances for his early work. Both Perkins and Wheelock wanted to keep him as a writer in their firm and pleaded to let them consider the next book. But Erskine sided with Lieber; the rejected author was too badly stung to forgive his editors and felt he had been betrayed— "I'll be a little more careful where I lie down next time," he promised Gordon Lewis in Charlottesville.

Caldwell did look wistfully back on his association with Perkins and eventually forgot the bitterness he felt when "Autumn Hill" was turned down. After they left the publisher's office, Lieber reminded his client that he was now a free man. Over coffee, to ease frayed nerves, Erskine was told that he must make moves that best would serve his own interests. Writers had to have their books published or they would cease to be authors.

*God's Little Acre* came in a rush. Begun in late May of 1932, it was the first work of his that didn't require several drafts. The story was close to the surface of his consciousness and the characters were familiar enough to give him the confidence he needed to achieve immediate results. "I was certain it could be done that way," recalled Caldwell. "I took the sheet of paper from my typewriter, placed it upside down on the floor, and did not look at it again until the final page had been finished."

Someone else had gathered the pages, claimed Caldwell, and sent them off to the publisher—that someone was his wife. "Skinny was a god-awful speller," replied Helen when asked what her role was in making these literary repairs, "and there were the usual grammatical corrections. Then I retyped the manuscript. The book was written in two months, and the Morangs were up several weekends that summer."

Painter Raymond Skolfield from Hallowell, Maine remembered a weekend visit at Greentrees when he was a teenager.

It was at the Morangs' that I first had the pleasure of meeting the Erskine Caldwells, and a few weeks later I received an invitation to spend some time with them in West Mount Vernon. Alfred told me to bring some eatable things with me as the Caldwells were rather low on necessary edibles.

Rejmor Nielson, a secretary at Huston's bookstore on Exchange Street in Portland, was also a friend of both couples, and her young brother had a small Ford truck. So we all set out for a weekend visit at the Caldwells.

There were stories about the Caldwell house; stories told in the evening as we sat by the big table in the large living room. They said the building had once been an Inn on the old Post Road and how the room we were staying in had been a barroom tavern where lumberjacks gathered to drink and carouse. Many fights took place there, I was told. Then they said that skeletons of some of the victims had been found sealed up in the walls. How slaves fleeing to Canada were hidden. Erskine informed me that there might be dungeons. I was made to feel I was in a real haunted house.

Afterwards, I was given a small room upstairs with a small iron bed to sleep in—to be honest, young and impressionable as I was then—I slept with a kerosene light on. They had told me that two ghosts walked through the old inn at night. Then there were these laughing loons on the small lake that was part of their property—those birds were so spooky and noisy!

"The house is definitely haunted," said Erskine's grandson, David Caldwell, the present occupant of Greentrees. "There was a ghost that we always called upon named Henshie. I don't remember anything more about him other than if you lost something in this house—and this house swallows things because it's so huge—Helen would have me call on Henshie to find it for me."

In mid-September, two months after leaving Scribner's, and having been turned down at Harcourt, Brace and Simon and Schuster, Lieber aroused the interest of a publisher. "Maxim Lieber has had a nibble," Caldwell wrote Alfred Morang. "When it becomes a bite, he says he's going to pull up a contract!"

The appointment was with Harold Guinzburg and Marshall Best at Viking Press. "After an abundant and leisurely lunch" Erskine was persuaded to give them first chance on his next two novels and they would give him an advance of one hundred dollars for each book. The up-front money was only a third of what Scribner's had advanced Caldwell for *Tobacco Road*, but he was in no position to negotiate vigorously. "Autumn Hill" was not included as part of this contract with Viking, but Guinzburg and Best agreed to consider it. When the signing was over, Caldwell returned to Mount Vernon still harboring some lingering regrets that he had broken his association with the ever-helpful Perkins.

Guinzburg and Best rejected "Autumn Hill" faster than Perkins, and though their refusal disappointed Caldwell, he had nearly given up on this novel. He had decided earlier that the manuscript had served a purpose: it cleared his mind and gave perspective to the experience of having written *Tobacco Road* and assured him of a heightened incentive.

"The book Scribner's and myself got sore about is laid aside temporarily," Caldwell wrote Morang, "and Viking's publishing in March a novel called *God's Little Acre*." All the editors at Viking were unanimous in their response to the book: they gave it rave reviews, and not one of them suggested softening the more explicit passages as Wheelock had done when editing *Tobacco Road*. "I'm beginning to think that Scribner's was a mistake to begin with," an elated Caldwell wrote Milton Abernethy. "Viking is much more decent about everything."

Ty Ty Walden has been digging up his farm for nearly fifteen years in search of gold. He and his two sons, Shaw and Buck, have excavated great pits, but Ty Ty always sets aside an acre of land for the church—any profits from God's little acre will be his charitable contribution. Inevitably, this plot looms as a potential mother lode in Walden's mind and he gives God a new acre, usually on some unproductive corner of the farm.

Pluto Swint, an obese and sweating candidate for sheriff, appears on page three: he has come to "count votes" and to see Ty Ty's daughter Darling Jill. Pluto wants to marry the girl, though her wildness with men worries him; she never lets him touch her and often makes fun of his big belly.

He asks the Waldens if they have struck gold, and when told the digging is poor, Pluto suggests they get themselves an albino—an all-white man with the knack of locating lodes—he's heard there is just such a person living in a swamp at the lower end of the county. Ty Ty's interest is aroused and the decision is made that he and his boys will kidnap this pale conjuror. But more people will be needed to help dig. His oldest boy, Jim Leslie, married to a rich syphilitic, would be an unlikely volunteer—he hates digging and is ashamed of his father. Daughter Rosamond and her husband, Will Thompson, might be coaxed into helping. Pluto and Darling Jill are enlisted to drive to Scottesville, South Carolina, a cotton mill town where the daughter and son-in-law are living.

All is not well with the Scottesville couple: there is a labor strike, Will is drinking heavily, and Rosamond's face is discolored where her husband hit her. Swint and Darling Jill stay the night, and the next morning when Rosamond goes shopping for hairpins and Pluto sits on the porch, Will and Darling Jill get better acquainted. During a flagrante delicto scene, Will's bare bottom is stung with a hairbrush—he rolls off Darling Jill and stares at an enraged Rosamond. The erring sister is next: six resounding blows leave her backside scarlet and blistered. Slapstick crowds a page when Rosamond pulls a revolver from the bureau and shoots at her husband— a bullet whines between his legs as he stands before her. "He looked down to see if he had been shot, but he was afraid to take the time to look closely." Will escapes through an open window and runs naked into the streets of Scottesville.

Rosamond absolves her sister and, with Pluto's help, rubs lard on Darling Jill's inflamed bottom. The husband returns home wearing a pair of borrowed trousers, barefooted and shirtless, and all is forgiven. But Will Thompson sees no such an amiable conclusion for the striking mill town. He "closed his eyes and saw the yellow Company houses stretched endlessly through Scottesville. In the rear of the houses he saw tight-lipped women sitting at kitchen windows with their backs to the cold cook-stoves. In the streets in front of the houses he saw the bloody-lipped men spilling their lungs into the yellow dust." Rosamond tells Will that Pluto is going to take them to Ty Ty's in Georgia, and Thompson is glad to get away from mill troubles temporarily. Perhaps when he returns he can break open the steel-barred doors of the factory and turn on the power for the workers.

Upon their arrival at the farm they find an excited Ty Ty. The albino, Dave Dawson, has been snared and the captive is guarded by Uncle Felix, one of Walden's two black sharecroppers. A twenty-foot hole has been sunk since that morning and Walden is hopeful. That night after dinner, Ty Ty has the young all-white man led from the barn so they can get a better look at him. Dave and Darling Jill are instantly enamored and they are soon together in the night away from the others—the albino has no intention of escaping now, though Walden fears they both may wander. The two are found by lantern under a water oak tree: Ty Ty and Will stand watching the lovers and are reluctantly persuaded by Buck's wife, Griselda, and Rosamond to leave the young couple alone. "Women don't like men to stand around and see one of them getting it," Will tells a perplexed Ty Ty.

Buck and Shaw have never been able to get along with Will, and the next morning when Walden leaves the diggings to help his two sharecroppers get some cotton banked an ugly fight begins. Before serious injuries are inflicted, the three are pulled apart by Ty Ty. "What in pluperfect hell have you boys got to fight about so much, anyhow?" he asks. Thompson has been taunted with the label "lint-head," Buck believes Will is interested in Griselda, and both brothers resent being called "countrymen."

Will now feels he must return to Scottesville immediately to turn on the power at the closed cotton mill—the workers want to take over the plant and he can't be wasting his time digging pits in the ground. "I'm no damn doodlebug." Then Will reminds Ty Ty that he should be raising cotton, and Walden admits that he first needs money. Jim Leslie is mentioned as a possible source, and though he is skeptical, the father is persuaded to see his rich son. Darling Jill and Griselda accompany him to Jim Leslie's showplace home, and stirred by Griselda's beauty the son is surprisingly generous. "I'm going to get you," he tells Buck's wife. "I'm coming out there and bring you back here."

Next day, Pluto appears at the farm puffing and sweating; Darling Jill persuades him to take Will and Rosamond back to Scottesville, and Griselda accompanies them. A jealous Buck threatens to kill the "lint-head" but Ty Ty orders his son back into the pit.

The moment they reach the mill town, Will instructs the others to wait and runs down the street. Hours later, he returns with "a painful plea in his eyes"—that of a wounded animal. At a meeting, the workers have voted to arbitrate: "We're going to turn the power on," he tells Rosamond, "and I'm man enough to do it." Thompson is possessed by an uncontrollable force, as if the starting of the mill machinery will make him "strong as God Almighty." The others stare at him, mesmerized.

"I'm going to look at you like God intended you to be seen," Will tells Griselda. "I'm going to rip every piece of those things off you in a minute." And true to his promise, Griselda soon stands naked, "the most beautiful woman God ever made...so God damn pretty, a man would have to get down on his hands and knees and lick something." Rosamond and Darling Jill witness this scene with an excitement bordering savagery. Then Will Thompson drives an unprotesting Griselda from the room to engage in an act of cunnilingus, probably the first to be performed in a serious American novel.

Next morning, Will invades the bastion of the mill doors while women and children hover round. All the windows of the cotton factory are flung open. When men of Scottesville go to work after a long layoff, they take off their shirts and fling them out the windows. Thompson is finally seen at a window tearing his shirt to pieces as he had stripped Griselda's clothing. "Turn the power on, Will Thompson!" excited voices scream. As the machinery turns, the crowd outside hears small explosions. Then there is silence. "Where is Will?" Rosamond cries, and she is told that one of the mill guards has shot him. When told of his son-in-law's death, Ty Ty says: "Trouble at the mill then, I bet a pretty. Or else over a female."

Buck suspects that something has occurred between Griselda and Will; after a prolonged ugly scene he leaves the house and stays away all night.

While going over the digging plans for the day with his two sharecroppers, Uncle Felix and Black Sam, Ty Ty finds himself obliged to tell them what happened to Will Thompson. After he leaves the two Negroes, they begin to discuss events in a chorus:

"Lord, Lord!"
"I was born unlucky."
"Ain't it the truth!"
"Trouble in the house."
"Lord, Lord!"
"One man's dead."
"And trouble in the house."
"The male man's gone."
"He can't prick them no more."

"Lord, Lord!"
"Trouble in the house."
"My mammy was a darky—"
"My daddy was too—"
"The white girl's frisky—"
"Good Lord, what to do—"
"Lord, Lord!"
"The time ain't long."
"Somebody shot the male man."
"He can't prick them no more."
"And trouble in the house."
"Lord, Lord!"

Caldwell's trouble-in-the-house motif is given further range when Jim Leslie appears at the farm in a shiny black car "with nickeled trimming that glistened in the sun like new half dollars"—he has come to take Griselda away and the returned Buck isn't going to stop him. The confrontation between the two brothers is harsher than the one with Will Thompson, and Ty Ty is unable to separate them. Buck threatens to shoot Jim Leslie: Instead of retreating, the elder brother shakes his fist at Buck. Ty Ty could feel his son's finger "tighten on the trigger" and as their father "closed his eyes prayerfully" he hears the first of two shots. Jim Leslie dies in his arms; Buck throws down the gun and disappears behind the house. Later, a fearful Griselda asks Ty Ty if he has seen the shotgun; it has disappeared; the implication being that Buck may have taken it to use on himself.

Caldwell's solution for the grieving Ty Ty is to have him return to the pit in search of gold and with this conclusion:

> There was a mean trick played on us somewhere. God put us in the bodies of animals and tried to make us act like people. That was the beginning of trouble. If he had made us like we are, and not called us people, the last one of us would know how to live. A man can't live, feeling himself from the inside, and listening to what the preachers say. He can't do both, but he can do one or the other. He can live like we were made to live, and feel himself on the inside, or he can live like the preachers say, and be dead on the inside.

A euphoria replaced the somber atmosphere at Greentrees as the leaves began their inevitable rusting and firewood was split and stacked. The long lean spell was behind them with the advance on *God's Little Acre* and future prospects. Then there was a small, unexpected windfall when Lieber sold "A Country Full of Swedes" to *The Yale Review*. By way of celebration, and to escape another cruel Maine winter, the Caldwells journeyed south. Pix and Dabney were left with their grandparents in Wrens while Erskine and Helen spent a week in a Florida beach house belonging to their friend Gordon Lewis.

There were reviewers who considered *God's Little Acre* to be a sounder novel than *Tobacco Road*. Jonathan Daniels in the *Raleigh News and Observer* hailed it as "one of the finest studies of the Southern poor-white which has ever come into our literature." A reaction which was shared by Louis Kronenberger in *The New York Times Book Review* when he emphasized the book's originality. But reviews of *Acre* contained some of the same adverse reactions that had pestered *Tobacco Road*; the shift in tone that Horace Gregory was finding objectionable in the *Brooklyn Daily Eagle*—"from violent, roaring humor to equally violent melodrama." It was a complaint Kronenberger conceded, in spite of his favorable comments: "no novelist of modern times ever made a more serious mistake than Caldwell did when he ceased to woo the comic muse and began paying stiff, self-conscious homage to the muse of tragedy." Faulted for its surrealistic components by several critics, *God's Little Acre* was defended by Robert Cantwell in *The New Republic*: "Caldwell is a satirist; his characters are all distorted and enlarged, closer in spirit to Don Quixote and Alice than to the farmers and merchants of Georgia and Carolina."

When asked if Will Thompson was fated to die in the novel, Caldwell admitted that he didn't know; the story had become increasingly complicated in the telling. "I had difficulty sorting it out myself as I went along because so many people were involved." Then with amusement, Caldwell concluded: "Sometimes I regretted that I allowed so many characters to get into the act—I couldn't control them all."

Edwin Rolfe, in the February 1933 issue of *New Masses*, observed: "All of Caldwell's previously revealed aptitudes and limitations" were crystallized in the novel. Rolfe felt the author had sought realism and failed—an assumption made by a number of critics in mainstream publications. The reviewer was perplexed with the emphasis placed on sex. While the approach was healthy, "he ought in the future to avoid this overemphasis" because of the "decadent possibilities latent in such writing."

Reaction to Caldwell's characters in their Southern settings left some readers amused and others revolted. More than ten years after the publication of *God's Little Acre*, Bennett Cerf, in his book, *Try and Stop Me*, included this exchange which appeared in the September 5, 1945 issue of the *New York Journal American*:

> Nunnally Johnson, perhaps the smartest producer in all Hollywood, is a Georgia product. So is Erskine Caldwell. One evening, an indignant Atlantan confronted Johnson. "I ask you to bear me out, suh, that our fair State of Georgia has never known morons like the characters in those libelous abominations, *Tobacco Road* and *God's Little Acre*."
>
> "Why, in the part of the State I come from," answered Nunnally, softly, "we regard the people Mr. Caldwell writes about as the country club set."

William Soskin's review for the *New York Post* under the heading "D. H. Lawrence and Erskine Caldwell" insisted that the latter's handling of sexuality as in the work of Lawrence was a conscious challenge—"back of all the Waldens' comedy and back of their hilarious antics one senses an essentially ominous note." Soskin believed that Ty Ty Walden's search for gold was a parallelism of man's search for spiritual realization.

Both *Tobacco Road* and *God's Little Acre* were more than social documents in their description of the despair during the Depression period. Joseph Warren Beach, in his *American Fiction, 1920-1940*, wrote: "Erskine Caldwell is probably the best example we have of the artistic imagination working consistently in matters of concern to the social conscience, and yet not subdued like the dyer's hand to what it works in."

*God's Little Acre* attracted unexpected attention: Will Thompson's cunnilingus with the fetching Griselda proved a too hearty fare for the New York Society for the Suppression of Vice. John Sumner, secretary and legal council for the society, demanded that Viking suspend sales. The book, claimed the attorney, was in violation of New York's penal code under Section 1141: it was forbidden to sell books that were "obscene, lewd, lascivious, filthy, indecent or disgusting." By directly charging the publisher instead of a bookseller, Sumner hoped to make the novel a test case nationally. Harold Guinzburg, Viking's president, immediately engaged renowned litigator Wolfgang Schwabacher to challenge the charge, and briefs were brought before Judge Benjamin Greenspan in Manhattan's magistrate's court.

The case hinged on whether the judge would rule that isolated sentences or paragraphs would be considered pornographic or if a book must be declared unfit in its entirety. Caldwell voiced concern that the ruling would go against his novel; he hadn't forgotten the furor over *The Bastard* during his Portland bookselling days.

Greenspan surprised Erskine and delighted a score of authors who supported Viking; among them were Max Eastman, Carl Van Doren, Dorothy Parker, Sherwood Anderson, H. L. Mencken, Lewis Mumford, and Malcolm Cowley. "In order to sustain the prosecution," Greenspan ruled, "the court must find that the tendency of the book as a whole, and indeed the main purpose is to excite lustful desire and impure imagination." The judge admonished Sumner and his society by pointing out that "those who see the ugliness and not the beauty in a piece of work are unable to see the forest for the trees."

The obscenity charge against *God's Little Acre* boosted sales, and prestigious journals, particularly *Vanity Fair* and H. L. Mencken's *American Mercury*, were quick to feature Caldwell stories. Another turn of good fortune came when Scribner's successfully landed a British publisher for *Tobacco Road*. Most lucrative of all was an offer from MGM. Caldwell was to write a screenplay on location in Louisiana to replace the temperamental and hard-drinking William Faulkner.

"Erskine went on a bus to New York for the trial," remembered Helen, "and came home very pleased with the verdict. But I was very upset with our situation. All the money we had, which wasn't much, was in savings and Roosevelt had closed the banks. 'What are we going to do?' I asked him. 'How will we possibly exist?' Then he told me."

Helen never forgot the abrupt way he announced the change in their lives. Caldwell casually handed her his train ticket and she read the schedule: "Boston to Akron, to St. Louis, to New Orleans." She was accustomed to his sudden departures on buses and to New York brownstones in order to write, but this leave-taking came at a bad time for her. She was eight months pregnant, with two active youngsters to look after, and she would be left by herself at Greentrees. She keenly felt the irony of this situation. Her reason for having another child was the hope it might save their faltering marriage. "I have a job," he told her in a flat voice. "I'm going to replace William Faulkner for Metro-Goldwyn-Mayer, and I'm going to leave tomorrow."

Unhappy as they were in their marriage, each clung to the other in fear of final separation. The trip to New Orleans and California for the screenplay threatened their union. They exchanged letters furiously—often twice, sometimes three times in one day. His were more detailed and bluntly practical. "Buy fertilizer," he ordered— "the garden won't grow without it, even if it costs $5. a sack. Have the hot water fixed, of course. Don't let the lawn and the garden get ahead of Clifford"—a hired neighbor. Then as a parting shot was the reminder: "Grass grows fast when it starts to grow." Even in his absence he had a precise awareness of what was needed at home. But these directives were not proprietary concerns; they were marching orders in his need to maintain control.

"Don't be foolish and kill yourself," he warned during her last

days of pregnancy. "It's silly to cripple yourself for life just to do
a few days wash." But his own clothing was more of a problem:
Two new seersucker suits were too light for the climate, "except
in the middle of the day, and I can't be jumping up to run home to
change."

Helen gave birth to a daughter—Janet—in the library room at
Greentrees on May 24, 1933. A woman in the neighborhood helped
in the delivery. As soon as word reached Erskine, he had a lengthy
list of instructions on infant care. "The trick now is to change her
sleeping time around," he wrote the new mother. "You can do that
by gradually keeping her awake during the day so she will sleep at
night. You can train a kid to do anything, just as you do a puppy
to do some things. And the younger they're trained the sooner will
they learn." Another exhortation was that Janet must have "all the
milk she can eat, and all the sunshine she can stand." There would
not be any sunlight after September, he reminded his wife. His new
daughter needed to be kept outdoors and "let her store it up for the
next six months to come." Pix and Dabney, too, needed fresh air,
"as much as possible."

With their father away, the boys became boisterous and often
naughty. Janet took much of Helen's time, and there were a number
of chores that her husband felt only she should do, but first and
foremost she must discipline Pix and Dee. "They can go wild in a
couple of months if turned loose," he warned her. "The idea is not
to let them tear up the place and burn it down." Pix, now seven
years old, must be made aware that he "was the man of the house
and to run things right."

Caldwell's salary at MGM was $250 a week and the contract was
for three months. "You know why I came here," he wrote Helen,
"and you know what I'm going to do." He was trying to get money
for her, and "I don't give a damn about anyone else." Yet her living
allowance was pitifully meager—twelve dollars came one week,
eight the next. When she begged him to send more his rejoinder
was "Don't worry about the money." But first, if she expected him
to send anything, he needed to know where it was going and if she

had planned wisely. "Figure out how much you will need now and June 15," he insisted. "Subtract what you now have on hand, and send me the figures for the net balance." But whatever the estimated amount, his enclosed check would be less than promised. Helen and the children often had to get by on vegetables from the garden and occasional small checks from her mother in Charlottesville. Finally, in desperation, Helen opened a charge account at the Mount Vernon grocery store, and when Erskine got the bill, he exploded. "I've tried to make it plain to you that you've been a damn fool, and that you ought to behave with some sense." How much did they owe on bills? She should pay them instead of trying to cover up. "I don't think you were born with much sense," he concluded. "And if you ever charge another dime I'll wring your neck off." Either that or he would insert a no-responsibility ad in the local newspaper.

Erskine may have dominated Helen on all fronts in financial matters, but he now relied on her totally when there were decisions to be made about his work. Without her editorial assistance, he would have blundered badly. Marshall Best at Viking was planning a short story collection for late 1933, and Caldwell passed the editor's report on to her. Later, when the publisher asked to have the final galleys returned, Caldwell fretted because she hadn't proofed the manuscript. "I can't find much wrong with it, but I have no doubt that you could find plenty. I wish you could have read it at least once before it goes to press."

Erskine demanded more from Helen than he expected of himself. Oblivious to the double standard that unbalanced their union, he played his domination game ferociously, and often with abusive behavior. Uncertain of her, he hid behind his anger and became unreasonably demanding. Their marriage appeared at times a mere conventionality, yet was more meaningful than both realized. In the emotional jungle of their relationship they were bonded, virtually cemented, by need. "Write to tell me how everything is and if you still love me," he begged her while having an affair with another woman. "When you discover that I care a hell of a lot more for you than you do for me, you won't be questioning my faith any longer. Don't forget that."

With good reason, considering how badly he behaved in Portland, Helen suspected that Erskine again was being unfaithful. There were too many starlets and scantily-dressed dancers on the MGM set. She had nothing to worry about, he assured her, but still Caldwell couldn't resist taunting her with such a possibility. He also increased Helen's deep uncertainty by harping on her lack of a trim figure; he didn't appreciate plumpness. "You ought to weigh between 140 and 145—not a pound more, not a pound less," and she had "better not refuse to step on the scales when I say I don't believe it." Yet there were compliments coming from his direction: "There may be fifty million other girls in the country," he wrote, "but none of them has a pussy as good as yours." And in another letter he confessed: "I'd be a fool to like anybody but you. It would take 100 girls to equal you—and I couldn't afford that expense."

Caldwell didn't blame himself for his infidelities. He was a helpless slave to his urges, and Helen must be made to realize the male predicament. If he liked another woman it was because of the contrast. He hoped she would be consoled in the knowledge that the only other woman he could imagine sleeping with was a prostitute. "And I wouldn't take anybody unless I asked or told you first," he taunted, "and gave you a chance to forbid it." He couldn't have any other woman but a streetwalker "because she would be too much like you—and I'd be dissatisfied." He never allowed Helen to forget that wandering from their bed in Charlottesville while he was involved with several women in Portland. It was totally up to her to keep their marriage intact, and if he strayed she would be at fault. "You seem to forget that I don't care about anybody else" and "as long as you don't let me down, I don't try to fool you."

Caldwell was asked in New Orleans to script the dialogue for a group of Creole fishermen. He carefully studied their speech patterns and was quick to discover that they spoke a French similar to what he had heard on a visit to Quebec. But no, the producers felt that "a sort of dog Spanish" would get better audience reception and make the film more profitable. "I refuse to do a damn fool thing like that!" Erskine wrote Helen when learning that he had been taken off the picture. "Who with any sense would?"

Then a new Hollywood assignment offended his artistic integrity and caused him to speak up again. This time the setting was a small farm, and in one of the scenes a colt was hitched to a post while its mother was free to roam. Caldwell pointed out the absurdity to the director, King Vidor: "Colts would never be tied up on a farm because they always stay near their mothers." Vidor gazed in the writer's direction and said nothing, but Caldwell soon was reassigned.

"This country is not a fit place to live," he informed Helen upon his arrival in Culver City. "There is no soil, nothing to put your feet on." He missed walking on dirt and seeing rain in the air. The thought of an earthquake terrified him, and he worried about the wooden fire escape in his hotel. But what troubled him most was his contract—would it be terminated unexpectedly? Finally, Erskine persuaded Lieber to verify it with the studio. When the agent sent him a copy of the agreement, Caldwell forwarded it to Helen with stern instructions for its safekeeping. "And don't lose the key!" he warned her. "It's the only piece of paper in the world that binds the company to pay," he exhorted. "I'll collect, or somebody will be sorry." The movie business had no dependability.

Caldwell was irritated by the lifestyle of fellow writers at the studio. There was too much partying and senseless chatter, and it wasn't long before his coworkers regarded him as a tedious and standoffish eccentric. His request for a chair with a straight back and no cushion at office meetings raised eyebrows. He didn't buy a new car immediately, wear tailored suits, keep a stable of girls, or drink hard liquor daily. "Most of them think I'm a 'funny' person because I won't fall in with the crowd," he wrote home. "I suppose most of them think I'm half, if not wholly cracked."

Erskine was never one to abandon a writing project when it was underway, and he did not have the temperament that allowed him to share a script comfortably with others. Screenplays were usually done in relays; each writer contributing his allotted section. "I'd thank god for a chance to complete a story," he complained to Alfred Morang. "But it seems that is not the way things are done in this racket." It was insulting to be pushed aside in the middle of a piece, and there was always the possibility of being considered inadequate for the task, even fired without warning.

Caldwell's fellow screenwriter on his first assignment was Jim Sprague, a veteran wordsmith whose lifestyle conformed to the usual late hours of play and careless disregard for punching an invisible Hollywood time clock. "Sprague is lazy as hell," he fretted to Helen. "He never gets up until 10 or 11, and I have to wait for him every morning to talk over the work with him before I go ahead." Often, such tardiness left Caldwell morose—he missed his tiny writing hut on Parker Pond and the hours alone with his yellow sheets and typewriter. Erskine was no person to work in the hubbub he described to Helen: "Joan Crawford was in the next room for three hours practicing voice lessons with a teacher. She did nothing but run the scales for three hours. If you don't think that will drive you crazy, add on top a crying girl in the same room with you (a rejected actress who got axed by the producer.)"

The hired author felt convinced that pictures should mirror the times, which was in opposition to what the executives were trying to achieve; comedies and romantic farces were prime properties; such motion pictures were distractions—they allowed the audiences to forget the Depression and long unemployment lines. Then came a screenplay that caught Caldwell's attention, and with his usual intensity he threw himself into the work, only to be told by Director Howard Hawks that the results were too realistic. Another promising Vidor picture, *Let the Hurricane Roar,* had "genuine life in it—none of this goddam tripe of (romantic) triangles and such" and he was ready to "hold out for it to the last ditch." Again, the film was abandoned, and Caldwell had the frustration of trying to adjust to another project.

In spite of all his ranting and irritation, Hollywood fascinated

Caldwell. Much of the time, he was in awe—just another farm boy loose in the big city. Better still was the money that crowded his pocket. He no longer had to count pennies. Caldwell may have had little patience for colleagues who wore tailored suits and came to work in expensive automobiles, but it wasn't long before he succumbed to the same temptations: his clothes had a finer cut, and in July he purchased a new vehicle and had it shipped to Mount Vernon with elaborate instructions to Helen on how the car should be washed.

Yet there were vexations that enraged him more than being shuttled about on movie sets. *Tobacco Road* and *God's Little Acre* were both ignored as potential film material. "All the directors and supervisors turned thumbs down on *Tobacco Road*," Caldwell penned an angry announcement to Alfred Morang. "I did not see the synopsis, but someone told me the reader had given this comment: 'Too Brutal.' They can't quite see TR, they can't quite see me, and they don't think anything I write is movie material, which does not make me cry." He further was stung by Nathanael West's success in selling the rights to *Miss Lonelyhearts*; he judged the novel to be unimportant, clearly not in the same league as his own work. Morang may have thought Caldwell's objection—that West's book had succeeded because of sexual elements—slightly ironic. "This business goes so far away from reality that most pictures even attempt to deny a man his stomach," he complained further to his friend. "Have you noticed that in the pictures people as a rule don't eat? But sex, sex, sex."

Caldwell promised several of his friends that he would never be a "literary whore." Yet there were feelings of guilt surfacing in his letters as the weekly checks were pocketed. "I have not gone Hollywood," he assured I. L. Salomon. "I thought when I left there might be danger, but since being here three weeks, I know damn well it's not my pie." He was "disgusted, dissatisfied and disgruntled," and felt that it would be "suicide" to linger in such an environment beyond his three-month contract. He detested all money-hungry screenwriters and considered himself a rebel; a serious writer who had no choice but to improve his lot financially.

Though his letters home and to friends were crowded with complaints about Hollywood, he said little on location. Even when a labor dispute between screenwriters and the studio erupted, Caldwell refused to join his colleagues in fear that it might jeopardize his contract. He preferred being the loner, not a troublemaker. "By God, they'll never get me," he assured Helen. "Each day I thank God that I've got one day less to stay in this factory."

During his three months with MGM, Caldwell completed only two scripts: one an original story and the other an adaptation—both were shelved and soon forgotten. Creatively, it was an unproductive summer for Erskine, but there were gains, in addition to the gleaming new vehicle waiting for him in the front yard at Greentrees when he returned in early September. He had from his screenwriter's salary, and the sale of short stories—minus Lieber's ten percent agent's commission—managed to squirrel nearly fifteen hundred dollars. Caldwell had been home only a few days when there arrived an unexpected bonus: a check for one thousand dollars. *The Yale Review* had given his story "A Country Full of Swedes" their 1933 award for fiction—it was the same work returned by the editor of a magazine with the comment: "This old nag will never reach the post." Clayton Dolloff heard a chorus "of excited voices a quarter-mile up the road" when the news came.

Caldwell's first financial transaction upon his return to Maine was with the Portland bank that had loaned him a thousand dollars when he opened the bookshop, but even more satisfying personally was how he spent the prize money: he purchased the Mount Vernon house from Helen's mother, probably in hope that it would end her "nagging about his living off her charity." "The two never got along," remarked Helen, "and I was caught in the middle."

In a letter to I. L. Salomon, he wrote triumphantly that Jack Kirkland considered *Tobacco Road* to be one of the best books in American literature. Erskine was understandably flattered, but hesitated when Kirkland asked for permission to write an adaptation for the stage. After being assured by Lieber that such an arrangement would cost nothing, Caldwell agreed and forgot all about the project.

Kirkland went to Europe while he endeavored to get the play underway. The young playwright carried the book in his pocket and soon knew it all by heart—he even wept over it. But how could one turn the novel into an "active dramatic tragedy?" Finally, in Majorca, Kirkland found a solution. *Tobacco Road's* Jeeter Lester loved the land, and had no fear of being evicted because the landowner didn't care if there were squatters on his property. Kirkland would introduce a new character, a villainous banker threatening eviction, and Jeeter's struggle to keep the farm would intensify the drama.

Caldwell's reaction to the adaptation was less than lukewarm, and he doubted that it would be staged. Kirkland was having extreme difficulty in landing a backer. No one was willing to risk money on destitute sharecroppers stumbling about on theater boards in the midst of the Depression—even musicals and light comedies were having limited runs. Finally, after agreeing to front six thousand dollars of his own money, Kirkland signed a contract with Broadway producer Sam Grisman.

The play went into rehearsal in late October, but Caldwell was far from optimistic, and felt disgruntled when Kirkland asked him to help stage the play in New York; he wouldn't go unless there was travelling money forwarded. His concern that Kirkland would blotch the adaptation abated as opening night approached, rehearsals intensified while the script tightened. Kirkland had sensed that the poverty theme in the play should be muted, but not the humor or sexual overtones. Caldwell was pleased to note that his adapter followed the novel as it had been written.

Erskine and Helen, along with the Morangs, drove from Maine to New York on December 4, 1933 for opening night. The ride down was a nightmare; from Massachusetts to New York the roads were glazed with ice. "When we got to the Masque Theater," recalled Helen, "the play had already started and wasn't very well attended—the place was only half full."

Caldwell's earlier uncertainty about the script soon rose full force when from the darkened theater came bursts of laughter. Not being able to see humor in his novel or the adaptation, he felt the audience was reacting negatively, and as the final curtain fell he fled in a rage, convinced that *Tobacco Road* was a fiasco. What greeted the Caldwells and Morangs under the lighted marquee was bewildering. A huge crowd lined the streets in a celebratory mood, some participants disheveled and drunk. Police were struggling to control the boisterous mob—Prohibition had been repealed and the law was only a few hours old.

Early reviews of the play were not encouraging, but Henry Hull's lead role as Jeeter Lester was praised by reviewers. Brooks Atkinson, in the *New York Journal American*, called Hull's performance "as mordant and brilliant as you can imagine." In this instance, Caldwell was cited as being "a demonic genius—brutal, grimly comic and clairvoyant." But Atkinson gave the adaptation low marks—it "reels around the stage like a drunken stranger to the theater" and assessed the work to be one of "the grossest episodes ever put on the stage." Percy Hammond, in the *New York Herald Tribune*, called Hull's character portrayal of Jeeter "as thorough a deed of acting as I have seen in forty years of professional playgoing." Walter Winchell's response was grimmer: *Tobacco Road* was "another of those familiar plays about Southern imbeciles, who never bathe, rarely eat and are generally disagreeable. For the most part the play is blabby and uneventful."

There were too many empty seats as the curtain rose night after night, but production costs were not ruinous as the play stumbled along. The whole cast wore tattered clothes, and two feet of topsoil shoveled onstage was an inexpensive prop. For a month, the Masque Theater sheltered the acting crew before notifying Grisman and Kirkland that they must close. Undaunted, and still confident of a recovery, the two persuaded the 48th Street Theater to allow them space to restage their production.

Within a week after opening in the new location, *Tobacco Road* was making a conspicuous improvement in sales: ticket requests doubled, and there was a flurry of reviews, these more favorable, and of the 26 plays that opened in December, *Tobacco Road* was the only survivor. By late February of 1934 the crowds continued growing, and within a month the theater was selling tickets weeks in advance.

No one could have foretold the huge success the play would become. *Tobacco Road* sold out its six-hundredth performance when only a year onstage and reached the one-thousandth mark twelve months later. By October 1935 it was listed third in longest running dramas, closing the gap on all-time favorites, *Lightnin'* and *Abie's Irish Rose*. When it finally closed, in March 1941, the last performance was a then record number 3,180.

*The New York Times* called it the "oath-begarnished, eighth wonder of the theatrical world." On every anniversary of its opening night, a count would be taken of how many turnips had been consumed onstage, how many rubber balls were hurled by Dude against the house—one report estimated twenty-five thousand without missing a shingle—even the dented automobile fenders on the new car were tallied for an avid newspaper audience that could never get enough trivia about the play. Dozens of celebrities saw *Tobacco Road* and gave the highest praise—among them were Mae West, J. Edgar Hoover, Harpo Marx, and Eleanor Roosevelt—one couldn't have a better mix of admirers. George Gershwin was so enamored with the production that he began a *Tobacco Road* opera which was planned to debut at the 1939 World's Fair, but he died before the composition was completed.

Though Maxim Lieber pushed hard for Caldwell when the play was considered for the Pulitzer Prize for 1934, the committee presented the award to Sidney Kingsley for *Men in White*, a choice that surprised many critics and disappointed Caldwell. "No prizes," quipped Sam Grisman—"only dividends." In December 1940, the producer estimated that *Tobacco Road* had grossed nearly seven million dollars in New York and with the road companies.

Many producers resisted the temptation of touring a successful play in other cities—road companies as a rule were financially unprofitable. Not so *Tobacco Road*—it usually had three groups criss-crossing every state but Upper New England, Rhode Island, Mississippi, Florida, and North Dakota. There were ten curtain calls on opening night in San Francisco, and Henry Hull got a twenty-three-minute ovation when he first appeared in Los Angeles. Cities in Middle America—Columbus, Cleveland, Cincinnati, Indianapolis—had the play booked six times in all locations, and it became a smash hit in such Southern bastions as New Orleans, Atlanta, and Memphis. Nearly eight million people saw *Tobacco Road* between 1934 and 1941. For Caldwell, this meant an income of at least $25,000 a year, while money coming in for short stories and longer works sold by Maxim Lieber increased his income another $3,000 or $4,000 annually.

Caldwell had great admiration for Henry Hull, the first Jeeter, and this seasoned performer carried the part straight. Actors who later followed Hull in the role, both in New York and the touring companies, played principally to get laughs. Caldwell and Kirkland were unhappy with this approach, but the producer always had the last word when box office results were favorable.

Young Dabney Caldwell saw comedy potential in Hull. Dee was seven when he went with his father to the play, and he excitedly helped raise and lower the stage curtains. Before the performance, Dee watched Henry Hull apply his makeup, and when the actor was through he asked the boy: "Well, what do you think of it?" Dabney paused for a moment and said to a grinning Hull: "I think you're a pretty good clown." The seven year old liked the play until he detected trouble between Pearl and her husband Lov.

"Isn't she going back to him?" He whispered to an offstage actor.

"No, she isn't," he was told.

"Well, why not?—he's her husband—she ought to go back."

"But she doesn't like him."

"Well," said Dabney, "I don't see why she doesn't."

After this exchange, the boy mingled with the stagehands and lost all interest in *Tobacco Road*.

"I don't know what prosperous means," Caldwell wrote Morang.

"Maybe it's hustling, because I have to hustle like hell to keep enough wood cut to keep us from freezing in this sub-zero climate." (Erskine's wood operation and garden never got high praise from neighboring farmers who watched the comings and goings of "that writer fellow.") Caldwell preferred to think of himself as a workman well acquainted with poverty. Regimented by the early work ethic and frugality instilled by his mother, the author, now nouveau riche, becomes an investor in the stock market, huddles for hours over financial journals, and avidly follows the progress of his portfolio. Characteristically, when escaping Mount Vernon in order to write, the lodgings he selects are modest, not unlike the ones he stayed in when he was nearly penniless.

*Tobacco Road* had its own momentum as audiences gathered and the play became legend. For the occasional theatergoer this was one they had to see. Henry Hull played the lead role with subtlety; he never allowed Jeeter's lechery to come between his audience and their values. Hull as Jeeter may have assumed a slapstick identity, but the actor was no hillbilly—his role was fully under control from curtain rise to fall. Caldwell, when explaining Jeeter to reporters, frequently offered the following: "When people laugh at the antics of Jeeter Lester, they're only trying to cover their feelings. They see what they might sink to." But this observation was given under pressure, and to avoid answering questions. In more relaxed surroundings, Caldwell suggested: "Well, everybody sees something of himself in it."

Not everyone found the explicitness in *Tobacco Road* amusing. Mayor Edward Kelly of Chicago saw the play during its seventh week in the windy city and was revolted. "It's an insult to decent people," he raged to reporters. "That show is not interesting nor artistic. It is just a mess of filth and degeneracy without any plot, rhyme, or reason for producing it except filth." Kelly worried about *Tobacco Road* because of its effects on "women and impressionable young people." Immediately, he ordered the show to be closed.

The producers of the play took Kelly to court—there had been too many embroilments caused by censorship against their author.

They were still cautious because of the bannings of *The Bastard* in Portland, Maine and *God's Little Acre* in Boston. "It's terrible that an honest, truthful expression of this kind is forbidden by men in power," Caldwell defended the work before reporters. "*Tobacco Road* is no more obscene than the truth," and the same applied to *God's Little Acre*.

Kelly's stand against the play created a flood of letters in Chicago newspapers, and many of these contributors questioned the mayor's right to monitor the city's morals. But Kelley had his following: "I'm with the mayor in his war on theatrical filth," wrote one outraged citizen. "A city can be liberal without being downright insane in its acceptance of dirt."

*Tobacco Road* had its day in a Chicago circuit court with nearly every newspaper in the country covering the case. The judge decreed that the show was not one of pornography: a restraining order against Chicago was issued and the play allowed to reopen. "Fighting the Catholic Church is like sticking your head in a cannon." Caldwell wrote to Morang. But he was premature in this assessment. The mayor's case against the play boosted ticket sales on every road show around the country and at the 48th Street Theater in New York.

The protest that got even wider exposure than the one that ended in Mayor Kelley's marching orders came from Braswell Deen, a congressman from Georgia. When the show came to the District of Columbia in 1936, Deen attended one of the performances and thought the play a disgrace. He was sufficiently outraged to rise in the House of Representatives and declare to his fellow congressmen: "I open my mouth and resent with all the power of my soul this untruthful, undignified, undiplomatic and unfair sketch of Southern life." He was angry because he felt his home state was being defiled. "There is not a word of truth in it. I denounce it and resent it." He knew poor families of twenty-two children and they were "decent and God-fearing citizens." Deen's speech was given national coverage in newspapers, and he was heavily quoted in Georgia publications, a political advantage that didn't go unnoticed by this seasoned politician who had aspirations of being elected for another term. Banning the show would give dignity to "the thousands of sharecroppers and their families who are not in the nation's capital to defend themselves against this infamous, vile and wicked web which they have been woven by those who would commercialize upon them." Deen's choice of words resonated well on home turf, and much to the congressman's irritation, at the ticket booth where Washingtonians stood in line.

*Tobacco Road* was hauled into court and banned in most sections of the country on various occasions. Detroit's mayor deemed the play "a conglomeration of obscenity, filth, putrescence; in short, a garbage pile of indecent dialogue and degenerate exhibitionism." When the cry came from an outraged church group that Jeeter's "By God and by Jesus!" was irreverent and shouldn't be heard in a public place, the producers of the show calmed the protestors with "By Gad and by Judas!" Then Ellie May's masturbatory crawl across the dooryard was made less obvious—it looked as if she had an itch. Both Grisman and Kirkland were particularly sensitive to the growls of officials in city and town government.

For Caldwell, these bannings were attacks on himself—he felt he was being persecuted. His response was to fight back, which he did by travelling around the country to defend the play wherever there were rumblings of outrage. Such protesters against the show he called fascistic—"little Hitlers" they were, all causing him trouble. "As long as we are able to tie tin cans to the little ones," he wrote Frank Daniel when the play was attacked in Atlanta, "there is not much danger of a big one getting a grip on America."

Caldwell did have reason to feel threatened during the years that *Tobacco Road* rose in popularity as well as controversy. Hundreds of letters were dumped in his mailbox, ranging from stern reproofs to death threats. Many Southerners considered him a traitor. "Any man who seeks to make his native state ridiculous merely for money holds no claim on the respect of the people of that state"—such an accusation was commonplace for Caldwell. One Gainesville, Georgia journalist called him an earthworm. "To turn against one's family is bad enough. But to turn against one's own state and section, holding it up to scorn and ridicule, is terrible. Phooey on Erskine Caldwell." It was easy enough to dismiss mild scoldings, but one letter disturbed him to the point where he alerted the FBI and requested that the Bureau investigate the threat. "Understand this you SON-OF-A-BITCH," the man wrote. "Write and talk fast, for when the time comes only the one you doubt will be able to save you."

Caldwell's first film assignment for MGM and the *Tobacco Road* production for the stage had diverted him from his writing. From early February to mid-December of 1933, he did not write a single short story—there had been too many distractions.

Through Max Lieber's efforts, his stories were now appearing in the better-circulated publications, such as *Vanity Fair, Redbook, American Mercury, Esquire,* and *Atlantic Monthly*. Shortly after the appearance of *God's Little Acre*, Viking brought out twenty of his stories in a collection entitled *We Are The Living*. This new book was hailed as surpassing his previous volume of short stories, *American Earth*. One of the pieces in *We Are The Living* was included in *O'Brien's Best Short Stories of 1934,* and six were named on O'Brien's "Roll of Honor." "A Country Full of Swedes," which had won *The Yale Review* award, appeared in the *O. Henry Memorial Award Prize Stories* collection for 1934. Caldwell's reputation was on the rise, and he was being lauded as one of the nation's most promising short story writers.

His New Year's resolution for 1934 was to begin working immediately. He had been away from words too long, and was dissatisfied with his present lifestyle. With the full realization that he had been doing a disservice to his craft, Erskine began anew. He often became short-tempered with his family when caught in the vice grip of creativity, and this was reason enough, he explained, to rent a basement room in a brownstone near Central Park—this way he could be alone when struggling with short stories from early morning to late night.

It was bitterly cold and the uncarpeted cement floor gave him chilblains. To keep warm, he began taking bus trips for several days at a time. On stretches of highway, Caldwell wrote with pencil and pad, and when stopping in the evening at a hotel he composed on his typewriter. Such journeys were made along the East Coast and into the Midwest.

One of the pieces that emerged from that prolific burst of creativity was his forty-page story, "Kneel to the Rising Sun." This would be the best story he would ever write, and it tells about the biracial friendship of two sharecroppers. One episode has a character being eaten alive by hogs in a pen. The gruesome description caused some readers to cancel their subscription to *Scribner's Magazine* when the story was published by a forgiving Max Perkins. Hamilton Basso, writing in *New Masses*, raved that the work was "by any critical standard whatsoever, one of the finest short stories any American has written." Caldwell's most thorough critic, Helen, felt that it was "by far his best," though she had a fondness for "A Country Full of Swedes." She admitted in an interview with this author that the $1,000 prize from *The Yale Review* may have influenced her. Caldwell, in a letter to I. L. Salomon, favored "Kneel to the Rising Sun." It would be the one he "would select if faced with the choice of taking only one to that desert island and leaving the other ninety-nine behind."

Erskine returned to Mount Vernon in February and soon was installed in the Parker Pond cabin with a glowing Franklin heater. Viking wanted a new novel, and he already had the title, *Journeyman*. It would be a story about an unordained, wandering minister who descends on a small Georgia town. The preacher, Semon Dye, stays at Clay Horey's farm and soon has the land, car, and Horey's wife. This man of the cloth shoots a black man, guzzles gallons of liquor, has sex with young girls, and rolls dice with the devious skill of a professional. Dye holds a revival meeting that soon becomes a debauchery of religious and sexual ecstasy. Finally, Semon Dye leaves town, and as cruel and debased a person as he is, Horey and his friends now realize that they will miss this spellbinding preacher.

His early fictional ministers as in *Journeyman* and *Tobacco Road* were inferior to their parishioners—whether they were wandering evangelists or self-ordained preachers. Semon Dye's cruelty and hypocritical behavior, and Sister Bessie's bawdy adventures in Augusta and her meddlesome ways reflect Caldwell's misgivings that the caretakers of the spiritual world were often unscrupulous or mean-spirited.

Critics found little in his work to reveal his religious faith, and he did his best to dismiss such probes: "Once in a while I get the feeling that people think I'm trying to reform something," declared Caldwell. "Well, it doesn't mean a thing. There is no meaning to it. The only meaning you can get out of it is what you can find yourself."

*Journeyman* had the same mingling of violence, sexual deviations, social concerns and humor as *Tobacco Road* and *God's Little Acre*, but when Marshall Best read the manuscript he clearly was disappointed. "You and Erskine both know that we don't think that *Journeyman* is as good a novel as *Tobacco Road* or *God's Little Acre*," Best reported to Lieber. "It is our opinion that it will not advance his reputation or his position in the book field." Best believed this was a book that should be set aside or revised extensively. If Caldwell insisted that it be published, the firm would bring out a limited edition for reviews but there would be no trade circulation.

Caldwell felt injured when he heard of Best's reaction to *Journeyman*. "I can't help being shaky all over from it," he declared to Helen. "I wish to god I knew about the book. I think it is good, and feel it is, but how can you be sure?" He was troubled enough to admit: "Maybe it's as rotten as that after all."

Lieber was busy behind the scenes: he let slip that Caldwell was interested in finding another publisher and there was immediate interest. Bennett Cerf at Random House and Patricia Covice at Covice-Friede offered contracts for *Journeyman* and first refusal rights for future books. But before Lieber could finalize a contract with Random House, the firm's lawyer convinced Cerf that the book would involve them in a legal wrangle with the censors and it could well be a costly skirmish. Covice soon came to the same conclusion, and Lieber was forced to deal with Best. Viking was adamant: they would not better their previous offer. *Journeyman* was published by Viking in 1935, and the edition was limited to 1,470 copies.

MGM came knocking on Caldwell's door in the late spring of 1934. It was another screenwriting assignment, and the offer was one that he greeted with mixed feelings. Checks from the *Tobacco Road* play were bulging his investment portfolio, but there was always the worry that what he had put aside so carefully could be lost in another Wall Street crash. Caldwell knew he was no longer a second-string hack who could expect a maximum of $250 to $300 weekly from Hollywood. He was well aware that his literary notoriety increased his value, and after agonizing over the offer with Lieber, Caldwell casually informed the studio that he would accept if the salary were increased to $600 a week. MGM quickly agreed, and he was assigned to the production of *Wicked Woman*, a film starring Mady Christians and directed by Charles Brabin.

His contribution to the *Wicked Woman* film was minimal, and Caldwell was soon pulled from the set for reassignment. He spent some weeks reading screen material and revising scenes for several completed scripts. Such literary chores were done perfunctorily, and his letters to Helen contained the usual batch of complaints. Finally, Harry Behn, a veteran screenwriter, asked Erskine to collaborate on an original story, and both were surprised when the studio gave its approval. Behn dictated one scene at a time, a secretary prepared the script, and Caldwell worked the revision. It was typical Hollywood fare: They had agreed on writing a story about lumbering in the Northwest. The foreman of the logging camp was their lead man and the actress playing a woodsman's daughter was the heroine. All went smoothly until Erskine and Behn discovered there was nothing more they could say. Inevitably—and what Erskine found so humiliating in the hierarchy of studio management—came the intervention. This time the story department was the culprit: the script must be benched while there was a full evaluation which later proved to be fatal.

Letters to his friends echoed those of his previous stint; he still abhorred the place and its insensitivity. Caldwell assumed the role of a renegade, but his rebellion was always under control—it never endangered next week's paycheck.

For many years Caldwell had wanted to tour America by automobile, drifting wherever he pleased and at his own pace. When his Hollywood contract expired in the summer of 1934, he drove his car in a zigzag pattern across the country. Some days he averaged two or three hundred miles, but when a town or area interested him he would stop and mingle with the people. As the landscape slipped past him, Caldwell soon realized that he must write about these road adventures.

*Some American People*, published in October 1935, was a book carrying twenty-four vignettes of what he felt were true Americans. Included in the cast of characters were elderly panhandlers from North Dakota, a gas-station owner in Spokane, coal miners in Scranton, a failed businessman in Oregon, a dump picker in Omaha, and an amateur philosopher from Illinois. There was even a hobo barber who cut hair for homeless tramps riding the rails on the Pacific Northwest Railroad. These were average citizens of the American drama, many of them victims of the Great Depression, but all clinging to their traditional American values. Hard work, not handouts from the Roosevelt administration, suggested Caldwell, would win the day. As a travel book, it was an unusual presentation. Caldwell was able to balance shame and pride, outrage and sympathy, sadness and laughter while mixing his reflections with honest and factual reporting.

The *Daily Worker* flew him to Detroit to report on the industry's assembly lines, and the editors were not disappointed with his coverage of the plant which revealed production speedups, starvation wages, company spies, and uncaring bosses. Inserted were first-person accounts, several obviously fictional, placed to provoke anger and to increase drama. Sexual exploitation and mutilation were exposed in his following article under the heading "Detroit The Eight-Finger City." This piece ruffled auto executives. "The Hudson plant, and every other motor products plant in metropolitan Detroit," declared Caldwell, "is littered with fingers, hands, arms, legs and crushed bodies." Another dark drama he depicted was that young girls were walking the streets to get food for their families. "In back-room beer joints they strip off their clothes, go through a few childish motions of dance routine, and reap a fistful of copper money from the floor." The name of auto magnate Henry Ford, Caldwell wrote the *Daily Worker*, "has been inscribed on the cornerstone of The School of Whoredom."

The commentary on *Some American People* was diverse. One reviewer in the *New York News* wrote that "the book reads too much like Mother India to be entirely credible." Perhaps the sternest comments came from Louis Haloff in the *Atlanta Constitution*—he hadn't forgiven Erskine for *Tobacco Road*: "Caldwell, not the American people, should hang his head in shame," for the author had "tried his hand at insulting the intelligence of our great nation." "*Some American People*," wrote Elizabeth Hardwick, "is more fact than fiction, but Caldwell is such a skillful writer that some of his sketches have a definite literary as well as a sociological value." Hardwick cited the author for his earnest desire for truth that had characterized previous works. "If anyone wants to know what one of America's foremost writers sees when he travels over our country, they will have to read this book, because his experiences are not found on penny postcards." Reviewer George Currie thought Caldwell should stay with fiction instead of giving readers a smorgasbord of "roadside philosophizing" with sharecroppers, tenant farmers, and workers in Detroit automobile plants. "One finds in these pages," wrote Currie in the *Brooklyn Daily Eagle*, "vaguely familiar things but one reads of them, conscious that to say, 'This is too bad' is no way of setting them apart."

A. B. Bernd observed in Georgia's *The Macon Telegraph* that

Caldwell did not have a high esteem for his native state of Georgia, but fellow citizens who had indignantly stomped out of the Broadway theater where *Tobacco Road* was playing would find some comfort in the author's critical material about the rest of the country. "Many of his sketches of men suffering under economic blight and places deserted because of the drought," wrote Bernd, "are scarcely distinguishable in form or treatment from tales in *Kneel to the Rising Sun* and *We Are the Living.*"

*Some American People* got praise from Charles Angoff in *The American Spectator.* He hailed it as the author's best book: a sound, honest, and simple rendering of words throughout. "It is therefore a pity that Mr. Caldwell has his heart so set on fiction, for which he portrays a very meager talent." All the short stories and novels were too incidental and "clumsily reworked" to be taken seriously. "Occasionally there is a kernel of sound reportorial observation in them, but most of the time they are a sort of proletarian chitchat."

The Montpelier, Vermont *Argus* declared the entire book to be "a breath-taking commentary on contemporary, restless America." Ernest Sutherland Bates, in the *New York Herald Tribune*, asserted that "the scenes, the people, their way of speech, their modes of living and dying are merged in well nigh perfect pictures." Such vignettes, declared Bates "should have their permanent place in American literature of this type." To Caldwell's surprise, *Some American People* was a journalistic forerunner: In the next four years, dozens of writers would be traveling the land in search of just such material, and six travel books mined in the same vein surfaced.

*Journeyman* was reviewed in leading New York publications and the response was decidedly negative. Hamilton Basso, who had raved about the short story "Kneel to the Rising Sun," wrote in *New Masses*: "There have been times when reading Mr. Caldwell that I have felt he has almost exhausted the soil from which all his writings have sprung. I felt it most strongly in *Journeyman.*" James T. Farrell curtly dismissed the book as "just another monster hastily rolled off Caldwell's typewriter." Perhaps the most cutting observation came from Horace Gregory, who in the past had been in the author's court, but now wondered in the *New York Herald Tribune*: "If Caldwell were a few years older...the present tendency to repeat himself would indicate the end of his career."

Thumbs down assessments continued. Critic Herschel Brickell in reviewing *Journeyman* warned his readers that if "the enjoyment of books about morons is not in your list of pleasures it is my advice that you stay strictly away from Erskine Caldwell's latest venture into the manners and customs and psychology of Georgia's poor whites." Brickell noted the limited number of copies published and felt the $4.50 price was exorbitant.

"Before I go on record with an official and pompous reaction to Mr. Caldwell's new novel, *Journeyman*," began William Soskin in the *New York American*, "I would like to explain this fact: that from the first I have considered him an important figure in American writing." For Soskin, Caldwell was "an unconscious writer," one who had "no clear idea of his own work as he creates it, but who writes from some deeply embedded intuitive, almost physical sense." Sadly, in *Journeyman* the author's intuition had failed him. "The situation in which an innocent bystander, as it were, is permitted to witness the most intimate and frank sexual seances and to comment casually or amusingly about the orgy, always provides a certain amount of comic material. In *Journeyman*, however, this device is used with a certain wantonness and unnecessary smacking of lips, and one loses the sense of the author's detachment." Such an approach, Soskin reasoned, plunged natural comedy into eroticism. "The story ends, incidentally, in a most brazen revival meeting, with screaming and holy-rolling and fits and low comedy. There, again, I think Mr. Caldwell overplays his hand."

Erskine was well acquainted with Sinclair Lewis's Elmer Gantry brand of preaching and exaggerated evangelism after those many excursions with Ira to witness tent revivals and a variety of denominational ceremonies. But the idea of a Semon Dye had other beginnings—while growing up in the South, Caldwell had seen many players of politics. "Georgia," he explained, "has always produced that quality of demagogue politician. And I always related evangelistic religion with politics. So Semon Dye, in my opinion, could either be a senator or a preacher."

Though the novel was soundly trounced by a majority of reviewers, there were those who applauded *Journeyman*. "If you've ever read a book like this," wrote Godfrey M. Elliot in the Mullins, West Virginia *Advocate*, "I'll eat it dry and unseasoned! Erskine Caldwell, who had such a phenomenal success with *God's Little Acre* and the dramatization of *Tobacco Road*, has completely outdone himself with *Journeyman*. Its force is astounding. It packs more wallop than a full-grown tornado."

Journalism was something he couldn't shake—it was in his bloodstream—a sort of fermenting residue of his days in Atlanta on the newspaper. This was the beginning: he wanted to put it into use before writing the next book. Max Lieber had committed him to a series of articles for the *New York Post*—a cluster on tenant farmers in East Georgia. Erskine left his family in Mount Vernon in December of 1934 and drove to Wrens.

It was sympathy rather than pity for the downtrodden that motivated him to produce his *New York Post* articles collected in the booklet format of *Tenant Farmer*. "In other words," he explained, "they were not people to be rejected and to be ignored, because not only I had a story to tell but they had an appealing personality which had a great effect on me." Their suffering was such an injustice. Why had this happened—was it due to ignorance, lack of education, ill health, or the economic decline brought forth by the Great Depression? Caldwell couldn't escape what he was seeing.

The quality of life on the tenant farms had deteriorated since his last visit outside Wrens. Sharecroppers who still planted crops had to trade half their harvest in exchange for fertilizer, seed, and rent. In the prison of their poverty and sickness, unable to free themselves from their new landowners, the Augusta banks, these tenants were a dispirited lot—a 1938 study revealed that in the Southern cotton states there were over 1,100,000 white and 700,000 black farmers who didn't own the land they planted; these farms belonged to retired farmers or the sons or descendants of pre-Civil-War plantation holders.

The abolition of slavery left the large farms and plantations with an inadequate labor force. Consequently, a sharecropping system arose in which landowners would furnish the land, housing, seed, and fertilizer while sharecroppers provided the labor and sometimes the farming equipment. One-fourth or one-third of the farm profit was the landowner's share, and often the tenants had to buy on credit against the following year's crop.

Though the Civil War brought legal emancipation to the slaves, World War II probably did more to free Southern blacks: large numbers of them were inducted into military service and others found better job opportunities in Northern industrial areas. As rural labor became scarce in the South, small farms were sold to landowners who had mechanized equipment, or the holdings were converted to the raising of cattle because such operations required fewer laborers.

The national wage in the summer of 1935 was thirty dollars a month, but a worker in the cotton belt received ten dollars a month if white and seven if black. Labor union organizations set up to improve salaries and working conditions in Southern mills were ineffective, and as a consequence industry could pay workers far below the standard wage. Cotton, which reached a high of 60 cents per pound, plummeted to 4 cents by 1932.

Aware that assistance was needed, the Roosevelt administration in its first term signed into law the Agricultural Adjustment Act in hope that it improve the plight of depressed farm families. The AAA program was based on the premise that by planting fewer crops farmers would get higher prices for their products. Though well-intentioned, the program did not aid those most in need—the farmers who rented the land or had to share their harvest. By law, sharecroppers were entitled to half the funds, but in setting up the program the AAA gave the supervision of funding to landowners.

In fear of being evicted, many of the croppers were afraid to ask for their rightful share.

Left-wing newspapers and journals gave only cursory coverage to the plight of Southern tenant farmers and sharecroppers; though an occasional article appeared in mainstream publications, top billing usually went to striking coal miners or Northern mill workers. Caldwell's series in the *New York Post* shocked its subscribers, and when his articles were reprinted in *Time* magazine the entire country was alerted.

He explained the differences between a tenant farmer and a sharecropper to his readers, and pointed out the faults in the AAA program, but his foremost motivation was to prove the credibility of *Tobacco Road*. Caldwell placed up front, in the first of his four articles, a warning that in parts of Georgia human existence had reached its lowest level. "Children are seen deformed by nature and malnutrition, women in rags beg for pennies, and men are so hungry that they eat snakes and cow dung." In the fourth and final article to the series, unable to resist a Romulus and Remus shocker for his *Post* audience, he describes what is happening in a sharecropper's cabin:

> On the floor before an open fire lay two babies, neither a year old, sucking the dry teats of a mongrel bitch. A young girl, somewhere between fifteen and twenty, squatted on the corner of the hearth trying to keep warm.
>
> The dog got up and crawled to the hearth. She sat on her haunches before the blazing pine-knots, shivering and whining. After a while the girl spoke to the dog and the animal slunk away from the warmth of the fire and lay down again beside the two babies. The infants cuddled against the warmth of the dog's flanks, searching tearfully for the dry teats....The girl on the hearth moved back from the intense heat. The dog got up and shook herself and lay down several feet away. The babies crawled crying after her....The girl then asked herself a question. What wouldn't I do for a heaping dish of hog sausage?

When the articles were reprinted in *Time*, Southern readers were outraged. "Until now," wrote Thomas J. Hamilton, editor of the

*Augusta Chronicle*, "no one has taken the trouble to call Caldwell's hand, but I think it is now high time to do so." Though there were a few letters defending his *Post* series, most were bluntly hostile, particularly those written by citizens of Wrens. Erskine's answer to Hamilton's challenge was an invitation. He would take the man on a conducted tour, and if conditions were not as he had described, "let the editor of the *Augusta Chronicle* hang me, with a suitable inscription pinned to my coat tail, on the highest pole in the city." If anything, he had understated the conditions in East Georgia communities: "I could tell of men, with tears in their eyes, begging fruitlessly while their children starved. I could tell of teenage girls without job or home, offering 'french-dates' for a quarter on the streets of the editor's own city."

The controversy over Caldwell's articles reached such a pitch that the paper decided to make an investigation of their own. Two reporters accompanied Ira and Dr. Pilcher to Jefferson, Richmond, and Burke Counties, the areas hardest hit by economic decline. A four-part series was published by the *Chronicle* in mid-March, and the reporters did attempt to present a balanced assessment of their findings. Most of the residents of these counties had an average standard of living, but the newsmen admitted that "there is some basis for the writings of Erskine Caldwell. While we did not observe the details of what he said in his writings, we did observe the conditions under which depicted events could have happened." This acknowledgment delighted Erskine and his father, though Ira took issue with the *Chronicle*, stating in a contribution to their letters section that the reporters "counted the unfortunate by tens when they ought to have been counted by hundreds or thousands."

The *New York Post* asked Caldwell if he would travel South again and write another four-part series. He was happy to oblige, and this time included rural areas in Alabama and Mississippi as well as other parts of Georgia. The *Post* had agreed that his articles would have greater impact if accompanied by photographic illustrations, and though the pictures were grainy and amateurish—Caldwell was not a photographer—they had eye-catching blurbs:

"Hopeless" was one caption under the photo of a couple sitting on a dilapidated porch. Erskine also inserted first-person lines to illuminate his findings.

2 THINGS ARE CERTAIN
—DEATH AND BOSS'S BLOWS

ALABAMA TENANT FARMER: "I'm sixty-three and not fit to do a lick of work any more. All my life I worked for the landlords, and now when I'm all broken down from hard work, I can't get a mite of help from anybody. I went to the relief office and told them my foot is broken and the doctor says it won't heal, and that I've got a stomach cancer and piles and fainting spells. They told me they couldn't do nothing for me. Me and my wife don't know what to do except wait to die."

GEORGIA LANDOWNER: "We know how to treat the blacks like they ought to be treated. I had a black tenant last year who moved into one of my cabins, and the first thing he said was that he wanted some steps built. I didn't pay any attention to him and he said something about it again. I told him to shut up. He talked back, and I jumped on that nigger and gave him the worst beating he'd ever got in all his life. He was in bed a week, he was that beat up. The next time I saw him he was as meek as a scared kitten. That's all they need—just a showdown to see who's running things."

GEORGIA TENANT: "My children had one meal of meat sometime before last Christmas. I brought home four pounds of liver, and they grabbed the bag and ate up every bite of it before my wife could get hold of it long enough to cook it."

Senator Ellison D. Smith, a plantation owner from South Carolina, took exception to the series on tenant farming. Caldwell's description was propaganda. "A sharecropper," Smith explained to his colleagues from the well of the United States Senate. "is furnished a home, clothes, farm equipment, and the fuel he needs, and given half the crops. He pays no taxes and has no expenses of up-keep." In concluding his remarks, the Senator accused the *New York Post* of "a blatant attempt to disturb the morale of our people." But praise for the new series exceeded negative responses, and when the left-leaning Phalanx Press published the thirty-page pamphlet entitled *Tenant Farmer*, Caldwell became known overnight as the spokesman for sharecroppers. Hamilton Basso of *The New York Times* felt that *Tenant Farmer* should be read by all Southerners interested in the welfare of their region. "If any further condemnation of the tenant-farmer system is needed and the whole plantation economy as it is now practiced, here it is." The pamphlet gave a graphic picture of what men with pride and decency should eradicate—"a system based upon exploitation and greed and a total disregard of human beings."

Ezra Pound, who was lobbying the Works Progress Administration to fund regional presses, declared the twenty-five-cent publication to be "precisely the kind of work which needs region-wide distribution and national consideration." W. T. Couch, editor at the University of North Carolina Press, differed with Pound's assessment. Caldwell was grandstanding, Couch accused, and as a parting shot wrote: "Whether he is interested primarily in reform or royalties, it is certain that he has achieved only the latter." But the North Carolinian underestimated Caldwell's impact on other writers. Shortly after the second *Post* series, Henry Wallace, former Vice President, published a well-received article in *The New York Times Magazine* entitled "The Danger of Tenancy," and Cecil Holland caught attention in *Survey Graphic* with "The Tenant Farmer Turns." This depressed segment of the Southern population, for Holland, was a disgrace.

The publication of his third short story collection, *Kneel To The Rising Sun,* by Viking in June of 1935, did much to solidify Caldwell's literary position. *The New York Times* book reviewer, Harold Strauss, felt that the book unquestionably contained Caldwell's most powerful work. The stories would be acclaimed both by critics who upheld traditional standards and those of left-wing viewpoints. "The battle of mediocrity—artistic as well as propagandist, but in the work of a major writer, one with the power and range of Caldwell, it becomes evident that the theorists have once again been quibbling."

The new collection of stories gave Lewis Gannett of the *New York Herald Tribune* more faith in Caldwell's talent than *We Are The Living*. "For sometime I have been puzzled by this man's almost morbid absorption in the sub-human representatives of the human race, and have wondered if, like the ghastly audiences at *Tobacco Road*, he, too, could be laughing at them." Gannett could never understand why Caldwell was called a humorist. "I think he is the most profoundly tragic writer on contemporary America."

Hamilton Basso, in *New Masses*, pronounced that Caldwell had "exhausted the soil from which all his writings have sprung." Basso felt it strongly in *Journeyman* and in some of the short stories. "But each man to his own plowing. Only Mr. Caldwell could have written *Kneel to the Rising Sun*, it could only have come out of that part of the world he has made his own and it is a contribution of first importance to the literature of our time."

Harry Hansen, in a *New York World-Telegram* review, declared that Caldwell's forte was invention. *Kneel* seemed to be pieces of life gathered here and there on the byways where no other American writers traveled. "One recalls his tales not as elaborations but as crisp yarns that stick in the memory." Though Caldwell wrote with a disregard for form, he managed to round out an episode and to select the most telling incidents. "This new book is typical of his writing," wrote Hansen, "even though it does not answer the question, Is he going forward or standing still?"

Phillips Russell, in North Carolina's *Charlotte Observer*, wrote that Caldwell perceived the people of the South with a "silhouetted sharpness." *Kneel to the Rising Sun* were stories written with an unemotional detachment and with a bitter suggestiveness that had an incisive edge. "In these new stories," declared Russell, "Caldwell reveals a surer hand and a better control than ever before. He is one of the younger writers who is laying the beams for a new kind of observation and of writing."

Such laudatory comments may have helped soothe Caldwell's suspicion that *Journeyman* had been hastily done and flawed, but what no one knew then, nor could have judged without viewing his entire work in retrospect, was that the stories in *Kneel* would never be equaled.

Published in 1936, *The Sacrilege of Alan Kent* was illustrated with eight wood engravings by Ralph Frizzell. The work had three sections which had been contributed to magazines as experimental pieces: "Tracing Life with a Finger" (1929), "Inspiration for Greatness" (1930), and "Hours Before Eternity" (1931). In its entirety, it is a series of epiphanies as the central character recalls experiences and emotions. Kenneth Burke, in his chapter on Caldwell, in *The Philosophy of Literary Form,* called *Kent* "a sport," but Leon Tebbetts, publisher of the Falmouth Book House in Portland, Maine who brought out this early edition of the slim volume declared to this author it was "Mostly poetry, which sells miserably—we lost money on that one!"

There is a compression of language in *The Sacrilege of Alan Kent*, and part of its strength lies not so much in the well-placed words as what is left unsaid—this gives the telling a prose-poetry quality and adds to the flight. Often overlooked and underestimated, *Sacrilege* is an extraordinary achievement, and though Caldwell never again would use this method to deliver a story, he did go back to the style at times for descriptive passages in novels or to emphasize a detail in essays. An example can be found in *Some American People* when he attempts to place an action in syntactical means: It is August 1934 and the federal government has rounded up ten thousand head of cattle and pastured them in places not destroyed by drought. "The last great roundup is over," wrote Caldwell, "the bones of the culls that fell by the wayside have been picked clean, and painted canyons of the Badlands are unchanged."

Until he found the long-pursued girl of his dreams, Alan Kent was a wanderer. He discovered life as it is in the raw: brutal, lonely, pathetic, harsh, joyful. The rhythmic prose style is often striking as in the sentence: "Once the sun was so hot a bird came down and

walked beside me in my shadow." *Kent* is fragmentary, broken into
one-, two-, and three-sentence paragraphs, each of which is a separate fragment of the story—it was an attempt to write idealistically
of the imagined world, and by injecting realism the author hoped
to project himself. When asked why he didn't continue developing
the *Sacrilege* style, Caldwell explained: "I had given up trying to
write poetry, as every young man should. *Alan Kent* came out of
that experience, you see, because I realized that I had no ability as
a poet while I still had the inclination to write poetry, so the transition from poetry to prose occurred at that point."

Critics have labeled *Sacrilege* as a prose poem, probably because
the work was too episodic for fiction. Kenneth Burke found parts
of it to be "purest poetry," author Gerald Sykes called it "the poetry
of unfeeling," and Malcolm Cowley felt it was "on a lesser scale
to Whitman's 'Song of Myself.' " Cowley did object to some of the
work; he found himself moved "to personal fury against the author
by the awfulness of the bad part" and saw in the "violent poetry"
a uniqueness seldom displayed in American prose.

Harold Strauss, in *The New York Times*, considered the work "a
youthful and unsuccessful experiment," though *Sacrilege* threw "an
interesting light on the technique for which he is now known. Its
publishers have issued it in a handsomely designed quarto format, and the wood engravings by Ralph Frizzell superbly echo the
author's subtle counterpoint of dream and reality."

The Dayton, Ohio *News* declared *Sacrilege* to be a book "you
will want to own, one to read through for the beauty and strength
of lines" such as "I loved my mother and father and I wanted to be
with them but I could not stop living with myself." Another was:
"In a yard where roses bloomed a dog went every day and smelled
the ones that he could reach, but the people who lived in the house
never knew that there were flowers there."

Ira had illustrated the article he published in *Eugenics* with photographs, and when Erskine did the same for his second *Post* series
he realized how effective the mix would be if the illustrator were

a professional photographer. The idea of a collaboration was unappealing to him, for there were always pitfalls and risks when one became involved with another person. After agonizing over it and discussing it at length with Helen, he told Lieber to find someone who could work with him on a more extensive study of Southern sharecroppers.

It was at a New York cocktail party in January of 1936 that the famed photographer Margaret Bourke-White excitedly approached Max Lieber. She had heard that Erskine Caldwell was in search of a pictorial illustrator, and Bourke-White told the agent how much she would enjoy working on such an assignment. But when Lieber relayed the message, Caldwell hesitated—he was not sure that this project would be suitable for a female photographer.

He couldn't have been more mistaken; Bourke-White was anything but squeamish. Her antics had made Margaret the darling of her trade. She dangled from airplanes to get panoramic shots, crawled out on the windswept gargoyle of a swaying Chrysler Building with photographic gear in hand, and went down an elevator hundreds of feet to get pictures of coal miners at work. Attractive, then in her early thirties, charismatic, she had an effervescent personality and possessed a stamina that distanced her from most male competitors. Bourke-White advertised products on the radio and in magazines, was chased by reporters, had a niche in *Who's Who*, and drifted in and out of affairs after an unhappy early marriage.

Though well aware of her fame, and flattered that she should be interested in such a collaboration, Caldwell was put off by her advertising photography, and told her so when the two met. But she already knew this; Lieber felt Bourke-White should be aware of the objection before they negotiated, and had confided in her. As they discussed the project, she studied the author carefully. In *Portrait of Myself*, her autobiography, Margaret recalled the meeting: "I could hardly believe this large shy man with the enormous wrestler's shoulders and quiet coloring could be the fiery Mr. Caldwell. His eyes were the soft rinsed blue of well-worn blue jeans. His hair

was carrot—subdued carrot. The backs of his hands were flecked
with cinnamon freckles—cinnamon which had stood long on the
kitchen shelf."

Bourke-White decided Caldwell would be difficult to work with
but it didn't matter to her, as long as the project flourished and they
collaborated well together. She was not stung by his criticism of
her advertising photography—there were many of her pictures she
didn't like either, particularly the grinning models. Because he had
reservations about working with a woman, surmised Bourke-White,
he was taking along a secretary on the trip across the South: Sally,
who had worked for him at MGM. (Not her real name, but called
that by Caldwell, Margaret, and Helen). Erskine and Sally, according to Helen in an interview with William Sutton, had been lovers
in Hollywood.

Bourke-White was delighted when Caldwell relented. A date was
set for the trip: it would be in June when the summer heat "made
the Southern climate at its best for such observations." Viking
Press liked Erskine's choice of a collaborator and agreed to advance
them one thousand dollars to cover expenses in gathering material
for *You Have Seen Their Faces*, a title Caldwell had in mind from
the beginning. Margaret attempted to harmonize the partnership
with a little public relations footwork. "This is just to tell you," she
informed Caldwell, "that I am happier about the book I am to do
with you than anything I have had a chance to work on for the last
two years. If I had a chance to choose from every living writer in
America I would choose you first as the person I would like to do
such a book with."

Caldwell had several writing projects he wanted to complete before the trip, and being meticulous in scheduling future plans—he
sometimes made appointments a year or more in advance—he and
Bourke-White set the date to start work on June 11, 1936. They
would meet at the Richmond Hotel in Augusta, Georgia early in
the morning and talk about the route they would travel.

Margaret was carrying a heavy workload of her own for the next
five and a half months. She had to sublet her penthouse studio,

there was a South American assignment scheduled, she needed to exit gracefully from the advertising business portion of her photography, and her boss, Henry Luce at *Fortune* magazine, was involving her in his new publication, now in the planning stages—*Life* magazine.

Her crowded schedule became increasingly complicated as the months went by, and twice she had to arrange a new starting date. "As with any change of direction in one's life," wrote Bourke-White, "there were a thousand insistent last-minute details." She needed to clear her mind for their book project, and for this she had to set her house in order. "A few more days would wind up everything. After all, it was nearly half a year ago that we had set our starting date. Maybe Mr. Caldwell also had extra things to do; I could always ask."

She telephoned Lieber who informed her that Erskine was already in Georgia and was staying with his parents in Wrens. The news startled her, and when she got Caldwell on the line and told him that she was delayed because of the starting of *Life,* her explanation was given the silent treatment. There still were things that she needed to do: Would he mind if they went a week later? Instead of the eleventh of July, could they begin on the eighteenth? "The frozen wordlessness at the end of the line conveyed to me we might never begin at all." Bourke-White professed. "Heavens, I had been planning toward this for all these months!"

She soon learned from Lieber that he and Caldwell had talked and the project was off. To Helen, Erskine wrote: "I consider it the last straw. I hate to see the trip broken up, but I think it was the wisest thing to do under the circumstances." Bourke-White panicked—the book meant too much to her; she knew something had to be done immediately to solve the dilemma. Her only chance was to drop everything, hurry to Georgia and "corner him for a little heart-to-heart talk." Margaret packed her bags and caught the first available flight to Augusta.

She checked into the Richmond Hotel and asked how far it was to Wrens. "Six miles," she was told—it was thirty-five. When she

learned Caldwell couldn't be reached that day by telegram, she induced a young lad who swept floors at the post office to deliver
her message on his bicycle and gave him five dollars. Bourke-
White sat all day in the hotel lobby watching and waiting.

In the evening at six o'clock a heavy-shouldered man in a loose
blue jacket entered the hotel lobby. Together, the two went into the
coffee shop and ordered coffee. The shy man looked down at his
hands while they waited to be served. Caldwell turned to Bourke-
White when their cups were empty. "That was a big argument,
wasn't it?" he said with a smile. She nodded. "When do you want
to leave?" "Now," she replied, and they did.

Erskine's secretary, Sally, and Bourke-White were at odds before
the journey got underway. The seating arrangement needed to be
settled as one of the passengers would have to be squeezed into
the backseat with Margaret's mountain of camera equipment and
luggage. The photographer gave no ground, and finally Sally declared: "Hired help sits at second table." Her statement was left
dangling in the tense humid air as they finished their packing.

One incident aroused Erskine's amusement. Bourke-White had
brought along two glass jars containing egg cases of praying mantises. She was photographing their life cycle, and since they were
due to emerge soon she couldn't leave them behind. As Margaret
placed them carefully into the boot where they would ride smoothly, the lid of the trunk came down on her head. "Not hard enough
to do any damage," she recalled, "but hard enough to make me
want to avoid trunk lids from then on." Caldwell chuckled for the
first time, saying that he hoped something like that would be a
daily occurrence. "Why, he can laugh after all," wrote Bourke-
White when recalling her thump on the head.

Tempers were ragged while the threesome crossed Alabama and
Mississippi, and the atmosphere in the cramped Ford became so
unpleasant that Caldwell was sorely tempted to cancel this adventure. He felt that Bourke-White had no social depth and he was
"a tourist guide just showing someone around." Margaret was

unfamiliar with the South and Southern ways, and Caldwell's long silences unnerved her. A resentful Hollywood-secretary-mistress in the backseat further complicated the journey. "This is the worst trip I have taken so far," he wrote Helen when complaining about the photographer. "We had a scrap in Montgomery that could be heard for miles around—naturally she cried—but promised to follow my suggestions. She had another spasm the next afternoon near Meridian, Mississippi, and then we had a second big scrap that night in Jackson....The trouble is Bourke-White is in the habit of getting her own way—and so am I—what happens when we fall out is all that can be imagined."

The three took a meandering course off main highways from Georgia to Arkansas in search of sharecroppers' hovels and weathered faces. During this time, Bourke-White was trying her best to read the mind of her enigmatic collaborator. She understood the broader outlines of their book as well as Caldwell, but it was difficult to get him to talk about it. Taciturn and moody, hours would go by before he could dredge from his depths a suggestion or observation.

In Little Rock, Arkansas, Caldwell decided that he had more than enough of the whole project; he felt they weren't getting anything accomplished. When he went to Margaret's hotel room to help carry down her camera equipment on the morning of the fifth day, he suddenly lost his silence and shared his frustrations. He was nothing more than a tourist-guide chauffeur, Caldwell told her as they sat on her second-floor windowsill overlooking a street lined with trees. In *Portrait of Myself*, Bourke-White recalls this momentous encounter. "I tried desperately to tell him how much this meant to me, this opportunity to do something worthwhile, but I wasn't making much sense, because, of course, I was crying. Then suddenly something very unexpected happened. He fell in love with me. From then onward, everything worked out beautifully."

"She seduced him," was Sally's embittered description of the predictable beginning, and Maxim Lieber was less generous with his "she raped him!" But Caldwell was now infatuated by Bourke-

White's glamorous presence; Helen, at home with three children, and taken for granted by a husband who had frequently strayed, was no competition.

On the sixth day, the hotel clerk handed Caldwell a note and explained that "the other young lady" had checked out at three o'clock in the morning. Sally remonstrated that she was tired of the seating arrangement in the cramped Ford. One temperamental  photographer or writer she could work with, but not two in the stifling heat of summertime Arkansas.

Alone together, "there were no more surprises," wrote Bourke-White, "except personal and pleasant ones. The work was flowing along, a wide stream with the deepening understanding between us." Caldwell was introducing her to a whole new concept of information gathering and photography. His interest in a person was not limited to what was said but the mood in which the words were given. Erskine hung over a fence while the farmer leaned on his rake in what Margaret supposed was conversation—"one remark every fifteen minutes." She lurked in the background with a small camera, and when rapport was established in the halted exchange of words, Bourke-White was free to capture her portrait.

Caldwell was able to put their subjects at ease with a Southern drawl and casual demeanor, but Margaret was handicapped with her unmistakable Yankee accent. More than once he had to explain that his companion was "down South on her vacation." The people being interviewed and photographed were frequently suspicious of strangers and thought they were being ridiculed when the camera was pointed in their direction. "Reassuring them was a very important part of our operation," recalled Bourke-White, "and a reassuring voice in their own mode of speech eliminated many a barrier." She also learned from Erskine not to set up her photographs; spontaneity and undoctored pictures were important to him. It was a fresh point of view for Margaret, and she recalled taking an interior shot: A black woman was combing her hair beside a dresser made from a wooden box with a curtain tacked to it, and on the bureau were "lots of little homemade things." Bourke-White rearranged these before taking the picture. "Erskine spoke to me about it. How neat her bureau had been. How she must have valued all her little possessions and how she had them tidily arranged her way, which was not my way."

Bourke-White's precious cargo of mantis eggs began to hatch on a backcountry road, and she photographed the insects as they were crawling from their protective sheaths. Soon the car was "surrounded by a solemn ring of little children" who stood by, amazed at the tiny river of mantises. "Oh, look at the little devil horses!" they cried out, delighting both Erskine and Margaret.

Caldwell's early doubts about working with her gave way to admiration and pride: she seemed to know instinctively what he was after as they toured the more destitute areas of the South. Bourke-White was now balancing her aesthetic quest for perfection in each photograph with a newly-learned social empathy. "I was learning," she wrote, "that to understand another human being you must gain some insight into the conditions which made him what he is. The people and the forces which shape them: each holds the key to the other."

Bourke-White's portraits gave Caldwell's prose a discipline that would strengthen the book: there was no need for sensationalism this time; a device that had been detrimental in earlier journalistic attempts. The six short essays that separate gatherings of full-page pictures are considered by many critics to be his best nonfiction. These essays would be further illuminated with fictional, first-person accounts following each piece. This time he valiantly resisted exaggeration for the sake of comic relief. Both authors would supply captions for the photographs: Under one picture of a hard luck sharecropper couple is "A man learns not to expect much after he's farmed cotton most of his life." The worn face of an elderly farm woman is subtitled: "I've done the best I knew how all my life, but it didn't amount to much in the end." There was also the photograph of a grinning boy with stained, crooked teeth who is saying: "School is out for spring plowing and Pa said I could go fishing." What had begun as an irksome collaboration was fast becoming a magic mix of pictures and words as the two prowled south through Louisiana, north into Tennessee, and east to South Carolina.

Bourke-White was given a new nickname. Her friends and colleagues called her Peggy or Maggie, but Erskine felt the new love in his life should have a special name, one that only he would use. Kit, he decided, was perfect for her because she "had the contented expression of a kitten that has just swallowed a bowl of cream." It was more challenging for Margaret to find a new name for him. "Nothing can be made out of 'Erskine' but Skinny, and even though he was anything but skinny, he had been called that by everyone most of his life. I disliked the name and searched for another. We tried 'Skeats' for a while, but it never seemed to belong to him."

The two hoped to photograph a chain gang but had little luck in locating one. Local sheriffs were not interested in sharing such information with a camera-carrying Northerner; the idea of chained men frequently fired controversy. But one day on a back road in Tennessee when rounding a curve they came upon a group in tattered stripes, chained man to man, "each with his soup spoon tucked in his iron ankle cuff." The beefy Captain with the paunch demanded a photograph permit, and when Caldwell said they didn't have one, the guard furiously waved his rifle at them and threatened. "When he yelled that he would blow off our tires," wrote Bourke-White, "Skinny and I left, and returned, driving past in a zigzag course." Several shots were fired at the car, but they made their escape without damage. Then Caldwell remembered an acquaintance from school days in nearby Atoka who had political influence, and who introduced them to the Commissioner. Armed with a permit, sealed and stamped, they went back to where the prisoners were digging a trench, Bourke-White waving the document from the car window much as one waves a flag of truce. The Captain "looked at the document with rage and felt the seals with an exploring thumb. 'The Commissioner, what the hell,' he hissed, 'he knows I don't read.' So it was up to us to read and reread the permit aloud with such dramatic expression there was nothing the

Captain could do except allow us to bring our cameras and take photographs."

Caldwell and Bourke-White wanted to include interior photographs of churches while the parishioners were being whipped up by fiery sermons. They had no difficulty getting into Negro houses of worship—the two were welcome to attend with camera in hand. But some of the white denominations were standoffish and discouraged visitors. In South Carolina the wandering journalists came upon a small church that "matched the town—bleak and built of splintery boards which had never been painted." They arrived while the morning service had reached frantic proportions, and finding the front door locked, used an open window as their entrance. What was happening staggered them as Bourke-White took pictures and Caldwell changed flashbulbs. Women in cotton-print dresses were throwing themselves about with abandon, one nearly knocking Margaret's camera from her hands. The chorus of "Praise Be" grew louder. Bourke-White recalled the "gamut of religious frenzy from exaltation to torpor. Some were writhing on the floor" as they began the hysterical process of "coming through." The minister by this time was so exhausted that he "sank down on the platform of his pulpit, where he held his head in his hands." Men and women were rolling wildly on the floor shouting "Amens" in hoarse voices. "Finally, the hallelujahs began dying away, and each amen was fainter than the last." Skinny and Kit knew it was time to disappear. "We sailed out through the windows the way we had come in, and in a matter of minutes we were out of town."

The leaves were about to flame into shades from deep red to yellow when Caldwell returned to Mount Vernon in late September. But this time back he was a stranger in the presence of his own family, and there was the temptation of leaving without a word of explanation. Helen was her usual self, loving and excited to have him home. She was also curious about his summer and travels with the temperamental photographer and unhappy secretary. When his answers became somewhat evasive, she asked him to describe their clothing and how they competed to get his attention. Then she wanted to know which one he considered to be the most attractive. "You must remember, Helen," Erskine replied, "we were working all the time on the book." Her retort was heavy with sarcasm: "Book my foot! Two unmarried girls and you on the loose—day and night—and all that time together. Oh my!"

His two sons were soon sniffing his clothing "like inquisitive puppies," for there was an odor that puzzled them. Caldwell remembered doing the same when his father returned home after long train journeys—perhaps it was gasoline or exhaust fumes, maybe onion or garlic the boys were smelling. But Helen wasn't fooled and remained unsatisfied with his explanations. When the sons left the room, she said: "Do tell me, Skinny-boy," fluttering her eyelids, "what was the name of the perfume you were exposed to? I'd like to try it myself."

Aside from helping Helen in the garden and gathering apples for making cider, Caldwell spent much of his time, day and night, at the Parker Pond cabin working on short stories, *You Have Seen Their Faces*, and letters to Bourke-White. "Dearest Girl in All the World," Caldwell began. "I love you. That's little enough to say, and it does not fill much spaces, but it is what I feel. I love you. I love you. I love you. I love you." Another fervent message proclaimed: "You must know that I love you so deeply that living does not hold any promise without you in it. The trouble now is that I want to share everything with you—every minute, every look, every step." He wanted to hold her in his arms every night and wake to find his Kit still there. "And all day long it is the same way. I want to see you, talk to you, feel you every minute."

Bourke-White was now torn between two loves: Erskine and her career. But as always, work had to come first; without it she would be lost. Her job on the new magazine, *Life*, became increasingly demanding, and she was its star photographer. Margaret's lifestyle was hectic and there were many rushed assignments as she flew out of New York for faraway places. Yet her physical attraction to Caldwell intensified, and a cable to him announced: "MY PUSSY

GROWS COLD FOR YOU." Hand in hand, they were seen strolling the streets of New York, and when Malcolm Cowley saw them at a party he thought they were "radiantly in love so that their presence transformed the crowded room." There was now another person in their lives—Patricia. She was the child they planned to have one day, and to seal this pledge they dedicated *You Have Seen Their Faces* to her.

Caldwell no longer tried to hide his affair from his wife, and when she threatened to divorce him he seemed unperturbed. They no longer slept together, and the atmosphere at Greentrees became increasingly tense. Clayton and Dorothy Dolloff spent an evening with the Caldwells and saw that Helen was unhappy. "Skinny didn't appear any different," recalled Dolloff, "but once during our visit Helen mentioned his frequent *business trips* to New York City, and I sensed that she was being sarcastic."

Erskine was now spending more time in New York than in Mount Vernon, and his parents learned from Helen that the marriage was in trouble. Carrie was unaware that another woman had entered her son's life and blamed her daughter-in-law. Helen had no reason to be jealous over nothing; they were "false impressions." But in her next letter to Erskine, she scolded him: "I am hoping and praying that you and Helen will consider the children before anything else in the world. I am appalled when I think of what would in all probability be their fate if they should be deprived of close companionship and supervision."

Caldwell and Bourke-White were now living together in the Mayflower Hotel, later to move to the Beekman Towers, and he was urging her to marry him—it would make Patricia "real." Assignments for *Life* kept her away and busy, and deeply as she cared for Erskine, Margaret had reservations. She was troubled by his moody silences which sometimes embarrassed her when in the presence of friends. Once in a fury, he struck her, and during one argument he squeezed her arm so angrily that he left deep bruises. "Please help me," he pleaded after an unpleasant incident. "I want to be able to make up a hundred-fold for what I have done." Forgive him, she

did, but he continued to freeze her out in spells of ugly silence—
the customary punishment of his childhood.

The more Bourke-White resisted him the more depressed he became. When she went on trips he could not sleep, would not eat
properly, and some days he stayed in bed all morning. "Kit, try to
understand," he wrote her, "I'm afraid I'm cracking up. I can't stand
it much longer." In his desperation, Caldwell even hinted that he
might commit suicide if she left him. On a trip West with him in
the late summer of 1937, she severed relations. "You can't leave us,
Kit," he begged. "You can't leaves *us*." Finally he was told she
would come back, but first he must see a psychiatrist.

Margaret had been in analysis for several years with Harry Stack
Sullivan, a well-known therapist, and Erskine agreed to see him.
After a few visits, he wrote her that progress was being made. "I
feel a lot better. I have eaten for the first time in a week, and hope
to sleep tonight for the first time in eight days." But these assur-
ances were designed to quell her doubts; he had little confidence
in Sullivan, hated spending the money, and was reluctant to reveal
himself to another person, especially a professional. After a few
weeks of treatment, he began cancelling appointments and then
stopped going entirely. Sullivan, who was a close friend of Margaret's, advised her to leave him. If Caldwell couldn't dominate her,
he warned, the man might resort to violence. While her lover had
"outstanding merits and attractive attributes," he did show "a fundamental lack of consideration that cannot be expected to improve"
without extended treatment.

His mood sometimes shifted, and when the warmth he usually
kept hidden surfaced, it nearly melted her resolve to remain the famous photographer that reporters chased or the Bourke-White who
endorsed products in national magazines. Once he filled her apartment with pastel balloons, and deluged her with hothouse bouquets.
On her trip to the Arctic Circle he sent telegrams to "HONEYCHILE,
ARCTIC CIRCLE, CANADA"—they all reached her. Then on a flight
from the West Coast to New York, when changing planes in Chicago, she heard the public address call: "Paging child bride! Will

child bride kindly step to the ticket counter!" Suspecting Erskine, she went to the desk and the clerk handed her a telegram which read: "WELCOME, WELCOME, WELCOME, WELCOME!"

Erskine still needed Helen, and when he and Bourke-White were at odds or she was on an extended assignment, Caldwell would be in contact with his wife. "Needless to say," he wrote Helen—the letter was written in Bourke-White's apartment—"I miss us (you and me) more all the time." He hinted that things might well be different one day. Being away was much like being on a chain gang, and he promised to come back to her if she would just be patient enough to wait for him. "Anyway," he assured her, "I love you. And I miss what we should be having now." When his affair had run its course, he and Helen would "have plenty of time to celebrate. I owe you a lot," he confessed, "and God speed the day when I can repay you—with interest plus a bonus."

If Caldwell had feelings of guilt for having left Helen, he kept them hidden much of the time. Typically, he blamed her for his straying, and when she begged him to leave Bourke-White, he stalled her plea with financial jargon: "I believe the long term, if not the near term, trend is definitely upward. Don't worry about anything in the meantime because we wish to keep the stock going up."

Erskine's implication that he and Helen might one day be "us" again was just another jolt on her emotional roller-coaster ride with its endless twists and breakneck slides. When he and "that other woman" quarreled, Helen defended him and blamed Bourke-White. "I'll spend the rest of my life trying to repay you for being the finest person in the world," he wrote, and the declaration left her hopeful. Caldwell became so despondent in the summer of 1937 that Helen was deeply worried. In a voice heavy with desperation, he telephoned her from New Mexico. Bourke-White had left him and he was in no condition to get back East on his own. Would she come fetch him? Without a moment's hesitation, Helen flew down and drove Erskine back in his car. When Margaret let it be known that her Skinny was missed, he hurriedly left Mount Vernon to be with his Kit.

Caldwell's income from *Tobacco Road* and his books was prodigious, but he continued to nickel and dime his way when Helen needed money for herself and the children. He also could be peevish, blaming her for mismanagement in running their home. "Good intentions won't buy clothes and food for three of the best kids in the world. I'm interested in the future, because I look forward to the time when you and I get straightened out." When Greentrees became unbearably cold and the firewood supply ran low—Erskine had ignored her plea to pay someone to cut several extra cords—she and the children were forced to spend another winter in Charlottesville.

"I have just finished the four stories," he wrote Helen from New York, "and I am sending them to you in another envelope. If you are satisfied with them, correct them and send them to Lieber right away." Such literary directives Helen took for granted, as she had from the start of their marriage. The galleys of *You Have Seen Their Faces* arrived while "Honeychile" was in the Arctic, and Caldwell needed Helen to help with the proofs. She came to New York at once, and together they made corrections. Helen did take careful note of the sumptuous love nest and particularly noticed the black silk sheets on the wide double bed.

She received an unexpected telephone call one morning shortly after returning to Mount Vernon from Virginia. The man on the line was a bank official from New York; he had a question about a lease agreement signed by Mr. and Mrs. Erskine Caldwell. When Helen asked the name of the apartment, he said it was Beekman Towers—the very one her husband was sharing with Bourke-White. "I was pleased to inform him," said Helen with a bitter chuckle, "I knew of only one Mrs. Caldwell and the signature he had was a forgery."

Her marriage to Erskine had declined to the point where it was no longer salvageable as he became more callous and intentionally tried to injure her feelings. When Helen developed an edema in her lung, Caldwell visited her in the New York hospital where she was being treated. She was astonished when her husband spent the entire time talking about all the things that he and Bourke-White had done in bed the night before—"a blow by blow account."

Helen filed for divorce in January of 1938 on grounds of "cruel and abusive treatment," and the papers were signed three months later. She was given custody of the children and retained possession of the Mount Vernon property. A $25,000 trust was set up to guarantee that payments would be made promptly. Caldwell had to give Helen $2,600 a year, and an additional $12,000 was to be paid in four installments. He was awarded visitation rights of one month during the summer with his children, then aged twelve, eleven, and five.

The divorce left Helen with a lifelong bitterness: "You can certainly afford to go to Europe, Hawaii or Lima—theaters, plays, expensive house and deluxe entertaining," she once wrote when asking him to send money for school clothes. "But any sacrifice of your personal comfort for the kids, or to keep your word to them, you will not make. You owe all of them more than you can ever repay. For self-gratification, you wrecked their home, their life and mine, as well as your own creative genius."

# LIFE WITH BOURKE-WHITE

*You Have Seen Their Faces* was published by Viking while Caldwell was on his way to the West Coast for another engagement of screenwriting. The Whittier, California *News* took note of Erskine's arrival at Paramount Studios in their November 22, 1937 issue:

> Reporting for work, he went to the office of Adolph Zukor and was shown into the inner sanctum during the executive's absence.
>
> A photographer had been working there, presumably taking pictures of Zukor. The place was littered with lights and cables and screens. Caldwell sat down and waited. After several minutes a man came to the door and bellowed:
>
> "Whaddaya think this is—the electrical department? Get that stuff outa there, and quick—every bit of it!"
>
> Presently Zukor returned to his office. He was astonished to find Caldwell, his new and expensive writer, on his knees rolling up electric cables.

*Faces* got immediate attention with the pleasing layout, high-quality paper, and prose which electrified the photographs. The book established a new genre—text always had dominated illustration, but now the two were balanced as equals.

The very virtuosity of Bourke-White's seventy-five photographs was partly a distraction for Herschel Brickell in his *New York Post* review. They were "simply magnificent, and many of them are so splendid as technical achievements that the edge is taken from their sociological value; they are mostly pictures of ugly things—not all—made beautiful by the sheer art of a skillfully manipulated camera." Caldwell was given polite notice for his contribution to the book though faulted for the presentation: "His theories are often sound," wrote Brickell, "but they also suffer from his lack of historical background."

"It is difficult at times to decide which carries the most force," observed Sigmund Arnold Lavine in his *Boston Evening Transcript* review. "The author's journalistic ability to make men, both white and black, owner and tenant, guard and a chain gang member, old and young, talk or the photographer's skill at catching unaware the people of the Black Belt country as they work, play and pray. No social document is seen; each one is a story in itself. And as a writer about these forgotten people Erskine Caldwell stands out among his contemporaries."

The Southern critics were far less positive, often hostile, when judging the book, and most of the snarls were directed at Caldwell. "Selling One's Birthright" screamed the *Dalton North Georgian* review. *You Have Seen Their Faces* was written by the same man who "wrote a disgusting sordid play, which, to the discredit of New York playgoers" had been running too long. "Why pick out the South when you can find want and poverty rampant in the slums of big Northern, Eastern and Western cities?" Donald Davidson's article in the *Southern Review* found Bourke-White's "strong irregular faces, often beautiful with a wild and touching nobility," but the coauthor could be labeled as "a treacherous, traitorous propagandist." Caldwell, Davidson decided, "would make a splendid curator of a Soviet park of recreation and culture."

Communist and left-wing reviewers praised Caldwell's appeal for "collective action by the tenant farmers themselves, or government control of cotton farming"—they were pleased with his admonishments and grateful that he had refrained from using burlesque humor as a tool for emphasis. "I am so anxious for you to be with us now that I have grown to understand your work with some degree of thoroughness," wrote critic Edwin Seaver. "When I first read *Tobacco Road* I had to overcome a lot of ingrained resistance." For Seaver, *You Have Seen Their Faces* was "even considering the captions for the pictures—an example, for sheer writing, unsurpassed by anybody in our time."

*Faces* did come under assault from an unexpected quarter, which could be dismissed as photojournalistic sour grapes. Photographer Walker Evans and writer James Agee had spent the summer of 1936 in the South collaborating on the same type of book, but with the appearance of *You Have Seen Their Faces* and its popularity, their *Let Us Now Praise Famous Men* was overshadowed and the publication temporarily suspended—when the book did appear in 1941, it lost money. Evans accused his competitors of exploiting people who were already exploited, and Agee included in *Famous Men* a tidbit of Erskine and Margaret bribing one downtrodden couple with snuff in order to take their picture. Yet it is ironic how the passing years have reversed this acclaim. *Let Us Now Praise Famous Men*, more intellectual in approach, is considered one of the literary milestones of the nineteen thirties; *Faces*, more popular and theatrical, was difficult to find until its reprint by the University of Georgia Press in 1995.

With Margaret away, and only the writing of short stories to console him, Caldwell felt the need of distraction. When Frances Gossel, manager of a lecture agency, asked Erskine to undertake a public speaking tour, he surprised himself by accepting the invitation. But there soon were regrets of having consented—it was the last thing he should have done, Caldwell told himself as the premiere loomed. Night after night, in dread of the ordeal, he tried to think of some escape. Just as the jaws of circumstance were about to snap shut, the engagement was canceled by mutual consent. Carl Sandburg was beginning a lecture tour that season, and Hamilton College where Erskine was to speak had also booked the poet. Would Caldwell agree to a cancellation? Relief and elation were instantaneous; he had no thought of asking why Sandburg was chosen—this was a poet with a guitar.

Gossel had also asked Caldwell to sign an agreement for the dramatization of *Journeyman* by Alfred Hayes and Leon Alexander. Caldwell read the script hurriedly, and though he had reservations, gave his approval accompanied by suggestions. Sam Byrd, who had the lead in *Tobacco Road* for four years, contracted with Hayes and Alexander to produce *Journeyman*. With the *Road* play still very much on the boards, Erskine had no desire to have another stage involvement, but Byrd barraged him with pleas by mail, telephone, and in person until he finally relented. "I thought Sam would be satisfied if I invested a few thousand dollars in the production, but he said this was not sufficient." In addition to investing, Byrd insisted that Caldwell help revise the script and attend rehearsals. It was a two-month commitment, "from midmorning to midnight."

On January 30, 1938, a wintry evening that slowed Manhattan traffic, *Journeyman* opened at the Fulton Theater. The cast was still in a state of shock: The dress rehearsal had been hissed so loudly that the actors had to belt out their lines, and later a shouting match had erupted during which both dramatists and the director "had loudly renounced any connection with the play, at the same time denouncing the personalities of anyone within hearing distance, all in terms barely short of physical violence." Sam Byrd was hopeful that the near brawl was "a temperamental flare-up"—jitters were common on the eve of an opening.

The theater column by Arthur Pollock in the *Brooklyn Daily Eagle* had a next-morning reaction: "If the first audience did not gasp, it held its breath. It held its breath for a long time, but nothing startling happened." That was the play's curse for Pollock—it began as the most outspoken work a dramatist could dare write and collapsed. "It seems to be just a bad play."

Drama critic John Anderson was even harsher. "I am minimizing its faults when I report gently that it is a dirty and noisy bore." Anderson found the work "duller than ditch-water" and not quite as clean. "Several of the scenes and many passages are frankly and deliberately filthy and playgoers who enjoy stable drama should find this one reeking."

After Brooks Atkinson of *The New York Times* declared *Journeyman* to be the worst play ever to open on Broadway and with little kindness questioned the author's direction, Caldwell sent a letter by messenger to Atkinson. In the epistle, he admitted that it was understandable for critics to be perplexed when *Tobacco Road* appeared because few people then knew what was happening in the South. But after four years of debate and the publication of *You Have Seen Their Faces,* he could not excuse critics for their ignorance—their response to *Journeyman* indicated they still reviled the play "instead of the condition out of which it stems."

One of the anecdotes told at the time of the opening surfaced in several theater notices: A drama critic was on the way home after writing his column and a friend asked him what he thought of the play.

"Dirtiest show I ever saw," said the critic.

"How dirty?" asked the friend.

"Well," said the critic, "one character says to another: 'You dirty lousy son of a bitch.' "

"That's not so bad," said the friend. "I've heard worse on the stage."

"But that," snapped the critic, "was the only clean line in the play."

The reviews of the premiere were so unfavorable that it seemed irrational to keep the doors open another day. Many critics viewed the play as a cheap spinoff from *Tobacco Road*. The *Brooklyn Citizen* declared *Journeyman* to be "Aimless, Shoddy, Sickening, and Very Childish." Robert Coleman, in the *Daily Mirror*, wrote that it was "reminiscent of the literary efforts of adolescents trying to be smart with crayons on a blank fence." But the producer was stubborn and told a troubled Caldwell that such adverse responses were all part of theater history and the play could be turned around. It was Byrd's intention to raise enough money to meet expenses for another full week or longer. Erskine was persuaded to write a check for five thousand dollars, but this amount, he later claimed, was only one of several installments. "As I watched the scenery being hauled away," professed Caldwell, "I vowed to be more careful of my investments in the future. And especially to shun the privilege of backing a play on Broadway."

The *Daily Worker* was now labeling Caldwell "an artist in uniform." His *Tenant Farmer* pamphlet and text in *Faces* had elevated him in left-wing circles, even in the eyes of critics who had gazed at him suspiciously because of his uneven reactions. He was seen attending meetings of the American Writers' Congress, sponsored at that time by the American Communist Party, and Caldwell was delighted when the Congress nominated him an honorary vice president to their 1937 session. For him, these political outings were social activities, rather than a joining of the fold.

Early in his career, his only publishing outlets were little journals, and it didn't matter to him whether they had conservative or liberal leanings—just as long as he could get a story into print. When the Marxist publication *New Masses* poled thirty of the contributors in 1934, asking if the magazine's criticism was helpful, Caldwell replied that such writing was "about ninety percent soap suds and that a Marxist critic can work up just as much lather from a cake of soap as a capitalist reviewer."

Michael Gold at *New Masses* became a close friend during the time when Erskine was living in a cold-water room in New York's Village. "He did not proselyte me," recalled Caldwell. "Mike Gold was a person who had a deep feeling for people, a deep feeling for writing about life, the economics of living, the sociology of living, and he was just my kind of person."

Though Caldwell would not be investigated by Senator Joseph McCarthy's subcommittee during the nineteen fifties, scripting the film *Mission to Moscow* would place him in a sensitive position. The studio cautioned him not to write anything that might jeopardize the film—a needless warning since Caldwell knew nothing about the internal workings of Communism nor thought of himself as furthering any doctrines. His position was that the stories he wrote were truthful statements about people he had observed in Georgia and Maine. "I am glad," said Caldwell, "if the communists like my books, but they are not propaganda."

It was through Bourke-White's influence and urging that he participated in panel discussions on the future outlook of American letters with other prominent writers and appeared in a cameo on the radio program *Author Author.* When the Columbia University Writer's Club—a group that had banned *Tobacco Road* only a few years earlier—invited him to speak, he accepted readily due to Margaret's insistence that it was excellent therapy. For a time, he taught a weekly course at the New School for Social Research in New York City on "Farm Tenancy and the Negro in Transition."

Having been confined to New York for more than a year, Caldwell was eager to travel again. Viking wanted a new novel, but the thought of settling down for a number of months to write one had little appeal. Though he was thirty-four years old he had never been abroad, and when he came up with the idea of another *Faces* book, similar but different in subject, Margaret was enthusiastic. They decided on Czechoslovakia and would spend two months there gathering material.

Hitler's troops already had entered Austria, on March 12, 1938, and if Germany could neutralize Czechoslovakia's defense system, the balance of power would be destabilized, and make possible a Nazi invasion of Poland and Russia. Three and a half million Sudeten Germans in Czechoslovakia were being stirred up by Nazi propaganda for an *Anschluss* with Germany. Caldwell and Bourke-White worried that time was limited as they hurriedly booked passage on the S. S. *Normandie*.

It was June when they arrived in Prague, and there was still snow on the slopes of mountains. Margaret's camera needed no translator, but Caldwell had the disadvantage of speaking only English. Jiri Poher, a literary agent, and newspaper editor Franz Weiskopf, were frequently helpful as interpreters.

They were given an official escort, much to Margaret's annoyance, and in typical Bourke-White manner she displayed her displeasure with tears. They weren't "planned," she wrote—it was the "result of weariness, but quite effective."

Officialdom was the least of her worries as the trip got underway. Caldwell's moods were making him a testy traveling companion. A government press officer and his wife, a warm hospitable couple, had taken them to a small village and had done their utmost to be helpful, even treating them to dinner in an inn, when much to Margaret's embarrassment Caldwell suddenly became rudely quiet and froze everybody out. In *Portrait of Myself*, Bourke-White wrote: "I am sure Skinny did not intend to cause this distress. I believe he was largely unaware of what was happening, for basically he was sensitive and almost uncannily perceptive about others. But this ungracious behavior prevented the closeness to the people we should have had."

She plotted their course as the two crisscrossed Bohemia and Moravia and roamed into the eastern provinces of Slovakia and Carpathian Ruthenia. It was a land of small farms and villages framed with evergreens and birches, but with all this beauty there was poverty and a heaviness of spirit as war threatened. On a train, a German couple ordered a woman to leave their compartment so they could be more comfortably seated, and when she refused, the man slapped her face, spat on her, and yelled: "You Jewish swine! You'll be taught your place!" Bourke-White's aggressive style of getting pictures attracted attention, and was particularly noticed by the local military police now under Nazi control. They were often shaken awake and interrogated on night trains. "They probably would have made it tougher for us if we had looked a little more non-aryan," Caldwell wrote Alfred Morang. "The thing is, they suspect everybody of trying to smuggle money out of the country for the Jews."

Caldwell, unlike many journalists of that time, didn't dodge the anti-Semitism he had witnessed. Both he and Bourke-White tried unsuccessfully to assist their Jewish interpreter in obtaining a visa to the United States. "Certainly you will find no prejudice against your race here," Margaret wrote the woman. Bourke-White herself was half Jewish—a fact that she kept secret. Included in their collaboration, *North of the Danube*, was a photograph of Talmudic students, and when Margaret lectured about Czechoslovakia upon her return she warned her audience: "Pick up any newspaper of this last week and you will be able to guess what is happening to those orthodox Jewish families in the area which Hitler has 'liberated,' as he likes to call it."

Caldwell's fourth collection of short stories, *Southways*, was published in June while he and Margaret were in Czechoslovakia. The sixteen stories, most of which appeared originally in such diverse publications as *Atlantic Monthly, Sunday Worker, Redbook, College Humor,* and *The New Yorker* were dedicated to Bourke-White.

"The customer won't get much print for his money," complained John Selby in the Tampa, Florida *Tribune.* The 206 pages were read at "one sitting in 58 minutes flat and didn't hurry." Readers "won't get quality either," commented Selby, "for Mr. Caldwell has snatched up whatever lay under the work table and stuffed the handful into his new book."

"A Knife to Cut the Corn Bread With," the story of a starving man who decides that a slice from his paralyzed leg will satisfy his wife's hunger, was cited as one of Caldwell's more powerful inclusions, and "The Fly in the Coffin," a tale that poses the question whether the fly that has been locked in Old Dose Muffin's coffin can tickle Dose's nose, one of his weakest. "A Small Day," "Nine Dollars' Worth of Mumble," and "The Night My Old Man Came Home" were perceived as having elements of bawdy and deadpan humor, some bordering slapstick.

"*Southways,* it is evident," declared Arnold Shukotoff in *New Masses,* "has more of the local color of *You Have Seen Their Faces* than of the caustic social criticism of *Kneel to the Rising Sun.* Though it displays a rich insight into the milieu, mores, and the physical details of Southern living, and though Caldwell has developed a more dynamic control of setting, the volume lacks power."

Frank Daniel, old friend and stalwart admirer, was predictably positive in the *Atlanta Journal*: "These stories, terse, eloquent, stirring, are realer for their laughter, for Mr. Caldwell knows how to employ this quality not as decoration, but as a medium for heightening his moods and his character delineation, and for winning a reader's sympathy for the fundamental ideas which the author expresses."

*Southways* seemed a return to *You Have Seen Their Faces* for Wilbur Needham in the Pasadena, California *Star News.* "He is experimenting with short stories of white and Negro tenant farmers," pronounced Needham, and is "not always entirely successful." Several of the tales were judged so slight that without Caldwell's touch they would be dismissed. "But they are all with amusing, satiric, or of compelling readability."

Another lukewarm response came from Edward Radenzel in the *San Francisco Chronicle*. "Slight as most of the stories are they reveal the folkways of the South as well as a living writer is able to convey them to us." Caldwell's chief virtue in the way he practiced the short story lay in his effortlessness, but the flaw was in the "clumsy way" his tales were written. "Perhaps never to be a great writer," observed Radenzel, "he succeeds without the limitations he has imposed upon himself, being the only representative story writer in the field he has chosen."

Caldwell and Bourke-White returned from their European trip on the *Aquitania* and were accosted by a number of reporters and photographers who had hurriedly boarded ship. Margaret was annoyed when two cameramen got out tape measures to check the distance between her cabin and Erskine's. Once the press discovered that the two had booked passage as Mr. and Mrs. Caldwell and had adjoining accommodations the questioning became more intense. Bourke-White was reclining on a deck chair, fashionably dressed, and holding a lapdog; Caldwell stood by in a tailored blue suit, his expression dour as Margaret assured the reporters that she was still single. "I'm not going to marry him," she snapped when one reporter persisted in catching her out. "I want to be single and that's all there is to it." But the newspapers headlined the two celebrities as purposely evasive. The *New York News* inquired "Is it Miss or Misses?" Caustic columnist Walter Winchell dropped a one-liner in his column to Bourke-White: "Go ahead and marry the guy."

Why should she marry "this fascinating, difficult man?" Bourke-White asked herself. There were several reason why she shouldn't: his frozen moods; his jealousy, not toward any man, but to *Life* magazine for the time it took her away from him; and the role he expected her to play as his wife, and mother to unborn Patricia.

But her resolve to remain independent was weakening, and he was increasingly determined to have his way.

Caldwell rented a cottage on a Connecticut island shortly after their return, and they both liked the area with its proximity to New York City so much that they purchased property in nearby Darien, Connecticut. The house and grounds were located in an upper-class neighborhood where homes had genteel names, such as Round Hill, Blueberry Hill, Rolling Hills. Not to be outdone, Margaret and Erskine decided to call their abode Horseplay Hill.

Their new home was a low white New England structure with peg floors and with three steps ascending or descending into various room levels. There were stone fireplaces, and from the living room one could see a sparsely wooded countryside. The dining table and stands were glass and there was a sizeable collection of glass ornaments. The front windows overlooked rock terraces, and behind the house were lawns and a swimming pool. Caldwell loved the sun and spent much of his time writing out of doors on a stone ledge where he could conveniently place his typewriter. Bourke-White decided on the layout of the grounds and how the house was furnished—this was her domain and one that he gladly granted her.

Their Darien neighbors assumed that they were a married couple, and when a New York friend asked if she had married, Margaret replied: "I am always trying not to." She wasn't against marriage, but it was of the utmost importance that her career be preserved. She needed an inner security, and this wouldn't be possible if she were "torn apart for fear of hurting someone" every time she was given an assignment.

In *Portrait of Myself*, Bourke-White concluded that "a woman is most strongly drawn to the man who needs her the most." Perhaps if she became his wife it would end his feelings of insecurity—if marriage had this kind of healing power for him, Margaret was willing to consider it. She had a general plan and wondered whether Erskine would consent to its terms. He did, and when they boarded an airplane for Nevada, a state where marriage licenses were issued immediately, Margaret worked this plan into a marriage contract. Number one declared that when there was a disagreement between them, they would settle it before midnight; number two had to be that all her friends would be treated as courteously as his—there should be no more moods that froze people out; and number three, the one most important to her, was that he would never interfere with her photographic assignments—she must be free to come and go professionally without notice. "We were flying over the great desert reaches of Utah and Nevada when Skinny signed this formidable document," wrote Bourke-White, "and at least that was behind us."

Both felt that Reno was no place for a wedding, and while still aloft they borrowed the pilot's chart and hunted for a town within a radius of a hundred miles that had a pretty name. Silver City, they decided; this had an appealing ring. After getting their license at the Reno courthouse, they flagged a taxi and told the driver their destination. It was a ghost town, he warned, and suggested they take the minister with them. A man of the cloth was found sitting in the lobby of an old hotel in Carson City, and he was delighted to be a part of the bizarre festivities. Their driver and a local tobacconist stood up as witnesses in the tiny Silver City chapel. "The seat cushions had slid off the benches onto the floor," remembered Bourke-White, "and the dust of years had accumulated. Through the windows we could see the glorious panorama of bluffs and mesas and desert patches, stretching as far as the eye could reach." It was her kind of landscape; one she might have photographed. The next day, February 28, 1939, the newlyweds flew to Hawaii for their long-awaited honeymoon.

The Silver City visit did come under criticism. The Rt. Rev. Thomas Jenkins, Episcopal Bishop of Nevada, charged the couple "broke into the chapel" and were not married by an Episcopalian pastor but by a Baptist, and that both bride and groom "were divorced and possessed no claim on the church." The Bishop termed it "a breach not only of manners but of morals, and an unwarranted invasion of a consecrated building." Caldwell was too surprised to respond sharply. "It's ridiculous to make such a charge," he told reporters. "We were permitted the use of the church by the caretaker. We did not break in."

Czechoslovakia was still a nation when Caldwell and Bourke-White prowled the provinces in search of material, but when Viking published *North of the Danube* in April 1939, Germany had occupied the country. This made the contents of the book more poignant, and at three dollars a copy it sold briskly. The reviews were laudatory, and Viking was delighted with the timeliness of *Danube*.

"It is a thin book," observed Maurice Hindus in *The New Republic*, "with comparatively little text—eight short sketches (there should have been twice as many)—and with not too many photographs. Yet it is one of the most extraordinary travel books I have ever read." Hindus was impressed with Caldwell's economy and ability to present a panorama of places and people but thought the photographs better than the text. "Miss Bourke-White has caught all the drama and pathos of an aspect of the Munich agreement and its aftermath which no journalist has as yet bothered to record."

The fifty pages of text and sixty photographs got a positive response from the *New York Post*. "Needless to say, the pictures are swell and the text is deeply felt and moving. As a flash of light upon, rather than an illumination of, troubled Central Europe, *North of the Danube* is required reading."

Caldwell and Bourke-White had reservations about the book in spite of good reviews. Erskine sensed that his inability to understand the language had severely limited him in producing a perceptive narrative. He hadn't grasped the humor of his subjects and was bewildered by swirls of different dialects. Simple factual details had to be used as captions for the photographs, not fictionalized, first-person blurbs as found in *Faces*. Bourke-White felt Caldwell's solemn, freezing moods had distanced them from the Czechs: there had been painful, awkward moments caused by his rudeness, which she had tried unsuccessfully to ease. "I am not sure it is as good as the other book," Caldwell wrote his parents when comparing *North of the Danube* with *You Have Seen Their Faces.*

It was a time of happiness for both of them when they returned to Connecticut. The two took long walks, saw plays, entertained friends, attended political rallies, and made love every night—often outside under the stars. But the world was intruding as Mussolini tramped into Abyssinia, Spain fell to Franco, and Hitler invaded Poland. Bourke-White, the star photographer of *Life*, was needed overseas, and in October 1939 she sailed for Europe on a six-month assignment. Caldwell saw her off with a huge bouquet of roses. A *New York Post* reporter covering the leave-taking commented: "Miss Bourke-White did much better with the stiff upper lip than did her bridegroom."

Margaret loved playing house with Erskine, and though her European assignments were crowded with excitement, she did think wistfully of her love nest in far-off Darien. She wrote to assure him: "This time away from you has really done something very important to me. It has shown with surprising vividness how very essential is darling Skinny to his adoring Kit." They had brought home four coon cats, the long-haired, Maine variety with six or seven toes, and the pets became surrogate children. Margaret, remembering the Connecticut scene, wrote: "I miss the house and the cats and the garden and the china and table linens and the alphabet on your wall and the Sunday papers and you and the tray of after dinner coffee and the red stars and your kisses but most of all I miss you."

Caldwell relentlessly continued his campaign to make Patricia a reality. He knew this was the only way to keep Kit home, and his efforts were never done with subtlety. When was she going to "do the wifely thing?" he kept asking; she must know their Patricia was waiting. To further his cause, he sent Bourke-White an advertisement of nursery furnishings with their child's name written on the clipping. Patricia was asking for her every night. "She has inherited her mother's persistency."

Motherhood was never far from her thoughts, and many of her friends felt that if she hadn't been the famous photographer rushing about the globe, Margaret might well have become a devoted mother. Whenever Pix, Dabney, and Janet visited their father in Darien, Bourke-White lavished them with clothes, let them assist her with photographic assignments, and took them on outings in Connecticut and New York. But there now was a war to cover, and their coon cats, Suzy, Fluffy, Johnnie, and Lottie, must stand in for a waiting Patricia:

> Suzy, you must keep on helping him write books as that is the most important thing in the world to Mama. Johnnie, you must try not to be sick and you must try not to do anything naughty in the house, and you *must* keep Papa good company in the car and stay awake when he is driving....And Lottie, your job is the most important of all because you are learning to make your way in a new life. You must learn to climb trees because this amuses Papa....Take care of Papa, all four of you. Your devoted Mama.

Wartime London with its bombings and assignments to air bases provided Bourke-White the type of lively theater she flourished in, and the longer Margaret was away the less she wanted a child. Her career threatened Caldwell, and the urgency to have her back home increased in every strident letter. He was beside himself when a thoughtless acquaintance said teasingly that his wife had forbidden him to accompany her to England—he wanted Bourke-White to "show the world" that they were married. Return she must, he pleaded and cajoled. But Margaret was no Helen; she guarded her independence ferociously. "Surely you can see daylight by now," Caldwell pestered. "Won't you tell me something and give me a time to look forward to?"

Bourke-White was on the London streets night after night to record pictorially the bombing raids, and when daylight came she would rush back to her quarters and write long letters to a jealous, frustrated husband. "I want to be sure you're seeing people frequently to keep in practice so when I come back I'll find a very sociable husband." But Caldwell was unhappy and needed sympathy. "I can't hide it," he wrote her. "Everywhere I go, I'm told I look lonely. I am. I'm very lonely. I don't think I could live without you....I couldn't stand it if there were more than a day over six months of this."

His moods of depression worried her to the point where Margaret wanted him to get "things fixed" for the sake of their marriage and Patricia's happiness. She suggested her new psychiatrist, Clara Thompson. "You must do those important things about those sides of yourself you don't know about. You must must must!" Reluctantly, he agreed, and she was overjoyed. But Clara Thompson soon realized, as had Harry Stack Sullivan before her, that Caldwell was having therapy to please Bourke-White. For him, the only way to get "things fixed" was to have her back home.

Margaret left England in December of 1939 for assignments in Rumania, Turkey, and Syria; she now seemed further away than ever to Erskine, but her absence didn't hamper his creativity—he was writing up a storm with new short stories and had just completed his novel, *Trouble in July*. There were, however, rumors that Bourke-White was homesick for Darien. In February, Leonard Lyons's gossip column had an item for *Life*. "Margaret Bourke-White, now in Europe on assignment from your magazine *Life*, yesterday sent a valentine message to Erskine Caldwell, her husband. It read: 'Adoration, adoration, adoration, adoration, adoration, adoration, adoration, (signed) Your-want-to-come-home wife.' It was sent from Ankara and cost 70 cents a word." When *Life's* General Manager C. D. Jackson cabled Bourke-White to ask if she wanted to forego another planned assignment, she replied that all was well. Emotionally, though, she was already back in Darien— soon, she and Erskine, their six- and seven-toed children, and waiting Patricia would be together.

Some reviewers of *Southways* suggested that it was imperative for Caldwell to write another novel to prove that he was indeed one of the leading fiction writers of his time. It had been five years since *Journeyman*, and though *You Have Seen Their Faces* and *North of the Danube* had been favored by critics and sales were brisk, more and more he was being urged to produce another *To-*

*bacco Road* or *God's Little Acre*. Among those who felt he should write what he knew best was his father. "It occurs to me that it is time you were undertaking a great Southern story," wrote Ira. "You can write about the South better than you can of any other section. I suggest you come down while Margaret is away and make a careful study of things Southern."

Several of Caldwell's best short stories had sprung from his fascination with racial incidents—ingrained during his youth; among them was "Candy-Man Beechum." Such a tale of violence brought out Caldwell's raw energy. In "Savannah River Payday" two Southern rednecks, Jake and Red, knock out the gold teeth of "some nigger" who was killed in a mill accident. This dentistry is done with a monkey wrench, and the corpse is stuffed in the back of their car while they get drunk on moonshine, try to rape a black field hand, and drive into town to play pool. When the local marshal sends word that they had better get rid of the body before it "stinks the whole town up," Jake and Red are insulted. "Say," the drunken Jake responds, "you go tell that marshal that I said for him to take a long running start and jump to hell—Me and Red's shootin pool!"

Such renderings were purposely warped, but there had been numerous barbaric incidents. The Ku Klux Klan had a stranglehold on many Georgia counties when Ira began his Wrens parish duties in 1919, and lynchings were commonplace. There had been 454 lynchings in America from 1918 to 1928, and 416 of the victims were black. Georgia and Mississippi led all the Southern states in hanging parties, and there seemed to be a correlation between higher religious participation and greater numbers of lynchings. Mob violence fermented Caldwell's magic vat of fiction, and throughout his life the bacchanalia of the lynching act haunted him. "I've been an unwilling witness at a number of lynchings," he told Robert Van Gelder in a 1940 interview, but in the same year Caldwell informed a reporter from the *Darien Review* that he had never actually encountered one. "I only witnessed one lynching in my life," he responded forty-two years later in a conversation with Richard Kelly and Marcia Pankake. "But I had read about and I had heard about—newspapers and word-of-mouth and many other instances of violence of that nature."

Caldwell once explained why he didn't choose to highlight the lynchings in *Trouble in July*, "Kneel to the Rising Sun," and "Saturday Afternoon." It was because "I never saw one myself. For me, they happened offstage, you might say. I heard all the tales about them because people would take sides and argue for days. These lynchings were like a pebble dropped in a pond that makes waves; they sent ripples through the community."

The prime source of Caldwell's knowledge of cruelty to blacks came from Ira and what the boy saw when he went on long rides with his father outside Wrens. "My knowledge of Negro life was limited," said Caldwell, "because the people I came in contact with were usually servants or working men. But I trusted the Negro more than I trusted the white man. The Negro was always—I suppose you'd say—naive, but basically sincere, and I have always had the feeling that you could trust the black man if he wanted to be trusted."

Ira Caldwell was fearless in his lifelong battle to have blacks treated as equals. Erskine never forgot Moses Coffee, a black man who worked as janitor for the church in Prosperity, South Carolina. Moses had scars on his face and neck from blows of a chain—compliments of an angry white landowner—and whenever Coffee was in the presence of white strangers he trembled and stuttered. Ira was one of the few who treated the janitor with respect. The previous parson had made Coffee sit in an unheated room until it was time to clean the church after services, but Ira led the trembling man to an empty pew while the congregation looked on in disgust. When the church fathers threatened to cut their parson's pay for this vile act, Ira ignored them. He provoked their displeasure even further by attending the elderly janitor's funeral. Their parson, the flock decreed, had gone to a "nigger burial."

Erskine always remembered the "cigar-smoking, florid, 250-pound landowner" in whose office he once sat with his father. A black sharecropper was being punished for buying a cow and fencing a strip of pasture without the owner's permission. "Clamping the cigar tightly in the corner of his mouth," wrote Caldwell, "the flush-faced landowner took a heavy black leather strap from the wooden peg on the wall, ordered the man to take off his shirt and drop his overalls to the floor, and then he was told to get down on his hands and knees." The incident outraged Ira—he wasn't able to help the black man—and later he commented to his son that "there'll be that kind of cruelty in our part of the world until people like that man in the plantation office become enlightened enough to be ashamed of their meanness."

Several lynchings took place in Wrens and vicinity, and when a black man, accused of raping a white woman, was dragged behind a speeding automobile and the sheriff did nothing, Ira targeted the lawman in several sermons in his church. Predictably, such protests riled his parishioners, and more than once the Caldwells were labeled "nigger lovers." But their pastor was undaunted, and what he could do to help he did. When a landowner severely beat a sick tenant for leaving the fields early, Ira dressed the man's wounds and denounced the landowner for his cruelty.

Caldwell defended the blacks in both his fiction and journalistic pieces, but he was more preoccupied with the South's economic difficulties than social problems in the 1930 period of his writings. Black-white associations were given little attention prior to *Trouble in July*, though *Journeyman* and some of the short stories show a concern that would loom largely in the later novels.

While Erskine and Helen were in Wrens in late 1933, there had been several lynchings in nearby Bartow, Georgia. A mob of enraged whites killed three blacks, severely injured five others with lead pipes, and burned to the ground fourteen houses. Caldwell spent several days in Bartow, asking questions and writing dispatches to *New Masses*. It was a town "where men butcher hogs with more humaneness than they kill Negroes," and he criticized the local newspapers for not covering the violence. Soon, threats were made on Erskine's life, and like his father, he shrugged them aside.

Ira Sylvester Caldwell, c. 1895
*Courtesy of Virginia Caldwell Hibbs
and Dartmouth College Library*

Caroline Bell Caldwell, c. 1901
*Courtesy of Virginia Caldwell Hibbs
and Dartmouth College Library*

Erskine with his mother, Caroline
Bell Caldwell, c. 1908 *Courtesy of
Virginia Caldwell Hibbs and Dartmouth
College Library*

Erskine in Staunton, Virginia, c. 1910
*Courtesy of Virginia Caldwell Hibbs
and Dartmouth College Library*

Caroline and Erskine, probably in Staunton, Virginia, c. 1911 *Courtesy of Virginia Caldwell Hibbs and Dartmouth College Library*

From the 1923 Erskine College Yearbook: Caldwell in his football uniform *Courtesy of Erskine College Library*

Caldwell, his son, Dabney, and Borzoi,
the family dog, in Mount Vernon, Maine,
c. 1928 *Courtesy of Helen Caldwell Cushman*

Erskine Caldwell, c. 1931
*Courtesy of Helen Caldwell Cushman*

Erskine (left) and Helen Caldwell (far right)
with a neighbor. Sons Dabney (left fore-
ground) and Erskine Jr., Mount Vernon, Maine,
c. 1931 *Courtesy of Helen Caldwell Cushman*

Left
Ira Sylvester Caldwell, c. 1930
*Courtesy of Hargrett Library,
University of Georgia*

Erskine Caldwell in Burbank,
California *c. 1934*

Helen Caldwell in Hollywood,
Florida, 1939

Left
Janet Caldwell c. 1943. Photos
on this page *Courtesy of Helen
Caldwell Cushman*

Caldwell and Margaret Bourke-White
in Moscow, 1941 *Courtesy of Dartmouth
College Library*

Caldwell broadcasting from Moscow, 1941 *Courtesy of Dartmouth College Library*

Erskine and June Caldwell, Tucson,
Arizona, 1944 *Courtesy of Dartmouth
College Library*

Alfred Morang, c. 1955
*Courtesy of Dartmouth
College Library*

Maxim Lieber, early
1930s *Courtesy of
Mrs. Minna Lieber*

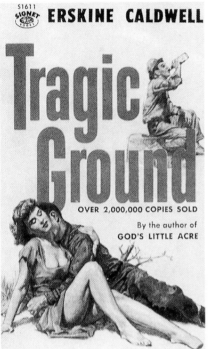

Paperback covers for the
"World's Best-Selling Author!"

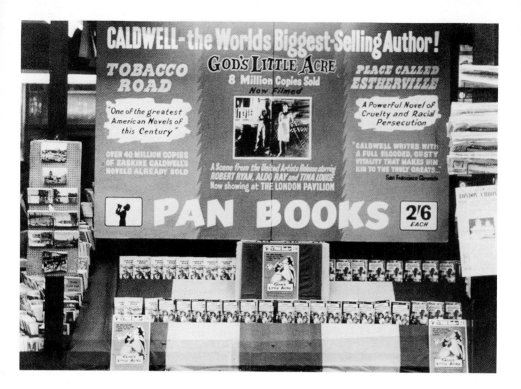

Above
London display of Caldwell's
books promoting *God's Little
Acre*, 1958 *Courtesy of Dartmouth
College Library*

Signet book cover of
*The Sure Hand of God*

Erskine Caldwell with Robert Ryan
during filming of *God's Little Acre*,
1958 *Courtesy of Virginia Caldwell Hibbs*

Virginia Caldwell and son Drew
(rear), Erskine and son, Jay Caldwell,
1958 *Courtesy of Virginia Caldwell Hibbs*

Erskine and Virginia Caldwell, 1963
*Courtesy of Virginia Caldwell Hibbs and
Dartmouth College Library*

Erskine Caldwell, Scottsdale, Arizona, 1980. *Photograph by Mark Morrow and courtesy of Virginia Caldwell Hibbs*

Caldwell felt that when he wrote for *New Masses* about the killing of blacks in early 1934 his investigative work placed him in a vulnerable position. As a writer, he received more than his share of hate mail, but it rarely worried him. The nearest he ever came to personal injury, asserted Caldwell, was at a New Hampshire gathering when he failed to stand as Kate Smith sang "God Bless America."

Erskine didn't let up. In *You Have Seen Their Faces*, he accused the Southern whites of causing a "retarded and thwarted civilization." While he and Margaret were gathering material for *Faces* they drove into Kelly, Georgia and saw a mob of whites in search of a black man accused of raping a white prostitute. The incident wasn't included in their collaboration, but Erskine mentally filed it away for future use in fiction; *Trouble in July*, it became—a conventional but sophisticated novel and clearly his most straightforward.

Sonny Clark, an innocent black boy, is accused of rape by a promiscuous white girl, and he is lynched by a mob while a paunchy sheriff looks on. Even before Sonny is caught, all the blacks in town disappear. The lawman, Jeff McCurtain, makes it a point to go fishing whenever his white brothers are in a lynching mood. It is good politics to turn one's back, he reasons, but the sheriff also has feelings of guilt. When the mob takes a black man hostage until the boy is found, lawman McCurtain is no longer lethargic. "Sam Brinson is a sort of special friend of mine," he informs the lynchers, "even if he is a colored man." The cry of "nigger lover" is immediate, but McCurtain stands his ground by declaring that "there are brother whites in this county a heap meaner than any nigger I ever saw." And the sheriff isn't the only person who has a conscience; the farmer who finds Sonny Clark and turns him in is ambivalent. He knows that the mob will praise him for finding the black boy, yet realizes that he will "probably hate himself" as long as he lives. "I hate like the mischief to have to do it, Sonny," he tell his young captive, "but this is a white-man's country. Niggers has always had to put up with it, and I don't know nothing that can stop it now. It's just the way things is, I reckon."

*Trouble in July* was the first work of Caldwell's fiction without Helen's editorial guidance. He keenly missed her careful editing and tried to enlist Bourke-White as the replacement. "I wish to goodness I had the benefit of your valuable help in correcting galley proofs of the new book," he wrote Margaret. "This is the last chance to make changes in Trouble in July—your book! The first novel I've done under your spell—and I want it to be perfect."

There was unexpected trouble for Caldwell's *Trouble in July* and it came from Viking—both Harold Guinzburg and Marshall Best felt the novel was uneven. At a conference to discuss the book's publication, Guinzburg leaned back in his chair and said: "I suppose we'll have to publish the new item." Caldwell and his agent, Lieber, were nettled by the remark: the man was treating *Trouble in July* "like a gross of stockings or a side of bacon." When Lieber negotiated for more money Viking quickly turned him down.

Caldwell and his publisher had not been on easy terms for the past five years. He blamed Viking for poor marketing of *Journeyman* and for delaying *North of the Danube* a few months beyond the set publication date. Caldwell believed this was the reason for disappointing sales. He also was unhappy with their handling of *Danube* and accused the firm of giving John Steinbeck's *The Grapes of Wrath* more publicity than his book. Lieber, who felt that Caldwell was overreacting, wrote: "I am in complete sympathy with you and you have never known me to favor the publisher against the author, yet I must give the devil his due." Viking had, Lieber reminded him, spent the same on the promotion of his book as *The Grapes of Wrath.*

Guinzburg and Best were tired of dealing with their complaining author. Caldwell questioned the pricing and advertising, and when he found a printing error was quick to register displeasure. Viking felt he was spending too much time writing nonfiction when the emphasis should have been placed on novels. Both men were acutely aware of the profit margin—novels sold better and were

easier to promote. When a new publishing house learned that Caldwell was unhappy at Viking, and offered to buy his contract and
the right to all future books, Guinzburg and Best swiftly negotiated.
They were relieved to see their author stabled elsewhere.

Charles Duell, Samuel Sloan, and Charles Pearce had worked in
New York publishing houses and were now established as Duell,
Sloan & Pearce. DS&P was planning to bring out a series of books
with the emphasis on topics which were typically American. The
three men realized that Caldwell was difficult to handle, but they
felt his reputation would advance the new firm. They offered him
a guaranteed salary of twenty-five hundred a year for three years
and would settle all unearned advances that Caldwell had received
from Viking. The contract was further sweetened with the promise
of a collection of short stories, a new edition of *Tobacco Road* and
a "heavy and consistent promotion" of *Trouble in July*. The three
also persuaded him to attend book signings and to speak before literary clubs.

This liberal contract temporarily eased Caldwell's worries about
money—after a record run on Broadway, the play *Tobacco Road*
was declining in popularity. The failed adaptation of *Journeyman*,
divorce settlements with Helen, and monthly checks he sent to his
parents for doctors' bills and their trips to see the grandchildren in
Mount Vernon cut deeply into his savings. The house in Darien
had cost twenty thousand dollars, and his and Margaret's lifestyles
were never modest. She loved fashionable clothes and insisted that
he upgrade his wardrobe. The Ford had been replaced with a luxurious convertible, and the hotels and restaurants they frequented
were always the most expensive.

Caldwell was pleased with the new publishing firm's willingness
to allow him full scope in his creativity—they didn't urge him to
follow *Trouble in July* with another novel. Encouraged by their
attitude, Caldwell revealed a plan that Viking had rejected: a series
of books, each dealing with a particular area of the country and
written by an author familiar with the region and its culture. To his
delight, DS&P readily endorsed the idea. American Folkway Series

it was called, and Caldwell would be its editor.

The series came at the right time for him. Alone in Darien, with only four coon cats for company, he desperately missed Margaret. The job would help defuse his bouts of depression with travel. Caldwell loved exploring the countryside, usually by car, and this was his chance to see new regions. He also liked the opportunity of reversing roles; to be editor, not a compliant writer. He would do the work conscientiously, and would never abuse his newly acquired powers. "You know far more about the writing of any book than I could possibly suggest," he wrote one of his astonished authors, "and I now leave the matter in your hands." Such responses were appreciated. "Caldwell is a wonderful editor to work for," one of the authors told Charles Pearce. "I haven't had anyone spur me on to my best efforts in the way he does since H. L. Mencken was editing the *American Mercury*."

Twenty-four contributors were published between 1941 and 1954. Each book, wrote Caldwell, tells "the colorful story of America... through its own galvanic medium, the customs of the people." Some of the books in the American Folkways Series became regional best sellers. *North Star Country* by Meridel Le Sueur handled the Great Lakes region, *Corn Country* by Herbert Croy had the setting of the Nebraska plains; others were *Ozark Country* by Otto Ernest Rayburn, *Blue Grass Country* by Jean Thomas, *Yankee Country* by Clarence Webster, and *Golden Gate Country* by Gertrude Atherton.

Most critics viewed *Trouble in July* as a well-crafted and moving novel. Edwin Berry Bergum in *Newsweek* hailed the book as Caldwell's best, and Richard Wright in *The New Republic* wrote: "Hovering grimly in the background of the lynching is King Cotton, an inanimate character whose influence is as fatal as that of any living being, and whose rise and fall on the commodity market set the narrow channel through which the political, social, and even the personal destinies of the other characters flow."

Constance H. Curtis told her readers in New York's *Amsterdam Star News* that Caldwell's people often reached the point of being unbelievable because they are so completely elemental. His cast of characters seemed earthbound, folks not capable of glossing over the harshness. The lynching topic of *Trouble in July* had caused the author to write in a fury. "There is controlled wrath," along with the conviction that such practices will cease only when "economic exploitation of minorities and corrupt politics have been destroyed."

There were a few negative reviews. Harold Strauss in *The Nation* saw *Trouble in July* as "a definite falling off," and Clifton Fadiman in *The New York Times* declared that the author was "beginning to repeat himself." But the biggest uproar came in letters from Southern white readers who threatened Caldwell for "stepping out of line." He was a "negro-loving Bastard." One livid supremacist sent Erskine a flyer warning against "integration, amalgamation, and miscegenation." At the bottom of the paper the man wrote in a scrawl: "You have sold your soul to the devil a long time ago—you cannot recall the dirty books you sired."

One congratulatory comment came from far overseas, but it was only a brief notice, and probably seemed all too brief for the man adrift in the sprawling house in Darien, Connecticut. THRILLED, Margaret telegraphed, THAT CRITICS APPRECIATE OUR TROUBLE.

There were stops in Arkansas, Oklahoma, New Mexico, and California on his cross-country trip in search of regional writers. Caldwell spent several days in Arizona and then drove east. Outside El Paso he began to have spells of dizziness and seizures of feverishness, some episodes so intense that he had to stop along the highway until he could see clearly. It was nearly midnight when he checked himself into the City-County Hospital in El Paso. Upon waking the next morning he was informed by a staff doctor that he had chicken pox and would be quarantined for a week. "By the end of the first day," wrote Caldwell, "I felt so good to be alive that I could even smile when I saw that the doctor or perhaps a nurse had hung an Infants Ward sign on my door."

While Caldwell was in Florida towards the end of 1939, he was interviewed for a University of Miami student publication. An attractive, raven-haired senior asked the questions, and Mildred Zinn impressed him. "She talked so interestingly and intelligently during the hour-long interview that, when she was leaving," Erskine recalled, "I told her there was a job for her as an editorial assistant anytime she wanted to come work for me." Zinn would graduate at mid-term in February and was delighted with the offer. She would help him select stories for his upcoming collection, *Jackpot*, and engage new authors for American Folkways. "Mildred came to Darien at the end of February," wrote Caldwell. "She was pleasant company in my loneliness."

*Jackpot*, a 756-page collection of 75 short stories, was a brisk seller for DS&P and on the whole was well-received. The stories gathered from his four previous books, with a handful of new tales, gave reviewers a clearer perspective of Caldwell as a spinner of yarns. A short introduction to each story, often no more than a few words, came from a fictional professor called Horatio Perkins. This character was somewhat like Alexander Woollcott, the bête noire of New York in the twenties and thirties. Caldwell liked the man personally, though as a critic Woollcott's wit and bite overawed many young writers. The fictional professor was labeled a parasite; one who lived off the work of better men, "tearing flesh from the bone," and with a smile as he sought "the secret of writing fiction."

"Probably the average quality of Erskine Caldwell's short stories is as high as that of any American practitioner," wrote John Selby for the Ottawa, Illinois *Republican Times*. "But Mr. Caldwell is no exception to the rule that a string of 75 stories, all in one book, must contain some pretty thin matter." What did surprise Selby was embedded humor in the tales. "The essential fact about *Jackpot* is that there is good fun in it, if it is taken in small doses."

The Lexington, Kentucky *Leader* felt that Caldwell "certainly ranks among the best American story-tellers, and the short pieces in this omnibus show him at his peak." His people were funny, in love, and often had little purpose in living—the kind of folk who were going nowhere. "One of the things which make Erskine Caldwell stories outstanding is that their characters are people whom readers have met—in New England, Georgia, Kentucky's mountains or the Mississippi Valley. They are believable."

Milton Rugoff, in the *New York Herald Tribune*, pointed out that the collection was equally at ease in studies of social justice, the folk yarn, adolescent love, and sagas of degradation and lust. One discordant note for Rugoff was the introductory material mouthed by Professor Horatio Perkins. "A number were ostentatiously in the manner of the plain-speaking country-boy genius telling them slick city critics where to get off." A few were "to put it gently, silly."

A Swiss Hermes typewriter was Bourke-White's coming-home gift for Caldwell, a machine small enough to be stuffed in an over-coat pocket. After carrying the cumbersome standard typewriter around on buses and trains, he was eager to test out this new possession. He didn't have long to wait: two weeks later *Life* had a new assignment for Bourke-White—a tour in Mexico. Since they had been separated for so long, it was decided they travel together. For several weeks they journeyed by trains, buses, and rented automobiles through the states of Coahuila, Chihuahua, Durango, San Luis Potosi, and Zacatecas. While Margaret photographed, Er-skine wrote six short stories—"all of them typed of course to good advantage on the Hermes"—later placed by Max Lieber for pub-lication in *Harper's* magazine, *Esquire*, and *Town and Country*.

Travel books continued to be popular, and in 1940, *Life* decided to finance Caldwell and Bourke-White in their third collaboration. This book would be a sequel to his *Some American People* pub-lished in 1935, a tour that would give the "feel of America." *Say, Is This the U.S.A.?* would be the title, and like *You Have Seen Their Faces*, the book would contain pointed criticisms—captions that would awaken national consciousness. Under a Bourke-White photograph of a tiny school for black children in Mississippi, Cald-well wrote: "They wonder sometimes why the white children ride in big yellow buses to the big brick school where there are swings and big, hot stoves, while they have to trudge along the best way they can."

"This America," Caldwell cautioned, "is a jungle of men living in the extreme of good and bad, heat and cold, wealth and poverty." Both optimistic and pessimistic views were encountered as the couple crossed the continent from Vermont to California. "In a certain light," Caldwell observed, "America's cheeks look gaunt and the seat of its pants is sometimes threadbare," but it was also "a healthy, rip-snorting, slam-bang America slinging freight trains across the country a mile a minute." The two for a time rode in freight cars to close in on their material; to capture it obliquely, and grasp the significance of what they were seeing, hearing, feeling. Their Christmas card that year showed a photograph of the two perched on the roof of a train, each holding what they were about: typewriter and camera.

"Regardless of whether his life is unusual or ordinary," Caldwell wrote, "almost every American today realizes that the small world he once lived in has vanished, and that now he had come to grips with a larger world." The war in Europe threatened small-town America, and no matter how ardent some were in their isolationism there was the apprehension of vulnerability.

Caldwell and Bourke-White focused on communities and groups of people that they felt would leave lasting recollections: in St. Johnsbury, Vermont, there were craftsmen who still made wooden pails without using machinery; in Bryon Lake, South Dakota they found an isolated religious group, the Hutterians; and the two mingled with Rotarians in Pretty Prairie, Kansas. A Missouri filling station attendant handed Caldwell a card that was flippantly double-edged in tone:

> I am 36 years old. I smoke about a pack of cigarettes a day, sometimes more and sometimes less, but it evens up. I take an occasional drink of beer. I am a Baptist, and Elk, and a Rotarian. I live with my own wife, send my children to school and visit my in-laws once a year on Christmas Day. I wear No. 9 1/2 shoes, No. 15 1/2 collar and No. 7 1/4 hat. I shoot a 12 gauge shotgun and have a 27 inch crotch. I like rice, sweet potatoes and pork sausage. I vote for FDR, pull for Joe Louis, and boo Diz Dean. I wouldn't have anything against Hitler if he stayed in his own back yard. I don't know any Japs, but I've made up my mind

to argue with the next one I see about leaving the Chinese alone. I'm in favor of the AA, the CCC, the IOU and the USA. If I have left anything out, it's an oversight. My business is selling gasoline and oil. If you want your tank filled, just nod your head. If you don't want anything, please move along and give the next fellow a chance. I thank you. Hurry back.

Even more fervently than in the past, Bourke-White wanted this collaboration to succeed, concerning, as it did, the emotional involvement of their marriage. She wrote: "And with all the temperamental difficulties none of it seemed as important to me as the fact that here was what I believe was a very creative and harmonious work that we were doing." The prenuptial contract Erskine signed was badly crumpled when an ice-age mood overcame him. "The frigid wave surged upward," wrote Margaret, "once begun there was no staying it. Until hard as I tried to stay aloof—as one can do with a stranger—when so close and in the same household there is no holding apart. In retrospect that seems to have been the goal. When I was ground down to fine dust then he magnificently, with spaciousness and good humor would raise me up." His wish to dominate her, to force her into a submissive role as he had done with Helen, just didn't work on Bourke-White. Her career came first and was a safeguard from subjugation.

*Life* didn't use the material, though they paid the expenses, and DS&P published *Say, Is This the U.S.A.?* in the summer of 1941. On every right-hand page of the book was a Bourke-White photograph facing Caldwell's text on the left. Curiously, the illustrations and text had no link with one another; it was as if the collaborators had been on different assignments. Americans, however, were ready to establish a national identity to distinguish them from nations in Europe, and publication of *Say, Is This the U.S.A.?* came at the best possible time. For a week in July 1941 the book was a national best-seller. The *Boston Herald* hailed it as "an unparalleled record of this land of liberty" and felt the book provided "a sweeping and panoramic picture of our land and of the people who make it what it is." Ralph Thompson in *The New York Times* had both praise and blame: "I don't see why, for example, Miss Bourke-White spent so much film on a single horse-and-mule auction in the South as she did on New York, New Jersey, Pennsylvania, Ohio and the New England states combined, and I don't always follow Mr. Caldwell's emphasis and am left completely buffaloed by the item he calls 'Sign of the Times.' But they had to pick and choose somehow among the results of a 10,000 mile trip, and they have managed it brilliantly, on the whole. The answer to the title is yes. This is the U.S.A."

*Tobacco Road* on the movie screen appeared in February 1941. Producers of the play had no desire to share ticket sales with the film industry, and production had been delayed for seven years. When the road companies of *Tobacco Road* began to lose money, Caldwell gave Lieber permission to negotiate a motion picture deal. It was a more opportune time than in the mid- and late-thirties— *Gone With the Wind* had made the South a box office commodity—and three companies, Warner Brothers, Twentieth Century-Fox, and Paramount began bidding for the property of the longest-running play on Broadway. Twentieth Century-Fox won the bid, and immediately hired John Ford as director and Nunnally Johnson for the adaptation. They had been a successful team in *The Grapes of Wrath*, and Darryl Zanuck began an advertising campaign implying that this *Road* version would be a sequel to *Gone With the Wind.* When Margaret Mitchell learned that Fox was exploiting her novel to generate preliminary interest in the film she wrote Caldwell asking him to intervene, and her attorneys threatened to file suit. Caldwell at once cabled Zanuck.

Henry Fonda was asked to play the part of Jeeter but he refused, and Zanuck hired Charles Grapewin who had brilliantly played Tom Joad's father in *Wrath*. Gene Tierney was miscast as Ellie May—to disguise her glamorous presence they rubbed stage dirt on her arms and legs; the character's harelip was ignored. Ford and Johnson wanted the end of the film to conform to the book, with both Jeeter and his wife dying in their burning shack, but when

Zanuck saw the film he insisted that it be changed. Instead of a tragic end, he had the two Lesters join arms and serenely march into a sunset on their way to the poorhouse.

Some critics were content with its modest format and buffoonery. It was "a hundred times better than its theatrical prototype," declared the *New York Herald Tribune*. But *Time* felt the film had been given "a moral scrubbing"—an assessment that many readers of the novel shared after seeing the movie version. Caldwell was delighted with the thirty-five thousand dollars he received in royalties but found fault with the rendition. "Hollywood," he said, "murdered *Tobacco Road*."

Bourke-White's editor at *Life*, Wilson Hicks, believed the non-aggression pact between Germany and the Soviet Union was only temporary. He wanted Margaret in Russia for the invasion. Hicks also felt that she could make a valuable contribution in comparing the country she had seen on her three previous trips with present-day Russia.

Caldwell should accompany her, Margaret suggested; they would be together as they had been in Mexico. Though he missed her keenly when she was away on assignments, Caldwell resisted the idea of collaborating with her on a fourth travel project—he was deeply involved in developing a series of connected short stories about boyhood in the South, the book which would be called *Georgia Boy*.

"War is going to happen there, Kit," Caldwell warned her. "Of course!" she exclaimed excitedly. "That's it exactly. Now don't you want to go, Skinny? Please say you do!" Did he want to be excluded from monumental events? Along with Ernest Hemingway and Jack London, translations had made him a celebrity in Russia. So much admired was Caldwell for his stand on capitalism and race equality that people would recognize him in the streets. The state publishing house had put away his accumulated royalties, and since the rubles couldn't be taken out of the country, he could use this money while he was there with Margaret. When *Life* agreed to pay his passage, Caldwell was ready to make the trip.

The Soviet Ambassador in Washington opposed the idea of such an adventure. Constantin Oumansky pointed out the many pitfalls: she and Caldwell would have to cross China to enter Russia, the war between China and Japan made travel routes extremely hazardous, and they could be shot down by Japanese planes or taken prisoner and interned. As a final discouragement, Oumansky told Bourke-White that foreigners were not permitted to take photographs within the Soviet Union. But Margaret had confidence in her powers of persuasion—so many times she had changed the minds of stubborn officials. Finally, the ambassador reluctantly decided to send instructions to Russian representatives in Chungking. If the two could get that far, visas would be issued.

Prior to their flight to the Orient, Caldwell spoke at a public meeting of the Inter-Professional Association, a business club for Honolulans. Instead of a prepared talk—as he preferred at all his public appearances—Caldwell invited questions from the floor and his remarks revealed his national concerns. "The whole country is so stirred up with preparations for war that socialization has been put aside and it may never come back." Sharecroppers faced a situation that was deteriorating because of mechanization. "A tractor, for instance, displaces six out of every eight families, and about half of those displaced find work in factories. The other half have no place to go." In the South, Northern capital dominated industry but not agriculture, and the only secure way of conserving wasted land was through government regulations. Attitudes about drafting young men for a possible war varied, he told his curious listeners. "The South is in favor of anything connected with war, more than any other region. The New England states are in favor of the draft and war for economic reasons, while in the Middle West and West Coast opinions differ widely."

The American Writers Congress went on record against "the imperialist war" while meeting at the Hotel Commodore in New York City on June 8, 1941. Dashiell Hammett was elected president and Theodore Dreiser was selected as honorary president. Among the seven vice presidents nominated were Richard Wright and Erskine Caldwell. "We recognize the present war," the members declared, "as a brutal and shameless struggle for the redivision of empire—for profits, territories and markets. We brand the attempts to drag us into war as a mockery and betrayal of the American people." The members were conscious of their obligations as writers and asserted that their art could not be bought and sold. The Congress sent greetings to the writers of the Soviet Union and China and cheered a reading of the text which the aviation strikers of Southern California sent to President Roosevelt defending their right to strike. Dreiser, Wright, Caldwell, and Hammett were not the only prominent names among the sixty notables who had endorsed the program: other signers were John Dos Passos, Malcolm Cowley, Langston Hughes, and Lincoln Steffens.

Margaret and Erskine flew to Los Angeles, and on March 20, 1941, they sailed to Honolulu on the SS *Lurlene*. Bourke-White didn't travel lightly: she brought along over five hundred pounds of camera equipment and an extensive wardrobe. Caldwell had seventeen pounds of luggage, including his tiny Hermes typewriter. The air flight on the amphibious *China Clipper* was for them a trip of eleven days due to delays caused by typhoons in Guam and the Philippines. The only seats available in the plane were on stacked piles of newly printed currency for Chinese soldiers. The crew of three with their nine passengers spent the nights at Pan American Airways hostels on atolls and flew only during daylight hours.

An official of the Chinese National Aviation Company in Hong Kong took one look at Bourke-White's five hundred pounds of camera equipment and shook his head—it was too heavy a load for the flight. Margaret immediately turned on her charm but this time her cajoling failed to overcome the man's inscrutable composure and it took a cash settlement to elicit his reluctant approval. The Caldwells departed at 4 a.m. in a tossing cargo plane to avoid Japanese fighters.

An apologetic official of the Chinese-operated Eurasia Aviation Corporation in Chungking explained that there was no record of a confirmed passage for the Caldwells to Hami, and there would be a wait of six days. They were assigned a teahouse for accommodations and were quickly adopted by a smiling houseboy, Sonny, who mysteriously arranged a photo session for Margaret with "stern-faced" Chiang Kai-shek. While Bourke-White photographed the Chinese leader, Sonny and Caldwell reclined at the far end of a reception hall where they "were served tea and cookies by the unsmiling Madame Chiang Kai-shek."

The flight to Hami was eventful. Somewhere over the Gobi desert region near Mongolia, they plunged into a roaring storm that pelted the windshield of the airplane with sand and pebbles. Forced to turn around, they dove earthward—the windswept Gobi hurling itself toward them. Minutes later, they landed at a military airfield where soldiers sealed the door of the aircraft, and they were forced to wait for two and a half hours while their fate was being decided.

Finally, the Caldwells and their fellow passengers were ordered from the plane and led to a truck which drove them to a barracks surrounded by barbed wire and guard towers. Each passenger was assigned a cot, large pitcher of water, slop jar, washbasin and a strip of cloth.

The sandstorm caused them to miss their connecting flight to Moscow from Hami, and the courteous airport manager's translator told them the next flight would be within a week. "It is too cruel for Americans visiting us to be delayed for such a long time," the interpreter told them. "Americans need to be in a hurry at all times because they are Americans. I am sorry this delay had to happen anywhere in China."

Alice-Leone Moats shared in several of these adventures on the journey to Moscow. She was an independent correspondent for a variety of magazine publications, and she caught up with the Caldwells in Hami after a visa delay in Chungking.

Moats liked Caldwell; she thought him handsome, but always out of his element—a bit of a "hayseed." When they took off after one of their delays, Caldwell "presented a picture of such sartorial perfection that he took my breath away. He had on powder-blue gabardine trousers, very wide in the leg and with seams hem-stitched in navy blue thread; a blue-and-white striped shirt; a white tie; a jacket with huge navy and light blue checks, and navy suede platform soled shoes cut at the sides." Caldwell's appearance—clothing selected by Margaret—caused his wife to gush: "Skinny darling, I bet you're the best dressed man who ever traveled on this route."

The correspondent did not care much for Bourke-White and accused her of finagling. When a room shortage threatened to part the couple, Margaret declared in a plaintive voice: "But Skinny darling, I want to sleep with you! I don't want to be separated from you!" Her cries did not go unnoticed and Alice-Leone Moats soon was assigned a less comfortable dormitory room.

Moats also recalled that when the Caldwells were told there would be no transportation for several days, Erskine wired his Russian publisher and various high officials in Moscow. After finishing each wire he handed it to Margaret "who read it with gasps of wonder. 'Splendid, Skinny darling, simply splendid!' She would exclaim. 'What a great writer you are!' The admiration she felt for her husband was quite awe inspiring." Though his efforts to snip the bureaucratic red tape of Communist Russia were never successful, Moats could see that Caldwell was pleased with his wife's commentary on his talents.

The Union of Soviet Writers couldn't do enough for Caldwell upon his arrival in Moscow. That aspect of his writing which centered on racial and class oppression in a capitalistic society gave him a hero's status in Russia. He and Margaret were mobbed with invitations, and since the Soviets were very well acquainted with Bourke-White's earlier photographs of their country, she speedily got permission to take her camera into some sensitive areas that were closed to other photographers.

After a vodka-wild party at the state publishing house, Caldwell was given his accumulated royalties and a suitcase to carry stacks of rubles back to his luxurious suite at the National Hotel. He gave half the money to the hotel manager for safekeeping and hid the remaining bundles under a white bear rug, behind pictures on the wall, and in a closet. Erskine sent word to his parents that they were "well and living on the fat of the land." With bundles of rubles at his disposal, money that had to be spent, it seemed foolhardy "to ask the waiter not to bring caviar and champagne for a midnight snack."

The Caldwells had planned to wander through the Ukraine, the Caucasus, and into Siberia, but all travel required permission and the necessary documents were inevitably delayed. After three weeks of waiting, they were notified that their request for a trip of two thousand miles to Kharkov, Tbilisi, and the Black Sea was approved. Most foreign newspaper correspondents and photographers were lucky to get beyond the Moscow suburbs.

Erskine and Margaret were in Sukhumi, a resort on the Georgian shore of the Black Sea, when Germany invaded Russia. The news of the invasion thwarted incipient plans of collaborating on another travel book. Hurriedly, they packed their bags and took the first available train back to Moscow. The two secured berths in a sleeping car, but food was in short supply. Caldwell spent most of his waking hours dashing to the hot-water spigot and standing in line for boiled water to make tea each time the train stopped at a station. Their ride northward through the Ukraine lasted four days and nights. On the morning of June 28, 1941, the Caldwells were back in their suite at the National Hotel.

There were a number of radiograms waiting for Erskine—most of them frantic messages from American newspaper syndicates and magazine editors offering him jobs as a war correspondent. Few reporters were covering Moscow: only two permanent ones, Henry Shapiro and Henry Cassidy, from UP and AP. Dozens of newsmen were eager to get inside Russia, but no one was granted an entry visa. Caldwell consented to file daily radiograms for a syndicate, the North American Newspaper Alliance; to broadcast twice a day for the Columbia Broadcasting System (CBS); and to write articles for *Life*.

The North American Newspaper Alliance (NANA) willingly agreed to pay him a thousand dollars a month, but after a short time on the job, when Ralph Ingersoll, the editor of PM newspaper, offered to double that amount, Caldwell couldn't resist. Erskine had written several articles on wheat harvesting in Kansas for PM and instead of money had accepted twenty-five hundred dollars in common stock. It would be in his best interest, he reasoned, to work for his own company, and Moscow correspondent Eugene Petrov was quickly enlisted to be the replacement.

The Soviets were in need of American aid and realized that Caldwell could reach a large radio audience. It was an extraordinary move on their part to allow his broadcasts as there had been no transmissions from Russia for two years. The only other Moscow broadcast heard in the United States had been at the time of the 1939 opening of the World's Fair in New York. Though Caldwell was trusted more than any other American journalist, he still was heavily censored. Stories of food lines, casualties, and German advances along the wide front were not allowed; the authorities encouraged tales of high troop morale and heroism—these were never censored. He was given two broadcasts—one at 3:00 p.m. and the other at 3:00 a.m. It was a difficult schedule to follow in Moscow with the day and night rain of bombs.

He lacked the polish and sense of drama that made Edward R. Murrow's broadcasts from London so sensational, and Erskine's slight Southern accent didn't forcefully project the contents of his scripts. His timing was frequently off, and he sometimes crowded the microphone. Margaret was there on the night of his first broadcast. She stood beside him with a stopwatch and signalled when he should slow down or speak more rapidly.

A portion of Caldwell's royalties were used to buy a secondhand car, and another bundle of rubles engaged the services of a chauffeur and secretary. Erskine soon discovered that the chauffeur carried a pistol under his jacket, though some weeks passed before he learned that the man was a corporal in the Red Army and had been assigned as a bodyguard. An English speaking secretary had been recommended by the press office and came daily to the large corner suite at the National Hotel, which had a balcony overlooking the Kremlin and Red Square. The bathtub was used to develop Margaret's films, while the bedroom and parlor became a newspaper office.

The Germans began bombing Moscow two weeks after the land invasion began—200 planes every night, the raids lasting three or four hours. Caldwell admitted being afraid for the first ten minutes, but after that he went about his business. The bombing runs usually coincided with his broadcasts and the radio station seemed a favorite target. "Every plane that came over dumped a few bombs toward it."

On the night of the first German bombing of Moscow, Caldwell and Bourke-White were ordered by rifle-carrying wardens to go down to the subway between their hotel and the Kremlin. They sat with hundreds of people from midnight until three in the morning. "Nobody and nobody will ever make me come down here like this again," said a determined Bourke-White. When reminded that the wardens had complete authority and also carried guns, Margaret replied angrily: "The only thing it says to me is that we let them herd us down here in this subway like so many sheep. I'm ashamed of myself for letting them do it. Well, I'm not going to stand for it another single time. I just won't! That's what!"

On the second night sirens wailed, and, according to Caldwell, the two crawled under an enormous wooden bed and remained out of sight for the next half hour while maids and wardens searched in closets and behind sofas. When the hunt was over, Erskine turned out the lights, barricaded the bedroom door with a large chair, and Margaret happily mounted her camera on a tripod at a window facing the Kremlin.

She quickly got permission to photograph wartime Moscow, and was the first foreign war photographer to have this distinction. Her earlier pictures of the country were greatly admired, and being the wife of Erskine Caldwell opened doors closed to others. She would prowl the streets of the besieged city, parks, and subways with camera in hand, but there were restrictions: Bourke-White wasn't allowed near the front lines, and she had to arrange her itinerary with the authorities in advance. Sometimes, so many officials were involved that a convoy of three cars was necessary to carry all of them to her photographic shoots.

There were irritations for a foreigner trying to conform to the Russian way of life. Nothing seemed to be free: one had to pay an admission fee to enter a railroad station or stroll in a public park. Then there was the inexplicable rule that no one could wear an overcoat in a public building, which required paying a garment charge to a custodian. Caldwell refused to take off his coat one evening while attending the theater—he had a severe cold. The manager was sent for and they argued. Finally, the man relented. "I think," Caldwell speculated, "that I am probably the only person in the new Russia who ever sat through a performance with his overcoat on."

Boris, Caldwell's armed chauffeur, usually drove him to the studio for the 3:00 a.m. broadcast, but when Boris had worked all day or they were unable to get through the bombing debris, Caldwell walked to the studio and back in the midst of air raids. He soon got used to the sounds of demolition bombs exploding around him, but his first reactions were different: "I had not experienced such fear since the time I was very young and was taken on a snipe hunt one night by a group of older boys who ran away and left me alone in the darkness of a forest far from home."

Caldwell soon was recognized by the wardens who flashed their dim lights on him in the blackened streets. But early one morning he was challenged by a new warden, who took him to a lighted room in the basement of a dark apartment building where he was interrogated and forced to remain until his pass could be verified.

On one occasion, as he and Boris were driving with no headlights during an air raid, their auto became tangled in an iron fence. The two got out to push free the vehicle while a storm of shrapnel pelted nearby buildings. More than once, bombs exploded within a block from where he stood, and it was common to see "buildings and streets rise into the air."

Caldwell's stories about the Moscow bombings and tank battles in *PM* and *Life* were hugely popular. So were the heroic exploits told him by soldiers who had returned from the front—he repeatedly tried to get permission to cover the front lines, but in spite of his reputation all requests were denied. His blunt style had a way of making the bombing raids come alive to readers at home, and he could dramatically relay tales of human interest. Caldwell's accounts were given graphic headlines in *PM*. A typical heading would be: "Rammed Tanks Reared and Buckled, Houses Toppled Like Duckpins in Battle Lasting Through Day."

His articles and broadcasts had, at the outset, been more propaganda than journalism. He mollified the censors and remained emotionally unaffected by the turmoil around him. Most of his early stay in Moscow had been spent pounding out on the Hermes typewriter stories which would be later published as *Georgia Boy*. "It seemed to me," wrote Bourke-White, "he was barricading himself against new experiences and tending to withdraw into this world of his earlier activity where he felt...at home...making a retreat to Tobacco Road." It was nearly a month, according to Margaret, before he would come "out of his protective shell and take note of the world around him." But once he did, Caldwell was caught in the drama and excitement of the war. His interviews with factory workers, Red Army commanders, and heroes back from the front were gripping documents of that time and horrendous place.

On September 15, the Soviet authorities told the couple to prepare for a trip the following morning. When they reported to the address given, there were five British and six American correspondents waiting; they were all going to the front lines as observers.

A convoy of five cars drove them to the battle sector near Smolensk. The autumn rains began when they started and didn't stop for long throughout the trip. Bourke-White tried to take photographs in a drizzling haze, and estimated there were only sixteen minutes of sunlight during the entire week.

Their visit to the front was crudely staged for propaganda purposes and not one of the journalists was deceived, though all were delighted to have a limited glimpse of the front lines. While enemy planes soared overhead, Red Army officers entertained the newsmen with endless toasts of vodka. Before them was the plain of Yelnya where twenty thousand Russians and fifty thousand Germans had perished. One reporter from *The New York Times* observed: "Rain pools in the trenches are stained with blood. The battlefield smells. A decaying hand sticks out of the mud."

It was late afternoon on their last day at the front that the group reached a ruined town. Bourke-White knew the shrapnel-scarred buildings would photograph well, and just as she prepared to take her pictures with the sun finally out, one of the journalists shouted that they were going back to Moscow in five minutes. But Margaret was not about to lose her chance; she played the well-known, time-tested Bourke-White game: she wept. A stern Russian official did what he was expected to do; he quickly melted and arranged to send everyone but Margaret and Erskine to a banquet; then he appointed several soldiers to help the tearful photographer in stringing up lights.

Bourke-White had tried to photograph Stalin on previous trips to Russia but all her requests for permission went unanswered. Success finally came through Harry Hopkins who was in Russia as a personal envoy for President Roosevelt—Hopkins had been helpful to Margaret when she took photographs at the President's home in Hyde Park. She put on red shoes and wore a red bow in her hair to honor the Soviet leader. His office was a long, bare room which contained only a long table with chairs and a globe of the world on a pedestal. Margaret had seen so many giant statues of Stalin that she had difficulty recognizing this five-foot-four man with a pockmarked face. When she asked the dictator to sit for his portrait, he said nothing and remained standing. "As I sank down to my knees to get some low viewpoints," wrote Margaret in *Portrait of Myself*, "I spilled out a pocketful of peanut flashbulbs, which went bouncing all over the floor. The Kremlin interpreter and I went scrambling after them. I guess Stalin had never seen an American girl on her knees to him before. He thought it was funny, and started to laugh."

By September, Caldwell realized that he would be unable to continue his hectic schedule of writing for *PM* and *Life* and doing two broadcasts a day for *CBS*. The ruble supply was running low, while his nontransferable correspondent and broadcast salaries were accumulating in America. It was time to contact new Folkway authors, and he needed to see Lieber about foreign royalties and editions. There now were more reporters in Russia and the race to get news exclusives was more competitive. Margaret's assignment for *Life* had been fulfilled, and both were ready to return home.

Caldwell and Bourke-White went by train to Arkhangelsk and on September 23 boarded a British ship which was part of a convoy of twenty-two vessels escorted by two destroyers and a cruiser. Their route was across the Arctic to the Firth of Clyde in Scotland. It was a hazardous journey—several ships had been sunk by German submarines in this shipping lane—but after the flight across China and heavy bombardments in Moscow, the two had become accustomed to danger.

Caldwell had completed a prodigious amount of writing during his five months in Russia, but the number of pages he produced during his two weeks in London was staggering. The *Daily Mail* asked him to write seven articles on his observations in Moscow and at the Smolensk front. A messenger from the *Mail* had been stationed in the hallway outside his room at the Savoy Hotel, and as soon as a piece was finished it was rushed to the editorial office. A full-time typist was hired so that his project could be completed punctually.

Hutchinson and Company, the publishing house, requested that Caldwell expand the articles, and Bourke-White agreed to contribute a selection of her photographs to serve as book illustrations. The seventy-eight she chose were not her best, much to Caldwell's irritation, for she planned to use her favorite pictures in a book of her own. Their fourth collaboration, *Russia at War*, was completed within a week and scheduled for publication in December.

With only four days remaining in London, Caldwell was asked by Hutchinson to edit his Russian diary of several hundred pages for another book to be published the following January—no writer was more in demand. Two full-time typists were needed, and Erskine hurriedly put together *Moscow Under Fire*.

Lael Wertenbaker, a *Time* staff member, met Erskine and Margaret on their stopover in London. She thought Caldwell was "what one would call rude. It was not pleasant being with him. She (Margaret) was trying to cover this socially, whatever one does, and to palliate him." Wertenbaker considered "his Kit" subservient to her husband. "He was very bad tempered, and she was trying to be the sweet wife. You'd think she was the original faded lady department if you didn't know she was Margaret Bourke-White."

From England the two flew to Lisbon—then the safest flying route out of Europe. After a wait of several days, they took the *Yankee Clipper* home with stops in the Azores and Bermuda.

There was not time to enjoy Horseplay Hill in Darien. After a Sunday dinner, Margaret immediately had to fly to St. Louis for her first appearance on a lecture tour. Both had contracts with agencies, and Caldwell was scheduled to speak in Detroit two days later. Bourke-White signed her contract eagerly, Caldwell hesitantly. "Margaret is crazy about lecturing," he wrote his parents, "but I certainly am not."

Before crowds, Erskine had a way of fumbling with his necktie, mumbling and slurring words, and there was little eye contact with his audience. Margaret demanded attention and got it from all who crowded the auditorium to hear her talk. Sometimes she would sing a song about her foreign travels, and in a voice that got laughter and roars of approval.

The four hundred dollars Caldwell got for an hour-long talk was incentive enough for him to squirm his way through a public appearance—Margaret got at least two hundred dollars more. His lectures billed as "What I Have Seen in Russia" or "I Saw Russia in Action" consisted of material taken from articles that he had contributed to *PM, Life* and *CBS* broadcasts. They were mostly pieces of propaganda designed to silence critics who had not forgotten Stalin's truce with Hitler and the cruel treatment countless Russians had suffered under their dictator's ruthless regime. On a *CBS We The People* program he told his audience stories about old women circling a German parachutist with pitchforks and "children fighting for the honor of putting out fire bombs." Many of these Caldwellian tales were imaginary and easily had passed the strict Soviet censorship in Moscow when they were first presented.

Caldwell's war experiences in Russia, his frequent talks before audiences eager to learn more about the Communist country, and his popularity as an author gave him spokesmanship status when America declared war on Japan and Germany the day after Pearl Harbor. The State and Treasury Departments of the U.S. Government were now soliciting his presence at bond rallies. He donated his manuscripts for fund-raising auctions and never turned down a request that contributed to the war effort.

"I've called various other editors," Max Lieber told him, "and there is no getting away from it. You must submit to being lionized. After all, not many people have been in the Soviet Union in these months, and certainly none have yet come back except the Caldwells." It was a reminder that neither Erskine nor Margaret needed; both were very aware of the monetary advantages, particularly Caldwell who kept investing his huge earnings into a bulging portfolio.

He had promised himself not to rush into any book project or deadline writing—his fortnight marathon of two books for Hutchinson and Company in London and the many weeks as a correspondent and broadcaster in Moscow had been enough. But Duell, Sloan and Pearce urged him to give them a manuscript based on the Russian experience.

Mildred Zinn was asked back to Darien to help as secretary and editorial assistant, and by the end of November several chapters of *All Out On the Road to Smolensk* had been completed. This book was another London hustle, and the manuscript was turned over to

DS&P at the end of December.

*All Out On the Road to Smolensk* was rushed into print by February, 1942, and promoted by the publishers as "the first uncensored work" and "the untold story." In spite of its blatant propaganda and fanciful journalism—Caldwell's automobile teetering at the edge of a bomb crater—*Smolensk* got friendly reviews: a majority of critics felt it was their patriotic duty to praise the work.

Ralph Thompson in *The New York Times* was amazed with Caldwell's "complete and utter trust in the Stalin regime," and the *New York Herald Tribune* cited the book for having "the most realistic account of a modern tank battle that has yet been written." There were sour notes from leftist reviewers—Samuel Sillen in *New Masses* declared Caldwell's latest to be "frequently amateurish, contradictory, and unconvincing." Lillian Smith, who had found *Smolensk* a stunning read, couldn't resist saying that the author was a "whopping candidate for the Southern Liar's Bench."

Albert Goldstein, in the New Orleans *Times-Picayune*, felt the book "had a good deal to offer in the way of frontline experiences" but gave "no clear picture of war's disruption of peaceful pursuits, no feeling of its effects on the mind and spirit of the man in the air raid shelter." *Smolensk* in treatment and style was not stimulating for Goldstein. "A reading of this chronicle forces one to conclude that Caldwell the creative artist and Caldwell the reporter unfortunately are not one and the same character."

While Erskine was autographing copies of his book he was approached by a *Philadelphia Evening Bulletin* reporter. The date was March 25, 1942, and what the author said surprised the newsman: The Russians, Caldwell predicted, ultimately would throw the invading Nazis out of their country and invade and defeat Germany. America was lamentably slow in meeting the war emergency. In Russia, food, clothing, and other essentials were turned into army channels within forty-eight hours after the war began, and the sale of all automobiles was stopped. "People rushed in to beg the government to take their cars."

In Virginia's *Lynchburg Advance*, one anonymous letter writer responded with bile after reading *All Out On the Road to Smolensk:*

> Mr. Caldwell likes Communism. He thinks it would be a fine thing for
> the world to be Communist, including the United States. But he likes
> money. He has made a great deal of money and likes to spend it to help
> other people with it, such as his chauffeur, two secretaries, and porters
> whom he tips $12 for handling his enormous amount of luggage.
>
> Like so many other men, Mr. Caldwell believes in imposing certain
> totalitarian systems of government upon other people, meanwhile being
> convinced, of course, that under that system he would be at the top and
> immune to the discomforts.
>
> Like so many other men who like Communism, Mr. Caldwell spends
> most of his time in the United States, where he can buy what he wants
> with all that money he makes writing about people who have no money.

Caldwell didn't pause for breath; the moment *Smolensk* was in
the publisher's hands he began his Russian novel based on guerilla
warfare. "The new novel," he recalled, "the title of which was *All
Night Long*, was written in three and a half months in Darien and
the manuscript was delivered to Duell, Sloan and Pearce in April.
It was listed for publication in the early fall of 1942. *All Night
Long* became a selection of the Book League of America that season and the motion-picture rights were purchased for fifty thousand
dollars by Metro-Goldwyn-Mayer."

*All Night Long* held little polish for critics and was considered
inferior to Caldwell's novels based on the South. The story line
covers a bare two weeks. Sergei Korokov and his wife, Natasha,
wake one morning in early winter to find the German front has
swept past their house on a collective farm. It is time now for
Sergei to take up his part in the guerrilla work for which he has
been especially trained during the preceding spring. At dark he
escapes through sentry lines, and after waiting for two nights in the
hope that Natasha will join him—she has been taken to a bawdy
house by the Germans—he goes to the hidden headquarters of a
partisan brigade. The remaining pages of the book are about two
raids which Sergei leads. "They will kill me, too, someday," says

fellow resistance fighter Fyodor Smirnovich whose pregnant wife was raped and killed by the Nazis. "But another Fyodor will take my place." The bawdy house is raided by the partisans, and in the end Natasha is freed.

Several reviewers, caught in the patriotic fervor of that time, considered *All Night Long* to be in the same league as Ernest Hemingway's *For Whom the Bell Tolls.* "It isn't a great book," Howard Fast admitted in *The Nation,* "but you can't rip a novel out of the guts and blood of this hellishness and make a masterpiece." Fast felt a million copies of the book should be issued to American fighting men—the work "would do more good than a new cruiser."

But William Du Bois in *The New York Times* was clearly unhappy. "War creates strange by-products, and a book like this is one of them." There was a place for the propaganda novel, Du Bois conceded, and "if thrillers like 'All Night Long' must be written, they should be left to the carpenters who know the tricks. Woodpulp fiction is not Mr. Caldwell's trade."

Lewis Gannett proclaimed that Caldwell had done "a good and interesting job" in writing *All Out On the Road to Smolensk,* but the *New York Herald Tribune* reviewer reacted negatively to its Russian sequel. It was "the sort of thoroughly bad novel" that a serious, and original writer sometimes produces. Gannett declared *All Night Long* to be as bad as *Ramsey Milholland* by Booth Tarkington, *The Roll Call* by Arnold Bennett, and *One of Ours* by Willa Cather.

Although the book was uneven and written hurriedly, it was part of the times and had extraordinary appeal: within a year, more than 175,000 copies were sold. But the movie version that MGM called *Vengeance of the Earth* was never released. By the time the film was completed, the war was over, and the Cold War had deteriorated U.S.-Soviet relations.

Caldwell and Bourke-White were frequently at odds while *All Out On the Road to Smolensk* and *All Night Long* were in the process of completion. Lee Scott—she was secretary to them both for

a time—recalled the tension between the couple. Erskine would
sometimes talk to the secretary while pointedly ignoring his wife.
Scott thought him a "shy violet" of a man and felt Bourke-White
incited his resentment by her self-centeredness. Erskine wanted
another collaboration, but "his Kit" resisted and in 1942 she came
out with her own book, *Shooting the Russians*, a work that had
more text than photographs. When *Shooting* was acclaimed by
critics for its prose, Caldwell was stung: now the wife was invading his territory. "Somewhere along the line she decided she
wasn't going to collaborate on a book," wrote Lee Scott. "She was
going to do her own book. (I could have advised her that wasn't the
smartest thing to do.) She didn't tell him. I found about six drafts
of that letter. I didn't type that one."

Four books in one year and a frantic schedule of public appearances were taking their toll on Caldwell. He felt drained, and his
recent books, popular as they were, lacked the vigor and conviction
of his earlier work. Bourke-White recalled one of Caldwell's "favorite sayings which he repeated very often—so often that I think
he convinced himself of the truth. 'The life of a writer is just ten
years,' he would say." Margaret couldn't agree; to her vibrant personality and ambition, people should take total control of their own
careers, and rule their own lives.

Caldwell had become lonely and morose. Margaret was again on
assignment, and by the time Erskine had finished and delivered *All
Night Long* to DS&P he had no desire to begin another book immediately. To escape the loneliness at Horseplay Hill, a call was
made to Harry Behn in Tucson; it was time to buy a house in the
desert; he and Bourke-White had fallen in love with sunsets and
the Catalina foothills when they were gathering material for *Say,
Is This the U.S.A.?*

A few days before the journey to Tucson, Hollywood agent Al
Manuel informed Erskine that Warner Brothers had made a lucrative screenwriting offer. The studio wanted Caldwell's expertise
in adapting *Mission to Moscow* by Joseph Davies. The book was
a chronicle of Davis's two-year appointment as U.S. Ambassador

to Russia; a work that presented Stalin as a strict but avuncular leader whose purge trials were necessary to eliminate Nazi sympathizers in the Soviet Union. *Mission to Moscow* was propaganda, and President Roosevelt, aware that its influence would strengthen ties with Russia, heartily endorsed the project. Caldwell's first reaction was to turn down the offer, but he was lured into accepting when Manuel told him the contract guaranteed a salary of twelve hundred and fifty dollars a week.

"I wanted Erskine very much to do something overseas," wrote Bourke-White, "but he had just gotten a big job in Hollywood and I was rather disappointed that he cared about that so much because he had always said that Hollywood was a place that you could go to but you could just stay a short time and it would corrupt you if you stayed too long."

Margaret believed her husband knew his ten years as a writer were up and he wanted the "fattest job" he could find in the movie industry. Caldwell, in an attempt to keep Bourke-White from accepting another overseas assignment, maneuvered a studio contract for her that paid a thousand dollars a week, but she wasn't tempted. By July 1942, Erskine was pleading her by cable to accept the job, and he was "deeply hurt" that she had made no commitment to have "a little Kit." Bourke-White ignored the pleas, and by August she was on her way to England to photograph an American air base operation.

Caldwell and Robert Bucker, the producer of *Mission*, wrote an outline of the story, and Erskine began the preliminary screenplay. He warmed to the book in the beginning. The task of changing the dry memoir into a film script was so challenging that he could ignore the close supervision given the work by the studio and government. But Davies's self-centered and pompous chronicles began to irk Caldwell, and to Bourke-White he confided that "the guy is certainly crazy about himself," and the ambassador was an "Ego #1." Since there was no narrative or plot in the memoir, Caldwell had to treat the work not as an adaptation but an original story. "I've put everybody in it from Roosevelt to Stalin," he wrote in his tongue-in-cheek report to Margaret, "and that includes Hitler, Hess, Goebbels, Trotsky, Molotov, Voroshilov, Tukhachevsky, von Rib-bentrop, Shigemitsu, Matsoaka, Timoshenko, Rykov, Bukharin, Yagoda, Vyshinsky, and Henry Shapiro." Erskine even threw in a Southern congressman and a black shoe-shine boy who said: "I declare. Those Russian folks sure must be up-and-doing people!"

Caldwell was fired after completing a first-draft adaptation and some of the dialogue. Howard W. Koch, who had such script cred-its as *Casablanca* and Orson Welles's broadcast of *War of the Worlds*, was Erskine's replacement, and when *Mission to Moscow* was released the following year, Caldwell's name did not appear in the film's credits.

After being fired by Warner Brothers, he remained in Hollywood for a few more weeks to work as an adviser for several other films with Russian settings. Caldwell briefly thought of enlisting in the military but realized that he could make a greater contribution and simultaneously better his finances by serving as a writer and speak-er at war bond rallies.

Caldwell revealed to several journalists at book signings in Feb-ruary of 1942 that he would prefer the "shooting branch" of the military to a desk job in Washington. "That's the only way to ex-perience and feel the war. In Russia, every newspaper man and photographer has been up to the front."

In early spring of 1942, he was warning whoever would listen that within a year Japanese sentries would be knocking people from the sidewalks of New Orleans, and soldiers of the Rising Sun would be ordering Americans to obey curfews. But war corres-pondent Quentin Reynolds objected: "Caldwell has not the right faith in this country. It is the best country on earth....We'll come through. We have resources. America will win the war. The way we are turning out planes and other things is little short of a mir-acle. And certainly our men can fight as hard if not harder than the enemy."

Caldwell believed that America needed a centralized military con-trol as a means of quickening the war effort. He was not optimistic.

"The way things are going now, we'll be beaten. Singapore lost today, Java tomorrow, Australia the day after"—the country was being hustled into a vulnerable position.

A rhetorical question Caldwell posed for reporters after his Moscow experiences was whether they preferred to have a temporary dictator or be completely under the control of Hitler. Americans were too lackadaisical, he felt, and it was the duty of the government to wake them up if they couldn't do it themselves. Most people were unaware of the conflict's rapidity: "A rolling army like Hitler's can swallow nations in a few hours. We think of 1943-44. They think of 3 p.m. to 5 p.m."

It made him angry that he could still go around in his civilian clothes. He felt the country should have drafted him: America needed an army of 10,000,000 men, equivalent to Russian forces, and strong leaders like General Douglas MacArthur to take over a nation in a state of siege. "Sure, I think we can learn a lot from the Russians," Caldwell concluded. "And I'm not advocating Communism. I'm just being realistic."

*Mission to Moscow* earned Erskine more than twelve thousand dollars, but this was only part of his income in 1942. There were royalties from new and reissued books, and the sale of short stories in the better paying magazines. His income during that year exceeded thirty-three thousand dollars.

"Of course I want enough to eat and a place to live," he stated, "but that's all. I don't write for fame—in fact, I'd rather not have it." His financial bookkeeping was more precise as he became successful—Caldwell sometimes charged fees for interviews and drove hard bargains for his fiction. Large royalties were a writer's fair-weather barometer, but there was always the fear of an unexpected downpour on the horizon. Those who knew him were well aware that he was tightfisted: he badgered his publishers over royalties or if he felt that they were not sufficiently promoting his work, gate receipts of *Tobacco Road* plays were carefully checked, and Lieber was hounded constantly to be more vigilant in collecting foreign royalties. Erskine was furtive about his taxes, and the IRS examined his returns suspiciously; in 1940 he was penalized for deducting the total cost of an automobile and claiming that his personal telephone expenses were work-related.

Maxim Lieber was a frequent victim of double-dealings—on a number of occasions, Erskine submitted manuscripts directly to publishers in order to dodge his agent's fee for placing the work. Caldwell behaved with perfidy when Al Manuel wanted to negotiate the contract for *All Night Long*, and Caldwell gave him permission, fully aware that his East Coast agent was trying to sell the same book to studio offices in New York. When Lieber got an offer and Manuel came up with a better one, Erskine then tried to end his commitment to his East Coast agent. "My idea," Caldwell informed Manuel, "is to tell him (Lieber) that I'm going to take the novel to Hollywood myself and try to place it. That will take the picture sale right out of his hands completely." When a hurt Lieber asked if he was being sold "down the river," his defensive client responded: "I suppose you were joking about the Warner deal. As you know, it was something I handled myself."

Caldwell's *Georgia Boy* had its beginnings in the 1937 short story "The Night My Old Man Came Home." Morris "Pa" Stroup, the "old man" of the tales, is a shiftless, lovable lazybones. At times, when consumed by schemes of getting rich, he rises from his lethargy with surprising energy. Hired as dogcatcher at a salary of twenty-five cents a stray, Stroup roams about town with a chunk of raw beef and soon crowds the pound with yelping canines. He sleeps half the day with his mouth open, chases women, and is blatantly dishonest. Mrs. Stroup has to take in laundry to keep food on the table, and she is forever frustrated with her husband's transgressions. The poor woman finally gets revenge by baking Stroup's favorite fighting cock in a pie, then watches him eat it. Handsome Brown, the black yard boy, is a frequent butt when the good-for-nothing Stroup follows some absurd notion.

*Georgia Boy* was written over a period of several years. During their long travel delays in China, Erskine kept to his room and worked on the sequence. One short story after another was stacked around a central theme, which began to build like a novel. The same consuming concentration returned when he and Bourke-White arrived in Moscow; she couldn't get him to leave their hotel suite—it took their trip to the Ukraine and the beginning of hostilities to jolt him. Upon his return to America, whenever he could find spare moments in his hectic schedule, Caldwell worked on the manuscript, and as his screenwriting assignment came to an end, he began to fit the tales into a collection.

Duell, Sloan and Pearce were delighted with the book. "It is really a swell job," Charles Pearce wrote Erskine, "and so altogether entertaining and well done that I would be hard put to say which chapter I liked best....Boy are we pleased with our old man." Lieber, too, was enthusiastic and had no difficulty in placing six of the fourteen stories in leading magazines. DS&P called the collection a novel. "You have read *Tobacco Road, God's Little Acre,* and *All Night Long,*" the publicity notices announced. "But you haven't read Caldwell until you've read *Georgia Boy.*"

Erskine's new contribution with a Southern setting drew mixed reviews. "In this slight but neatly turned volume," wrote Stanley Walker of the *New York Herald Tribune,* "Mr. Caldwell goes back to the vein of his familiar 'Tobacco Road.' " Walker felt the present offering seemed pale, but did have genuine aspects. "He knows these people—their futile posturing, their snide tricks, their astonishing language and their essential hopelessness."

"Featherweight," was *Time's* verdict, and Diana Trilling in *The Nation* called the book "an innocuous collection of extended anecdotes." Another biting commentary came from Mark Schorer in *The Yale Review*: "There was a time when it seemed possible that Caldwell might grow into a kind of Breughel in prose, that out of the grotesque miseries of our submerged populace, he might develop a genuine and individual satire. That has not happened."

William Du Bois of *The New York Times* saw it differently: "Erskine Caldwell has come back from the steppes at last." Du Bois found *Georgia Boy* "heartwarming" and was delighted that the author's role as a correspondent in Russia was over. "This reader," the reviewer admitted, enjoyed Caldwell's new book "for its laughter, and the overtones fall where they may. Taken in that spirit, it is an unalloyed delight."

Reviewer W. M. Frohock called *Georgia Boy* "a sort of *Tobacco Road* sweetened down for the carriage trade." It was something Mark Twain might have done had he come from Georgia and found himself in a playful mood, and if he wanted to be sure of not offending his public.

Caldwell was uncertain as to how long *Georgia Boy* had been in the making—he told one interviewer "four years" and another estimate was "seven to ten years." As the stories gradually accumulated, he had no idea that he was fashioning a connected story line. Erskine was carried along by repetition buried in the shaping. For him, there was comedy in tragedy and tragedy in comedy—the two were inseparable and interchangeable. It was like the old saying: "I couldn't laugh for crying; I couldn't cry for laughing." Handsome Brown, the black yard boy's complaint of his arches hurting whenever Ma or Pa Stroup asks him to perform some unpleasant task is workable repetition. Caldwell compared this to a refrain in music; it was useful in making a point and heightening drama.

The comedy-tragedy motif is vividly illustrated in the chapter "Handsome Brown and the Aggravating Goats." (Goats are on the roof and Mrs. Stroup is mortified because she will be giving a ladies' circle meeting momentarily. Handsome is told by Pa Stroup to climb up and chase the creatures down. The big billy butts him and the yard boy falls off the roof and into a well—luckily he escapes serious injury.) "I wouldn't set out to try to write a comic or tragic interlude," Caldwell insisted. "By the time I got halfway through the chapter I still wouldn't know whether the effect was going to be funny or sad." For the author, it served an "ideal form" and "the most complete book" he had ever written.

In *Portrait of Myself*, Bourke-White wrote that Caldwell had bought her a house in Arizona but she was unable to accept it. He wanted them to leave Darien so that Margaret could have little Patricia. They would commute to the West Coast and live well on screenwriting jobs. "You are my wife and I want to take care of you," Erskine wrote her. "When are you going to begin staying instead of going? I think it's about time you began staying. Life isn't much without you around. Maybe you can't understand that, but that's exactly the way it is."

Margaret was swept into the tension and excitement of wartime England. She photographed Churchill and Haile Selassie—he was the only emperor who ever carried her camera gear. "Who is that woman with the remarkable hair?" asked the British monarch when seeing the startling white streak crowning her forehead. Meanwhile, alone in the new house in the desert, Caldwell sensed that Bourke-White was pulling away from him and his pleas grew in urgency. "There is no finer thing in the world than having someone close to you and that's the way I feel about you. No matter where you are, you know you can always feel that I am as close to you as if we were the same person."

Erskine kept Margaret fully informed on the decorating of their new home—"Casa Margarita." He had purchased a silver tea service that she could one day give to Patricia, and the master bedroom had been done just the way she planned it. The Mexican decor in the guest room was completely in place, and the chairs had been upholstered with the black and yellow material Bourke-White had selected. There was a screened porch facing south, and at night the lights of Tucson were spread out for miles. "I can't get much good writing done without you here," he reminded her. "I need you around to put me to work. I seem to do better books when you are here, so I guess if you want me to do a good one, you should come home."

The transatlantic mail was slow and some of Caldwell's letters may never have reached Margaret. On October 2 he telegraphed: LAST LETTER RECEIVED SEPT 10. LAST CABLE 20TH." But Bourke-White had now become a captive of her assignment for *Life*; she was photographing American bombers at a secret air base in England and had been too busy to notice that Caldwell's last letter had come in early October. But on November 9 a cable from him got her attention:

"HAVE REACHED MOST DIFFICULT DECISION OF LIFETIME STOP DECIDED THAT PARTNERSHIP MUST DISSOLVE IMMEDIATELY SINCE PRESENT AND FUTURE CONTAIN NO PROMISE OF ULTIMATE MANIFEST STOP NO SINGLE FACTOR OR COMBINATION COULD RECTIFY UNTENABLE SITUATION STOP BELIEVE ME WHEN EYE SAY EYE AM TRULY SORRY AND INCONSOLABLE STOP PLEASE NOTIFY WEISS STEPS YOU WISH TAKEN." (Julius Weiss was Margaret's lawyer.)

Bourke-White cabled back: "EXPLAIN REASONS MORE FULLY AND PLEASE TELL ME HONESTLY IF ANYONE ELSE INVOLVED."

Caldwell replied on November 12: "HAVE WAITED FOUR YEARS FOR SOMETHING BETTER THAN THIS AND THE PRESENT AND FUTURE HAVE BECOME DISMAL APPARITIONS STOP SUCH IS LONELINESS."

Bourke-White cabled again, and this would be the last communication: "SUCH IS LONELINESS AND SUCH IS POETRY BUT SUCH IS NOT ANSWER TO DIRECT QUESTION STOP THEREFORE CAN DRAW ONLY ONE CONCLUSION AND SORRY YOU COULD NOT TELL ME OPENLY."

Margaret's secretary, Peggy Sargent, claimed to have heard that Bourke-White was "ravaged" by the unexpected cable. After waiting a week for Erskine to reply to her last sally and hearing nothing, she wrote Julius Weiss:

> In a world like this I simply cannot bear being away from things that happen. I think it would be a mistake for me not to be recording the march of events with my camera when I have such remarkable opportunities, and when my work is put to such good use. Erskine has become interested in such different things lately. I do not understand his passion for big houses and comfortable living.
>
> ...I care a reasonable amount about how it looks. While I'm not doing any worrying about public opinion I might as well be realistic about it. I suppose it does look better if the wife brings suit....
>
> The only thing I really care about in all this is the Connecticut house, which really seems like home to me. If I could keep it as a home I would be glad.

The swift change from decorating a new love nest in the Catalina foothills of Arizona to a cable demanding divorce was not an overnight decision. Caldwell had long been aware that he had no control over Bourke-White. She had reached the top rung of her professional ladder and couldn't possibly settle in a peaceful desert home away from a world at war. "I feel so right, somehow," Margaret told Wilson Hicks, her photo editor, "that nothing, not even personal considerations are going to interfere. The work has always been first with me as you know. But now it is FIRST FIRST."

There were other reasons behind Caldwell's sudden announcement that all was over: one was that Bourke-White had an abortion sometime after their return from Russia and before she left for England. Somehow, Caldwell found out what she had done, and in the ferment of his unhappiness he was unable to forgive her for "killing their little Patricia." Years later, a friend overheard him say that "it was the worst thing she ever did when she got rid of that child."

He had to accept the fact that their marriage no longer existed. The legal procedures were handled quickly and without acrimony. For Caldwell, the biggest sacrifice was the loss of Horseplay Hill. But Margaret did make sure that his personal belongings were shipped to Arizona and with them came the long-haired, black-and-white cat, Fluffy, that "divided her time between people in the house during the day and with the gophers and rabbits on the desert at night."

It had been no oversight that Erskine neglected to answer Margaret's cabled question whether anyone else was involved; he had met an attractive young woman who was eager to take up the domestic role that Bourke-White resisted. Caldwell had spoken to a creative writing class at the University of Arizona, and in the front row sat June Johnson. She greatly admired his work, and he invited her to Casa Margarita for horseback riding and a swim.

The young student came frequently and soon there were daily visits. After that it was not unusual for June to spend the night in a lounge adjoining the bedroom of his secretary—Polly Stallsmith.

For her convenience, Erskine provided the girl with his smaller sedan for traveling between Case Margarita and the university.

Caldwell's divorce was finalized on December 21, 1943, the day before a troopship was torpedoed on its way to North Africa— Margaret was one of the survivors in a crowded lifeboat. Two days after the divorce, Erskine and June were married. The *Norwalk* (Connecticut) *Hour Newspaper* published an article, datelined Phoenix, Arizona, that began:

> Playwright Erskine Caldwell, 40, was honeymooning today with his 20 year old bride, the former June Johnson, following a marriage which revealed for the first time that he had been divorced from Miss Bourke-White, photographer and writer. The bride is a brunette and a senior at the University of Arizona. She has been active in school dramatics and will graduate in June.

The photograph of Caldwell with his young bride could have confused readers of *PM*—dressed in a charcoal-gray, pin-striped suit, he looked more like a father escorting the bride than a groom about to receive her. "Meet the New Mrs. Caldwell," *PM* headlined its article about Margaret's replacement. The former Miss Johnson was five feet six inches tall and had brown hair and hazel eyes. She was a graduate of Phoenix Union High School and Phoenix Junior College and a member of Pi Beta Phi Sorority at the University of Arizona. June's ambition was to become a writer, and she had done radio scripts for a local broadcasting station. The overseas newspaper for servicemen, *Stars and Stripes*, carried a story about the newlyweds, and this was how Margaret Bourke-White learned of the marriage.

# THE MIDDLE YEARS

Erskine had committed himself to a lecture tour starting in early January, but when informed by Al Manuel that Twentieth Century-Fox wanted him to write a screen treatment at a salary exceeding five thousand dollars a month the lecture plan was hastily dismissed. Two weeks after their wedding, he and June moved to Beverly Hills where the former screenwriter began his fifth assignment. Again, as on previous stays in Hollywood, his contributions were ignored, and he was shifted to different adaptations without receiving any screen credits. At Dartmouth College Library there is a Caldwell script based on Thomas Wolfe's *Look Homeward Angel*. He worked on it while in Tucson, but had nobody to confer with about the film. The producer, an independent, visited him only once, and after Erskine had worked for three months in a vacuum the project was dropped.

The glamour of her new lifestyle impressed June, and Caldwell during the early months of their marriage was lavishly generous. He bought a new automobile, hired a full-time maid, and encouraged frequent trips to fashionable shops for expensive clothes— Erskine was determined to shrug off all the outer wrappings that Bourke-White had bought for him. Their luxurious accommodations at the Beverly Wilshire Hotel soon proved too confining, and they rented a house on the beach in Malibu.

Caldwell stayed nine months in Hollywood, ignoring his contention that no writer should dwell there longer than three months— beyond that one risked becoming a "hack." It was the money that lured him; his film contracts in 1944 paid him $50,000. But by the fall of that year, both he and June had had enough of their fast-lane California existence, and she was missing her parents and college friends.

Casa Margarita was traded as partial payment for a new and larger house with four bedrooms and situated on a higher elevation of the Catalina foothills. It had ample service quarters, library, office, bar, and lounge. "A lot of money has been spent for a place to live," he wrote his parents. "But I think it is worth it, if only for the fact that at last, and for the first time, I feel that I have a place to live in that I am satisfied with."

There had been several failed attempts to cast *God's Little Acre* as a stage replacement for *Tobacco Road*, and Caldwell hadn't forgotten the money he fronted for the sinking production of *Journeyman*. But Max Lieber was urging him to "fill the void," and Caldwell finally agreed to reconsider a grant for *Georgia Boy* to an eager Jed Harris, a leading Broadway director and producer.

The seduction of seeing his work performed again proved irristible, and Caldwell was soon involved in every detail of the production. He shuttled between Arizona and New York for set designing conferences and casting. Erskine wanted Nunnally Johnson to write the script but was turned down, and after several other dramatists couldn't be enticed, Jack Kirkland was hired. The original Jeeter Lester of *Tobacco Road*, Henry Hull, would play the lead role of Pa Stroup.

*Georgia Boy* opened in Boston and crashed. The reviews were all bad and the play so poorly attended that the scheduled two-week run was cut in half. Every backer lost heavily, and though Caldwell's losses were not comparable to the *Journeyman* fiasco, he had invested more than three thousand dollars, as well as considerable traveling expenses and time away from the writing table.

There were other business ventures which proved troublesome. Ira had long wanted to edit a newspaper, and Erskine had first inquired about purchasing the *Augusta Chronicle* as early as 1938. A local bankruptcy auction in 1943 finally gave his father the chance of fulfilling this dream of a lifetime. Backed with his son's money, he made a down payment toward the purchase of the Hampton County South Carolina *Guardian*, the Allendale, South Carolina *Citizen*, and the Jasper County South Carolina *Record*. Several weeks later a fourth paper was added to the chain, the Beauford, South Carolina *Times*, and in association with Carrie's sister and brother-in-law, Kathleen and Lawton Maner, Ira began the formidable task of trying to revive four newspapers in decline.

Ira had enormous energy and loved the challenge of running a business that the three of them knew little about. Caldwell's father was now sixty-eight and his eyesight so poor that he had difficulty seeing the keys on his typewriter when composing editorials. Erskine wanted to step back from the venture and not become involved, but felt he couldn't refuse when his father asked for advice and assistance. Ira also persuaded him to accept the presidency of the Caldwell-Maner Publishing Company.

The son soon was confronted with a myriad of problems: the woman in charge of one office complained that her typesetter was "a liquor head," a labor dispute erupted when Ira hired a black typesetter to run one of the presses, and decisions had to be made in advertising and distribution. Did the format of the paper require a change?—his father needed to know. There was also the constant financial drain; machinery had to be repaired, and money rolled into advertising to boost a waning circulation.

"I am very anxious to know something about your new book," wrote Al Manuel with a movie sale in mind. "I hope you can understand my feelings in this matter and that you will cooperate to the best of your ability." His New York agent, Lieber, was also pressuring him: serializations were lucrative, and Caldwell had the name to get top billing in national publications. Even a substandard novel would sell in the thousands, Lieber assured him. Charles Pearce at DS&P was also anxious; within three weeks he must know whether the firm would have the prize novel of the fall season or no book at all. "Don't prolong the agony," wrote Pearce, "we're beginning to show the strain." In June 1944, to silence all three, Caldwell sent them manuscript copies of *Tragic Ground*.

This novel was one in a series of stories that Caldwell had been planning as a "cyclorama of Southern life." Spence Douthit, a poor white farmer, and his family are lured from their desolate surroundings to work in a munitions plant on the Gulf Coast. When the plant closes, the Douthits are left stranded in a shantytown called Poor Boy. Unable to find work, the family is reduced to grubbing for food as best they can while the situation fosters dishonesty, lechery, and indolence. Douthit's wife, Maud, wanders about their dismal shack, swearing and naked—she is heavily addicted to Dr. Munday's Miracle Tonic. Thirteen-year-old Mavis Douthit has left home in order to become a prostitute, and next door, Spence's best friend has daughters who want to tramp the streets for a living. Another neighbor peddles marijuana—he's the one who started little Mavis down the path to whoredom. Libby, the elder daughter, works and keeps her parents from starving with an occasional five-dollar bill. When a social worker arrives and gives Spence money to buy bus tickets back to their farm, the inevitable occurs—he spends it at the White Turkey where he hoped to rescue daughter Mavis. He doesn't find her but gets acquainted with a grinning character who expresses willingness in marrying the girl. Such a respectable solution to his daughter's problems strikes Spence as a wonderful idea. He takes the young scoundrel home and a murder results to finalize "Tragic Ground."

Hypocrisy abounded in the editorial office of DS&P when the new Caldwell novel was evaluated. The editors knew it was bad, yet they praised him—the author was, after all, one of the heavy investors in the firm. Charles Pearce offered a few timid suggestions: maybe "a thread of affirmation" could be slipped into the story "to balance the hopelessness of the Douthits and the other people of Poor Boy." But he did not want to rile his number one author. "Whatever you decide to do, brother, my hat's off to you," Pearce soothed him. When Caldwell agreed to perform minor surgery on a paragraph or two, Pearce was effusive. "What a man, what a man!" he declared. "I couldn't be more delighted than I am with your reaction to our suggestions. I know you'll work out that main point of thread of affirmation in a masterful fashion."

Al Manuel had no comment on the quality of the manuscript and busily tried to land the work with some studio. But Maxim Lieber was less cautious and wrote in a detailed critique that the story was "rather slight" and had "a faulty dramatic structure." The Douthits, Lieber contended, were "not unicellular amoebae, but rather human beings prone to a variety of reactions, to a variety of impulses, and even to the suggestion of improvement."

This reaction angered Erskine, who felt his agent was paying him back for some unintentional slight or misunderstanding over a commission. It was treachery and not easily forgiven. But Caldwell did make modest changes after Lieber's critique: the final chapter was altered and had Spence Douthit's eldest daughter with her new husband helping her parents to get out of Poor Boy and back to the land. Nevertheless, Caldwell's agent had learned an important lesson: he still spoke of their "warm and loyal friendship," but was resolved to shroud his honesty when called upon to evaluate his client's work.

The novel was rushed into print with careless disregard for detail. *Tragic Ground* went out of control in the early pages, and the story content was patchy and riddled with clichés. At times, Caldwell seemed to be elsewhere—preoccupied as he was with the *Georgia Boy* dramatization failure and the running of four newspapers. On page thirty-four he described a social worker, whose "dark brown hair was carefully combed." But ten pages later the same young lady had blond hair that was "piled on top of her head in a mass of curls and waves." Such fatal errors never occurred when Erskine had Helen to work revisions, and Bourke-White certainly would have noticed such incongruities, but June may have been too much in awe of her husband's place in the literary world to pass editorial judgements.

"Don't misunderstand me. I like this stuff," Bernard De Voto told his readers in the *New York Herald Tribune*. But critic De Voto questioned the author's treatment of his characters: making them laughable morons and knocking them about in a burlesque farce. "Mr. Caldwell is always saying, 'Jeeter's baby died, yippee!' or 'I like to bust a gut, the pay doctor says grandmaw's got cancer.' " With everybody doubled up with laughter, the pity evaporates. "If Mr. Caldwell doesn't think it's funny, then his is a badly confused mind. But not so badly confused as the critics who refuse a laugh when he hands them one."

*Tragic Ground* was less lively for Harry Hansen in the *New York*

*World-Telegram*: "This is one of the saddest books of the season—saddest because of Caldwell's desertion of standards when treating a theme that demands something besides a leer." Even Jack Conroy, usually one of Erskine's loyal defenders, called the book "pathetic, ominous and terrifying."

However, the reviews were not uniformly discouraging; there were several commentaries praising the author's skills. Hal Steed in *Tomorrow* hailed the new book as an event. *Tragic Ground* was one of Caldwell's best long stories. "It is much better than *Georgia Boy*, his last previous work, which it resembles, and it has more length, breadth, and warmth than *Tobacco Road*."

Herbert Kupferberg, in the *New York Herald Tribune*, asserted that Caldwell "manages to steer pretty clear of the farcical. His Southern crackers may be shiftless and spineless, but he keeps the flicker of humanity in them burning like an eternal light." Malcolm Cowley emphasized the tension between "the sociologist and reformer" in "Two Erskine Caldwells," and Nelson Algren thought the author of *Tragic Ground* "a cracker-barrel humorist." Algren told the readers of the *Chicago News* that here was the spiritual heir of Mark Twain and Stephen Crane, "yet as a storyteller he is something less than either." Caldwell's comedy was "frontier hijinks" and his tragedy came from a "consummate pity tempered by a contemporary social consciousness."

"Spence Douthit, his wife and two daughters are the principal characters in Caldwell's new book," wrote Orville Prescott in *The New York Times.* "A more foul-mouthed, feckless, ignorant, useless family had rarely been described in print....But they were always thoroughly alive; what happened to them was nearly always interesting and dramatic." Caldwell was a master of cruel and sardonic humor for Prescott. "So much of his work has been superficial and repetitious, and some of it has been sickening. But all of it seems to have been written with the honest intention of portraying human wrecks as the unfortunate victims of environment."

There had always been a closeness in the Caldwell family, in spite of the three marriages and Erskine's frequent travels while interviewing new Folkway authors, his home in the desert of Arizona, and screenwriting in Hollywood. Ira and Carrie doted on Pix, Dabney, and Janet—Helen was always delighted to have her former in-laws at Greentrees, especially "Dad Caldwell." Bourke-White was not overlooked either, and Erskine once said to Margaret that he "wouldn't be surprised if they (his parents) loved you more than they do me." His ties with his father were immensely strong, and though his mother sometimes irritated him, he was forever generous and concerned for her well-being.

Ira's pride in his son's writing career highlighted his existence in small-town Wrens, and he frequently defended his son's novels from the pulpit. It gave him pleasure when he could tell strangers that he was "Erskine Caldwell's father."

Erskine wanted his father to retire and offered to buy his parents a comfortable home in nearby Augusta, Georgia. Caldwell, who was known for his financial caution, was just the opposite when it came to Ira and Carrie—he often sent them checks and paid their travel expenses when they visited their grandchildren in Mount Vernon. "I should think that when the war is over you should seriously consider giving up school work, so both of you can have time to do some traveling," he urged. "As it is, I hope both of you will let me present you with a six months trip to Europe. It will certainly be worthwhile, and I can easily afford the cost." (In an *Atlanta Constitution* newspaper article of April 25, 1967, M. C. McCollum, ninety-three-year-old head of Wrens Institute, had only praise for Carrie and Ira as educators: "Erskine's mother taught English and French, and her husband, I. S. Caldwell, taught history. They stayed about fifteen years and were among my best teachers." Ira was remembered as having a tart tongue. To one student, he said: "Your head is a nest from which the brains have flown.")

Ira was too involved with his four newspapers, pastoral duties, and the small A.R.P. school to think of retirement. His days were eighteen hours long, and he thrived on a heavy workload. "The job ahead of us is both large and hard," he happily wrote when reporting recent developments at the four newspapers, "but I think we can make it a success."

He did, however, admit to having small setbacks with his health: there had been one "spell"—probably a heart episode—and his eyesight was growing worse. "I can see objects but not details," he wrote Erskine. "I can see people in the church, but I cannot tell who they are." Poor health was an inconvenience, he confessed, but never a reason for doing less in life. "I am hoping that when I go to the doctor Monday I will be able to get glasses that will make it possible for me to see," he wrote his son. "My left eye has not bled in nearly four weeks." When a physician found a blood clot on his coronary artery and recommended surgery, Ira elected to ignore it. There was chest discomfort, but he would relax for a few minutes, and "if that does not stop the pain, I can take a tablet of nitroglycerine, and this stops the pain immediately."

Caldwell had to suppress grave second thoughts when he purchased the four newspapers for his father; Ira had so much desired them that the son was unable to turn him down. But Erskine had been attempting for years to get Ira into a relaxed lifestyle—checks were sent more frequently to Wrens. On one occasion, when worried about his father's increased burst of energy, he sent $1000. "Under no circumstance must you think that it should be saved," he scolded. "This particular sum is to be earmarked for a trip and nothing but a trip."

By August 1944, Carrie was clearly worried about Ira's declining health, and to silence her he finally agreed to have a thorough heart examination at the Johns Hopkins Medical Center. As much as he hated to take precious time from work, the trip to Baltimore excited him. Ira and Carrie had supper on the train, and in his letter to Erskine he reported having "a great array of dishes, a meager amount of food, and a large beer." The patients and medical equipment at the hospital interested him more than the depressing results of his medical tests. "I am going back tomorrow to see a specialist," he wrote Erskine, "and I hope that good will result." But it didn't, and on the train journey back to Wrens, Ira Sylvester Caldwell suffered a massive heart seizure and died.

Carrie received hundreds of telegrams and letters from former students, sharecroppers, church members, and strangers who had been touched or rescued by Ira's kindness and generosity. Many of the letters were difficult to read—the handwriting untrained but the sentiment poignant and heartfelt. One condolence deeply touched Carrie: "Father's passing away," wrote Margaret Bourke-White, "is a loss to all whose lives he touched. He was one of the finest men I've ever known"—after the divorce she had continued writing to them. "People like Father really helped to leave the world a better place. The partnership between you two was always so close that my heart goes out to you in this loss."

Because of wartime restriction, Erskine was unable to book a flight for the funeral, and he had shown no emotion when June told him that his father had died. But Ira's passing was a greater anguish to him than his waning powers as a writer. The one person he loved—more than mother, former wives, children, and present wife—was gone.

Duell, Sloan and Pearce published *Stories by Erskine Caldwell* in the late summer of 1944. The introduction to these twenty-four selections was written by Henry Seidel Canby, board chairman of Book-of-the-Month Club and first editor of the *Saturday Review of Literature*. "I myself regard Caldwell as primarily and essentially a short-story writer," declared Dr. Canby. Caldwell was the product of sociology and wanderlust, evenly mixed, who produced material that was not naturalism, realism or romanticism but something entirely new. "His fame among masses is due of course to the incredible success of the play 'Tobacco Road,' written by another, but based on a long short story or nouvelle, as the French call such stories by Caldwell. But at his most original, most effective, and certainly at his best, Caldwell belongs in the distinguished list of American short-story writers who have made their place in world literature, beginning with Irving, Hawthorne and Poe."

Reaction to the twenty-four tales was positive, and DS&P were pleased with sales. Among the selections were "Handsome Brown" and "My Old Man," chapters from *Georgia Boy*; and there were several widely-read tales, such as "Candy-Man Beechum," "Kneel to the Rising Sun," "Maud Island," and "August Afternoon."

"This collection of many of his stories should make it clear that he should be known, and remembered, as one of the best of the short story writers of this day," Marjorie Stoneman Douglas told her readers in the *Miami Herald*. Caldwell had neither the slightly arty tenderness and deliberate drama of John Steinbeck nor the steely distortions of William Faulkner. "He conveys the feeling that he has no bias at all, what he writes, with the exception of the obvious fantasies, are the truth, so help him."

"That Erskine Caldwell can leap from the oppressive, the brutal, the seamy and the vicious to the rich deep humor of American folklore," John C. Fuller wrote in *The Boston Post*, "is but one of the many virtues which stamp him as a leading short-story artist of the day." Praise also came from the *St. Louis Globe-Democrat* but with the warning: "Time is scarcely personal, and has a way all its own of discarding the standards of a time as being but a passing fashion in their relation to time's tradition."

There was a discordant note from John Chapman in the *Dallas Morning News*: "What one finds lacking most of all in Caldwell's study of white domination and Negro subjection is motivation." Caldwell—and Dr. Canby—didn't understand why white men behave badly. "It is to beg the question to dismiss a lynching as sadism only," declared Chapman, "yet that is the inclination of most southern writers."

*The Commonweal* pointed out to its readers that "The People vs Abe Lathan, Colored" and "The End of Christy Tucker" were tales deserving to rank with the best of the time. But Caldwell's stories of lynching and violence did not carry "the sense of reality," and the New England yarns were less convincing than those with a Southern background. *The Commonweal* also pointed out a carelessness: "If the maple tree the Swedish child climbs (this is in "A Country Full of Swedes") is slight enough to bend dangerously under his weight, how is it possible for a woodsman to chop 'chips as big as dinner plates' out of it?"

Dan S. Norton in *The New York Times* partially agreed with Canby's high regard by saying cautiously that the book had "a few first-rate" inclusions. But Norton couldn't resist telling his readers that it was "only slightly inaccurate to say that if a happy Negro appears in a Caldwell story he is about to be starved, beaten, shot or lynched."

Jay, Caldwell's fourth child, was born shortly after Ira's death. The father-son relationship was of an entirely different kind—untainted by the tense and sometimes brutal disregard Erskine had for Pix and Dabney. Now that his work had diminished in quality and range, he became more accessible to the new son—outbursts of anger and woodshed paddlings were parcels of the past. Caldwell still had spells of writing in his study, but little Jay wasn't trained to speak in whispers or to tiptoe about in their Tucson home. As the child grew older, the two would play games on the rug in the living room and there were baseball outings and time together at carnivals. Erskine didn't insist, as he had with Pix, Dee, and Janet, on being called Skinny—for Jay, his father was Papa.

After Ira's demise, Caldwell made a determined effort to narrow the emotional chasm between him and his three older children, but the wreckage of his marriage to Helen made it difficult. Erskine Junior, Dabney, and Janet visited their father over the years, but they were unable to forgive him for leaving them or for his cruel behavior to their mother. The three had served as witnesses for Helen in the divorce trial, and also in several attempts to renegotiate a better financial settlement. They had become extremely fond of Bourke-White but were uneasy with their new stepmother—June was closer in age to them than to their father—in 1944, Pix was eighteen, Dabney seventeen, and Janet eleven.

Erskine Junior had been more injured by his parents' divorce than Dabney and Janet, and though Norman Cushman, Helen's second husband, brought love and stability into the home, Pix had trouble shrugging his wildness. He didn't care for school or classmates, dropped out, lied about his age and joined the Marines at sixteen. After World War II, he had a brief marriage with a lounge singer and there was an encounter with the law. Drifting from one job to another, he finally settled in Hollywood with the unfulfilled dream of becoming a writer. Caldwell sent checks regularly to Al Manuel for Pix and assured his elder son that he always was welcome to be with him in Tucson. In time, the son remarried, became a salesman (for Chesterfield cigarettes), and like Erskine Senior, lost much of his anger.

Dabney dodged some of the emotional turmoil in the wake of the broken marriage. He liked being alone, out in nature, camping and exploring the woods surrounding Mount Vernon. He was an outstanding student and got a doctorate in geology at Harvard; this career preference originated from his closeness to Ira who had frequently taken him on fossil and Indian artifact hunts. Dabney intentionally distanced his father and preferred to tell him little about his personal life. When he planned to get married, he sent a letter to Erskine—though not about the coming wedding or the bride— the young man needed twenty-five dollars for a new suit. This quiet and private second son couldn't forget or condone the difficult early years at Greentrees. "It's the truth, Skinny," he wrote—Dabney was then nineteen—"you don't look a day older than the first time I can recall your face—the day when you beat the daylights out of Pix and me in the wood shed."

Caldwell preferred having Erskine Junior and Dabney make their own decisions in life; he felt it necessary that they learn self-reliance. But this wasn't the case with Janet, and he was often meddlesome, insisting on being informed whenever choices had to be made. Erskine was unduly preoccupied in Janet's selection of colleges and in his letters directed her which courses to take. When she decided to drop a Bible class, he immediately wrote the president of the college and urged him to dissuade the girl. Janet was, however, spirited and fiercely independent; she dropped the course and made arrangements to attend a different college. "Don't let it be such a long time between letters," he complained. "I worry about a lot of things when I don't hear from you." (It could have been a letter to Bourke-White.) Yet, when least expected, Caldwell showed flexibility. When his daughter was seventeen and wrote him that she soon planned to get married, his reply must have startled her. "If you have made the decision, that's the way it will be, and you can always be certain that you have my love and blessing. Don't ever feel that you can't write to me about your troubles or your happiness, and as long as I live you can be assured that I hope it be little of the former and much of the latter."

Erskine brought his mother to Tucson for a visit after Ira's death. Carrie was not always an easy person to be with and she found fault in the way June brought up Jay and her son's decision not to attend church. Set in her ways, Carrie insisted that the house be run in the same orderly fashion that she was accustomed to in Wrens: everything had its place, down to the crockery on the shelf, and punctuality in serving meals was no detail to be overlooked. She was a woman who demanded attention and when Carrie felt that she was being ignored she made her presence known. Her frugality and meticulousness were more trying for June; Erskine shared his mother's careful concerns in the waste-not, want-not world of managing a home.

June was far more sociable than Caldwell and loved entertaining friends and going to parties. She soon became a member of the Tucson Junior League, and the two were charter members of the Old Pueblo Country Club, known as Tucson's "high society" clique, where they participated in champagne suppers and dances.

Caldwell was asked to join a group of businessmen to help establish a new broadcasting station in Tucson. Harry Behn, who had collaborated with him on a Clark Gable script for MGM, planned the operation with the intention of making it both a commercial enterprise and a project for civic betterment. There had to be several costly hearings with the Federal Communications Commission in order to obtain a license—the FCC had granted permits to three other groups—this, along with the outlay of equipment for the station, necessitated a great deal of front money. Many of the supporting members backed out of the Catalina Broadcasting Company arrangement, and Caldwell was advised to follow suit. Instead, he bought out most of the investors and became the leading stockholder. Though it was an expensive decision—nearly $50,000 was involved—the running of a radio station appealed to him at this time in his life, and he soon purchased shares in several Phoenix stations.

Erskine was uneasy in many of these social gatherings, but he did his best to be part of the crowd. He mingled shyly, drank heavily, and didn't resort to deep-freeze moods that had frequently overcome him during the Bourke-White days. He became one of the leading sponsors of the Tucson Press Club, a group of radio and newspapermen who enjoyed hard liquor, pool, and all-night poker. Caldwell felt more at ease with these cronies—there was no need to make an impression or play famous author for curious socialites. Whenever the Press Club had financial troubles he rescued it with sizeable contributions, and the camaraderie he had here was more important to him in this time of life than his writing; being with the boys became a sedative for the concern about his waning power over words.

With June, he seemed in the early years of their marriage to have found emotional stability. She cared for him deeply and loved being the young and devoted wife. June brought meals on a tray if he needed seclusion to write, and when he felt depressed she was quick to brighten his mood. Their home, in spite of Carrie's demanding presence, was not an unhappy household—Caldwell's income was steadily on the rise and there was an atmosphere of prosperity.

Caldwell had no major writing plans in the weeks following his father's death. He signed his contract to produce the adaptation of Thomas Wolfe's *Look Homeward Angel*, and later, tried to arrange a musical comedy of *Tragic Ground* for Broadway—Agnes de Mille and Aaron Copland were picked to do the choreography and the score—but he had had too many failed adaptations of his books since *Tobacco Road* to attract investors.

In the Dartmouth College Archives can be found the script for a musical written by Caldwell. "The Strong Man of Maxcatan" depicts Mexican politicians and the lead singer was to portray the President of Mexico. But someone in the State Department felt it would create a diplomatic stir if Broadway showed the President of Mexico singing songs and chasing girls around adobe walls.

New Folkway books were published during 1944, and the series increased in popularity: among the releases were *Far North Country* by Thames Williamson, *Lake Huron* by Fred Landon, and *Deep Delta Country* by Harnett T. Kane. At year's end, Caldwell's novel, *Tragic Ground*, was given the best possible form of advertising: it was banned in Boston.

Miss Margaret Anderson and one of her clerks at the Dartmouth Book Stall in Boston's Back Bay area were charged with possessing and selling indecent literature shortly after a copy of *Tragic Ground* was sold to Detective Edward Blake of the city's police department. Wilfred E. Pratt, an agent for the New England Watch and Ward Society, underscored twenty paragraphs he considered to be in violation of the Massachusetts obscene book statute. But members of this watchdog group were surprised and disappointed with Municipal Judge Elijah Adlow's ruling.

"I refuse to agree that *Tragic Ground* is an obscene book," he told the court, "and I find nothing shocking in a scene where a female sees a man stripped to the waist." Then turning to Detective Blake on the stand, Judge Adlow asked: "Have you read *Anthony Adverse*?" The detective had not. "That," said the magistrate, "is the trouble with the police department—they haven't a big enough library." *Tragic Ground* was dull but not indecent, the judge ruled— "you would have to be chained to a chair to read it. But I'm getting tired of books being banned. It is getting so this court's business is divided between booksellers and bookmakers. The police would do better to bring in a few pickpockets and burglars."

If the book had dirt, Erskine defended, it was because he had tried to make it real. Yet there was something wrong in *Tragic*

*Ground*, though he was unable to find what flawed it. Vitriolic reviews of his work were to be expected and rarely helpful. "Maybe, after all," he wrote Morang, "the best that can be done is to plug along, doing the best you can, writing one book after another, and then, God willing, at the end of fifty years, maybe one book of the lot be worthwhile."

Penguin Books published a paperback edition of *Trouble in July* in 1945, and this twenty-five-cent book was a sensation. The major problem in the past, going back for decades, was that large numbers of copies had to be sold in order to realize a profit. Robert Fair de Graf fathered the paperback publishing in 1939 when he founded Pocket Books.

De Graf's scheme was to reissue popular hardcover editions in a twenty-five-cent softcover format with reduced margins, so that these 4 1/4- by 6 1/2-inch books printed on lightweight paper were small enough to fit in a person's pocket. The publisher's distribution approach included drugstores, grocery stores, and newsstands. De Graf hired commercial artists to produce colorful covers for his first ten books; among them were an Agatha Christie novel, a self-help book, *Wuthering Heights* by Emily Brontë, and *The Bridge at San Luis Rey* by Thornton Wilder. On the day before their release, *The New York Times* carried a full-page advertisement. "Out Today," the ad ran, "The New Pocket Book That May Revolutionize New York's Reading Habit."

Sales were spectacular. Bookstores sold out within hours, and Macy's moved nearly 8,000 copies before they could set up a window displaying their pocket wonders. Even a small neighborhood cigar store sold 100 copies in a day and a half. The ten titles were distributed to cities and small towns across the country with the same success, and within three months 500,000 Pocket Books had been purchased. De Graf started his enterprise on $30,000, and when he sold the business five years later the asking price was $3,000,000.

The Armed Services Editions of pocket-sized books were hugely popular during World War II. Printed on magazine presses and stapled, more than 35,000,000 copies were distributed to military camps in this country and overseas. "The books are read until they're so dirty you can't see the print," declared one soldier. "To heave one in the garbage can would be tantamount to striking your grandmother." (The first book this author ever owned—other than the Bible his mother gave him—was one of these Armed Services Editions: a battered copy of Caldwell's *God's Little Acre*.)

Erskine had been urging both DS&P and Lieber to arrange inexpensive reprints of his work. There was an untapped audience that would welcome his out-of-print books, he assured Lieber. "We are all most interested to hear you express your ideas about cheap edition business and the future of books," Sloan soothed Erskine. "Every few days we make one sort or another of good effort in the direction of Caldwell cheap editions. We'll try to make it every day from now on."

His persistence finally nudged the publisher into action; the firm signed several contracts with houses between 1943 and 1945— with Random House, Avon Books, Pocket Books, Garden City Publishing Company, World Publishing Company, and Grosset and Dunlap—but sales of reprinted editions of *Tobacco Road, God's Little Acre,* and *Journeyman* were at first disappointingly light. It took *Trouble in July*, under the direction of Victor Weybright and Kurt Enoch at Penguin Books, to initiate successful paperback ventures for Caldwell. Following de Graf's idea of a striking cover, they engaged painter Robert Jonas to design one that would ensnare readers. A fiery orange-red sunset revealed a man hanging from the branch of a tree with a second rope leading from the victim's neck to a courthouse on the left side of the cover. Another innovation that Weybright and Enoch worked out with Fawcett Publications, a magazine distributor, was the "Spin-It" rack; this was a revolving four-sided tier of shelves that saved wall space.

The sparkling cover of *Trouble in July*, inexpensive price, and a rack that one could twirl proved irresistible to browsers. Within the short span of six weeks, 350,000 copies of the book were sold. It was a bonanza that exceeded expectations, and called for an immediate follow-up. Weybright and Enoch chose *God's Little Acre* and were instantly compensated; within a year of its Spring 1946 release, a million copies were sold. Caldwell flew in from Arizona to attend the New York celebration hosted by Penguin, and he was back six months later when the two-million mark was achieved. *God's Little Acre* was Penguin's best-selling item, and over a five-year period nearly six million copies were purchased.

Part of the credit for the success of both Caldwell books in the series belonged to Robert Jonas. His arresting covers and the fast method of distribution made an unbeatable combination. Jonas's design for the *Tobacco Road* edition was a weathered wood fence with a peephole revealing a sharecropper's cabin in a landscape of stunted pine, discarded automobiles, and cotton-depleted soil. This hole-in-a-fence presentation was imitated by artists throughout the late forties: dozens of designers would be influenced by that front cover.

There was trouble in the book-selling paradise that Penguin had created. British top executive Allen Lane and the American branch, run by Weybright and Enoch, were at odds over cover illustrations and marketing. Lane felt that Caldwell's books were blemishing Penguin's conservative and respectable image; he was convinced the editions were too racy for the firm. When Lane suggested that Weybright and Enoch should "have a pornographic imprint detached from Penguin—perhaps 'Porno Books'—for such material," Weybright was livid. He admired Caldwell's work, and being a Southerner understood the author's intent and considered him a close friend. Finally, it was agreed that Penguin and the American branch sever relations, and in 1948, Weybright and Enoch renamed their venture the New American Library of World Literature—NAL. With Caldwell as their top-selling writer, they were instantly transformed into one of the giants of paperback publishing.

Caldwell often complained that his royalties of 1 1/2 cents per paperback were embarrassingly meager; Lieber and Weybright were told this repeatedly, and so were the editors at DS&P. His earnings,

however, exceeding any other author in the paperback industry—
for every million books sold, Erskine realized about $15,000. In
1948, his share was $33,000, and the following year total royalties
exceeded $95,000.

Yet there was a downside to his success: inferior novels such as
*Journeyman* and *Tragic Ground* had blockbuster sales, and this
lowered his standards of excellence in producing new work; he was
fast becoming a hack for the sake of royalties. Erskine scheduled
his writing hours much like a weary office worker, placed himself
on robot while developing his Southern cyclorama of novels, and
every time he completed one after nine or ten months, he would
reward himself with several weeks of travel, book signings and
appearances to boost sales for NAL. The lackluster *A House in the
Uplands* followed *Tragic Ground*, and the four concluding novels
in the series (one each year) were *The Sure Hand of God*, *This
Very Earth*, *Place Called Estherville*, and *Episode in Palmetto*. He
saw his cyclorama as a merging of life and visions—not as single
themes but a progression: "I was just picking out various phases of
Southern life to write about as exemplified by the small-town politicians, the schoolteachers, the boardinghouse keepers, by a colored
brother and sister in one of those little Southern towns."

There were other distractions for Caldwell as he fretted over radio
station affairs. The NAL publicity department kept asking him to
make guest appearances in cities around the country and to attend
book signings—he never turned down a request and had promotional ideas of his own. Could the Fawcett Distributing Company get
him to sign a few copies of *God's Little Acre* in Arkansas?—maybe with an inscription of "for the best wholesaler in Little Rock."
Would he pose with a dog for a Calvert Whiskey advertisement as
a "Man of Distinction?" Caldwell accepted the request with pleasure and was paid three hundred dollars and a case of Calvert. He
also autographed his paperbacks in small-town drugstores, gave
short promotional speeches for NAL and Fawcett, attended cocktail
parties, and posed for publicity shots. "From my own experience,"
wrote a manager of book sales, "I can tell you that no other author

is as well known or has met, personally, the many wholesale distributors you have. This is most beneficial to our cause."

Caldwell's novels and short stories continued to increase in popularity overseas, particularly in England, and translations of his work were available in most European countries, the Far East, India, Turkey, and South America. One aspect of foreign publication that exasperated him was the pirating of editions, and to combat this he took regular trips abroad after the war in order to expose these literary thieves and to collect accumulated royalties. Frequently his earnings could not be taken out of a country, and his only option was to go there and spend the funds. Caldwell didn't tarry longer than two or three days in most locations. He attended hurried conferences with distributors, autographed books, and engaged in translated radio interviews. During these brief stays, he lived lavishly in the best hotels and ordered the most expensive entrées on the menus—he hated to think of his money wasting in editorial offices and banks.

The new manuscript was proving to be a joyless task, and when *A House in the Uplands* appeared in DS&P's 1946 spring list of books, the evaluation of his new segment of the cyclorama depicting life in the South was far from encouraging. Though several authors who had been assisted by blurbs from Caldwell offered flattering reviews, harsh negative responses found their way in a variety of journals and newspapers.

This novel centers on the decay of Southern gentry. The protagonist, Grady Dunbar, a man in his thirties and the last of a line of "big house" whites, has the handicap of being overly fond of hard liquor and gambling. The Dunbar mansion, now in decline on what was once a flourishing plantation, is dominated by Grady's bigoted and overbearing mother, Elsie. Added to this domestic mix is Lucyanne, Dunbar's wife; a young, beautiful girl who needs love and understanding but is neglected cruelly by her husband—Grady prefers Sallie, a "high-yaller" who lives in the Negro quarter.

Dunbar goes on a three-day bender, loses $50,000—which he

doesn't have—at Skeeter Wilhite's gambling den, browbeats his plantation overseer, and is abusive to Lucyanne. After finding Grady and Sallie together, the young wife runs heedlessly into the night until, exhausted, she falls in a field and is rescued by a young poor white, who later visits her in an off-the-balcony bedroom.

Finally, Skeeter Wilhite shoots Grady when he refuses to settle his gambling debt, and as one disgruntled reviewer of the book concluded: "the reader can't feel even a perfunctory regret."

Paul Crome came out swinging in his *Dallas Morning News* review of *A House in the Uplands*: "This novel is some kind of event in American letters. It is the first time a writer of talent has ever managed a worse book about the South than *Uncle Tom's Cabin*." The *Hartford Times* agreed with Crome: "It seems incredible that the man who wrote 'Tobacco Road' and 'God's Little Acre' could have concocted this inordinately bad novel."

This reaction was amplified by Maxine Baxter in the *Cincinnati Enquirer*: "Personally, and without taking into consideration the vulgarity and lack of taste in this novel, I found it tiresome and stalely familiar. Caldwell's oft repeated premise that the Southern white male of the upper classes is a degenerate drunken lecher who delights in romping with the colored girls on his plantation, becomes boring after reading it in every one of his books."

Some critics decided that Caldwell's new novel needed no more "than a few strokes of emotional shorthand" to portray for the informed reader the charming Grady as he makes life hell for the lovely Lucyanne. "Grady may be charming," wrote Sterling North in *The Washington Post*, "but the author has failed to show him in any role except that of Simon Legree." "It is a book you can put down, period," wrote Charles Lee in the *Brooklyn Daily Eagle*. "Rarely—indeed almost never—in the history of American literature has so much talent squandered itself to so little effect. It is almost impossible to write a novel of violence, Negroes, sex, gunplay, and Southern aristocratic decay, and at the same time be dull, but Mr. Caldwell has at last succeeded in this difficult task."

The paperback editions of Caldwell's novels, which were selling briskly in bookstores and small shops across America, got an additional publicity lift in February 1946 when *Tragic Ground* was declared obscene by the Attorney-General's Department in Toronto. William Collins Sons, one of Canada's oldest book publishers, had been distributing a hardcover version of *Tragic* for nearly two years before the book was deemed unfit. "It was done," explained attorney Leslie Blackwell, "to curb the flood of obscene and salacious books and magazines which has become a pressing problem in this country." Caldwell was always an easy target for such proceedings, and most Canadian booksellers felt the move was a copycat decision based on an earlier banning of *Tragic Ground* in Boston.

St. Paul, Minnesota was next in generating a scramble to acquire NAL's twenty-five-cent edition of Ty Ty Walden's gold-digging antics on his Georgia farm. Frank Mondike, chief of police for the department's morals squad, obtained a copy of *God's Little Acre* and asked patrolman Don Wallace to read and review it. Wallace, who had no literary background or leanings, underlined in pencil the passages objectionable to him and declared the work "immoral, obscene and lewd." Immediately, the American Civil Liberties Union offered to defend the book, and an editorial in the *St. Paul Dispatch* carped that an "up-to-date city" was "sticking its neck out" when it bans "a work by an established author a dozen years after the original publication date." Later, when the book had been cleared, the former ban was a bonanza for booksellers in neighboring Minneapolis—they couldn't keep copies on their shelves.

"After 16 years of being harassed by censors, I am sorry that I ever wrote or heard of *God's Little Acre*," said Caldwell in a 1949 *Publishers' Weekly* interview. Personally bitter he was not, nor did he feel any animosity toward the judges who must do their jobs. But censorship in cases where obscenity is not clearly evident was a threat to freedom of the press. "A really objectionable book," declared Caldwell, "rarely survives. It feeds on itself—just as magazines which appeal to offensive sensationalism rarely last—and is inevitably consumed by its own salaciousness."

For all the ballyhoo generated by his notoriety and the accusations of pornography in the courts, he was surprisingly uncertain and uncomfortable in rendering sexual scenes in his fiction. Semon Dye in *Journeyman* and Will Thompson in *God's Little Acre* were "sexier" than Darling Jill or luscious Griselda. Caldwell understood exploitation: the woman was there to be chased and the man pursued her because she was desirable. But the propelling force was grounded to burlesque engagement—there were no emotional complications or subtleties.

Why Philadelphia should attempt to ban a book cleared in Boston puzzled him. His only explanation was that regionalism prevented the country from having common standards of interpretation. Potshots had been taken from all directions, but none of his books had been publicly charged in the South—only Southern librarians acted as official judges. *Tobacco Road*, as a play, had difficulties in both Atlanta and New York—but visual presentations were analyzed in a different manner.

When a book was impounded by local authorities, Caldwell felt this required public involvement. Bookselling was a service, not a money-making business with profit the main objective. When a civil functionary declared a literary work indecent, a representative group—lawyers, doctors, churchmen, educators—should form a panel to consider the objectionable item before it was brought into court. A cross section of prevailing standards would be less arbitrary.

If a character in one of his stories acted or talked in a certain way, Caldwell was being faithful to his creation, and when a censor came along and said: "You can't print that," officialdom would be destroying his fictional character. Any piece of trash, like X-rated movies, dodged the courts by claiming freedom of speech, the First Amendment. But pornography written under the guise of literature had always been less defined. He believed there should be stoplights, some control, though the legal and moral aspects perplexed him.

There were signals—red, yellow and green: "You don't go up to a yellow traffic signal and barrel through it, do you?" asked Caldwell. "If you do, you're nuts, crazy." He realized that there was a crowd of quick-change authors who wrote for the dollar, but they were practicing a con game—literary burglars. "I always have considered myself to be my own censor," he insisted, "and I am just as qualified as anybody else. I think I have been, and still stay with that theory, that I'm a good censor."

Caldwell now began claiming that he was "a writer not a reader" and this statement would be repeated over the years in many of his speeches, appearances before college classes, and interviews. Although he had read widely when reviewing books, and the claim was partly a Caldwellian exaggeration, he indeed seemed to have little interest in what was current with his contemporaries after World War II. When his editors asked him to provide a blurb for a fellow writer, Erskine would leaf through the work quickly and come up with some tongue-in-cheek flattery. He rarely unfolded a newspaper, and the only book he took on a two-month's stay in Europe was his dictionary which he perused as a minister does the Bible when preparing a sermon.

In response to an assertion that critics often associated his fiction with that of William Faulkner, Caldwell was unable to further the analogy. He had read only one of the author's books—*As I Lay Dying*—and thought it "a very fine exercise in writing." This reading, however, was only to see what Faulkner was doing. Perhaps he and the Mississippian were "dealing with the same kind of people," although it was beyond him to hazard literary comparisons. He and Faulkner had met only twice—in France and New York. They said little, and the single recall Erskine had was a brief conversation on the "difficulty of talking to anyone in a foreign language when a person has the use of only his native language."

(Helen Caldwell Cushman once claimed that Caldwell didn't have the vocabulary to read writers such as W. Somerset Maugham and Aldous Huxley. But in a letter to author Guy Owen, she wrote of her first husband's partiality for D. H. Lawrence: "I do know that

Erskine read with enthusiasm *St. Mawr* in 1925, and that he gave it to me. That winter we also read *Fantasia of the Unconscious*, *Women in Love*, and *Aaron's Rod*. The next year we read and discussed two plays, *Touch and Go* and *David*. About that time, too, we read *Kangaroo, Sea and Sardinia*, and *Tortoises*....I know, too, that Erskine read *England, My England*. Sometime later, perhaps in 1927, we did read *Plumed Serpent*. Yes, we did read some of the short stories.")

His comfortable insularity during the Tucson years, sustained by the Old Pueblo Country Club dinners and poker games at the Tucson Press Club after his scheduled hours at the writing table, didn't dull his commentary on politics and conditions in his native South. While vacationing with June in Miami, prior to a trip to South America, Caldwell warned Milt Sosin of the *Miami Daily News* that a reborn Ku Klux Klan could sweep the country if not stopped in time. "There is no basic difference between the people of the various sections of the country, just as there is no difference in the peoples of the various European nations. In troubled times," he told Sosin, "nations will seek a leader. Thus a klan or any similar organization can take advantages of the fear of the people."

In Buenos Aires, Caldwell predicted another financial depression, partly because of the coming obsolescence of cotton as synthetic yarn takes its place, which forces cotton growers to find alternative means of livelihood. When questioned on the motive behind his writing, he told a reporter from the *Buenos Aires Herald* that it was "the economic and social study of people"—this structured his present cyclorama of novels.

Caldwell believed that the major impetus for every writer was an economic one. "You know you have to make a living," he shared with an interviewer. "It's like digging ditches or anything else....It's the only job I've got, and I have to work at it full time just like a doctor or a lawyer." Both Lieber and Al Manuel hoped one of the books in the series could be scripted for a film or the stage; Caldwell optimistically shaped the novels with adaptations in mind. Yet he sometimes regretted his contract with DS&P—the production of five novels—would the task ever be completed!

Waybright and Enoch urged Erskine to expedite his novels; the books were skyrocketing off the sales chart, and there always was need for another Caldwell production. The marketing buzzword at NAL now was "sex sells." An elaborate and dignified Robert Jonas cover was a thing of the past: a book sold better if it had a woman showing plenty of leg and being fondled by a grinning cotton planter or horny merchant. The blurb on the cover of *This Very Earth* had as a come-on: "I'll talk as I damn well please to high-yellow wenches. Now strip off to your skin and quit answering me back." *The Sure Hand of God* front cover displayed a blonde in a flimsy dress; she is sprawled at the feet of several scowling men. The crotch of one man is positioned directly over the woman's head while another lecher is unbuttoning his fly—this cover was hot enough to sell 1,400,000 copies in its first year of print.

Sex, violence, comedy bordering vulgar burlesque, and melodrama became the magic mix for the five novels concocted during the mid to late 1940s. Another essential was length, and this was important for the packaging; the books were designed to fit snugly in the "Spin-It" rack at the local drugstore. The longest novel of the five was *This Very Earth* which ran 254 pages, and the shortest was *A House In the Uplands* at 238 pages.

The public obviously gave no credence to what critics were saying—the novels were selling by the millions. Victor Weybright, the editors at DS&P, even Lieber, were dripping with praise for their money-making trotter in this horse race of words. "I can only repeat that there is only one Caldwell," wrote Pearce, "and that he seems to get better all the time." Lieber declared that *The Sure Hand of God* had "the perfection of a Bach Fugue," and Weybright proclaimed: "We rise to cheer! It's wonderful to know that the old maestro has delivered another great book in the series of novels."

Caldwell's first trip to Europe after World War II was in the early summer of 1947—he had just completed *The Sure Hand of God* and could reward himself with travel. The purpose of the visit was not only to become better acquainted with editors and translators of his books, but also to collect royalties from publishers who had issued unauthorized editions. The business part of the tour was a success for Erskine, but there were difficulties. June accompanied him and was homesick—she seemed indifferent to her surroundings. In Italy, according to Caldwell, when not expressing a desire to return to Tucson, she spent her time in long conversations with English-speaking porters and bellhops.

Molly Bowser, Caldwell's over-the-hill trollop of *The Sure Hand of God* has just been made a widow. Putt, her elderly husband of two years, has been killed by a streamlined train. Molly is grief-stricken. She comes home from the funeral, wiggles out of her girdle—with the help of her seventeen-year-old daughter, Lilly—rips off her brassiere and slings it across the room, and then, crushing some of the funeral chrysanthemums to her ample breasts, sits down to have an honest-to-God cry. Molly had been ready to enjoy life with old Putt and now she is on her own again; the house is a morgue without a man in it; baked beans and red wine lose their flavor; and the "vitamin" injections she gives herself no longer provide a titillating bounce.

Now, with Putt dead, widowed at 35 and "big as a ginhouse roof," Molly must marry off her daughter before calamities befall them. Then complications arise: Putt's brother, Jethro, arrives from a faraway country to settle the estate and is surprised to find that the only asset is a wheelbarrow. Jethro looks Molly up and down, even sideways, with a practiced eye and is anxious to give this "widow-woman a special helping hand and comfort." But Molly takes one look at the slack seat of Jethro's trousers and decides his southerly exposure is too scant. When Putt's brother makes something more serious than sheep's eyes at Lilly, Molly lambastes the lecher with a kitchen chair.

The two Bowsers, mother and daughter, might have achieved respectability if the churchgoers in town weren't so disapproving. Lucy Trotter, teacher of the women's Bible class, often warns Molly that the sure hand of God will eventually lead her to the bad end she deserves.

Erskine's firm stand for racial justice and his sympathetic handling of the minority characters in his fiction did little to budge black novelist James Baldwin—he headlined his review in New York's *The New Leader* as the "Dead Hand of Caldwell," and began his blistering review by pointing out that *The Sure Hand of God* was the author's twenty-third published volume. The book was "almost impossible to review" because it was "almost impossible to take seriously." Baldwin wondered why *Sure Hand* was written: "Certainly there is nothing in the book which would not justify the suspicion that Mr. Caldwell was concerned with nothing more momentous than getting rid of some of the paper he had lying about the house." Baldwin elaborated further his "Dead Hand" banner at the conclusion of the review: "His career is almost a study in the slow conquest of immobility. Unless we hear from him again in accents more individual we can leave his bones for that literary historian of another day who may perhaps define and isolate that virus so deadly to the growth of our literature in general and our writers in particular."

Not all reviewers had Baldwin's negativity. Dudley Jenkins, in the *Philadelphia Evening Bulletin*, told his readers: "It's always an event when Erskine Caldwell marches out a new batch of his motley and unorthodox characters, and in 'The Sure Hand of God' he lives up to his past efforts in that respect." Robert Martin of the Waco, Texas *Times Herald* felt the author had returned to his earlier vein: a book resembling *Tobacco Road* and *God's Little Acre* in theme and characterization. The characters in *Sure Hand* "are real and vital, strangely enough, for they are extremely weak people. In *A House in the Uplands* they were silly and unbelievable."

Caldwell returned to Georgia for a brief visit in the middle of June of 1948 after being awarded the "keys of the city" in New Orleans. June and young son, Jay, had remained in Tucson while he got reacquainted with Wrens and Tobacco Road. "There has been some economic progress," replied Caldwell when asked if he had seen changes since his last visit in 1940, "but socially and politically the South has, if anything, retrogressed. In the back country, you see the same undernourished kids, the same diseased old folks who have always been there."

He had accepted an invitation to appear at the Kansas Writers' Conference held on the state university campus at Lawrence, but Roscoe Fawcett and Edward Lewis, field representatives for NAL, asked him to first visit Kansas City and help promote their reprinted books in an unusual publicity stunt that got national coverage— Erskine spent time in one of the large Katz drugstores autographing copies of NAL's twenty-five-cent editions. He signed books for more than four hours, chatted pleasantly with employees and customers, and winked at several grubby children who were staring at him in open-mouthed amazement. Twice, the supply of books had to be replenished, while reporters and photographers huddled with Caldwell at the soda fountain.

Margaret Young, literary editor at the Kansas *Beaumont Enterprise*, wrote that the staff of the writers' conference was "conspicuously absent" when Erskine rose to give a lecture on Russia. Later, Caldwell asked fellow conferee Walter Van Tilburg Clark what was wrong. "The Kansas City newspapers are widely read here," replied Van Tilburg Clark. One professor felt the drugstore appearance was an "undignified publicity stunt" and another said it was "disgraceful and shameful" to be signing twenty-five-cent paperbacks.

Erskine was not alone in riling reviewers and stirring controversy—June was criticized locally when she contributed a twenty-four-page chapter on Tucson for an anthology called *Rocky Mountain Cities*. With the arrival of the Southern Pacific railroad, the city was no longer the hub that it had been in happier days. "Thereafter Tucson became, not a center of trade, but a town through which the train passed en route from El Paso to Los Angeles." Members of the Old Pueblo Country Club chided Caldwell for his wife's contribution to the book, which was not her first venture into print—two of her short stories had previously appeared in national magazines.

The DS&P edition of *This Very Earth* was published on August 22, 1948, and some critics were quick to growl at Caldwell's latest offering. The story was described in *Time* as "a scrawny literary turkey."

Chism Crockett, a widower who likes corn liquor, possum hunting, and an occasional woman, sells the farm and moves his father, three grown daughters, and an eleven-year-old son to a slum section of a nearby town—he is sick of grubbing a livelihood off the farm which had been in the family for several generations. With no job, Crockett mooches off an elder son—who practices law in a small way—and promiscuous daughter Vickie who finds work as a waitress in a cheap restaurant. Daughter Dorisse marries a drunken swine named Nobby Hair, and he soon sends his adoring wife streetwalking so she can support his drinking and gambling habits. Daughter Jane, a pretty high school girl, is nearly raped by this drunken Nobby, but Grandpa Crockett comes to her rescue with a flourishing cane. Chism takes his young son, Jarvis, on a possum outing and forces the contents of half a quart of corn moonshine down the boy's throat to give him a taste of manhood. Later, father and son sneak down to the railroad yards to "have fun" with two mulatto girls. Subsequently, Jane is fondled by her father, but two passersby foil the incestuous woodshed molestation. Towards the end, Nobby Hair smashes his wife's skull with a flatiron when she threatens to leave him, and the murder of his granddaughter causes Grandpa Crockett to have a fatal heart attack. "It looks like the only thing on the topside of the world I want to do is hunt possums," Chism defends himself. "I can't help it if I like a simple thing of life the best of all. I'd rather be proud of what I am than ashamed of what I'm not."

Nelson Algren in the *Chicago Sun & Times* was one of the reviewers who felt the book was sounder than *Tragic Ground* because it pointed up more sharply, and without a loss of humor, the forces of bigotry rising from poverty. "Chism's native cunning," wrote Algren, "is well-matched by that of Daniel Boone Blalock, a congressman intent on defending southern womanhood in his own strange fashion. When he and Chism do a bit of horse-trading over Vickie we have the sort of cracker barrel humor, shadowed by pathos, that no one but Caldwell does so well."

"Erskine Caldwell's latest novel," wrote Lon Tinkle in the *Saturday Review of Literature*, "sharply arrests the distressing nose dive taken by his talent in the two preceding novels, 'A House in the Uplands' and 'The Sure Hand of God.' Chism Crockett and family are powerful Caldwell creations." But Tinkle also observed that the book had shortcomings. "It will prompt instinctive admiration from any but the intellectual snobs, who ought to admit that as a craftsman Caldwell perfectly frames the exact picture he wants to paint. But what he paints is not 'this very earth'; it is the world of Erskine Caldwell. And that world is becoming increasingly artificial instead of deeply felt."

Joseph Henry Jackson of the *San Francisco Chronicle* called *This Very Earth* "a pretty dreary, grim business. The book might come to something if it were developed a bit more. But as it is, it isn't good enough—not for me, at any rate, nor, I suspect, for other readers who prefer a novel to be reasonably three dimensional."

Neil M. Compton in the *Montreal Gazette* mauled Erskine further by pointing out that "there have been too many signs that Caldwell had found a commercially profitable formula that will guarantee a wide audience without the necessity of attempting anything more ambitious than a series of vaguely salacious episodes loosely connected to form what purports to be a plot." And the *Gazette's* rival newspaper, the *Montreal Star*, concluded its review with this admonishment: "Why a man who is admittedly an able writer should continue to prostitute his talents by exploring such repulsive fields of human disintegration, he alone knows."

Caldwell at a book signing, surrounded by pocket reprints of his earlier editions and a stack of *This Very Earth*, reacted with some bitterness to what his critics were saying: "During my first few years as a writer," he said, "99 out of 100 reviews were favorable—but no one bought my books. In my second decade, 99 out of 100 reviews are unfavorable, but everyone reads my books."

Esther Henderson of *The Magazine Tucson* wrote a portrait article about Caldwell around publication time of *This Very Earth*. Henderson was surprised to find the man who could be so brutally realistic in his fiction to be a pronouncedly reserved, soft-spoken and mild-mannered individual. "Actually taller than average," wrote the columnist, "Mr. Caldwell's stocky build creates an illusion of shortness. His graying hair and craggy features are emphasized by a healthy tan that belies the long daylight hours spent at his desk. When he smiles, he does a good job of it, his face crinkles into innumerable 'laugh lines' and his eyes really sparkle." Henderson concluded her article with a description of Caldwell's desert home and family: "The rambling ranch home in the El Encanto Estates, in a setting of peace and tranquility, form a perfect background for his quiet mode of life and reserved demeanor. In addition to Mr. and Mrs. Caldwell and their three-year-old-son, Jay, members of the household include his mother, Mrs. I. S. Caldwell, a son by a former marriage, Erskine II, now a student at the University of Arizona, and Eloise, the cook. And there's Crackerjack,—'Crackers' to his intimates—a four year half collie, half police dog import from Los Angeles."

On the day that *This Very Earth* was published by DS&P, three of Caldwell's novels, *God's Little Acre, Tragic Ground,* and *Journeyman*, were taken from a Portland, Maine bookstore by Police Inspector Leon T. Webber after a citizen complained that "salacious reading material" was on sale. This banning got wide coverage when City Manager Lyman S. Moore ordered the books returned to the shop five hours later. "It is not proper of the police and city government to censor adult literature," declared Moore. The decision delighted Portland booksellers, including Francis J. O'Brien who was later to sell books in the same shop that Helen and Erskine had rented in 1929. "The City of Portland couldn't do anything about it," O'Brien told this author. "The police were disgusted with Moore and red-faced when they had to take the novels back. But it would have been more interesting to see someone go to court."

Nine days later, a group of 146 clergymen from 28 states protested the Philadelphia police's seizure of more than 2,000 books earlier that year. They termed the action "police censorship." William Faulkner, James T. Farrell, and Harold Robbins were among several who were charged with having authored "blasphemous and indecent books"—Caldwell's *God's Little Acre*, dependable in riling obscenity hunters, was pulled from the shelves with the others. A Protestant committee of sixteen clergymen had been behind this effort to ban "not only filthy and anti-American literature but blasphemous books." Reverend Donald Harrington of the Workers' Defense League declared the seizures were largely inspired by church groups that had no right "to impose their private views and standards of good taste and morality." Six months later, Common Plea Judge Curtis Bok ruled the books be returned to shop proprietors. "Obscenity," explained Bok, was "sexual impurity, and pornography is dirt for dirt's sake."

Denver was next on the banning list of cities out to get *God's Little Acre*. Captain John F. O'Donnell, head of the Police Morals Bureau, directed book distributors to withhold the pocket-sized edition of Caldwell's best-seller from newspaper stands and drugstores. No action was taken against the hardcovers, and the move to suppress paperback copies was, explained O'Donnell, "to keep it out of the hands of teen-agers." As a consequence, Denverites eagerly bought the more expensive edition, and Caldwell's Colorado royalties soared.

Attorney General Francis E. Kelly sought court authority to keep *God's Little Acre* off Massachusetts newsstands, and Caldwell flew to Boston in March 1949 to testify as a witness for Robert W. Meserve who was defending the book. Despite government objection, Erskine was allowed to testify as an expert on living conditions in the South. Under cross-examination, he stated that "so far it has seemed most readers of the book have been those seeking sensation, but some day I hope those for and of whom this story is written will have an opportunity to read it."

Though cleared by Boston Judge Charles Fairhurst, that decision was overturned a year later by the Supreme Judicial Court when *God's Little Acre* was charged with being "obscene, indecent, and impure." At a news conference in 1962, years after the Massachusetts banning, Caldwell was asked if the ruling had angered him. "No," he said, "but I think it's time for this democracy to decide about literary censorship." Then he added: "I could not write some of the books being written today. I'm a little old-fashioned that way." And what did he think of Henry Miller's *Tropic of Cancer* and *The Carpetbaggers* by Harold Robbins? "Don't know," he responded. "Haven't read them. I don't read other people's books. I'm too busy with my own." Later in the conference, Caldwell noted that while many of his novels and short stories were popular in Russia, *God's Little Acre* had never been published there. Then returning to the original question, he reflected, "If that book were to go to trial today, I would imagine that it would be quickly exonerated. There is nothing obscene in this book. I act as my own censor and I prohibit in my fiction, to the best of my ability, the misuse of the English language and the craft of storytelling."

Sensitive about his reputation as the author of indecent literature, Caldwell would point out that his books had been less in court than generally supposed. On a stopover in the nation's capital after testifying at the Boston trial, he told *The Washington Evening Star* reporter Mary McGory: "I write with as much decorum and restraint as people who are guided by the customs and mores of civilization behave in their everyday lives. The letters I get are from the people who milk cows and pick cotton. They don't feel that I'm laughing at them or that the books are pornographic. They thank me for writing about them with sympathy and understanding."

Caldwell's next cyclorama offering, *Place Called Estherville,* was published by DS&P on September 7, 1949, and Erskine was in New York at the time of publication for a radio appearance and several autograph sessions. Advertising for the book included full pages in the Sunday literary sections of major newspapers which prompted brisk sales.

Reviewers were not enamored with this new tale—"without a plot" it was appraised—and several critics thought this eleventh novel was a slender book containing a slender story. The *Chicago Herald-American* opened with a typical salvo: "Ever since 'God's Little Acre,' the line of descent has been steady. Let's hope 'Estherville' is rock bottom. This story, without Caldwell's name, would never have passed a publisher's first edition."

Ganus Brazemore and his sister, Kathyanne, two mulattoes with some education, have moved to Estherville from the country. Not having acquired the defensive humility of city Negroes, they must learn the hard way about being minority members of a Southern town. Ganus is a tall, graceful young man of eighteen "with handsome fulvous coloring and closely cropped hair"; Kathyanne, too, attracts attention with her petite presence, golden complexion, and blue-black hair that doesn't curl. Estherville becomes a hellhole for these two new arrivals. Ganus is pursued by white girls—these pursuits get him fired from several jobs and beaten by malicious rednecks. His destiny soon overtakes him: he is murdered by a brutal farmer whose nymphomaniacal wife tried to seduce young Brazemore. Meanwhile, Kathyanne has her own dilemmas: employers chase her, she is gang-banged by several drunken businessmen and left pregnant. Dr. Plowden, the only decent white man in Estherville, delivers her baby, then stumbles out into the cold December night and dies of a heart attack on Kathyanne's doorstep. The young mother eventually marries a Negro admirer and she is given a hundred dollars—atonement money—by one of the rapists. The good Dr. Plowden, shortly before his death, confronted this philanthropist, possibly the father of the child, with the admonition: "We're all human beings, Will. You're going to have to learn to treat people alike, white or colored, or else there won't be any place for you one of these days. I know that you and a lot more like you think you can keep this a white man's town, but you're wrong. The world has changed, a great deal in the last generation, and it's going to change a lot more in the next generation."

The Pittsburgh *Post-Gazette* was one of the few newspapers that had kind and encouraging words for *Estherville*. "Erskine Caldwell has probably written his masterpiece. It lacks the sardonic humor of 'God's Little Acre.' But in place of that earlier, almost playful approach to human degradation, it has the pure passion of true tragedy."

David Daiches in *The New York Times* mentioned Caldwell's ability of distilling a sense of nightmare that "haunts the mind like a vision of some secret hell lying deep within all of us." But Daiches concluded that there was no such quality in this new novel. "The characters here are abstractions in a parable and the reality of their life escapes the reader."

In a letter to the editor, subscriber Peter Harris expressed displeasure with Charles Dameron who reviewed *Place Called Estherville* for the Dallas Texas *Times-Herald*:

> Mr. Caldwell's books have exceeded all book sales with the one exception of the Bible, for just one reason. Mr. Caldwell's succeeding books continued to sell for the same reason. Last week a drugstore on Jefferson Ave. stocked 100 copies of his latest book, and there were just 13 copies left one week later. Imagine a book that outsold the national weeklies on the newsstand! Also, in restocking the shelf, the publisher showed his continued faith in Caldwell when he stocked in dozens of new copies of all the other books, all the way back to "God's Little Acre." Why, indeed should Mr. Dameron suggest that Mr. Caldwell would have a book "we" would like better if he cleaned it up a little? Have you really and truly reached the distinction of reviewing his work without comprehending this momentous phenomenon? You are arguing the theory of the long hair, while Mr. Caldwell is selling books and making a living. Do you stop to think that the thing you would take out is the thing which makes any lame title sell like popcorn at the movies so long as it has Caldwell printed somewhere on it? If you did, you certainly wouldn't blame the author.

"Hatchet work" was what Caldwell's editors called the blows his novels were undergoing from critics. "The reviewers seemed to be swinging their tomahawks in your direction," Pearce at DS&P admitted—"the book sellers and public don't seem to agree with the reviewers anymore than I do." There was room for optimism in spite of all the literary hectoring—by 1950, American readers had purchased more than 22 million paperback copies of his fiction. But Erskine was sensitive to adverse criticism and easily injured. In the early days, when his cyclorama of novels was first being condemned, he felt a certain relish at lashing back. Caldwell now realized the futility of such reciprocation and tried to ignore his assailants.

He was under heavy fire when the last novel of the Southern series, *Episode in Palmetto*, was published in 1950. Many of his detractors felt the book had an overdose of superficial psychological commentary on small-town life. The plot, constructed within a time frame of two weeks, centers on the mores of random lusts concealed by unhappy husbands and gossipy wives who use sex as their weapon. Into this muddle steps a young, sexually attractive schoolteacher, Vernona Stevens, and she becomes the focal point of jealousy and violence. Schoolgirl Pearline Gough falls in love with the "well-stacked" schoolmarm, and when repulsed attempts to destroy her teacher. During the heated fortnight, Vernona runs afoul of a variety of males. 10th-grader Floyd Neighbors, a football hero, has an enormous crush and sneaks into Miss Stevens's bedroom at Blanch Neff's boardinghouse. But Floyd is unable to learn the complicated rules of deviousness and hypocrisy which make seduction possible in the grownup world; as a consequence he kills himself. Next is Jack Cash, Palmetto's Mortimer Snerd character and the town's one-pump filling-station attendant—he is known to have a weakness for pretty marms with blackboard erasers; Jack calls upon her and soon finds himself more involved than expected when the teacher teasingly offers to sleep with him. Along comes Thurston Mustard to intensify the drama—he's a county agent eager to earn a trip to Chicago by persuading some farmer in the area to raise millet—Thurston is also wanting to plant a crop of human seed. Next is Em Gee Sheddwood, the farmer who worked his first wife to death and now needs a replacement. Other characters in the

cast are Reverend John Boykin Couchmanly; Cato Pharo, the mail
carrier; and Milo Clauson, the principal who reprimands Vernona
for wearing a tight yellow sweater yet flirts and makes passes. But
Mrs. Clauson has seen her husband on the prowl before, and when
she finds out that he is interested in the young teacher, the deceived wife raises her special, furious brand of hell.

Critical response to *Episode in Palmetto* closed his hope of
furthering the range of the cyclorama. After a two-month holiday
between books, he began writing *Call It Experience*.

"The purpose of this volume," wrote Caldwell in the preface, "is
to set forth some of the experiences of an author which may be of
interest to curious readers and would-be writers who seek visions
of the wonderland in which all authors are believed to exist." It
wasn't his intention to detail all the happenings in his life, he explained. "What is to be found here is less a personal history than
it is an informal recollection of authorship."

Though labeled autobiography, *Call It Experience* at times bor-
dered fiction: Caldwell had little patience for meticulousness if it
impeded his eloquence in a passage. The struggle of becoming a
successful writer during those Mount Vernon years, his experiences
as a newsman for the *Atlanta Journal*, and the close relationship he
had with his father were straightforward and moving accounts. The
fiction crept in as it did in his second autobiography, *With All My
Might*, whenever he felt an incident needed to be enhanced theatri-
cally: then a paragraph or several pages would take on the sem-
blance of a story.

There were omissions in *Experience* which baffled readers who
had knowledge of Caldwell's life. Helen, June, and his four children were never mentioned, and while he did include Bourke-White
and their *You Have Seen Their Faces* collaboration, he neglected
to tell his readers that he and Margaret were married. Curiously,
Helen appears and reappears in nearly a hundred pages of the last
autobiography, and this book of Caldwell's was published after her
death. There are readers who wonder if some of these later Mount

Vernon recollections of Helen and the children had been written at the time of *Call It Experience* and were set aside.

*Experience* was the last book that Maxim Lieber worked on as Caldwell's literary agent. In 1951, Lieber gave up his office and moved to Mexico. Though he had been ailing for several years, and a second heart attack was his reason for giving up the business, his political position was another factor in seeking a sanctuary outside the country. In the Alger Hiss trial of 1949, Lieber was called "a secret Communist spy" by Whittaker Chambers who was a witness for the prosecution.

Both DS&P and the NAL were glad to see Lieber out of Caldwell's life. The agency was in shambles, and most of the authors connected with it had found new agents. Caldwell's publishers had felt uneasy about Lieber since the mid-1940s, and the worry was one of association: a politically suspect bedfellow could seriously damage their best-selling author's reputation. Weybright and Pearce had more than once hinted that Erskine would be better served with a different literary representative but he resisted. Lieber had worked hard for him in the past twenty years, and they shared a friendship.

Generally disregarded was Caldwell's record of affiliation with leftist groups. He had tainted himself somewhat in 1947 by serving as cochairman with Joseph North, editor of *New Masses*, for the Progressive Writers Group, an organization that defended First Amendment rights for authors. Howard Fast was among those who benefited from bail money when he was arrested and jailed for not cooperating with the House Un-American Committee. With anticommunist hysteria on the rise, Erskine began to take a low-profile position. When Lieber and Fast had asked him to add his name to an open letter in *The New York Times* backing presidential candidate Henry Wallace, Caldwell turned them down. He had also instructed Lieber not to submit a story to the new leftist outlet, *New Masses-Mainstream*, though his agent argued that this publication had many subscribers. But Caldwell was not swayed and remembered Charles Pearce's warning that appearing in that sort of magazine would be disastrous.

Lieber had irritated Weybright and Enoch when he began urging them to reprint a paperback edition of *All Night Long*. Such a move would be poor medicine for the raging anticommunist fever; it was no time to decorate "Spin-It" racks with a book lauding Russian resistance fighters. Weybright suggested the book be rewritten with a Korean or Greek background and let the resistance fighters be forces against a Communist regime. This idea was too repugnant and bizarre for Erskine, and he lost all interest in Lieber's endorsement of a reprint.

Weeks after Lieber's retreat to Mexico, Caldwell received a letter from his agent saying that business was being conducted as usual and the new location would not in any way be an impediment. But Erskine had grave doubts about Lieber's effectiveness, and he was thinking of severing all ties. However, in a letter to his agent's wife, who was still in New York, Caldwell confessed that he felt "lost in a world of confusion without his help and advice."

One applicant hoping to replace Lieber insisted that Caldwell change his name to a pseudonym that carried more literary significance (perhaps factual, but more likely a storyteller's fabrication), another agent wanted to be paid a fixed monthly salary instead of the usual percentage of royalties, and a third suggested that Erskine write mystery novels exclusively. The search for a responsible agent necessitated several trips between Tucson and New York. Each time he left home, Caldwell felt "increasingly deprived of June's assistance and companionship. However, try as I did, no amount of pleading would persuade her to go with me during that period."

James Oliver Brown, a youthful, educated, and aggressive man, who was conservative and matched the tempo of the time, was hired. Weybright, Enoch, and Al Manuel were delighted with the choice. "It must be a great relief," wrote Weybright, "to have someone to cope with the details as well as the promotion of your best interests, who is young, vigorous, well-connected—and unpolitical." Erskine did hear from Lieber again: months later when his former agent requested a story for an anthology. "I hope Maxim in his boredom does not attempt to build up a correspondence with you," wrote a worried Brown. "I see no reason for acknowledging this letter." With reluctance, Caldwell heeded his new agent's warning and the split became final.

Another breakup in long-established relations was occurring while Caldwell was in chase of a new literary agent. DS&P was financially on the skids and had to reduce office staff, cut salaries, and severely budget their advertising and promotional program. The difficulties came about inadvertently: the firm had relied too much on one author, Caldwell, and the hardcover sales of his books were undermined by NAL's cheap paperbacks. Book customers knew that if they waited for a few weeks, the "Spin-It" racks would be stocked with the inexpensive editions. DS&P had been more interested in raking in their large slice from reprints than trying to maintain a balanced level of sales. Grossett & Dunlap also had problems with hardcovers of Erskine's better-known novels when they marketed a series; in 1948 they sold 24,000 copies, but in 1951 sales had plummeted to less than 5,000.

Relief for DS&P came quickly when they merged with Little, Brown and Company of Boston. The move resulted when Little, Brown realized that this merger would add a number of conservative authors to their publishing list—a safe and protective cover at a time when Senator Joseph McCarthy was in search of literary leftists.

Caldwell had several meetings with Little, Brown's president, Arthur Thornhill, Sr., and James Oliver Brown attended these conferences. The two men had enjoyed a friendly business relationship in the past, and Erskine found this an encouraging sign for the publication of his future books. Both Thornhill and Brown assured him that they were determined to rekindle his flagging reputation, cover his novels with dignified wrappers, and that NAL would be obliged to allow the hardcover editions more sales before bringing out a glut of cheap paperbacks.

Caldwell's association with his new publisher had a shaky beginning. Little, Brown wanted a novel and Erskine was reluctant to produce one after five years of being mauled by disgruntled reviewers. Unfortunately, his marriage had ceased to be a haven—he and June were increasingly at odds, and he felt hurt when she refused to accompany him on business trips or holiday travels. A numbness of creativity had settled in, and he was unable to force himself to limber his pen. Instead of a new novel, he brought from storage the Mount Vernon manuscript, "Autumn Hill," and tried to peddle it as *A Lamp For Nightfall*—the very work that had caused his breaking away from Scribner's. Caldwell insisted that "Autumn Hill" and *Lamp* were different books. "The two are the only ones I can recall that I completed but never published. And they were not good enough to be published." Yet the first six chapters and the ending of "Autumn Hill" are the same as those in *A Lamp for Nightfall*, and the names of the characters and their circumstances are identical. Over the years, this novel with a Maine setting had been turned down by Simon and Schuster; Viking; Harcourt, Brace; and even DS&P. Caldwell now asked his new agent to submit *Lamp* for magazine serialization, and it was spurned by *Redbook, Woman's Day, Collier's, Country Gentleman, Cosmopolitan,* and *The Atlantic*. Thornhill and Weybright detested the story and were convinced that its publication would plunge Erskine's critical reputation further into the literary cellar. But Caldwell persisted and with much reluctance Little, Brown agreed to bring it out.

Thede and Rosa Emerson, descendants of stern Yankee stock, exhibit their nastiness as the tale unravels. Four chapters of the book take place in Robinson's store where the menfolk gather and complain about foreigners who run the town—those detestable Frenchmen, Swedes, and Finns are a threat. Other chapters are crowded with illicit sexual affairs, stinginess, incest, suicide, and madness. The sensitive brother and sister, Howard and Jean Emerson, are powerless in the family atmosphere to cope with a domineering father and a spiteful, unbalanced mother.

An incongruity is Jean's wedding to a French Canadian—Thede's daughter is permitted to wed a "Canuck" because if she married someone from a decadent American family, Thede would have to support them. Howard has dreams of attending an engineering school in the fall, but he needs a loan from his father. Thede tells his cronies at the store: "I'd be a solid fool taking good money out of the bank to give to the boy to spend on learning how to build roads and bridges." Besides, Thede would have to pay a hired man for doing Howard's chores. As the novel closes, the trapped son takes his own life, uneven Rosa runs off to live with another man, and an embittered Thede Emerson is left alone at Autumn Hill.

There were few reviews of *A Lamp for Nightfall*. Publications such as *Newsweek, The Nation,* and *The New Republic* had been compelled to cover his books in the thirties, but it was now the fifties and *Lamp* was ignored. David Dempsey, in the April 20, 1952 issue of *The New York Times*, called the novel "standard Caldwell" and "work that was beginning to run thin." Dempsey's complaint was that the seriousness of this offering failed because the author was "seldom convincing when he moralizes." Poet Paul Engle, in the *Chicago Sunday Tribune*, believed the book's design was all too obvious—"we are told every circumstance in the first chapter," and it "makes the novel far less a discovery than it should be." *Time* sarcastically pointed out that Caldwell "plays no regional favorites...sniffing out fictional meanness and degeneracy with the zest of a Berkshire in a barnyard."

Caldwell now induced the new publisher to bring out collections of his short stories, not new works but reprints and altered pieces from the past. Examples of such doubling can be found in *The Humorous Side of Erskine Caldwell*: The tale called "A Sack of Turnips" is a reworking of the first four chapters of *Tobacco Road*; another is "Gold Fever," the first two chapters of *God's Little Acre*; and the third is "The Doggone Douthits," a pulling together of chapters 13 and 14 of *Tragic Ground*. Two other anthology collections of Caldwellian memorabilia from Little, Brown were *The Courting of Susie Brown*, and a bloated gathering entitled *The Complete Stories of Erskine Caldwell.*

Hardcover editions of his work were fast becoming unmarketable, but three paperback publishers were successful in compiling four collections of earlier tales: *Midsummer Passion and Other Stories, A Woman in the House, Where the Girls Were Different,* and *A Swell-Looking Girl.* The garish covers and blurbs stressing Caldwell's notoriety as a "dirty writer" proved to move more of these books than did their contents—the paperback release of *A Woman in the House* had sales of 1.4 million during the first year. But such staggering numbers weren't making the author rich; royalty percentages were minimal and the paperbacks delivered a deathblow to the more lucrative hardcover editions. Word now was out—the literary community often bruises—that Caldwell's career was over. Now that he had fulfilled his ten-year prophesy of a writer's creative span, this dazzling word chaser had become a hack pornographer, and maybe a secret Communist. When Erskine's loyal friend, James Aswell, wrote a Caldwell profile for *Collier's,* the editorial board stalled and finally rejected it because they felt their readers no longer were interested.

James Oliver Brown was unable to land a Caldwell story in any of the slick literary publications. By the 1950s, the only receptive editors were those who brought out what Brown defined as "girlie magazines." *Manhunt* took three stories, and *Cavalier,* without permission, changed the title of "A Gift for Sue" to "Just a Quick One." Erskine managed to write eight new stories at this time while everything seemed to be collapsing around him, but when these halfhearted attempts were published they appeared in magazines that further damaged his image. *Dude, Playboy, Swank, Gent* were not credits he needed. When told that acceptance in these vehicles was detrimental to his career, Caldwell responded pragmatically: "I wish, selfishly perhaps," he wrote in 1951 to Brown, "to have my work published while I am alive, and don't care particularly about it when I'm dead."

Caldwell soon found himself in a financial predicament with NAL. By August 1954, he had received more than $50,000 in advances, and when he and Brown tried to negotiate a new contract,

Weybright and Enoch weren't tempted. NAL did not insist that Caldwell return the unearned royalties immediately, but no more money would come from them until the debit was paid through book sales. When Thornhill at Little, Brown attempted to act on Erskine's behalf, Weybright wouldn't budge—he regarded Caldwell as a friend and genius, but NAL wasn't the "Ford Foundation."

There were some royalties from the sale of books overseas, but when Weybright and Enoch stopped all payments to him, Caldwell was without a dependable income. Most of his earnings had been invested in Arizona radio stations and real estate, and additional money pressures would come when he and June were divorced in 1954—she got the luxurious Tucson home, thirty-nine acres of prime land, and $600 a month child support and alimony.

An unexpected rebuff jolted Caldwell when he requested passport validation for a Russian trip and was turned down. He had been invited to attend the Congress of Soviet Writers in Moscow, and such a visit would have given him access to his swelling accumulation of royalties. Someone in the State Department questioned his political sympathies, and it was known within the hierarchies of government that he had been under FBI surveillance since early 1943.

Weybright, Thornhill, and Brown were relieved when he was denied the trip. With anticommunist hysteria on the rise, his presence at a Soviet writers' conference would have impeded book sales. "Unfortunately," Weybright told him, "Communists are known to be devious and their motives very often concealed and cunning." Brown, tired of dealing with "girlie magazine" editors and anxious to halt the downward spiralling of Erskine's reputation, sent him a clipping on black singer Paul Robeson whose career had been seriously damaged by red-baiting forces. Frequently, Caldwell had disavowed any interest in left-wing politics and leftist causes, and after the passport denial he became more reluctant to accept speaking engagements at rallies sponsored by liberal organizations. "I have," he informed the State Department after their travel rejection, "no interest whatsoever in advancing the Communist cause; on the contrary I would do anything I could to hinder it."

Max Lieber recalled June Johnson as "the direct opposite" of Bourke-White, "young, pure, adoring. Caldwell was to be the complete master." The nineteen years' age difference seemed no obstacle; she was in awe of her world-famous husband and eager to be helpful in his career. He found in June what had been missing in his life with Margaret: togetherness.

June's talents as an artist and writer were useful when she energetically took on the role of helpmate in the early years of their marriage. She shared in answering the flood of letters, attended to details for new Folkway books, and gave marketing suggestions to DS&P. On her own initiative she wrote NAL recommending that the dedication "For Helen" be removed from an upcoming paperback edition of *God's Little Acre*. June also sent long letters to critics who she felt had wronged her husband or misunderstood his intentions, and when she was discomfited over the cover art of a NAL paperback she angrily corresponded with the publicity department and insisted that changes be made; the editors promised to "satisfy June 100% this time," but the First Commandment of a publisher was selling books, not mollifying the "pet peeve" of an author's wife.

Being married to Erskine Caldwell had aspects less satisfying: June endured the challenging visits of an exacting mother-in-law. Carrie grew more rigid as she aged and her fastidiousness increased—one habit was ironing money before folding it carefully in her purse. June, as previously mentioned, was frequently disregarded when household decisions were made, and amid the crush of admirers meeting her famous husband at public gatherings she became the awkward wallflower. On several occasions she was embarrassingly misidentified as his second wife—when she and Erskine went on their trip to South America, he asked the State Department to wire the reception committees that June was "NOT, REPEAT NOT, MARGARET BOURKE-WHITE."

After Jay's birth, June began planning to have a life of her own:

she tried to find work as a French translator, took singing lessons, attended courses at the University of Arizona, went to law school for several weeks, and corresponded with a number of politicians and government officials—Barry Goldwater was the recipient of several long letters. But most of her activities somehow backfired and she was left discouraged. When she began submitting her own stories to magazine editors, June was unable to stay clear of Erskine's reputation. An editor at *The New Yorker* when rejecting one of her stories wrote: "Please tell your husband that it seems a very long time since we've had the pleasure of reading one of his short stories." Another editor when giving her a cold rejection slip declared: "Your husband has a very great talent."

June began visiting a psychoanalyst in the hope that she could emerge from her tortoiseshell of self-doubt. The visits increased over a period of several years to three or four sessions a week. Caldwell admitted that he was in "an ill-tempered mood" the day he was confronted with a bill for three months of treatments. Failure to pay the psychoanalyst promptly, June argued, would create a strained relationship with her doctor. It might damage the progress of her analysis. "I fully expected eventually to pay in full what was owed," explained Caldwell, "but for the present I did not have several thousand dollars in hand for nonessentials."

June suggested they sell the second home Caldwell had bought in Santa Fe, New Mexico in order to pay off the debt. Reluctantly, he agreed, but it was a decision painful for him: Alfred and Dorothy Morang had moved from Maine to Santa Fe and lived in the house as caretakers. If it were sold they would have to move and the couple had little money.

It was emotionally devastating for Morang that he must leave his home and studio, wrote Caldwell, and the eviction was responsible for the hurried divorce of Alfred and Dorothy. But this was not the final disaster. While trying to recover from his separation, he married a woman with two teenaged daughters. This union lasted two years. Then came the end. Alfred, alone in a shack, went to bed one night with a bottle of wine and a lighted cigarette. He died in the fire, and his body was found days later when boys were playing in the rubble.

Erskine's marriage was beginning to lose its solidity as he felt June pulling further away from him. Since she refused to travel, he traveled alone—but not always: He was seen at the 1948 Kansas Writers' Conference, and elsewhere, with an attractive young woman reporter who gave him some of the comforts that a distancing wife denied. With his writing in a decline, he needed June more than ever while she tried desperately to be independent.

Caldwell developed a stomach ulcer, and in 1952 he had surgery. On the night before the operation he wrote June that they must somehow save their marriage. "I love you and want your love more than anything else in the world." He didn't understand why there now was so little between them. "It may be that you have grown to have different feelings or something but I have the same feelings for you that I've had all the time since I first knew you. I wish you could return to that and let us be happy together because that is all I want in life. I love you very much, Skinny."

Shortly after he returned home from his surgery, June asked for a separation, and Erskine packed a few clothes, took his typewriter and manuscripts, and moved to Phoenix. From there he sent dozens of letters asking her to reconsider and have him back. Finally, he had had enough and wrote no more.

It was early in the 1950s when he purchased a house with a gable roof on Central Avenue in the northern residential section of Phoenix. Oleanders and roses grew in profusion, and in addition to a swimming pool there was a guest house that Erskine used for his writing studio.

Lonely without June and Jay, he soon found some solace in the companionship of newspapermen at the Phoenix Press Club where he became a life member. Drinking and playing cards far into the night kept his depression partly in check, though his consumption of alcohol was alarmingly on the rise: he now averaged a fifth of bourbon daily, and there was often the fear that his liquor cabinet would not be amply stocked. On a trip to Poland he took three suitcases; one held clothing, and the other two were filled with whiskey.

In appearance, he was no longer the handsome author who posed in photographs with Bourke-White: his weight was out of control, bulging from his usual 185 pounds to 235; he now combed his hair straight forward to hide a skin condition. Erskine slept poorly, had an improper diet, and when he did write he worked listlessly. There were occasional meetings with James Oliver Brown to worry over his sinking royalties, and he sometimes weekended with Al Manuel in Nevada for lubricated evenings at the blackjack table and to see Las Vegas shows. Alimony was a constant irritant, and he was bitter over the loss of the valuable foothill property that had been awarded to June in the divorce proceedings. Finally, believing that he needed a medical evaluation, Erskine checked himself into the Mayo Clinic, stayed there a week, and returned home dispirited.

Caldwell had attended a dinner party as the guest of honor at Victor Weybright's home in Maryland. It was late 1949—June did accompany him on this trip—and one of the guests was a pretty twenty-nine-year-old woman named Virginia Moffett Fletcher. She had almost decided not to go because she expected the guest of honor would be loud, pompous, and foul-mouthed. Virginia wore an old dress and arrived late—"I wasn't going to kow-tow to anybody." Instead, she saw a shy man standing in a corner and mumbling his thanks to admirers eager to shake his hand. The awkward way he moved about disarmed her, and Virginia decided that this person who had written *Tobacco Road* and *God's Little Acre*, surprisingly, was a "Georgia country boy." Caldwell was enchanted with Virginia's vivaciousness, and he no longer mumbled when they got talking. "He liked Chevrolets and blackeyed peas," said Virginia, "but he's sure complex inside." At the end of the evening, Caldwell hurriedly asked Virginia to send him her address and telephone number, a request she did not honor. "One vow I made," she recalled, "was to have no married man in my life."

Three years earlier, Virginia had separated from her husband and with her young son, Drew, moved to Sarasota, Florida where she painted and tried to readjust her life. Erskine visited her there in March 1952, and they talked far into the night. He spoke of his feelings of rejection and compared himself to a turtle—a creature hurt so often that it feared coming out of the shell. Virginia wept when she read *The Sacrilege of Alan Kent*; the work confirmed to her that here was a man who always had been lonely.

It was at this time that Caldwell was finishing *Love and Money*, a novel, written in the first person, that his editor at Little, Brown feared might be mistaken for autobiography. Rick Sutter tries to conquer uncertainties and anxieties. Three obsessions consume the central character of the story: the ideal woman, a need for critical examination, and his disappointing writing career. Sutter is between books and can't find a suitable subject for his next novel as he searches for a woman who will sustain him "mentally, morally, spiritually and physically."

He finds her, and she is a woman who, like Virginia, has "thick dark hair, cut somewhat short and framing her face." The heroine, too, has a seven-year-old child, and mother and son are living in Sarasota. Sutter and this ideal woman spend a night talking, but she refuses his offer of marriage and runs away to New Orleans, Houston, and Colorado Springs—places where Caldwell himself had found female companionship in the past. Sutter has long conversations with his friend, Mizemore, a professor-critic, as they envision the perfect woman-mother placed on a pedestal. "There should be a worshipful statue of her at every crossroad, every hamlet, in every public place," says Mizemore, "for there is nothing to take her place in the life of a normal man." But another friend reminds Sutter: "There's no future in your frantic attempts, when you're between books, to find the ideal woman. There is no such creature ...you'll never be able to find her because she doesn't exist outside your imagination. Most writers have the same telltale occupational malady—you, too. You get in the habit of making fictional women so attractive and desirable—when you're not making them despicable and crude—that you'll always be disappointed with every last one of them in real life."

Both Caldwell and Sutter share a worry: "Is it better to write a poor novel than not write a novel at all?" Another question asked is whether millions of readers of "shoddy books" are only in search of a thrill. Sutter is told he is "second rate" and is advised: "If you can't write better novels in the future than you have in the past, you ought to shut up shop here and now." This critical enemy tells Rick that he is vain, selfish, conceited and contemptible. Sutter's life is mirrored in his novels. Near the end of *Love and Money*, the fictional author speaks for himself *and* Caldwell: "Sometimes I think writers like me ought to be kept in cages so they can't mingle with decent human beings. I've got to write—that's all I can do. I follow a bent. That's writing. It takes all of me to do that. And that's why I'm selfish and cruel and scoundrelly—I know I am and I can't help it."

In an interview with Edwin T. Arnold, Caldwell stated that he had a "low regard" for writers and their mentality—Rick Sutter "was just a bum." Authors were not special people nor did they have the qualifications of oracles. The protagonist in *Love and Money* isn't going to be content with a substitute; Rick wants the "real thing" and feels compelled to strive for perfection as he looks for this consummate woman. One didn't give up—"You still have that urge and that desire to continue your search until you reach your ultimate goal."

Virginia and her son moved from Florida to Arizona in 1953, and as the months went by she and Caldwell spent more time together. They swam in his backyard pool, and he would grill hamburgers for outdoor suppers. She wasn't dismayed by his long silences, and it calmed him to hear her talk as they sat under the desert stars. It was obvious that he was unhappy, and his heavy drinking and sudden departures to Las Vegas failed to ease the pain. He was hurt by the negative reviews of his novels and troubled with the fading of an aura that had once given a magical glow to his writing.

Virginia Moffett Fletcher was not the kind of person to make demands and never mentioned his excessive drinking. If he became sullen and locked her out, she remained placid and understanding; when he wished to be alone, she immediately disappeared. "As Virginia and I became better acquainted," wrote Caldwell, "we found that there was a distinct likeness in our lives. Our fathers had been ministers, our mothers had been teachers of English, our parents had moved from state to state every few years, and we had sons of the same age."

When Caldwell's secretary, Betty Pustarfi, gave notice and enlisted in the Women's Army Corps, Virginia volunteered to fill her post until a replacement was found. Pustarfi's leaving had depressed Erskine, and he found it difficult to stay for long sessions at his writing table. The temporary help proved to be a most capable editorial assistant—Virginia had an instinctive sense of what was needed—and the selection of another secretary was delayed. The sons, Jay and Drew, brought an atmosphere of family closeness, and Caldwell's depression eased. Jay made frequent trips to Phoenix, and the two boys splashed for hours in the pool. "At the end of the summer," Caldwell recalled, "Virginia asked me in a casual manner one evening at twilight if I had ever considered leaving Phoenix and moving to San Francisco to live. The question was a startling surprise because I had thought of the very same thing many times without mentioning such a possibility to anyone." It was agreed that San Francisco would be the next stopping place.

Virginia went ahead to California and was delighted to find a year's lease for Caldwell on a house overlooking the Golden Gate Bridge, the Embarcadero, the Bay Bridge, and Oakland. This home with its exceptional location became a private kingdom for Erskine. "Indeed," he recalled, "the view from Twin Peaks was so spectacular that until I could become accustomed to such entrancing splendor I had to force myself to draw the curtains over the windows day and night when I was determined to concentrate on my writing."

Caldwell was finishing *Certain Women*, a book which would be published by Little, Brown in 1957, and he had started a preliminary draft of *Claudelle Inglish*. His two previous novels, *Love and Money*, 1954, and *Gretta*, 1955, were selling so well in NAL editions that the Fawcett wholesalers produced a publicity cartoon of Caldwell perched on a cash register with the caption: "Undisputed King of all Paperback Novelists...Largest-selling author of modern novels...over 37 million sold." Caldwell's financial crisis was over, but paperback shares still remained less lucrative for him than hardbound royalties, and the reviewers continued to be relentless in their assessment that he would never write himself back to critical redemption.

San Francisco had healing distractions: the fog creeping inland from the Pacific, the high towers of the Golden Gate with its red glow in sunlight, and evenings out at various bars in North Beach and Chinatown. But there were times of loneliness; Virginia was living in a residential hotel, the Gaylord, in the downtown section, and though she came to Twin Peaks during the day, he felt lost without her. "Alone late at night," wrote Caldwell, "in the large three-level house after work had been put aside and the curtains opened to city lights below, I often had a strong yearning to be with her and be able to express my feeling intimately and without reticence."

Finally, on an evening at Shanghai Lils, Caldwell made his fourth proposal of marriage—promising himself it would be his last. Virginia accepted and the two made wedding plans; they would go to Reno, Nevada and begin their life together at one minute past midnight on New Year's Day (1957). From Reno they would travel to New York, take the *Queen Mary* to Europe, spend time there, and return by airplane to Florida. It was a typical Caldwellian holiday and one of celebration; the kind that he enjoyed most: a luxurious voyage at sea, the shifting panorama of sights, and the chance to confer with several translators and publishers.

Caldwell was never far from his admirers, even when reviews were unfavorable or critics were ignoring him. Virginia recalled an incident which occurred in Reno when they were checking out of their hotel the morning after their wedding. The porter carrying her husband's suitcase noticed the name tag. "May I just shake your hand?" he asked the author. "I've enjoyed your books so much." As the two pulled away in a taxi, Erskine turned to Virginia and said: "I would rather have a comment like that than the praise of all the great critics."

"We went to Europe on the *Queen Mary,*" Caldwell would later remark to Jack Castel in a relaxed interview for the *San Francisco News,* "and I ate nothing but steaks the whole voyage. The Cunard Line seemed to think this an affront to the variety of the cuisine." He and Virginia were leading a quiet life and didn't neglect restaurants, though he preferred to broil steaks over a hibachi in their expansive living room. "At the moment," said Caldwell when writing was brought up, "I have no ideas beyond looking at the Bay and trying to keep my weight down."

There was promising news waiting for him upon his return to San Francisco from Florida. Al Manuel was negotiating for a four-way partnership with producer Sidney Harmon, writer Philip Yordan, and director Anthony Mann for a film version of *God's Little Acre.* Though there would be no hefty advance, what appealed to Caldwell was that he would have a say in the production and a twenty-five percent share of all the profits. Manuel told him to be prepared to leave San Francisco on short notice to help search for a suitable location near Augusta, Georgia for the filming.

Caldwell had two novels in mind that he wanted to write, but he realized that any involvement in the film would hamper such efforts. This movie project was important to him—he hadn't forgotten the "false ending" given *Tobacco Road* by Twentieth Century-Fox. While waiting for the finalization of the film contract, he revised his story for children, *Molly Cottontail*, to be published in book form, and wrote several additional short stories for a collection called *When You Think of Me*. (Before she met him, Virginia had read "Molly Cottontail" to her son. The tale was first published for the general reading public, but she encouraged Caldwell to rewrite the story and have it brought out as a children's book.)

Caldwell thought of himself as a storyteller in the Southern-oral tradition: one person telling his cronies a whopper. This led him to believe that the short story should *improve* on nature; a remark which caused some critics to label him a naturalist—much to his bewilderment.

Short pieces parallel his longer works of fiction in subject matter and presentation. The cost of such a parallelism was found in the novels; they were too often anecdotal and episodic. The sudden end of an incident can be successful in a brief piece of fiction, though in a novel readers are left with the feeling that the author has failed them.

He liked the short story because he didn't have to conform to the commercial idea of a specified length. It could be one page or fifty. His publishers had repeatedly asked him to produce a long novel, but he resisted—the briefest way to completion gave him more time for travel. "The novel is subject to being too long for the subject matter," he observed. "I have always tried to write a novel no more than 200 to 250 pages."

Caldwell has been criticized for producing too much work—his one-book-a-year schedule raised eyebrows. There is some truth in the charge that he was a one-man industry, though he never increased his publication rate after achieving acclaim. Two-thirds of his total number of 150 short stories were completed before 1940 and eighty percent of them were in print a decade later.

Horace Gregory, in a *New York Herald Tribune* review, wrote that the humorous stories in *American Earth* were the best. This assessment followed Caldwell throughout his career. The departure from comedy to achieve greater book sales, along with the lurid NAL covers, did much to bring about critical censure. Comedy did not interest him—despite early joke writings at the University of Virginia; he didn't consider himself a raconteur and was reluctant to pose as the humorist Jack Kirkland proclaimed him to be in the *Tobacco Road* drama.

In his short story collection, *Jackpot*, Caldwell stressed the need for first-hand experience:

> A writer has to be a jack of all trades. He has to know how to harness a horse and snub a tractor; how to gig suckers and bait a taut line; how to point up a brick wall and shore up a cow shed. Furthermore, he has to know how to make crepes Suzette and Sauerbraten; how to change a baby and shroud a corpse; how to float stock and sink a catamaran. Further still, he has to know how to recognize a Piquet frock and a Suzy hat; how to make love and how to practice celibacy; how to take a time exposure and how to make a lap dissolve.

By March, the movie contract was signed, and Caldwell with the film's art director, Jack Poplin, were in Georgia on a preliminary search for an appropriate setting. Local reactions to *God's Little Acre* being filmed in the area were mixed—there still were residents who thought Erskine "a Georgia traitor" and his book "a dirty shame."

The *Augusta Chronicle* gave front-page coverage when Caldwell and the film party arrived at the Augusta airport on July 25, 1957. At the passenger gate a dozen or more attractive young women rushed the Hollywood invaders and unwrapped two sizeable banners. One read: "Why No Parts For Us?" and the other announced: "Southern Girls For Southern Movies." When asked his reactions to this homecoming, Caldwell replied that it was "the most surprising reception I ever received."

Thomas Wood of the *New York Herald Tribune*, in a January 8, 1958 article explained the eventual outcome of the search for that Georgia film site:

> Despite the fact that earlier the Augusta Chamber of Commerce had agreed to co-operate fully with the movie company—Security Pictures, an independent outfit which makes films for United Artists release—it pulled the rug out from under them when they arrived to nail down the specific locations—a cotton mill, a piece of farm land and a row of workers' shacks. The city council suddenly declared the project off limits, and everyone in town promptly withdrew the welcome sign.
>
> Not even the lure of exorbitant rental could change the citizens' minds. The owner of the mill decided he had other uses for his plant, the farmer refused to allow a camera near his fields, and the workers just slammed their doors in the production's face.

The Georgia expulsion was only a temporary setback. A few weeks later while flying in a small plane over the San Joaquin Valley, Anthony Mann saw the perfect landscape site for the filming, and in nearby Stockton, California he found an abandoned spinning mill which would serve for factory scenes.

Philip Yordan's screenplay closely followed Caldwell's dialogue and plot, although some of the more explicit events in the book were subdued. Instead of Darling Jill and the albino copulating under the nearest tree, the film script has the two floating serenely and romantically to the middle of a pond in a rowboat, and Will Thompson doesn't tear Griselda's clothes off in front of his wife. The factory scene was altered by having Will accidentally shot by a doddering old night watchman, instead of being killed by strike-breakers—though the McCarthy era was over there were lingering fears that Caldwell's original story material could be labeled by some theater critics as communistically tinged. The ending of the film was less violent: Buck doesn't shoot his brother Jim Leslie for trying to take wife Griselda away from him; Yordan's version has father Ty Ty separating the brothers when Buck goes after Jim Leslie with a pitchfork. The finale comes with Ty Ty's vow "never to dig another hole" in search of gold. He is determined to plant a crop, but while plowing he unearths his grandfather's shovel and is convinced that the old man buried gold nearby. Dreams of being a farmer again are forgotten, and Ty Ty starts digging another hole.

James Cagney and Jane Mansfield were among several Hollywood notables interested in joining the cast of *God's Little Acre*, but both had other commitments. Robert Ryan starred as Ty Ty; Will was played by Aldo Ray; Griselda, Tina Louise; Pluto, Buddy Hackett; Buck, Jack Lord; Shaw, Vic Morrow; Darling Jill, Fay Spain; Rosamond, Helen Westcott; Dave (the albino), Michael Landon; Jim Leslie, Lance Fuller; and Uncle Felix, Rex Ingram.

(This author worked as a desk clerk at the Sheraton Palace on Market Street in downtown San Francisco when the movie was being filmed. I recognized Robert Ryan the moment he entered the lobby with Aldo Ray. The two came to the front desk and I waited on them. Ray was in a jocular mood and his wisecracks amused Ryan. Later, while they were having lunch in the hotel's Garden Court, a man asked me if the actors had registered and I told him they had and where they could be found. The reservation clerk working on my shift had an autographed copy of *God's Little Acre*, and he informed me that the one I had just spoken to was the author of that book—Erskine Caldwell.)

Caldwell visited the set during the filming, and his downcast expression throughout a humorous segment was so distracting to Robert Ryan that the actor nearly forgot his lines. Ryan wasn't a temperamental person, but he finally took director Anthony Mann aside and said: "You've got to get Caldwell off the set. He gives me the willies. He looks at us as though we were missing the point. I can't go on while he sits there glowering." Mann agreed to draw Erskine out of range but instead placed him next to Ryan when the company broke for lunch. Caldwell said nothing for several minutes as he directed his attention to the food. Finally, he turned to the actor and told him how fascinated he was in the wonderful way Ryan was getting across the character of Ty Ty Walden. The astonished Ryan no longer resented the author's presence on the sidelines, and the two became good friends.

NAL and the distributor, Fawcett Publications, rarely missed a publishing opportunity; they scheduled a new paperback edition of *God's Little Acre* to coincide with the releasing of the film. The cover of the book had a photograph of a passionate love scene, and Caldwell was sent on a 10,000-mile tour to promote book and ticket sales.

Within a month of its appearance in neighborhood theaters, the movie was selling better than any current film in the country. Nevertheless, it got mixed reviews from the critics: some of the pundits were sympathetic, others condescended to the subject matter, and a cranky gang believed the story line had been distorted. Stanley Kauffman in *The New Republic* called it "God's Belittled Acres" and complained that the film "skimps the proletarian aspects of the book and treats the sex in that censored, suggestive fashion which takes out of the bloodstream of the characters and makes it a matter of Hollywood bosoms and fake fire." A. H. Weiler of *The New York Times* claimed that the characters in the story had "been treated with dignity and intelligence in a folk comedy that is actually funny, realistic, and rarely a lampoon." Bosley Crowther, who had assailed the film rendition of *Tobacco Road*, agreed with Weiler in the *Times* ten days later, hailing the *God's Little Acre* flick as "one of the best films of the year."

The movie was one of fourteen films selected by an international jury to compete for prizes in the Venice International Film Festival. Anthony Mann, Erskine, and Virginia attended, and an audience attired in evening clothes gave the American entry long applause. But again there was no unanimity among the critics. *Messaggero*, Rome's independent daily, declared the movie "failed to live up to expectations," and *Il Populo*, the Christian Democrat party organ, deemed it well photographed and splendidly acted, especially by Robert Ryan, but wondered "how much life, how much reality, and how much poetry are in all this we are not able to perceive."

For Caldwell, this film version of his book was totally gratifying—a far cry from the failure and limp ending of *Tobacco Road* in 1941. "I had plenty of previous offers for *God's Little Acre*," he told Jerry Gaghan of the *Philadelphia News*, "but I didn't take any of them. Now I've finally got what I wanted. I'm in the producing partnership and get a percentage of the gross." Left unsaid was his share—later reported to be a staggering four to five thousand dollars a week during the first year.

Caldwell and Virginia were on their way to Boston to deliver his new manuscript, *Certain Women*, to Little, Brown. "There it is," he said, pointing to a brown paper package. "It took a year to write and two hours to pack."

*Certain Women* has seven females of various stations in life, all living in a Southern town called Claremore, and each is contained in a separate story—only Claremore bonds them in a loosely-fitted novel: a frightened bride, the schoolteacher hungry for a husband, the disappointed prostitute, a brutal father who wants his daughter married and pregnant, the teenager yearning for a boyfriend, Nancy who says, "I'll never get married again," and a restaurant proprietor who behaves so badly that in her fury his wife disfigures a girl for life.

Luther Nichols in the *San Francisco Examiner* believed that the stories in *Certain Women* were "competently done, for Caldwell works hard and knows his craft. Yet there is a flicker of the gaslight era about some of them, a disturbing note of melodrama from the days when virtue was triumphant and titles ran to 'The Flower Girl' or 'Outwitting a Cad.' " They were not top grade, Nichols decided, not stories that gave readers an overwhelming illusion of experience—"Erskine needs only to restoke those old fires and write more burning passion and less tidy and consciously dramatic plottings."

*Gulf Coast Stories* (1956) and *Certain Women* (1957) were collections that had little humor and placed an emphasis on marriage and sexual tensions. Caldwell had no intention of giving up his burlesque light moments, yet by the end of World War II he was consciously slanting his stories in more somber directions.

Caldwell was often criticized for his portrayal of women in such novels as *Jenny by Nature*, *Gretta*, *Claudelle Inglish*, and *Annette*: they were females trapped by society and forced to conform. Beginning in 1946, with *A House in the Uplands*, he turned from the male character as his protagonist to the female. In explaining the switch, Caldwell said wryly: "Well, maybe because I began to have a lot of personal experiences with women. There was quite a large turnover there, you know, as far as being married was concerned; so maybe that had something to do with it." He did feel that women were victims in a male-dominated society. Even with feminism in ascendancy, females were second-class citizens, not in the role of responsibility but in the sense of personal liberation.

Caldwell's 1958 novel, *Claudelle Inglish*, like *Gretta*, explores the sexual habits of a young woman who is driven to repeat acts of prostitution by the overpowering forces of youthful vicissitudes. Claudelle returns to her small Southern community and lives in poverty with her sharecropper father and nagging mother. After her fiancé jilts her, she goes on a seducing rampage with every man in town. Girls without panties, ministers with frigid wives, and fights in which people are impaled on car hood ornaments are standard fare as the tale unfolds.

Many of his readers found it difficult to believe that the author of *Tobacco Road* and *God's Little Acre* could write novels as slight as *The Sure Hand of God*, *Gretta*, and *Annette*. Frequently overlooked is the writer's intent: Caldwell was entrapped in his stylized process of shocking a huge public—he was too taken up in the joy of storytelling to evaluate each evolving work. Unevenness dogged him throughout his career; *The Bastard*, *Poor Fool*, and *A Lamp for Nightfall* ("Autumn Hill") belong to the same time period as his two best novels.

John David in reviewing *Claudelle Inglish* for the *Houston Post* felt that only staunch fans of the author could warm to the book. "Because this is a Caldwell who has repeated himself so many times that he reads like a third-rate writer satirizing Caldwell. The tragedy," wrote David, "is not Claudelle's; it's that Caldwell, who emerged as the Depression's humorist of the grotesque, keeps on restaging the same old minstrel show after the impact and meaning are gone."

*New York Herald Tribune* reviewer Carol Field predicted that the novel would be difficult for a reader to take seriously because the author didn't place much faith in it. "The portraits of Claudelle and the others in the book are shallow and superficial; the direction of the plot wavering and uncertain; the denouement a little ridiculous."

Several reviewers called the novel "abysmal," though critic C. Hugh Holman judged it to be "an almost flawless sexual comedy with the skill of story-telling and the exuberance of a Chaucerian fabliau." Paperback sales were brisk, and Warner Brothers, basking in the success of the movie version of *God's Little Acre*, paid Caldwell $45,000 for film rights. The same Stockton farming area was selected for the filming, and though Natalie Wood was first mentioned for the starring role, the heroine was played by newcomer Diane McBain. Directed by Gordon Douglas, the result was a mediocrity. Caldwell was unimpressed with the script and refused to see the film.

*Claudelle Inglish* was Erskine's thirty-eighth book, and for an author whom many critics scorned as a literary disappointment, his sale figures were staggering. Royalties now were coming to him from all directions: novels, foreign translations, films, travelogues, short story collections, and anthologies. *God's Little Acre* led the way with more than seven million copies sold. When Virginia took the almost impossible task of counting all sales—this hemisphere and other continents—she found the total number was more than sixty-one million; this didn't include pirated editions. England, Italy, and France topped the foreign markets, and Caldwell's books had by now been translated into dozens of languages, including Hungarian, Hebrew, Slovak, Serbo-Croatian, Slovene, Icelandic, Danish, Bengali, Dutch, Japanese, and Korean.

Virginia was aware that her husband wasn't a cheerful person—

"Humorous, yes," she told Edwin T. Arnold in an interview, "but there's a difference. He was dependent upon me for the good cheer, and he let me know early on that that was important to him, and so I turned into a Pollyanna, which wasn't much trouble—by habit or by instinct I'm that way anyway." She seemed to know exactly how to short-circuit his bad moods. Over the years, he depended more and more on her and felt lost when she wasn't with him before and after his daily bouts of writing. In spite of his reluctance, she got him to attend plays and concerts and to socialize. Virginia never forgot his children on birthdays and she made sure they had regular contact with him. Dabney Caldwell marveled over his stepmother's ability of getting his father to laugh—she was the only person who could thaw those glacial moods that so often overcame him.

He never claimed to be a paragon in his role as husband before his marriage to Virginia. "When I was having domestic trouble," said Caldwell, "I did not hesitate to get out of it. I was not a nice guy. I considered my job more important than anything else. But I had to take a stand, selfishly, not thinking of anybody, just myself."

Unlike June, Virginia had her husband's love of travel, and they were away from home every year. In 1959, they visited London, Paris, Rome, Madrid, Moscow and Istanbul; in 1960, they were in the Far East and Japan; in 1961, they traveled to Finland, Sweden, Denmark, Italy, France, and England; one year after this journey they saw Australia, India, and China; and as soon as the next book was completed, seven months later, they prowled ten countries in Central Europe.

In late February 1959, the Caldwells sailed on the *Liberte* from New York for his European tour and conferences with translators and publishers. After the first night at sea, with most of the ship's magazines and newspapers read, they began perusing the passenger list, and there in bold print was MR. AND MRS. JOHN STEINBECK. Messages were exchanged and the four met. "I've taken quite a few compliments for *God's Little Acre* over the years," said John, and

Erskine responded: "And I've taken quite a lot for *The Grapes of Wrath.*" At first neither had much to say—Steinbeck looked down at his hands and mumbled while Caldwell spoke quietly, shyly, and looked off into the distance. John, who claimed to dislike being around other writers, soon warmed to Erskine. They both rose early in the morning and so got into the routine of having coffee and long relaxed talks. They playfully planned a collaboration to startle the literary establishment: the two would write a book of fiction allegedly authored by a fifteen-year-old prodigy who was still too young to shave. "Try as we did, however," recalled Caldwell, "we could not decide immediately if he should have a given name and surname or an added middle name or two initials and a surname."

Erskine didn't mingle with many writers because, he said, "it's a bad class of people." His friendships had been "with the young ladies of life." He felt that writers never talked about anything interesting; just about themselves and their work. The two authors he did enjoy having around, in addition to Steinbeck, were Nathanael West and William Saroyan; Sinclair Lewis also stopped by occasionally at the time of the Darien, Connecticut days. Pep West and Saroyan liked to keep the conversation ordinary and spoke of simple things, "including cigars."

Caldwell and Steinbeck met again two years later in Moscow when both were on tour for the United States Information Service. Erskine invited John and Elaine to have dinner with him and Virginia at the National Hotel. They had a lavish feast and there was an abundance of caviar and Georgian champagne purchased with an ample supply of rubles which Caldwell couldn't take out of the Soviet Union. Steinbeck was having such a carefree time that it was past midnight before he went downstairs and ordered a taxi to take him and his wife back to their hotel in another part of Moscow. But there was no available transportation at that hour, and when the night manager of the hotel refused to be helpful, Steinbeck went to the street and lay down in front of the hotel's entrance.

A gathering of people from the late performance at the nearby

Bolshoi Ballet theater surrounded Steinbeck, and suddenly one observer pointed at John. "I know who he is!" the man said in English. "That's Hemingway, the American writer." The beard was recognizable.

"Hemingway, *nyet!*" roared John. "Steinbeck, *da!*"

Another English-speaking Russian asked if John had been hit by a vehicle, and Steinbeck explained that he was protesting the treatment received from the hotel night manager.

"I know you really are Steinbeck, the American writer," said a man helping John to his feet. "And you have a better beard than Hemingway. Come with me. I'll take you in my car wherever you want to go."

Caldwell's *When You Think of Me*, a gathering of six short stories and nine sketches, got scant notice from reviewers. The title story tells about a returned soldier who cringes from the hero's role because he feels that the only heroes are the ones who do not return. Some of the sketches are American, some Czechoslovakian; the two capturing the most attention were about a dogcart trade in a Czech village (a carryover from the Bourke-White days) and a dialogue between American hobos watching a ball game.

Jennie Puryear Gardner, when reviewing the book in the August 30, 1959 issue of the Louisville, Kentucky *Courier-Journal*, deemed the stories to be "good models" in a composition class. "But they are almost too professional. They are like an instant mix, not to be compared with the heady home-brew of fiction like *God's Little Acre* and *Tobacco Road*." The collection had "something of the best and worst of Caldwell," declared reviewer Sam Ragan. "It will not add to his reputation as one of the leading writers of this generation, but neither will it ruin it."

An unexpected bonus, and one that would have bewildered the professors at Due West who had tried to discipline and awaken the intellectual curiosity of their rebellious student from Wrens, came on December 8, 1959 when The Euphemian Literary Society of Erskine College bestowed on him an honorary membership. He was only the second person in the society's 120-year history to be so recognized. The other honoree was General Robert E. Lee who accepted membership in 1868. Caldwell was chosen for his "services to the American novel of realism, to the enjoyment of millions in our own land and abroad, both by the media of the printed page and the several dramatic media." Left unsaid during the ceremony was his other membership years earlier at Due West: the chicken-chasing "Night Hawkers Club."

Throughout his life, Caldwell was never one to dwell long in the same abode; even the Twin Peaks view paled after three years, and when he learned that a townhouse on Nob Hill could be rented, he and Virginia moved. This home on Mason Street was located on one of the steepest slopes in the city, and shielded by an ivy-walled courtyard at street level. There were winding stairways, and a roof garden with greenhouse on the fourth level. Among the few guests who panted their way to the door for a visit were San Francisco columnist Herb Caen and novelist Truman Capote. (Caldwell considered Capote to have a talented hand, though the young Southerner tended to refine the state of things too much. "I'm from the barefoot school," he told *Houston Post* reporter Emmet Collins in a 1957 interview, and Faulkner, too, was barefooted. Then pausing, Caldwell added: "I don't want to talk about Faulkner characters. He's a fine writer. But when you're trying to sell Lucky Strikes you don't talk about Camels.") Caldwell was particularly uncompromising about interruptions, and never hesitated to withhold invitations to friends and strangers alike in order to hoard time for writing.

(Herb Caen, in his January 21, 1960 column of the *San Francisco Chronicle*, revealed an incident under the heading "Small Ex-World." At the opening of attorney Melvin Belli's sumptuous offices on Montgomery Street, Caldwell lifted his punch glass in a toast to author Niven Busch. "To your ex-wife," said Caldwell, "who played my ex-wife on television." The toast had wit and accuracy: Teresa Wright, the former Mrs. Busch, portrayed Margaret Bourke-White on the popular TV program *Sunday Showcase*.)

The Caldwells made three visits to Japan: in February 1960, in November 1971, and in April 1982. Their first trip was for only a week, and its principal purpose was to renew the copyrights on several of his books. Japan's ten-year-limitation law encouraged pirated editions and threatened royalties. "I think," said Caldwell before leaving San Francisco, "that I'm getting a bad case of public domain poisoning."

Upon his arrival at Tokyo International Airport, a number of reporters were waiting to interview him. "I have assured various Japanese intellectuals," he jokingly announced, "that I'm not over here gathering material for a Japanese *Tobacco Road* or a 'Buddha's Little Acre.' " When asked which of his books he liked best, he replied: "My next one." Then Caldwell gave his usual response when a newsman wondered if he had ever been influenced by another author. "No," he replied. "I very rarely read books. Years ago I divided the population into two classes, readers and writers. I wished to belong to the latter category."

Charles Tuttle, his Far East literary agent in Tokyo, had arranged book signings in several shops, and Erskine also spent a day with a group of Japanese students of English at Waseda University. There was still lingering antipathy toward Yankees among the older Japanese, but the young students, many of them avid readers of books written by Americans, were delighted to have his autograph and the chance to photograph him. "In fact," recalled Caldwell, "during the entire length of our visit, from early morning until late at night, there were few times when several polite but persistent students were not waiting in the hall of the hotel for Virginia and me to leave or return to our room."

Caldwell's short story "The Empty Room" was translated as early as 1932 and published in the Japanese literary magazine *Shin Eibungaku Kenyu* (New Studies in English Literature). A translation of *Tobacco Road* appeared in 1937, and one of *American Earth* followed in 1940. But it wasn't until after World War II that Japanese readers got a full dose of Caldwell's work. American soldiers of the Occupation Army often passed on their paperback editions to English-speaking Japanese, and by the mid-1950s at least thirty of his books had been translated. Further strengthening his Far East exposure was the publication of more than 60 inexpensive reprints for college students, and in the English textbooks for Japanese high school students one still can find Caldwell stories, such as "The Lonely Day," "Molly Cottontail," "The Strawberry Season," and "Vick Shore and the Good of the Games." There was gratification in being so enthusiastically acclaimed in a distant country. This first trip to Japan had been an exhilarating experience for both Erskine and Virginia.

Caldwell had unsettling news upon his return to San Francisco. He had asked his agent, James Oliver Brown, to negotiate a better contract with Little, Brown and Company when personally delivering the manuscript of *Jenny by Nature*. The request was bluntly rejected by the editor-in-chief and an incensed Brown snatched the manuscript from the editor's desk and returned to New York. Erskine felt his agent should have waited long enough to give Arthur Thornhill the opportunity to intervene, but what disturbed Caldwell more was that a frequent change of publishers might in the future cause a dip in royalties—first Scribner's, then Viking, a switch to DS&P, and now the rift with Little, Brown. But his agent had reassuring news: Farrar, Straus and Cudahy (later Giroux) were willing to publish the novel and enroll Erskine in their firm.

*Jenny by Nature* is the story of a onetime prostitute who runs a boardinghouse in Sallisaw, Georgia. Her star boarder is Shorty Goodwillie, a circus midget whose carnal high jinks so delight the hussy next door that she tries to get him to change residence—this causes Jenny and the woman to get into a hair-pulling scuffle. The other boarder is Betty Woodruff who is young, pretty, and so reckless that few men in Sallisaw can resist her—including the preacher. She was a schoolteacher but gave up the profession after being jilted by her boyfriend. Now the members of the church want her to leave town, but Jenny, the golden-hearted ex-prostitute, defends Betty.

A dark-skinned girl named Lawana Neleigh further complicates this tale—she claims to be part Indian, though the town suspects that she is a mulatto. Lawana is looking for work and becomes another boarder at Jenny's. The most influential citizen of Sallisaw demands that this intruder leave town, but the boardinghouse lady resists him.

Harold Bunting in the March 18, 1961 issue of the English newspaper, *Sheffield Telegraph*, provides a synopsis of the novel's switch from broad humor to fierce panic and tragedy:

> Here I come. Clanging a bell. Shrilling a whistle. Crying "Unclean! Unclean!" Giving every sort of warning that this is not a book about good people. Not the sort of book that would be given away as a Sunday School prize.
>
> The religious folk want to buy her boardinghouse to build a Sunday School, as an annex to their church!
>
> "I've told them over and over again that if they want my property they can get it by paying me my price for it.
>
> "But they won't offer me a single dollar. They say that if I do as they say, they'll convert me to their religion and save my soul, and then I can hand my deed over to the Rugged Cross Church and feel safe about the life hereafter."
>
> Jenny is confiding all this to Judge Milo Rainey, her slow-moving (towards the altar) suitor and attorney.
>
> The boardinghouse is burnt down by church fanatics, and Lawana dies in the flames. In the end, the heroine marries the Judge.
>
> "Jenny," he said, speaking slowly and firmly, "if you can do it, I can too. There are lots of things worse than having your house burnt down —and being a coward is one of them.
>
> "You and I are going to be together now and I want the same kind of courage you've got. And I'll get it, too."
>
> Life is not really like that even—I guess—in those queer patches of America where Mr. Caldwell gathers his stories.
>
> Yet this tale has a vigorous humor, for which much may be forgiven. I enjoyed it.
>
> But remember my warning: This is not a Sunday School prize.

Reviews of *Jennie by Nature* were varied. Day Thorpe, book critic for *The Washington Evening Star*, couldn't decide whether the novel was a "potboiler" or a "parody on inconsequential and out-of-focus writing." Thorpe felt the first sixty pages of the book would shame a backward weekly newspaper. "I thought it simply silly. But Erskine Caldwell is no hack—he is a writer of long experience." Gordon G. Stain of the *Columbia Missourian* was kinder when he stated that there were flashes recalling the heights found in *Trouble in July* and *American Earth. Jennie* had "a dazzling resourcefulness and a high skill." England's *Manchester Evening Chronicle*, however, declared the novel to be a "painful contrast to the author's short stories." Caldwell "can probably write this sort of stuff in his sleep—and that's where the reader will feel like joining him."

Erskine was pulled two ways as his writing career spun dizzily out of control. He was indeed the king of best-selling authors yet a man who hadn't fulfilled an earlier promise. He made foolhardy pacts with himself to average that one book a year between travels, and only his wastebasket could measure how difficult it was when the words were slow in coming. Caldwell realized that he was chasing the shadow of his former skill, and he tried to ignore the negative reviews. Readers came first, he said as he defended his position, not the critics. "When he did his first writing he had deep feelings about it," said Virginia Caldwell, "the people and the sadness he was writing about, and then to have it laughed at or criticized or banned, what would that do to any sensitive man?"

For Caldwell, critics were "superfluous commodities," and there often was an edge to his voice when he mentioned them. "I have always more respect for the book reviewers than I do for the critics," he said in an interview. "The book reviewer tells you what the book is about, and the critic tells you what's about himself." Caldwell once guessed that half the world would like him and the other half would not. Then with bitterness he added: "All except critics. They all hate me. I never get a fair deal from them. If they like my writing, I think they don't know what they are talking about; if they dislike me, they are just my enemies, that's all."

His commentary for "The Girl Ellen" in *Jackpot* had nothing to do with the story of a young man's infatuation and the death of his girlfriend: ("AUTHOR'S NOTE TO CRITICS: The publisher was doubtful of the wisdom of including this paragraph, but I succeeded in overcoming his objections by pointing out to him the traditionally high esteem held by critics for truth and honesty in an author's writings. So, with the comforting feeling of having fully discharged my obligations in that respect, I wish to quote my grandfather's definition of a critic. He said a critic was a man who had a perverted sense of smell, continually begged cigarettes, and kept a blonde mistress who had been locked out by every author in town.")

After Caldwell's death, Virginia wrote Japanese scholar Fujisato Kitajima: "He didn't have much peace in life, it was always a struggle and even though he declared that the critics didn't bother him I know that as sensitive as he was, all of the banning and anger in the beginning must have been very hard for him to bear. He was so young when it all began, young and naive about so many things."

Early in 1961, Erskine and Virginia traveled in Europe for six weeks: they visited all the Scandinavian countries, West Germany, Holland, Yugoslavia, Italy, France, and England. It was the sort of hectic tour that appealed to Caldwell as he met with his overseas publishers, accepted speaking engagements, and renewed himself for the next novel upon his return home. He met Henry Miller—a writer he admired—at a United States Information Service meeting in Germany. Was Miller an artist or a pornographer? Caldwell was asked. "Miller is a great writer," he replied. "I put him in a class with Steinbeck and Faulkner." Writers were either pros or non-pros, and he had little sympathy for authors who failed. Miller had succeeded because he knew how to write a good sentence.

Erskine dined with Swedish publisher Bo Wahlson, but most of the three-page recall of the trip in *With All my Might* dealt with an incident that occurred in Oslo: The Caldwells had eaten tainted oysters and the "disastrous aftermath" came at a dinner party of fourteen guests hosted by Norwegian publisher Harold Grieg. The banquet included salmon and its pungent odor caused the couple to take turns scrambling to the rest room. Virginia solved her embarrassment by taking "a morsel to her lips but no farther and then adroitly dispose of it under the table." Caldwell and one of the waiters exchanged knowing looks. However, the author was far less skillful; he had to brave the two-hour ordeal as best he could, but "abruptly left the table three times with unrelenting nausea."

*Close to Home* was Caldwell's 1962 contribution to his readers. The novel was timely, in the sense that it bravely dealt with black-white issues which were coming to the forefront in the struggle for equal rights.

Native Hunnicott, a bachelor and one of the more colorful citizens in the small Southern town of Palmyra, is about to complete what friends and neighbors feel is his greatest feat: Mrs. Frank Bowers, a wealthy widow, has agreed to marry the shiftless Hunnicott—she is lonely, and he knows she "sets a good table."

The two marry, but after the wedding Native tells his bride that he is going possum hunting overnight with some of his cronies. Maebelle Bowers, now Hunnicott, is furious but willing to forgive him until she finds her mulatto maid, Josene, with Native in his bachelor shack. "You're as bare as a plucked pullet!" she cries at the naked girl.

The outraged wife goes to the police and is determined to have her new husband and Josene arrested on a charge of "race-mixing," but Bill Parks, the jailor, tells her such things are better left private. Finally, Maebelle is promised that Josene will be arrested on a prostitution charge. One Palmyra housewife, when discussing this adulterous act, remarks: "It's embarrassing enough for a white woman to have a mulatto maid who looks like somebody you know, but it's even worse when the colored maid has a small child who looks like somebody too close to home for comfort."

When Clyde Hefflin, the sheriff's deputy, is ordered to arrest Josene he cannot find her. This lawman is known for his violent treatment of black men: "He'll go crazy if any Negro crosses him one word too many. That's why he's already killed so many of them—and he gets more proud of himself every time he does it." Deputy Hefflin questions Josene's black boyfriend, Harvey Brown, and when the interrogation proves unproductive and the Negro mildly reacts to a racial slur, Hefflin slaughters him.

In the end, nothing is resolved. Josene leaves town—she is urged to do so by a white lawyer who well may be her father; and Native, who could be the father of Josene's young daughter, returns to his new wife's house, raps hopefully on the door, and she takes him back.

The California *Oakland Tribune* called *Close to Home* "decidedly better than his last book, *Jenny by Nature*, but that is scant praise indeed. In spite of the fact that this new book concerns some important issues, it is surprisingly trivial and has little to recommend it." But the Glasgow, Scotland *Evening Times* when reviewing the Heinemann edition declared that Caldwell could add *Close to Home* "to his long list of popular successes." The Durham, England *Northern Echo* reverberated that assessment: "In this simple, entertaining and most successful novel both the comedy and the tragedy have much of the naturalness and universality of a folk tale."

In 1940, Caldwell had given typescripts of *God's Little Acre*, *Tobacco Road*, and *Southways* to Dartmouth College. This gesture was generated by a conversation Erskine had with Charles Pearce at DS&P. When asked what he wanted done with his manuscripts after publication, Caldwell replied: "I don't care what you do with them." The publisher reminded him that they were too valuable to throw away and suggested Baker Library at Dartmouth as a possible solution. This was the beginning of the Erskine Caldwell Collection which over the years has grown to more than 96 linear feet of books and 81 linear feet of manuscripts. The prize items are its books—the Caldwells have given this library every issue of his works, as well as seventeen stage and screen versions of the fiction. There are eighty-three editions of *Tobacco Road* in twenty-five languages, and fifty-seven copies of *God's Little Acre* in ten languages. The Dartmouth collection is still being assembled and many of the 1,059 catalogue items are not single entries. An entire set of papers on Virginia Caldwell's family, 1907-1972, is under one listing, as well as seven boxes of magazines containing early stories, business papers dated 1933-1938, and scrapbooks of newspaper clippings. A substantial variety of material can be found at university libraries in Georgia, Harvard, Illinois Urbana, Delaware, Nevada Reno, Syracuse, Oregon, and the Library of Congress. Erskine also gave Dartmouth a number of unpublished manuscripts with the stipulation that they were not to be published without permission. He had precise instructions when he turned over some of his personal papers in 1951: "1. Certain envelopes will be sealed by me and marked 'This material is not to be published or inspected until 15 years after the death of Erskine Caldwell.' 2. Certain envelopes will be marked 'This material is not to be published or inspected without the consent in writing of Erskine Caldwell, or until after his death.' 3. All other envelopes or material, which will be for the most part clippings, photographs, and manuscripts, will not be restricted as to any use the Library may wish to make of them."

The *New York Herald Tribune*, in March 25, 1952, carried a news item of his generosity and noted: "Caldwell's gifts in the past have included thirty-two proofs, manuscripts, and typescripts; 271 books, of which eighty-three are in foreign languages, eighty anthologies of Mr. Caldwell's short stories and twenty-nine different editions of his famous *Tobacco Road*. In addition there are twenty-six scrapbooks, largely of clippings relating to his works, collections of photographs relating to the author and his activities, and sixty-four magazines containing first publication of stories by Mr. Caldwell."

Erskine and Virginia made nine official visits to Dartmouth, and over the years their friendship with the college deepened. In the fall of 1968, Caldwell served as Writer-in-Residence for a month. He enjoyed visiting classes and the informal meetings he had with his students. But the residency didn't take him away from the novel he was working on *(The Weather Shelter)*, and his advice to aspirant authors was one he practiced himself when he started a new book: "Every writer must be selfish with his time if he is to accomplish what he sets out to do even though he runs the risk of being called rude and anti-social. If a person cannot take this name-calling, and maintain his dedication to his work, he should take up another trade to find happiness and forget the word business."

The new publisher, Roger Straus, was pleased to have the completed manuscript of *The Last Night of Summer* in hand, and when Caldwell proposed a new work of nonfiction Straus readily agreed. The proposed book, *Around About America*, would be a volume of travel observations in the same spirit as *Say, Is This the U.S.A.?* Erskine would develop the text and Virginia would provide pencil drawings.

After two years of renting the luxurious town house on Mason Street in the Nob Hill section of San Francisco, the couple decided that it was time to become home owners. They found a newly built seven-room, ranch-style house east of Berkeley in the hills near Orinda and Walnut Creek overlooking Rheem Valley. "I lived on the city pavement for seven years," Caldwell told a *Los Angeles Times* reporter, "and I wanted the country air and green grass growing all around me. Now I guess I like it well enough here to live it out."

The move to Orinda was done at the time that the Caldwells were busy with their passport renewals, travel reservations, and leaving instructions for their part-time secretary. Morrell Cody, European Director of the United States Information Service, had requested that Caldwell spend ten days appearing at USIS libraries and Balkan universities. But first there was an exhausting week at the Frankfurt Book Fair, which proved to be for Caldwell: "an orgy of eating and drinking from midmorning to midnight." It was during this trip that Steinbeck was to sprawl on the Moscow sidewalk and be mistaken for Hemingway.

Their field trips to assemble material for *Around About America* zigzagged across the continent: St. Johnsbury, Vermont was the beginning of the journey, then into the South and up to Minnesota and South Dakota before winding through Colorado into Texas, and concluding in Burn, Oregon and Rheem Valley, California. "The busy highways," wrote Caldwell, "will always lead to the hurly-burly of a metropolis where people have no time for strangers. However, in the hinterland there will be many times when an act of human kindness rarely fails to be offered to friend and stranger alike"—a West Virginia motel owner had no vacancies but took the time to find the Caldwells accommodations elsewhere, and in the Imperial Valley near the California-Mexico border a watermelon farmer filled their car trunk with fruit because they showed interest in the harvesting. The nine-thousand-mile route they followed was almost identical to the one taken with Bourke-White for *Say, Is This the U.S.A.?* The 224-page *Around About America* was given favorable and polite reviews in a scattering of national publications and would be the first of two collaborations, the other being *Afternoons in Mid-America*, 1976.

The central character in Caldwell's 1963 book *The Last Night of Summer* is Brooks Ingraham, a decent, middle-aged man who is soon romantically challenged. He had a humble background, but his station in life was immeasurably and materially raised by his marriage to the wealthy and frigid Maureen.

All the action in the novel occurs within the twelve to fourteen hours marking the end of summer's continuous and stifling heat. On this day, in his 48th year, Ingraham is told by his young secretary, Roma, that she is madly in love with him and asks Brooks to come to her apartment that night. He wants to go, but wavers, and finally makes up his mind that he does need love.

That last night of summer brings out all the animalism in human beings: Roma, who is overanxious about their meeting, goes to Ingraham's car to wait for him and is raped and murdered by an escaped convict. In the end, a contrite Brooks confesses his arranged tryst to Maureen and she is predictably vengeful.

Responses were mixed and some guarded—book viewer Michael G. Mattis summed up what many reviewers were thinking: "Well, if one enjoys reading Erskine Caldwell's novels, this one probably will be very appealing. If, on the other hand, one tends to dislike his work, this would rank as his worst."

"The book is disappointing," wrote Douglas Wynn in the *Delta Democrat Times*, "because it seems to lack the old grim humor of the earlier Caldwell"—Wynn faulted the author for changing the setting from the rural South to the metropolitan new South—the shift causing a loss of "perception and grasp of his characters."

"In the hands of almost anyone else," declared George Minot in the *Boston Herald*, "this novella would be a pretty trite effort." But Caldwell had skill and endurance: "Rape, murder, disfigurement, grossness, all follow one another, but instead of these all adding up to nonsensical melodrama, Caldwell produces a tragedy that comes close to being a minor classic. And there's not a wasted word in it."

Erskine and his literary agent, James Oliver Brown, mutually decided to sever ties; Brown was ill with hepatitis and requested a secretary to assist him. Caldwell disapproved: "Reasonable Jim's demand may have been, but nevertheless I insisted that if I paid the salary of a full-time secretary she should work in my office and not in the office of James Oliver Brown. Our friendly parting was toasted many times with martinis in the years to follow."

Since Erskine distrusted agents as much as he did publishers, it took him a while to find a replacement. Several years earlier, at a cocktail party, he had met Elizabeth Otis and Mavis McIntosh who jointly headed a literary agency. McIntosh had now retired from the firm, and Otis agreed to become his American representative.

At the time of Caldwell's negotiations with the agency, Harry Gilroy interviewed the author for a 1964 *New York Times* profile. Gilroy described the subject as having a square-shouldered appearance "from his football-playing days." With a look of "country boy innocence," he told his interviewer over lunch: "I made my first million before World War II, but I don't think I'll ever make another." Then he "presented his pretty, dark-eyed wife, Virginia. (She's a good bookkeeper) and asked her the latest sales figures of his books. The total has passed 67 million, she replied." This is Caldwell, the shy and uncomfortable publicist on the road for NAL,

Gilroy noted. "The paperback is the best thing that has happened to authors since the invention of the printing press," said Erskine. "They couldn't subsist without it."

The civil rights movement of the 1960s stirred Caldwell into another writing engagement on racial prejudice in the South. *In Search of Bisco* frames the hunt for a boyhood friend to shape a report on travel and people. The book structurally is an oxymoron: a collection of nonfiction short stories. He recalls three Negro boys: Bisco, from whom he was separated when he became too old to sleep in Bisco's bed; Sonny, lynched for alleged relations with a white girl; and Roy, sentenced to serve two years on a chain gain for supposedly stealing an iron washtub that was too heavy for one person to lift.

Bisco, probably a fictional character, took on real identity as Erskine searched for him while traveling through the South. The black-white subject matter seemed to energize him and gave readers and reviewers glimpses of a more powerful and earlier Caldwell.

Louis Untermeyer, who remembered "curing" him of poetry, now requested a children's book for a series he was editing. "I know you're out of poetry," wrote Untermeyer, "so perhaps you can write a good child's story." The nocturnal visit of deer to the twenty-five fruit trees on their Orinda property inspired Erskine to produce *The Deer at Our House*. Many readers found it incredible that the author of *Tobacco Road* and *God's Little Acre* could produce two children's books: the tale about a rabbit, *Molly Cottontail*, and now one about a nightly gathering of hungry four footers. "Our deer get fruit salad every night," said Virginia.

Shortly after the publication of *In Search of Bisco* in 1965, Caldwell submitted *In the Shadow of the Steeple* to Farrar, Straus, and Giroux—published in England with that title. The book was partly a biography of his father, Ira Sylvester, autobiography, and the author's explanation for having turned away from an organized religious practice.

Response to the manuscript was immediate: Roger Straus and his partners didn't feel that the book was one they wanted to publish without revision. Throughout the 1960s there had been debate and controversy over the influence of "white Anglo-Saxon Protestant-ism," and from this widespread reaction the acronym WASP had come to the public vocabulary with derogatory force. Straus was convinced that the publication of the book would signal that they endorsed the conservative religious view.

The rejection of the manuscript did not cancel the existing con-tract as Farrar, Straus, and Giroux had not committed the firm to bringing out Caldwell's books of nonfiction. Terms of the original agreement as negotiated by agent James Oliver Brown had already been met—three books of fiction—and there were no further ob-ligations on the part of the author.

Caldwell previously had sent a duplicate copy of the manuscript to Laurence Pollinger, his editor at William Heinemann in London, and it was accepted at once. Pollinger wrote that the publisher was particularly pleased with the book's title: it had "inherent implica-tions" that would appeal to readers.

During the time that Caldwell was writing *In the Shadow of the Steeple*, Victor Weybright had begun to maneuver him into accept-ing New American Library as the original publisher of all future novels. Weybright felt Caldwell owed some allegiance to NAL for the many paperback editions they had brought out in the past—it was no accident that he was "The World's Best-Selling Author!" In order to sweeten the deal, both *hardcover* and softcover editions would be part of a new contract.

He hadn't always been happy with his string of former publishers nor they with him, but he had a friendship with Roger Straus, and his new editor, Robert Giroux, was trustworthy and sensitive to Erskine's best interests. Yet Caldwell was well aware that Wey-bright and Enoch deserved consideration: they had printed count-less copies of his short stories and novels, never asking him to revise the material. There were several meetings in New York with NAL, and Weybright journeyed to Los Angeles for an anticipated consummation.

The congenial and persuasive publisher further tempted Caldwell by promising to bring out *In the Shadow of the Steeple* in return for NAL's rights to all future novels. To Erskine's surprise, a clause was attached to the offered contract indicating that all prospective *nonfiction* books would be published by a company not affiliated with NAL. "It was then revealed," wrote Caldwell, "that a company bearing his name (Weybright) was being organized and would soon begin publishing books in hardcover editions."

The wavering author surrendered and immediately delivered to NAL his new book, *Miss Mamma Aimee* and pledged to complete *Summertime Island* for early submission. But first, there must be repairs on the *Steeple* manuscript; Weybright insisted that it would be a "disaster" to bring out a book with such an "ominous title." When asked to explain, the publisher replied: "Because readers will avoid reading any book that bears the slightest suggestion of being a religious tract. The people with an emotional devotion of their personal religious beliefs don't want to risk having their tranquility disturbed by reading comments and observations by somebody who may have persuasive beliefs differing from their own." *Deep South* was Weybright's choice for a title because, he said: "It's safe."

*Miss Mamma Aimee*, Caldwell's new novel of 210 pages, was published on May 1, 1967. "Miss Mamma Aimee" Mangrum, as her disliked son-in-law, Woody, calls her and others echo, is a rattlebrained, faded but still attractive woman who is strong on family pride but weak on domestic economics. Aimee inherits all the family property of 8,000 acres and the stately mansion, but in order to support herself and numerous relatives and in-laws she is forced to sell large parcels of land from time to time until only a thousand unworked acres remain.

Besides her mentally impaired son, Graham, Aimee supports her daughter, Velma; the girl's guitar-playing husband, Woody Woodruff; her brother-in-law, Russell Mangrum; and Russell's bitchy wife, Katie. Complications arise when Miss Mamma becomes interested in a roaming preacher, Brother Raley Purdy, who is trying to establish his own brand of religion which he calls the Supreme Being Mission. Aimee offers to take in the horny preacher, and while she awaits his arrival, her daughter, Connie, who has been a call girl in Savannah, returns home for a visit until the hubbub abates after a police raid on her nightclub headquarters.

Evangelist Purdy who likes sex and God (in that order) plays havoc with Aimee's purse and lust and Connie's natural talents. But there are contradictions: When the preacher sees a naked girl he worries about what "if Billy Graham saw me now." The girl asks, "Who is Billy Graham?" to which he replies, "I can't talk about Billy Graham when you're stark naked—he wouldn't want me to."

Not one man in Aimee's home has a job and the women rarely help around the house—they leave the work to the Negro maid, Martha, who has been with the family for years. Tired of it all, and more liberated than black domestics were a decade earlier, Martha leaves to find work and a living wage with "Yankee Jews."

The tale shifts from comedy to tragedy: When Miss Mamma invites Brother Purdy to make free with her daughters—in order to keep the preacher from abandoning the mansion—Graham is opposed to her sleep-in plan, and a scene of Gothic horror culminates in the murder of Miss Aimee.

Caldwell scholar James Korges praised the book: "Perhaps the best of his novels since *Georgia Boy, Miss Mamma Aimee* is about the live past and the dead present." Korges saw the work as structured on "a complex series of reversals." Family histories endured while plantation tracts were being sold; race relations were changing along with traditional values.

John K. Sherman in *The Minneapolis Tribune* called this 41st book by Caldwell "stronger in character and conflict than some of its predecessors. If it isn't elevating it is entertaining by an experienced entertainer." Further positive commentary came from the Pasadena, California *Star News*: "Caldwell's humor is in full play in this latest novel," wrote Brent Howell who felt the characters in the work were "drawn and issues joined" with more skillful strokes than in much of the author's earlier tales. "The master story-teller is master still."

Predictably, publications that had come down heavily on Caldwell's cyclorama of the South series and his novels about women were not persuaded to favor *Miss Mamma Aimee*. Joel Clemons of the Charleston, South Carolina *News & Courier* concluded his review by saying that "Caldwell's South is one I, fortunately, do not know. And I doubt seriously that anyone—including the author—knows." The *Pittsburgh Press* reserved no space for kindness: "The book is gratuitously and deliberately obscene and reads much as if it had been written by a comedian who, realizing that he is losing his grip and his audience, lapses into vulgarity in a crude and futile effort to hold attention." Probably the sternest rebuke came when W. Emerson Wilson asked in the Wilmington, Delaware *News*: "How could such a promising literary career have ended in such a mess as this? One wonders and one feels a bit sad about it all."

Caldwell begins *Deep South* with the admission that he was untouched by the steeple's shadow:

> The experience of living for six months of a year or sometimes longer in one Southern state after another, in cities and small towns and countrysides, and being exposed to numerous varieties of Protestant sects which were Calvinist in doctrine and fundamentalist in practice proved to be of more value to me than the intermittent and frequently curtailed secular education during the first seventeen years of my life.

Modern Protestantism is viewed by a minister's son who soon becomes disillusioned. Though haunted by scenes of snake handlers, bloodlettings, and glossolalia, Caldwell pragmatically notes that such experiences are necessary rituals for ignorant and deprived millworkers and sharecroppers—their lives would be emptier without these ceremonies conducted by sly evangelists and tricksters. His father, an intelligent man of ethical attitudes, introduced him to the bush religions of fundamentalists, which then as now are closely allied to ultraconservative politics. (Viewers have only to turn on their television sets any Sunday morning for gospel hysterics.) Caldwell finds that these sects are splitting into ever more outlandish factions as he microscopes them. *Deep South* is a storyteller's history of white and black religious life in the South during the early years of the twentieth century—that is its grace and strength—and one of Caldwell's more adventurous journeys with words.

He was unable to determine the extent of his father's belief in God and traditional Protestantism, and had never asked, just as Ira had never quizzed his son about such matters. Christ was not dwelt on at home, and in the pulpit any direct reference was expressed symbolically for the purpose of guiding his flock towards ethical conduct. If a person fulfilled the requirements of the Ten Commandments, no further reading of the Bible was necessary.

In an interview, Caldwell was asked to distinguish his philosophy of life from the teachings of his father's church and he answered the question by identifying himself as a naturalist. "Of course, I know that a person has the ability to change his own life and to direct his own existence to some extent. But at the same time, I think, fundamentally, we are all people of nature and nature is going to get us one way or another."

A minister was expected to assume a variety of roles during the twenties and thirties in rural Georgia: financial advisor, marriage counsellor, social welfare worker, arbitrator between feuding families—Ira willingly did these, but he resisted all pressures by his critics to conform to the prevailing religious practices and spent much of his time on humanitarian projects, impartially benefitting church members and non-members, white or black. His frank way of speaking frequently got him in trouble with his parishioners and members of other denominations. A mild disagreement prompted his critics to call him unorthodox—which he was throughout his ministry—and a heated argument usually brought forth accusations that he was an atheist and Communist.

Caldwell had never known his father to criticize another person's religion, but on one occasion he heard Ira Sylvester say that some unfortunate people, like gluttons and alcoholics, would be better off if they could be cured of religious excesses. After the two had witnessed a snake-handling ritual, Erskine recalled his father coming away silent and subdued. There were times like this, Ira told his son, that he thought of resigning from the ministry to devote the rest of his life to teaching. The South was engulfed by primitive religious practices, and more education was needed to counteract such influences.

The legacies of frontier revivalism were evident in the South during the time of Ira's ministry; there still was that preoccupation with individual repentance and the tendency to dramatize religious ceremonies. But the world was threatening Southern self-centeredness; there were the pressures of labor unrest, industrialism, and agricultural inequities. The last bastion was the church, exclusively concerned with saving souls, far more concerned with preparations for the Hereafter than with social welfare or political reforms: it was aloof and unmoved by the injustices of an economic system which exploited sharecroppers and cotton-mill workers.

The church thus remains the sole arbiter of moral values. After the parson's exhortations to his parishioners that they must quell their appetites for drink, cards and promiscuity, followed by a rousing call to repent, the choir explodes with an old-time gospel of singing. A place of worship in the South is more than a meeting house for worshippers: it is also a social center for the neighborhood. When asked what people in her part of town did for recreation, a Southern woman replied: "Why, we go to church."

Both Caldwell and his father applauded the church services practiced by blacks while contemplating those intense discombobulated rituals; such theology was therapy and led to serenity. The prospect of the soul's salvation dispensed by a white Jesus Christ and an eternity in heaven under the auspices of a white God had very little appeal to blacks living in hostile environments. The only earthly place of temporary refuge was in a church of their own with religious services designed to gratify an illiterate membership: they had no need for hymnbooks and Bibles; instead of sermons and prayers, familiar biblical stories were enhanced along with the singing of spirituals.

Since blacks were unable to raise enough money to build their churches, they accepted help from white landlords. Such contributions were considered excellent investments—white Protestants were convinced that "religious niggers would be good niggers" and not troublesome ones. The theory, however, was not as tenable as anticipated: once a church was built, it often became a sanctuary from the rule of plantation bosses.

*Deep South* drew favorable reviews, as did *Bisco,* and for a short time critics wondered whether Caldwell would exorcise the curse of having written too many prescription novels for "spin it" racks. Anthologies prior to World War II usually gave his work space, but he was increasingly being ignored by the literary establishment. NAL's lurid covers aimed at the skin trade did little to repair his sinking reputation.

Virginia Caldwell believed that switching publishers had a "devastating" effect on her husband's reputation as a writer—if Erskine had stayed with Farrar, Straus, and Giroux, he would have been more secure in academic circles. When NAL sold to the Times-Mirror organization, Weybright was dislodged from his position as president, and "kicked upstairs." The hardcover project, which Caldwell had reluctantly accepted, never materialized, and as a consequence he had lost his publishing foothold.

*Deep South* is Caldwell's best nonfiction rendering of his native region, but it didn't fulfill the expectations of either author or publisher. Unfortunately, the book appeared at a point in his career when he was being excessively pummeled by critics. A reissuing of *South* in 1980 by the University of Georgia Press should have helped to rectify the neglect, though by that time the civil rights movement had outdated some of the book's impact.

One risks inaccuracy when labeling any memory and observation treatment by Caldwell as a departure from fiction. His practice of supplying imaginary monologues as a substitute for what he actually may have heard from people he interviewed for works of nonfiction often irritated critics. It was a method of intensifying impressions—to him, there never were borderlines between under-statement and exaggeration; what was and what might have been—in writing or life. Closer looks at his two previous autobiographical attempts reveal yarns and vignettes that could have been included in a collection of his short stories. In *With All My Might* his ob-serving Bugsy Siegel at a casino on the Las Vegas Strip is a first-draft story outline. *Deep South* is also packed with incidents that need only titles to make them tales. When these are taken collect-ively, with Caldwell's father as the protagonist, Ira emerges as the hero of an episodic novel.

Virginia Caldwell zealously guarded her husband's privacy when he was writing, and reporters found it difficult to arrange meetings with the author at his home. She kept diaries of their appointments and travels, even saved ticket stubs, invitations, labels from cham-pagne bottles, and business cards. Columnists Gene Robertson and Carrie Davis, along with photographer Ralph Flynn, were surprised when an ordinary scheduled interview at Orinda became a hospi-table and cordial visit. While Flynn wandered about taking photo-graphs, the four sat on the patio and chatted as if they were "long-time friends." Caldwell spoke of his writing habits and his days on the *Atlanta Journal*; Carrie Davis and Virginia were soon talking about cooking and exchanging recipes—included was a method of making gumbo. Later, the visitors were given a tour of the new home. "Several of Mrs. Caldwell's lovely paintings adorned the walls," described Robertson, "and this included a huge abstraction which is a dramatic departure from her previous work." A three-panel screen (Virginia's idea) was completely covered with colorful dust jackets of Caldwell's books printed in foreign countries; they all agreed that the Denmark jacket for *Georgia Boy* was the most attractive. Instead of a bar in the playroom, the dominant fixture was a billiard table—"The only time he relaxes," said Virginia. That, and when watching football. (He attended every home game of the San Francisco 49ers while living in the Bay Area and saw them on television when the team was on the road.)

The two columnists had expected the interview to be a difficult one: in public, Caldwell was often shy and had a hesitant manner when answering questions. But in the sanctuary of his Orinda nest there wasn't a vestige of that public stiffness and reserve. "If the mark of perfect host and hostess is to put their guests completely at ease," declared the impressed Robertson, "then Erskine and Virginia Caldwell score 100 percent in my book."

The daily schedule at Orinda was no different than the one they had kept in San Francisco. "My husband works from 9:30 to 6 or so, seven days a week," Virginia told Agnes Murphy of the *New York Post*. "After I've tidied up the house, I go to the village for the mail. Then I have office work." There were scrapbooks to keep current, formidable royalty logs to record, and a heavy correspondence. After a brief lunch, Caldwell returned to his writing and she to more letters, perhaps a little painting, or tasks around the house. "Supper is no set time—maybe 7, sometimes as late as 9. And it's likely to be simple—steak and a salad."

Readers who had been shocked by the violence and sexual explicitness found in his novels and short stories would have been bemused had they known his and Virginia's conventional lifestyle. As intentionally vulgar as Caldwell had been in his youth, and openly unfaithful during his marriage to Helen, after meeting Virginia he became increasingly puritanical. "I dislike a lot of my characters," said their creator. "I'm ashamed of them. They do things I don't approve of. But it can't be helped. They've got to be what they are."

Virginia was fascinated by some of the letters her husband had received, especially those from people who thought they knew one of his fictional characters. "The most wonderful letter," she recalled, "was from a man who wrote and offered a home to one of Erskine's fictional people. He said, 'If there is really such a person, we'd like to help her. She has such a terrible life in the South— we'd treat her much better than she was treated in the story.' "

Caldwell never shared a manuscript with his fourth wife while it was being written—the exception, during a time of failing health, was *With All My Might*. "If I go into his room," declared Virginia, "I so much want to look at that manuscript that it nearly kills me. But I am superstitious and I haven't dared look yet." Her first chance to read a new work came only after he had typed the final revision. Once, when going over one of his stories, Virginia called his attention to a paragraph and remarked that she didn't like the comment that a character made. "I don't like it either," he replied, "but that's the way the man talks." The paragraph went unaltered, and after that she left well enough alone.

"Do you like music?"
"No."
"Painting?"
"No."
"How about reading?"
"Just newspapers and a couple of the news magazines."
"No books?"
"No."
"Science? Philosophy? Literary Criticism?"
"No."
"Then what do you like?"
"People. I like to tell stories about them."

This 1967 exchange was with Keith Coulbourn, a staff writer for the Lakeland, Florida *Ledger View*. The brevity of his replies was gaged to emphasize his storytelling role—of course he read books, admired paintings, and had above-average intellectual curiosities. The Caldwells had been vacationing in a private home for a month, and their visit had been kept secret. "Who wants a lot of social-izing?" he asked Coulbourn. "So you go to a cocktail party and there's all this yackety-yak. Or you have to listen to yackety-yak." He didn't play golf, hunt or fish, and his one hobby was travel.

Over the years, he developed a sizeable pouch of pat answers for there was a considerable amount of repetition in the questions asked, and his shyness often led him to take on a persona that he thought best projected his image—former football player and sometimes local yokel. In a Baltimore *Evening Star* interview, he told reporters: "I'm just a simple country boy who is still fond of turnips."

For work, a bare room suited him best: All he needed was a table, chair, yellow pads, soft-lead pencils, dictionary, and typewriter. There were five or six typewriters in their Orinda home, and he bought a new one every eight or nine months. "Do you bang on your machine pretty hard?" "Oh no," he replied. "But I do a lot of rewriting. I rewrite everything about nine times. I'm never satisfied. I keep trying to get better. I keep going till it sounds right."

When asked if he had any superstitions about writing, Caldwell remembered the Maine years. "I have a red rug in my room. Wherever I've lived in life, I've carried my red rug with me. I keep it in excellent shape. I have it vacuumed; I have it dry-cleaned." He had lived too long on cold and splintery floors during his apprentice years in Mount Vernon. An unheated room in a New England winter was "a difficult dungeon." He remembered the moment that this luxury could be afforded. "And I decided then that I'd carry my red rug with me wherever I went."

Caldwell believed in allowing a rush of words to happen. If he came to his writing room and had nothing to say, he would patiently sit until thoughts appeared on paper. Over and over, he proudly announced that he had "the biggest wastepaper basket in town" (a half barrel), and at the end of each work session it would be full. When his eight-hour stint was successful, he might have as many as three typewritten pages, but it wasn't uncommon for him to sit at the typewriter all day and end up with scant results.

Writers have their individual craft habits—he never took notes or formulated plots—his way was to start with a few words: get that first sentence on a sheet of yellow paper and see what happens. "I don't know what my characters are going to do next," said Caldwell, "and that keeps my interest up in the book I'm writing." If he knew, he would be too bored to finish the job. Fictional characters needed room for expansion as they marched through his pages, and he never hampered them with preconceived ideas. "Once the process of creation is over the story is dead."

He felt the short story was the origin of fiction, and one had to perfect that before undertaking a novel. A short piece of fiction was the best teacher that one could have. "I don't know how many short stories William Saroyan has written, but in his early life there were times when he would write a short story a day. He learned he wasn't spending enough time on it, so he gave himself a week to write a short story. I had very much the same feeling about it, that I wanted to write as quickly as I could and then go on to the next one."

He usually gave himself a year for each novel and started work slowly—six or seven hours a day, four to five days a week. After two or three weeks the work schedule increased to eight hours, six days a week, and later ten-hour days all week long. Yes, the pace quickened but care had to be taken because the long story must be filtered through one "like moonshine whiskey."

Caldwell hadn't been a writer in the beginning; he had been a listener of tales told around the wood yard, store, and cotton gin. Southerners were skilled in the oral tradition of making a far-fetched idea believable or the smallest incident interesting—"it could be just a rooster crowing at a certain time of night or morning."

His principal concept of writing was to tell the story. People sometimes thought that he was trying to reform or change things, but his only motive was to make the tale interesting. He had his own way of working, and the method wasn't exact. Telling the story was a constant experimentation, and the things he needed most were "plenty of those yellow sheets and typewriter ribbons."

Another 1967 book, a strange companion piece for *Miss Mamma Aimee*, was *Writing in America*, a work from a series of lectures which partly fell into the category of autobiography as did his early 1929 broadside, *In Defense of Myself* and some of *Deep South*. Self-sketches and invented dialogues with his critics punctuated the presentation: "A literary eunuch or procurer" was one who kicks the author's shins and flails the readers' spirits whenever consummation between them takes place without his active procurement. A critic was "the lazy sparrow who moved into a ready-made crow's nest in the top of a tall tree." He asserted that the poverty of recent fiction had been brought about by the misplaced and stumbling attitudes of such literary judges.

Caldwell acknowledged to his readers that he was motivated by the need not just to fictionalize but to record the lives of people outside the mainstream. "*The Bastard*," divulged the author, "was conceived and written as an important and untouched phase of American *mores*"—it had been structured as literature that simultaneously beckoned to the sociologist, and could be labeled folkway history, "the personal diary of the people."

A national fiction of endurance was his hope and it would come perhaps from "a record and a revelation of the social, moral, political and economic history of America." Young writers should "dramatize and interpret and give meaningful direction to the unresolved economic and racial inequalities."

Any accomplishments he might achieve in his work were for himself, not for his readers or inept critics. His and the literature of fellow writers were tied closely to the contexts in which they appeared. "Fiction in America changes almost from one day to the next," he insisted. Perhaps his work would never be contemporary again, but if there should be a revival of interest in what he did, it would come from style as "historical appeal," not content.

Critics who camped in Caldwell's dwindling court found *Writing in America* praiseworthy, and predictably, those who were of the opinion that his heyday was behind him dismissed the book with sighs and grunts or ignored it entirely.

By the time of *Writing in America*, Caldwell had been categorized as a minor writer with few ideas, though the cruelest charge was that he did not really understand the humans he wrote about. Had he called it a day before the 1940s, the assessment might have been more generous. Perhaps fewer publishers would have been to his advantage. The generally conceived decline of his work in such novels as *Love and Money* (1954), *Gretta* (1955), and *Jenny by Nature* (1961) hardened the disapproval of reviewers and critics who had only praise for his earlier books.

Otis Ferguson, in his "Story-Teller's Workshop"—this was in the early forties and published by *Accent*—believed that Caldwell had not succeeded because the subject matter was too overpowering. It was the conundrum of sacrificing fiction for sociological reporting. Though Caldwell's preoccupation with violence was calculated to be sensational, his purpose was to alert his native region and nation of deplorable living conditions in the South while telling an entertaining story.

*Summertime Island,* like *Close to Home* (1962), was faithful in reflecting the 1954 Supreme Court decision of racial equality and desegregation. In these two novels, blacks were not subservient; they speak up for their rights and defend them with action. But prior to 1950, Caldwell characterized black-white relationships as they existed: Negroes were expected to be humble and shambling and were punished like children—anything to make them acquiesce to the premise of racial inferiority. Both *Trouble in July* (1940) and *Place Called Estherville* (1949) mirrored the times.

*Summertime Island* was Caldwell's 1968 contribution as the literary treadmill whirled in a cycle of interviews, promotional appearances for NAL, college campus visits, travels, and long (and sometimes sluggish) bouts with words—things were imperceptibly coming apart but sales were still staggering. The new book carried overtones of Mark Twain's river novel, though Caldwell declared that he was unfamiliar with this work and looked forward to one day reading *Huckleberry Finn.*

Troy Peckett is a lower-class, uneducated lout of a man who has a soaring hatred for Negroes. His sadism begins with kicks and punches and escalates to rape and murder. As the novel opens, Troy accompanies a middle-aged, mild-mannered white man, his nephew, and a young black schoolteacher on a fishing trip. Troy, who has been asked along because he has a truck, suggests that they bring along the black schoolteacher, Duke—a "colored fellow" would be helpful around camp. Guthry, the uncle, concurs, and the nephew, Steve, who narrates the tale is silent. All the way to the Mississippi River, Troy mistreats Duke. "An educated nigger!" his tormentor tells him. "Now ain't that something! You stand still and don't move so I can get a good look at you."

The outing begins on a vicious note: Troy leaves his companions and rushes into a nearby field to rape a black girl. A dozen Negro women, clutching hoes, stand by wailing at his action. Behind a curtain of saplings the three in the fishing party listen helplessly; "What can anybody do?" the mild uncle asks unhappily.

After leaving the mainland for Summertime Island, Troy is forced to rely more on Duke; the schoolteacher rows him across a treacherous river and saves his life when the boat capsizes. It is decided that as long as they are on the island Duke and Troy will be on a first-name basis.

The young black and Steve become friends, swim naked together in the river—as did Twain's Huck and Jim. The idyllic scene is interrupted when another fishing group invades the island and in that party is Bonnie, a beautiful loose young woman who soon initiates Steve in explicit and physical ways—unlike Huck Finn's innocent wandering eye for Mary Jane.

As the novel closes, the fishing four are back to the truck with their gear. Time now for Troy to behave characteristically: He runs Duke down with the truck, breaking both legs and some ribs—the cruel white man now demands to be called "Mr."

A routine physical examination in California revealed that Caldwell had emphysema, and his doctor suggested that he move as soon as possible to a semi-tropical climate where swimming daily would be beneficial. Since he and Virginia were familiar with various locations in Florida, they decided to go house hunting. The search ended in Dunedin where they came upon a builder who was pouring a cement foundation for a home that he planned to sell. Agreeing to Virginia's changes in design, the builder widened the foundation and installed a swimming pool. Five months later the couple moved into their new Florida home.

Five decades of smoking two packages of cigarettes a day and fifteen years of excessive drinking had damaged his health. But shortly after moving to Dunedin, Erskine was assured by a specialist that his ailment was nothing more than chronic bronchitis and the condition would be aggravated if the water in the swimming pool wasn't heated to body temperature. Erskine was tempted to fill the pool with gravel and loam and send the bill to the California doctor for a faulty diagnosis—it probably was the Florida physician who misread his condition.

Although he tired easily and had only a ghost of his old stamina, Caldwell was eager to complete another novel. First, there were travel plans: The United States Information Service wanted him to make another tour in Europe, a two week itinerary limited to Oslo, Stockholm, Milan, Amsterdam, and London. He and Virginia accepted immediately; both were delighted to be traveling again.

The setting of *The Weather Shelter* is Grover Danford's Tennessee breeding farm of Shetland ponies. The owner and his head stableman now want to introduce a stronger bloodline to improve the stock—the assumption is that crossbreeding gives vitality to decadent lines; an identical premise found in *A Lamp for Nightfall* with the mixing of Yankees and French Canadians. (Caldwell clearly had his Maine novel in mind: "Goddam lawyers," one character in *The Weather Shelter* tells Grover Danford. "Sleep late in the morning and read forty words out of their lawbooks and slap a lien on a poor man's chattels if he can't hand over forty dollars in cash when they snap their fingers." Few residents of Tennessee would say it quite that way. This clipped delivery of words only could be coming from Caldwell's Maine neighbors or from a person in *A Lamp for Nightfall*.)

The pony-breeding analogy applies to Grover Danford's affair with the mulatto woman, Kathlee, who bears his light-skinned son, Jeff. Grover's white wife is lesbian, and consequently the boy is the only son Danford will have to carry on the business.

Caldwell also explores the predicaments of race mixing: the rejection by whites and the resentment of blacks who are developing a militant pride in their own race. Black children taunt Jeff on the street with a song:

> I have a little brother
> With shiny brownish hair.
> My mama says she got him
> Out behind the county fair.

Jeff's black grandfather closes the door on him: "I don't want nobody in this town seeing a white-nigger hanging around my house. I'm a black man and I stay proud of it." No white restaurant will serve Jeff, and when he is seen riding in the front seat of his father's car, the two face the hostility of whites.

Grover is willing to leave his farm and go away with Kathlee to some place where they can marry, but before he can arrange this she unexpectedly dies. Danford rescues Jeff from a lynch mob and savors the feeling of the boy's arms around his neck. The father is now determined to raise his son openly and name him as the inheritor of the pony-breeding farm.

Caldwell had completed a six-week stint as writer-in-residence at Dartmouth, and early in 1971 he was asked to sit for a portrait to enliven the large collection of his books and manuscripts in the college's Baker Library. He assumed the oil would be painted on campus but was informed that it would be executed by John Gilroy in London. The timing was right: Erskine had planned to meet with his English publisher and agent in October, and from there he and Virginia expected to travel to Japan where Caldwell was scheduled to lecture at universities in Tokyo and Kyoto for the United States Information Service. They decided to go by way of the Middle East since it was approximately the same distance from London; stops were to be made in Lebanon, Pakistan, India, and Thailand on their way to Tokyo.

Before an informal group of professors and journalists at the American Cultural Center in Tokyo he shared his thoughts on fiction writing. Lecturer and Caldwell translator Fujisato Kitajima recalls the author becoming "hoarse and seemingly weary and guarded" as he addressed the gathering:

> I have written one book a year for the last fifty years and maybe one hundred and fifty short stories published in magazines and books. To me, fiction is the real heart of writing. I think I am a romanticist, though others say I am too realistic, too hard. The purpose of all the books of fiction I have written is to provide a mirror into which people may look. Whatever good or harm my books do depends on an individual's reaction to the image he sees in the mirror.

Caldwell's next offering, *The Earnshaw Neighborhood*, published in 1971, was in part a soap-opera farce reminiscent of "A Country Full of Swedes." The tourist bus pulls up in front of Medora Earnshaw's house, and she holds the camera-clicking gawkers at bay with her garden hose. Children, barking dogs, bicycles, and police cars appear in the scene—everyone is talking and no one is listening.

As in *Miss Mamma Aimee*, social changes along racial lines are acknowledged. Zerena White, the black maid, insists that her white employer call her Mrs. White, and she won't let her daughter model in the buff before a non-integrated group. Martin Luther King, Jr. and George Wallace are mentioned as Caldwell articulates his views on integration while developing what he said about blacks in the early thirties: "The Negro has yet to sink as low, economically and morally, as the white man....I doubt very much if the Negro will ever fall to the lowest depths of the white race."

Caldwell didn't bring out a novel in 1972 though one was underway, *Annette*, his last. There were the usual trips for promotional chores, interviews, and talks—he may have been trashed by the literary establishment, but there still was a wide following of readers. Erskine and Virginia usually celebrated their New Year's Eve wedding anniversary in chosen locations from New York to Honolulu. Memorable as these occasions had been, they agreed that the most practical way of commemorating the date would be for both of them to check into the Mayo Clinic for medical examinations. After three days of elaborate tests they were declared "fit for another year of living."

The United States Information Service arranged for Caldwell to visit cities in Scandinavia and behind the Iron Curtain, including a stop in Moscow. Unlike earlier trips where he attended receptions and gave readings, his assignment was to speak only at universities. Denmark, Finland, Poland, Czechoslovakia, Hungary, Yugoslavia, Bulgaria, and Romania were on the crowded schedule; Caldwell kept to it and returned to Dunedin exhausted—soon to face another batch of tepid and bleak book reviews.

The scene of Caldwell's *Annette* is a nighttime suburb with tree-lined streets. The heroine is a neurotic who in unable to jettison her upbringing: rejected by an insane mother who is eventually institutionalized and a father who is unable to return the love she so desperately seeks, the troubled girl sits naked before a mirror and for hours laments to Mr. Truelove, a life-sized teddy bear.

Annette's first marriage is a love match but husband Wayne is murdered. Her choice of a second husband is influenced by her friend Evelyn who practices astrology, but there is disappointment when number two fails to give her the three children she and Wayne had wanted—Annette's new man never mentions his vasectomy.

Then comes the night she decides to leave him: yet the moment that she steps into the unlit rainy street she becomes the victim of threatening men and a tease to males who would help her. Every dash for safety leads her into a more dangerous situation. She is assaulted by a boy when she goes to a house to telephone her best friend's husband. The rescuer makes sexual advances and abandons her in a park when she refuses him. But Annette, the victim, embraces the friend of the boy who had attacked her. These entanglements are not accidental; Annette is as much guilty as innocent in the mix of her neurosis. In the end, she is murdered. Women have no control over their fates, regardless of their improved lives and styles, Caldwell tells his readers, and they are vulnerable to men's mistreatment and violence.

Philip Henderson, in his *The Novel Today: Studies in Contemporary Attitudes*, assessed *Tobacco Road* as superior to any of Faulkner's novels: "Caldwell not only gives an unforgettable picture of the world in all the bitter humor of its ruin, but, by concrete social settings, shows us why his agricultural morons are as they are and indicates how their individual helplessness can be remedied by large-scale collective farming on the part of both whites and blacks."

When asked why he wrote so much about poor people and the unpleasant things of life, Caldwell replied: "Those enjoying the pleasant things in life are fewer than those enduring the unpleasant. When this social condition no longer exists, I'll feel there is no longer any purpose in writing about effects of poverty on the human spirit." With this attitude and his productivity, he soon became a scalawag to the Southern literary historian.

Erskine acknowledged that one could analyze his stories and come up with suppositions, but what he set out to do while writing them was entirely different. "If the reader comes along and reads a story, he may get much more out of it than I got because there is always the chance that he sees things that I don't."

Caldwell tried to write in a straightforward style. "I fail sometimes," he admitted, "because I get carried away with enthusiasm, and think maybe I have discovered a way to embellish something. But that's so false with me that when I go back to revise it I always strike it out and try to be simple."

In the early years of his career, his progress had become cloudy when he strayed from Hemingway's writing style. Thoughts had no sharp edges while the sentences lengthened, though he did manage to keep some syntactical integrity. His dangerous precipice was the unshakable conviction that whatever could be brought to mind *could* be placed on paper.

The simplest word was the one he preferred "to find out how to squeeze it." As an example, Caldwell proposed the word "entertainment," which he didn't like because of length. But "fun" was a word he didn't favor either. "So I have to get a word between those two that has the meaning I want." His passion for using small words was so intense that in one instance he went through a *Webster Collegiate* and crossed out all words that had more than four syllables: "I think, probably my main reason in crossing out the words of many syllables and of great length was because I couldn't spell them," he told an interviewer. Yet when asked to name his favorite author, Caldwell replied: "Noah Webster."

Automobiles were important props in his stories and he used them with pop-cultural frequency. Other influences were pulp magazines, the movies, and daily newspapers. Characters rush one another in his tales, fire weapons carelessly, and leap out of windows. If a story began to lose momentum, he quickly enlivened it with some humorous disturbance or violent happening. Another notable device to catch his audience was word repetition in substantiating characterization; noticeable examples were Jeeter Lester's "By God and by Jesus," Spence Douthit's "Dogbite my pecker," and Ty Ty Walden's "Why in the pluperfect hell."

As the treadmill slowed, critics all too quickly measured him a minor and limited writer, and this assessment caused much of his neglect. Caldwell was well aware of the decline. At a University of Georgia conference near the end of his life, he said more to himself than to those who were standing around him: "I hate to go in bookstores. I hate to see how many of my books aren't there."

# THE CLOSING CHAPTER

Caldwell began having annual physical examinations at the Mayo Clinic in Rochester, Minnesota while he was in Tucson. His first visit there was in order to find relief for a "persistent case of lingering amoebic tourista" that had plagued him after a ten-day stay in Mexico.

A few years later Dr. Llewelyn Howell, a Mayo consultant, told him there was a blocked artery in his left leg and prompt care must be taken in order to save the limb from amputation. When a startled Caldwell asked what should be done, Dr. Howell's response was immediate: the patient must stop smoking cigarettes. Erskine had tried to stop several times, but now there was no choice. He retreated to the nearest bar and fortified himself with two fingers of bourbon and his last cigarette. The final puff was blown upward in a gigantic smoke ring which hovered over the bar. Several years later, after the retirement of Dr. Howell, another Mayo consultant, Dr. Richard Weeks, persuaded him to give up bourbon and replace it with a moderate serving of wine.

Caldwell left the Mayo Clinic in the early spring of 1972 in good spirits and ready to enjoy a few weeks of meetings with publishers and translators, mostly in France. Shortly after their return home, he and Virginia travelled by automobile through several Midwestern states; Caldwell interviewed while she sketched for what would be their second travel book, *Afternoons in Mid-America*. While in Iowa, they decided that he should return for another series of tests that Dr. Weeks had been conducting periodically for the past year. Erskine thought these medical probes were routine but the doctor had voiced continued concern.

After five days of bronchoscopy, esophaguscopy, and X-ray tests, there was evidence of cancer in his right lung. Since it was Friday, and the surgeon didn't operate on weekends, Erskine was scheduled to enter the hospital on Monday. Virginia had telephoned Elizabeth Fawcett in Brainard, Minnesota where she and book distributor Roscoe had summer property, and on hearing about the pending operation, the Fawcetts invited their friends for the weekend. "For my part," wrote Erskine, "I was glum and apprehensive about life thereafter....The best I could do was to smile occasionally while most of the time wondering, if I did not survive lung surgery, what momentous events might take place in the world after my life had ended."

Half of his right lung was removed, and he was in intensive care for six days before being moved to a hospital room. He was grateful to be alive and well aware that there wouldn't have been cancer if he had stopped smoking cigarettes years earlier—crumpled sheets of paper in the wastebasket and a mound of butts in the ashtray were accoutrements of his long struggle with words. Virginia spent much of her time in Rochester answering the telephone: there were calls from Erskine's children, friends, and literary people involved in his life. One of the more unusual gestures of concern and respect was an anonymous telegram stating that a donation had been made in his name to have prayers said for an entire year at a Cleveland Catholic church.

It was seventeen hundred miles from Minnesota to Florida, a trip fatiguing enough for a hardy traveler, and both Virginia and his doctor had extracted from him the promise that he would not drive the car. "As much as I wanted to sit in the driver's seat," admitted Caldwell, "and envious of Virginia for having the privilege, I managed somehow to be moderately pleasant as we went southward through the states to Dunedin."

After a month of recuperation in Florida, he and Virginia left for Iowa—this time Caldwell driving while his wife resumed "her knitting, reading, and letter writing as usual when traveling by car." From the tall corn country they prowled in a southerly direction, ending their exploratory journey several weeks later in the Oklahoma Panhandle. The most exciting part of the trip, claimed Caldwell, was the Cow Chip Festival, a Dust Bowl annual extravaganza, in which contestants whirl dung cakes, and as an out-of-state visitor, he was offered the opportunity to fling a chip.

Upon their return to Dunedin, Caldwell rushed into the manuscript with his usual alacrity, though his work habits were not as rigorous; he needed further recuperation and was easily fatigued.

It wasn't until the early part of 1975 that Ed Lathem, editor for his current publisher Dodd, Mead and Company, came to Florida for the first glimpse of the partly completed manuscript.

In spring, and too soon to commence another field trip to finalize the travel book, Kazimierz and Wanda Piotrowski, his Polish translators, wanted him for an autographing session at a Polish book fair. Such an invitation was irresistible for the footloose Southern gypsy. "There was no difficulty about meeting the expenses of the long weekend trip," Caldwell recalled—the pragmatist throughout life—"which was to be at the height of the flowering lilac season in Warsaw, since my blocked royalty accounts were more than ample to pay for round-trip flights on LOT, the Polish airline between New York and Warsaw." His stint of book signing took place under a sheltered umbrella of trees in a park where he sat for two and a half hours and autographed a total of nine hundred copies. A Soviet novelist from Moscow, seated at another table, smilingly challenged Caldwell without much success.

After their return from Poland, the second field trip was planned to begin in the middle of June in the Dakotas. Erskine had another stop at the Mayo Clinic for his routine twice-yearly tests, and X-rays this time revealed cancer in the other lung. Again, immediate surgery was prescribed, but Caldwell insisted that the operation be delayed until he and Virginia had time to complete another phase of their field trip. His concerned surgeon reluctantly gave permission, and the Caldwells left Rochester for Brookings, South Dakota, and later traveled westward to visit the Standing Rock Indian Reservation. At the end of six weeks of travel, he returned to the clinic and Dr. Spencer Payne removed half of the other lung.

The doctors were amazed at his resilience and spirited frame of mind. His labored breathing was never discussed, and he refused the painkilling tablets they gave him. He stoically remarked to one doctor and with an edge of humor: "If I had more lungs, I'd probably have more cancer." His one concern was to get back to his typewriter, and Caldwell was adamant that he be discharged from the hospital as soon as possible.

He now was placed on a regimen that wasn't appealing to a man of his intemperate nature. The second period of recuperation in Florida gave him sufficient time to complete the text for *Afternoons in Mid-America*, and after his manuscript was turned over to his publisher, he had more travelling in mind.

Caldwell returned to Europe in the spring of 1976 and began his fifth and final tour for the United States Information Service. His doctors preferred that he be a more sedentary patient but there were editors and translators to see, and Caldwell refused to succumb to an armchair existence.

The trip started with Milan and Rome, ending in Paris and London after a tour through Scandinavia. In Paris, he was surprised to learn that Marcel Duhamel and Virginia had secretly arranged a meeting with Alexander Calder who had illustrated a French edition of *The Sacrilege of Alan Kent*. Though Pablo Picasso had agreed to do the drawings he died before this could be accomplished, and Aimee Maeght, of the publishing firm, got Calder to furnish the illustrations. This edition sold immediately—not as a result of an overlooked and experimental work by Caldwell, but primarily as art curios.

*Afternoons in Mid-America* received a scattering of positive reviews, and Virginia's drawings contributed to a balanced collaboration as in their previous travel book *Around About America*. The 276 pages of observations and impressions, with 17 letters of commentary addressed to Marcel Duhamel, revealed a more cosmopolitan point of view: Caldwell, the seasoned world traveler, viewing a changing small-town America as he returned to some of his enduring worries, such as race relations and conservation. The guise of simplicity was now dropped and the reporting became less harsh than in previous travel books, though some of the reminiscences displayed mixtures of an earlier Caldwell when he evoked scenes from his Southern background.

After his second lung operation, Caldwell had been told the best possible prognosis would be five years. This surmise had underestimated his stamina and will to live, and with every checkup at the clinic his physician was more optimistic. Still, the emphysema and diminished lung power caused discomfort, aggravated by the Dunedin climate which was sometimes damp.

On the occasion of another wedding anniversary, New Year's Eve, Erskine and Virginia vowed they would leave Florida in 1977 and live somewhere west of the Mississippi River. The search for a new home was a welcomed distraction for Caldwell and a chance for further travels. Colorado Springs and Albuquerque were envisioned but the chase ended in Paradise Valley, Arizona, near Phoenix. "One particular house had appealed to Virginia very much and, although all houses were beginning to look the same to me," wrote Caldwell, "I was pleased with her choice and was glad we had not bought a house elsewhere."

His reputation in America was somewhat eclipsed by a rising generation of younger writers and a glut of new books while the public furor over *Tobacco Road* had abated. An article in *The Atlanta Constitution* began: "Erskine Caldwell. There. We've said it. Not so very long ago any Georgian pronouncing that name might have been run out of the state on a rail. If he were lucky."

The University of Georgia Press looked favorably on this native son: In 1977, they bought a substantial collection of his books for their library and staged a campus production of *Tobacco Road*. Later, the university produced a documentary called *In Search of Caldwell's Georgia* for public television. Though older Wrens residents never forgave the author of *Road* for defaming their beloved state, the children of these seniors saw him as an important writer, not the despicable outcast.

Most of Caldwell's books were out of print in America—not so in Europe and Japan—but the stirring of interest in his work on college campuses did help to repair part of the damage done by thumbs-down reviewers. By the time in his life when reappraisal of his career would have been in order, most critics had written him off as an overrated minor writer, and scholars had decided his work was too mechanical and repetitious. When William Faulkner was asked to assess Caldwell's contribution to American literature at a University of Virginia seminar, he praised *Tobacco Road* for its plain and simple style but thought that later books were mostly trash. "The first books, *God's Little Acre* and the short stories," declared Faulkner, "that's enough for any man; he should be content with that, but knowing writers, I know he's not, just as I'm not content with mine."

Virginia Caldwell got excited when she read the encouraging notices given to *In Search of Bisco* and *Deep South*. "When he wrote *Close to Home* there were excellent reviews," she told Edwin T. Arnold in an interview, "and I can remember the idea that 'the old Caldwell is back and in good form again.' Also for *The Weather Shelter* and *Summertime Island*. I was so happy when I read these reviews because, as a wife who is working as a team with her husband, it makes it extremely worthwhile to know that your husband is having success and that perhaps you're helping him a little to come back to the strong writing he is capable of."

Shortly after Jimmy Carter's election, an editor at Dodd, Mead & Co. wanted Caldwell to write about the new President—since both were from Georgia, the publisher felt that it would be a meaningful biography with photographs; however, the project was too severely budgeted to afford what the editors needed to electrify the text. When asked whether the Carter family's Southern folkishness was authentic, Caldwell felt they were typical, and that he had known men like Billy Carter. "In fact, I'd probably rather do a book on Billy than Jimmy."

(In 1978, he and Virginia were invited to a reception at the White House to honor the Performing Arts. When Caldwell was greeted by Carter, the President remarked that he had looked forward to meeting a fellow Georgian whose public life was as controversial as his own. "I suppose we were born to be what we are," the author replied, "and whether writer or statesman we must live out our fate." When Virginia was presented to Carter, she impulsively leaned forward and kissed him on the cheek. "There was an immediate flurry among members of the security force," recalled Caldwell, "and she was hastily encouraged with stern gestures to step lively and shake hands with the President's wife. It is not know what Mrs. Carter said to Mr. Carter about the incident.")

Not to be outdone by Georgia, the University of Virginia sponsored a party on the seventy-fifth birthday of their famous alumnus. Caldwell had expected the celebration to be informal and with only a few people present. More than a hundred attended the reception and dinner. While deep in thought about what remarks he should make to express appreciation, Caldwell was surprised when library donor Waller Barrett, who arranged the event, announced that the honoree would read aloud his recently published essay "Recollections of a Visitor on Earth." "Nervously slurring pronunciation and heedless of cadence" he somehow got through the text which looked totally alien. The next morning's *New York Times* noted the celebration by saying that Caldwell was a "rehabilitated" Southern writer.

A few months after his birthday party in Charlottesville, Editions des Autres enticed Caldwell and Virginia to take the supersonic Concorde to Paris for a book signing tour of the recently released French translation of *The Bastard*. For six days the exhausted but travel-happy author attended book festivals in Brussels, Lille, at an industrial fair in Marseille, and a wine-tasting celebration in Bordeaux.

Kazimierz Piotrowski persuaded Caldwell to go to Warsaw in late 1981 to join in celebrating the publication of *Episode in Palmetto*. Upon their arrival, he and Virginia were whisked to the hall of the Union of Polish Writers where Caldwell was decorated with the Republic of Poland's Order of Cultural Merit.

There were other honors in the twilight of his long career: Governor Bruce Babbitt of Arizona declared November 1982 Erskine Caldwell month and held a weeklong celebration of his work, including a stage production of *Tobacco Road* at the Phoenix Little Theater. A further honor came on his last trip to Japan when he was asked to address the inaugural meeting of the Erskine Caldwell

Literary Society. (Caldwell was slightly bent, noticeably feeble but not completely succumbing to his years and two operations.) Fujisato Kitajima described him as "a man who had spent many years leaning into unfavorable winds—hurricanes of criticism and censorship."

His election to the fifty-chair American Academy of Arts and Letters in 1984 was personally gratifying and moved him deeply. (Norman Mailer also was elected that year.) John Hersey in an induction tribute described Caldwell's work as "balanced on a razor's edge between hilarity and horror...told in a quiet conversational voice, which speaks in rhythms of truth." In the presentation of this honor, Richard Wilbur stated: "Though his characters are driven, deluded, and luckless, there is no cruelty in his treating them as he does with the greatest comic gusto. This is because he celebrates in them the crazy solidarity and the will to assert in the midst of every privation the basic appetites of life."

At an annual ceremonial banquet of the American Academy and Institute in New York, Caldwell received what he considered to be a supreme compliment as a writer. The hall was crowded with famous and important authors and he and Malcolm Cowley were talking over drinks when a waiter approached with a tray of hors d'oeuvres. The waiter "was just a young punk," recalled Caldwell—probably a student hired for the evening. "Take one," said the young man, "and shake hands with me. You're the one person here I want to shake hands with." They did and Caldwell ate the hors d'oeuvre with much relish.

Caldwell read from his writings at Southern Methodist's Literary Festival in early November of 1983. He and Virginia were just back from France where he was decorated with the Republic of France's Commander of the Order of Arts and Letters. "I've already had my 80th birthday party," he grinned. "There was a gathering of 500 Frenchmen in Nice, and they all sang *Happy Birthday* in English with a French accent." Everybody held a lighted candle during the singing and among the guest were novelist Anthony Burgess and playwright Eugène Ionesco.

After he celebrated his 80th birthday, Virginia arranged the congratulatory message in two huge leather-bound volumes. Among the many writers who paid their respects were John Updike, William Styron, Robert Penn Warren, John Hersey, Malcolm Cowley, and Saul Bellow, who told Virginia that her husband should have won the Nobel Prize.

Norman Mailer's tribute was, "One of my first literary heroes and always one of the best." Kurt Vonnegut wrote: "In the 1930s, you and a handful of contemporaries pulled off a revolution for ourselves. I wonder if we could have had the guts or brains to pull it off."

Black novelist Ralph Ellison, in his long birthday letter, remembered the *Tobacco Road* play: "There in a darkened theater, I was snatched back to rural Alabama. When Jeeter Lester and the horsing couple went into their act, I was reduced to such helpless laughter that I distracted the entire balcony and embarrassed both my host (Langston Hughes) and myself....I became hysterical in the theater because by catching me off guard and compelling me to laugh at Jeeter you also forced me to recognize and accept our common humanity."

A reporter for the *Dallas Morning News* asked him if he had been married four times. It was true, Caldwell blandly responded, and was an unprofitable habit. "I lost three good houses—one in Maine, one in Connecticut, and one in Tucson. But I'm much smarter now. I put everything in Virginia's name, so I can never lose it."

"Well, sure, I'm hard to live with," he admitted. "I don't like to talk about the other people or about my complaints or what the circumstances might have been. But certain things exist in a writer's life that aren't conductive, in my view, to stabilized living or peaceful existence. I don't like to talk about it because two of these people (Helen and June) are still living."

Caldwell appended this note to his 1983 entry in Who's Who: "I am fully aware that my life has not been without fault and error; even so, in my present state of mind, I would hesitate to change anything in the past were I given the opportunity to do so. My reason for declining an opportunity to change the past is that I am satisfied with myself."

When asked what he wanted to be remembered for in his work, Caldwell hoped he had been a good influence for future writers. It had taken him ten years to break the publishing barrier, and perhaps his struggle might convince others to endure—it was so easy to give up unless one made a lot of money.

In answer to the question as to which of his novels he valued, Caldwell felt that *Tragic Ground* might be picked as the one having lasting interest and *Gretta* was another—work not ranked among his best. "But Virginia liked it so much that one night in Las Vegas she was playing dice next to Elizabeth Taylor and came over to me and said that we should try to get her to play *Gretta.* But we didn't follow up on it."

When told there seemed to be a renewed interest in his writings and asked if he had any specific books he would recommend for people who had not read his work, Caldwell responded: "No. Tell them to read all fifty. Then they can choose the one they like best."

"As you look back on your many years of writing," was one question, "do you have any regrets?" The author shrugged and replied: "I do regret a lot of technical matters that I was foolish to indulge in or to be taken into. I've had a lot of bad experience with publishers"—he was beholden to NAL because they held copyrights on several of his books but didn't get along with the new editors and had no direct dealings with them. "It sort of hurt my feelings that I got suspended high and dry, I would say hanging up there kicking my feet and can't touch ground as far as they're concerned. But it's just one of those publishing things that can happen to you."

*The Black & White Stories of Erskine Caldwell*, selected by Ray McIver, 1984, followed *Afternoons in Mid-America* and the *Sacrilege* edition in France. But there was one more story to be told: his own—*With All My Might.*

The idea came when he and Virginia were having lunch with

Pierre Belfont in Paris, and his friend asked: "Erskine, why don't you write your autobiography?" Caldwell told him he had—*Call It Experience*. "But that's all about your work. Why don't you write one about yourself, your life other than your work?" No more was said, but when Caldwell returned home, he wrote to his agent, Elizabeth Otis in New York, asking if she thought the idea worthwhile. She replied enthusiastically, and his last writing adventure began.

Momentum was the problem he had to face in his second autobiography, as he was not a talkative person and found it cumbersome to write about himself. It was the only book he shared with Virginia chapter by chapter. She had seen the beginnings of *In Search of Bisco* but had to wait for its completion before reading the rest. "Erskine would start writing," recalled Virginia, "and the next thing you knew he would be writing about his work." When it happened, she would tell him: "Well, here we go again. Another *Call It Experience*. How about a little personal talk here?"

Anxious to finish the book—Caldwell increasingly felt that time was limited—he hurried the span of years after the Mount Vernon era and his marriages to Bourke-White and June Johnson. Virginia admitted that she would like to have seen more of his personality exhibited because, "just like any other reader, there were a lot of things I never totally understood about Erskine." For the author, however, there was an abundance of personal material, and getting it on paper was often an ordeal. After a full day of work, he would come from his study and lie down on the floor in a state of exhaustion. Virginia felt the book was challenging him physically: he gave up riding his stationary bicycle and sat too long in one position while struggling with his life's story.

The project took nearly four years and the nucleus of the book came from a piece he wrote for Gale Research, an anthology gathering of writers' autobiographies. The right title for the book was elusive, and there were several working ones. Then one day he came from his study with a sheet of paper and on it he had typed *With All My Might*. "Well, what about that?" he asked Virginia.

And she thought "it was so perfect."

There were signs of deteriorating health as he plunged further into his last book. Checks were made on the sedimentation rate of his blood and the result proved there was infection. The Mayo Clinic doctors gave him a complicated barrage of tests whenever the sed. rate flared up, even a bone marrow examination because they sensed that something was wrong. Caldwell frequently ran a high temperature that an aspirin would bring down. "We had things like that going on all the time," remembered Virginia, "and that might have been a signal to him." In March 1986, Caldwell speculated that he would live to be 83, and she replied: "Oh let it be 85. It's a better number." And he said: " 'Well, okay,' to please me. But he had his 83 number in mind for some reason."

Caldwell didn't tell his wife that he had a sore throat when he came down with a cold. They were in Florida—it was July 22, 1986. His emphysema had progressed and there was fibrosis. "How he pushed himself to do what he did," recalled Virginia, "I simply don't know. He had an incredible willpower to keep going."

Upon their return to Arizona, the cold had turned into pneumonia. Their Scottsdale physician was out of town, and the substitute doctor didn't have the medical charts to make comparisons. Caldwell was hospitalized for six days before his fever came down, and during that time his undiagnosed cancer incubated further. A bronchoscopy proved inconclusive, but when Caldwell's doctor returned, a second test was performed which showed results. "This time you've got a bad one," he was told. "It goes like wildfire."

*With All My Might* was being published in France the following month, October 1986, and he wanted to be there. His first question after learning of his terminal state was: "If I take the chemotherapy, when will I be able to go to Paris?" Caldwell also had been looking forward to attending a writers' conference in Bulgaria. The doctors didn't want their patient wandering about Europe: they would lose control of the cancer and there were problems with a breathing apparatus on airplanes and the necessity of a wheelchair wherever he went. "He was on oxygen for eight months," explained Virginia. "He had a fifty-foot leash so he could go from one end of the house to the other, and he was never without it."

Arrangements were made in spite of the disapproving doctors, but another X-ray revealed that he was responding to the treatments. Caldwell had a choice, he was told: "If you go, we will have to cut your chemotherapy, and the cancer may get out of control and that will be it. So it's up to you. Do you want to live longer, or do you want to have a fine trip?"

It was his book and his life, and neither the doctors nor Virginia felt they had the right to intervene. Finally, *he* made the decision to fight for limited survival: eight more months of chemotherapy and alternate treatments at home and in the hospital—Virginia had a cot installed in his hospital room so she could be with him at all hours. "And he held up remarkably well until the seventh chemo," she recalled. "Then they gave him what they called a 'whammer,' and then he lost his hair and became so weak that he could hardly get into the wheelchair."

"They take the life out of you," he said when speaking of his chemotherapy treatments. The voice was still strong, but his eyes were pale and watery; he seemed easily distracted and when he shook hands the trembling of his grip was noticeable. Caldwell's doctor bluntly told him the chemotherapy wasn't going well and asked what he wanted done. Virginia remembered her husband's answer. "I want a miracle."

There was optimism for a while—X-rays showed some improvements, and on occasion the Caldwells got out the champagne to celebrate. But there came the time when his body was unable to tolerate more chemotherapy, and after three weeks without treatment all the old symptoms were back.

They both used the word *if* but knew his chances were not good. Under the circumstances, a strong and optimistic outlook was the only therapy left. His doctor recommended they both read a book on the practice of visualization, and Erskine said he didn't need it but relented when Virginia insisted—he read only two chapters and declared: "It's just simple Christian Science."

Caldwell kept busy writing letters and paying bills. When his shaky hand left his handwriting illegible, he would take the stubs from his checkbook and record them on the typewriter. Charles Trueheart interviewed him—published in *Conversations With Erskine Caldwell*—and several days later he sat at his desk and posed for a *USA Today* photographer. Afterwards, when the man had left, he said in amazement to Virginia: "I'm exhausted. All I did was sit here, and I'm exhausted."

Caldwell requested that his stepson, Drew, come see him—there were matters he wanted the young man to look after. His first task was to call several mortuaries and find the least expensive—"which was just like him," recalled Virginia. "But we did *not* take the least expensive." This gave her an opening to talk about a subject that bothered her: he had always said that he wanted cremation and to have his ashes scattered on water, just any body of water. "I had told him I couldn't do it," Virginia recalled in Edwin T. Arnold's interview with her, "that it went against something in me." She said to him: "Erskine, if something happens, do you still want to be scattered on the water?" And he replied: "No, that's a silly idea. Probably the best thing to do would be to find a shovel, find a dead-end street, and dig a hole." She asked: "A dead-end street?" And with a smile, he said: "Well, isn't that appropriate?"

He kept losing strength and reached the point where he couldn't shave and had to be dressed. Drew lifted him into the wheelchair and Virginia gave him breakfast. On a Wednesday morning, after having eaten, he said: "I'm going to have to go back to bed." The cancer had metastasized, there was pain, and his determination to live was collapsing. He had said to Virginia: "If you stay in bed one day, then it's going to be the next day and then you won't get up again."

Their next-door neighbors, a psychiatrist and his wife, had been helpful through the ordeal, and when Virginia realized her husband was sinking, she telephoned them. "I'm frightened," she told the psychiatrist. "I think Erskine is much worse tonight." The neighbor came immediately and stood by the bed and spoke to him. Caldwell mumbled something that was difficult to understand, at first, and then they realized the humor crouching behind the remark. "What are you charging for house calls?" he asked.

The following morning he was unable to speak, only a nod or shake of the head, and he refused sleeping pills and tablets to ease the pain. Gradually, he lost consciousness and was gone. It was Saturday, April 11, 1987.

# Appendix

1903   Erskine Caldwell, born December 17 in the church community of White Oak, near Moreland, Coweta County, Georgia, the only child of Reverend Ira Sylvester Caldwell and Caroline Preston Bell Caldwell.

1903-18   Ira Caldwell's appointment as Secretary of the Associate Reformed Presbyterian Church Home Missions Board causes frequent changes of address. Young Caldwell lives in White Oak, GA; Prosperity, SC; Timber Ridge and Staunton, VA; Charlotte, NC; Bradley, SC; Fairfield, VA; and Atoka, TN. In 1917, Caldwell works for a short time as a YMCA driver at Millington Army Base. He attempts his first work of fiction, "A Boy's Own Story of City Life."

1919-20   The family moves to Wrens, GA. Erskine attends the local high school but fails to graduate. Always eager to earn money, he works as a driver for the town's doctor, as a laborer in a cottonseed-oil mill, and for the local paper, *The Jefferson County Reporter*. Several weeks of one summer are spent helping a stonemason build a church in Calhoun, GA. He becomes scorekeeper for the Wrens baseball team and begins contributing reports of the games to the *Augusta Chronicle*. The poverty he witnesses on his rides with the doctor and Ira will greatly influence his future writing.

1921-23   With the help of his father, he gains admission to Erskine College, a Presbyterian school in Due West, SC. Caldwell plays football but shows little interest in studies. On weekends, he spends much of his time hopping freight trains and visiting nearby cities. In the spring of 1922, he leaves Erskine College without notice and is jailed for several days in Bogalusa, Louisiana on the false charge of being an I.W.W. labor agitator.

1923-25   After a restless summer in Wrens, he enters the University of Virginia on an overlooked United Daughters of the Confederacy Scholarship. Caldwell works in a poolroom to supplement living expenses. He shows little interest in studies. Summer courses at the Wharton School of the University of Pennsylvania lure him to Philadelphia. After time spent as a counterman in an eatery, janitor at a burlesque house, and paid companion for a wealthy Chinese student, he moves to Wilkes-Barre and works as a stock clerk for the S.S. Kresge Company. Caldwell fails to get on a semi-professional football team and breaks his nose in a pre-season scrimmage. He finds work as a short-order cook in the Wilkes-Barre train station before returning home. Then there is another semester at Charlottesville. He meets Helen Lannigan, the daughter of the University of Virginia's track coach, and they are married on March 3, 1925.

1925-27   Caldwell withdraws from the university when his father helps land him a job as a reporter on the *Atlanta Journal*. His first child, Erskine Jr., is born. In addition to his work on the paper, he begins writing short stories and reviewing books for the *Charlotte Observer*. He returns to the University of Virginia in the autumn of 1926 and attends classes long enough to receive grades for a first term. His essay "The Georgia Cracker," written for an English composition class, is published in *The Halderman-Julius Monthly*. A second son, Dabney Withers, is born. In the spring of 1927, the Caldwells leave Virginia to live in Mount Vernon, Maine at the Lannigans' summer house, "Greentrees."

1927-28  The Caldwells remain in Mount Vernon until midwinter when inadequate clothing and a cold house force them South. They return to Maine in early spring, and he begins another onslaught to write saleable stories. Early in 1928, he opens Longfellow Square Bookshop in Portland, ME, stocked with hundreds of review copies sent to him by the *Charlotte Observer* and *Houston Post*. They rent a house in nearby Cape Elizabeth, where Caldwell spends much of his time writing while Helen runs the shop.

1929  The breakthrough comes when *transition* and *The New American Caravan* accept his stories. Numerous little-magazine acceptances follow, and *The Bastard*, a short novel, is published by The Heron Press in a limited edition. The book is soon banned in Portland—the first of his many brushes with censorship. In response to the banning, he produces a broadside entitled "In Defense of Myself."

1930  "The Mating of Marjory" and "A Very Late Spring" are accepted by *Scribner's Magazine*. His second novel, *Poor Fool*, is published by The Rariora Press. Scribner's proposes to bring out his first collection of short stories, and with an advance in royalties, Caldwell travels to California and to Georgia. He begins a novel on an impoverished sharecropper family.

1931  *American Earth* is published by Scribner's and *Tobacco Road* is accepted by the same firm. Caldwell begins work on "Autumn Hill," the manuscript which will later be renamed *A Lamp for Nightfall*. He lives for a short time at Sutton Place in New York, a hotel run by Nathanael West.

1932  "Autumn Hill" is rejected by Scribner's, and Caldwell moves to Viking Press. During the summer, in Mount Vernon, he completes *God's Little Acre*.

1933  Viking publishes *God's Little Acre* and his second collection of short stories, *We Are the Living*. He is hired by MGM as a screenwriter and spends the spring and summer in Hollywood. His daughter, Janet, is born in May at

Greentrees. *God's Little Acre* is deemed obscene by the New York Society for the Suppression of Vice, but Judge Benjamin E. Greenspan rules in the book's favor after it is defended by sixty writers and critics. "A Country Full of Swedes" wins *The Yale Review's* annual award for fiction. The play, *Tobacco Road*, adapted by Jack Kirkland, opens in New York on December 4.

1934  He works on a new novel, *Journeyman*, and writes short stories. He returns to Hollywood in June for several months of screenwriting.

1935  *Journeyman* is published by Viking in January. Caldwell spends the first three months of the year in the South. He writes a series of articles on the plight of sharecroppers for the *New York Post*. The pamphlet, *Tenant Farmer*, and his first book of nonfiction, *Some American People*, appear. Viking brings out another selection of short fiction, *Kneel to the Rising Sun*.

1936  He and Margaret Bourke-White travel through the South for a photojournalistic book of impressions. In October, Caldwell leaves Helen and moves to New York.

1937  Viking publishes *You Have Seen their Faces*.

1938  The unsuccessful play, *Journeyman*, opens in January. *Southways*, a collection of stories, is published by Viking. Helen divorces Caldwell. He and Bourke-White tour Czechoslovakia on another collaboration.

1939  Caldwell and Bourke-White marry in February. *North of the Danube* is published by Viking. Duell, Sloan & Pearce becomes his new publisher, and Caldwell begins editing the American Folkways series.

1940  *Jackpot*, a selection of seventy-five stories, appears along with his first novel in five years, *Trouble in July*. He and Bourke-White tour the United States for their third collaboration.

1941  *Say, Is This the U.S.A.?* is published by DS&P. Caldwell and Bourke-White travel to Russia. When the Germans invade, they are among the few journalists to report the attack. Caldwell makes broadcasts for *CBS* and writes for *Life* and the newspaper *PM*. He and Bourke-White return to America in October. Hollywood produces the film version of *Tobacco Road*.

1942  His Russian exposure brings forth *All Night Long, All Out on the Road to Smolensk*, and *Moscow Under Fire*. His final collaboration with Bourke-

White, *Russia at War*, is also published. Caldwell goes to Hollywood to write a screenplay for *Mission to Moscow*, a propaganda film he fails to complete. Bourke-White continues her war assignments for *Life* in Europe, and this separation leads to divorce. He marries June Johnson, a 21-year-old student at the University of Arizona, on December 21.

1943 *Georgia Boy* is published. He and June settle in Tucson. Her reluctance to travel and dependence on psychoanalysis cause a strain in their marriage. He signs a two-year contract for screenwriting at Twentieth Century-Fox but asks to be released at the end of the year.

1944 *Tragic Ground* appears and is banned in Boston. *Stories by Erskine Caldwell*, with an introduction by Henry Seidel Canby, is released. He makes war bond rally tours. Ira Sylvester Caldwell dies. His fourth child, Jay Erskine is born.

1945-50 His New American Library paperback publishers with their drugstore "spin-it" racks accomplish a publishing phenomenon: Caldwell becomes known as "The World's Best-Selling Author!" Sales skyrocket when his books are banned. *A House in the Uplands*, 1946; *The Sure Hand of God*, 1947; *This Very Earth*, 1948; *Place Called Estherville*, 1949; and *Episode in Palmetto*, 1950, are published. As the number of his readers increases, his critical reputation sinks. In 1948, he autographs 25-cent paperbacks in a Kansas City drugstore, and in consequence he is shunned by fellow writers at a University of Kansas conference.

1951 His recollection of authorship, *Call It Experience*, appears. *The Humorous Side of Erskine Caldwell*, edited by Robert Cantwell, is published.

1952-56 Duell, Sloan & Pearce is sold to Little, Brown. Book publications are *A Lamp for Nightfall*, 1952; *The Courting of Susie Brown*, 1952; *The Complete Stories by Erskine Caldwell*, 1953; *Love and Money*, 1954; and *Gulf Coast Stories*, 1956. He separates from June Johnson and moves to Phoenix. There are travels in Europe to check on publications. He and June are divorced in 1956. Caldwell decides to live in San Francisco.

1957 He marries Virginia Moffett Fletcher, and they honeymoon in Europe. *God's Little Acre* is filmed in Stockton, California. *Certain Women* is published.

1958 *Claudelle Inglish* and his book for children, *Molly Cottontail*, appear. He and Virginia attend the showing of *God's Little Acre* at the Venice Film Festival.

1959  The Caldwells travel to England, Turkey, Greece, and Russia. *When You Think of Me*, a collection of stories and sketches, is published.

1960  He and Virginia go to Japan where he is honored for his work. Again, Caldwell changes publishers: he leaves Little, Brown and moves to Farrar, Straus and Cudahy, later Giroux.

1961-64  *Jenny by Nature*, 1961; *Close to Home*, 1962; *The Last Night of Summer*, 1963; and *Around About America*, 1964, are published. The Caldwells tour Scandinavia and other European countries. In November 1961 he begins the first of nine official visits at Dartmouth College. *Claudelle Inglish* is filmed by Warner Brothers. He and Virginia move to Orinda in Rheem Valley, California. *God's Little Acre* passes the ten-million mark in sales; *Tobacco Road* surpasses seven million copies.

1965-68  *In Search of Bisco*, 1965; *The Deer at Our House*, 1966; *Miss Mamma Aimee* and *Writing in America*, 1967; *Deep South* and *Summertime Island*, 1968, are his book publications. Caldwell's schedule remains unchanged: seven or eight months of writing and time for travel. Caldwell is told that he has emphysema and should move to a semi-tropical climate. He and Virginia buy a house in Dunedin, Florida.

1969-72  *The Weather Shelter*, 1969, and *The Earnshaw Neighborhood*, 1971, are his new novels. Caldwell and Virginia visit Japan for the second time. Margaret Bourke-White dies on August 27, 1971, a victim of Parkinson's. In 1972, Caldwell stops smoking and has surgery for lung cancer at the Mayo Clinic.

1973-76  *Annette*, 1973, is his last novel, and *Afternoons in Mid-America* is his second travel book with Virginia's illustrations. He goes to Poland in 1975 for an autographing session at a Polish book fair. Cancer is found in the other lung and there is more surgery. In 1976, he returns to Europe to begin his fifth and final tour for the United States Information Service; *The Sacrilege of Alan Kent*, illustrated by Alexander Calder, is published in France.

1977-84  The Caldwells move to Paradise Valley, Arizona. He goes to Warsaw in 1981 to help celebrate the Polish publication of *Episode in Palmetto*. In 1982, he and Virginia go on their last visit to Japan. Honors are bestowed on Caldwell: Arizona officials declare November as Erskine Caldwell month, 1982; France and Poland make him a Commander of the Order of Arts and Letters and present him with the Order of Cultural Merit, respectively, 1983; and he is elected to the American Academy of Arts and Letters, 1984.

1985-87  *The Black and White Stories of Erskine Caldwell*, Selected by Ray McIver, 1984, and *With All My Might*, 1987, are his books. In 1986, Helen Caldwell Cushman dies at the age of 81. Caldwell dies on April 11, 1987.

# ASIDES

Following her divorce in 1938, Helen Caldwell stayed on at Greentrees and soon married Norman Cushman, a childhood friend from Mount Vernon. Cushman, a modest man with conservative views and common sense, brought stability into the household. "He was a good father to the children," recalled Clayton Dolloff, "but she never got over Skinny."

Helen, in need of distraction and eager to fulfill talents which had long been suppressed, flung herself into creative activities: She became a correspondent for several Maine newspapers and soon had her own radio program. Helen's specialty was telling ghost stories, and she was hugely popular with young audiences when she masqueraded as "The Green Witch."

Over the years, a friendship with Margaret Bourke-White developed as letters were exchanged. Clayton Dolloff's daughter, Althea, recalls riding to Augusta with Helen to fetch Bourke-White for a visit. The girl sat in the backseat and watched as the two women "giggled and teeheed" about the past. A prized possession on the living room wall at Greentrees was a Bourke-White photograph showing a distant view of Cape Town in South Africa. Another trophy was an autographed copy of Margaret's book, *Halfway To Freedom*. The inscription read: "To the first Mrs. Caldwell from the second Mrs. Caldwell—'Halfway to Freedom' is only half the truth."

After Norman Cushman's death in 1968, Helen began spending her winters with her children—Janet in North Carolina, Dabney in Massachusetts, and Erskine Jr. in California. From these locations she sent postcards and loving notes to dozens of friends. This author has a bulging file of communications from Helen—not something to throw away.

This remarkable lady died in 1986, shortly before the publication of *With All My Might* and the death of Caldwell. In a poignant farewell service to his mother on December 5, son Dabney did mention his father: "It is said of famous authors that their first wife bears his children, the second shares his wealth and fame, and the third cares for him in old age. While this adage well describes my father, it doesn't do Helen justice. My father's early books and stories written in Mount Vernon were without doubt his best. Some scholar of the future will discover that Helen was his best editor and critic and helped to engender the spare, eloquent style that marked his early writing."

Margaret Bourke-White's daredevil lifestyle continued as she photographed the conflict with Germany in North Africa. After much coaxing and exuding her charm, she was given permission to go on a dangerous bombing run in a Flying Fortress. Later, in Italy, she hitched a ride in a small reconnaissance plane that flew over enemy territory. Her flamboyance thawed the glacial glances of General George Patton, and he requested a lesson in photography. Near the war's end, she took pictures of emaciated prisoners when Buchenwald was liberated.

She drifted in and out of love affairs—usually safe ones with married men—and *Life* with its ever-demanding assignments kept her prowling the globe. She photographed Mahatma Gandhi at his spinning wheel, the great migration in Pakistan, and two gold miners at work in South Africa. Her most poignant photograph captured the reunion of a Korean mother with her son who was believed dead. Bourke-White's extraordinary career ended too soon when she was diagnosed as having Parkinson's in 1954.

At the time of Ira Sylvester's death in 1944, Caroline Caldwell faced another full term in order to fulfill her teaching obligations in Wrens. When told that she was free to break the contract, Carrie declined: an agreement was binding, she insisted, not something to regard lightly. A.R.P. officials quickly made other living arrangements for Ira's successor so the teacher could remain in the home she had known for so many years.

(The manse was later used as a social hall and eventually became badly in need of repairs. Instead of restoring the structure, parishioners voted to sell it to a businessman who moved the building out of town. As an investment, the purchase proved unproductive—an accumulation of bat dung in the attic was too much for its new owner and the structure was burned. There now is a new building on the vacated lot and across the street, next to the A.R.P. Church—another manse.)

Carrie missed her teaching upon retirement, and a concerned son invited his mother to Arizona where she became part of the household. She was in Phoenix after Caldwell and June separated, and later stayed at the Gaylord Hotel in San Francisco. Her time on the West Coast was of short duration; an earthquake frightened her, and when Erskine and Virginia went on their next vacation of travels, Carrie moved to Allendale, South Carolina to be with her sister and brother-in-law, Kathleen and Lawton Maner.

Mary Maner of Louisville, Georgia was a child of five or six when she met her Cousin Erskine for the first time. He, Helen, and the two boys were visiting Mary's aunt and uncle in Wrens, and she was sent outside to keep little Pix and Dabney occupied. "I didn't have much contact with Erskine over the years," she recalled, "not until he married Virginia. That was because Carrie was living with us and he would come up to Allendale from Florida to see her." And what did Miss Maner think of Virginia? "I'm crazy about her," she replied. "Such a delightful person! I remember she called me and asked: 'Could you meet me in Williamsburg for my birthday?' I immediately said yes. And my father once remarked: 'It's a pity he didn't marry her first!' "

Mary Maner spoke warmly of Virginia's third husband, Ralph Hibbs, a retired doctor. She met Virginia's son, Drew Fletcher, when he was a teenager during the San Francisco time, and enjoyed an unexpected visit from Erskine's youngest son who is a doctor living in Anchorage, Alaska. "About two or three years ago," recalled Miss Mary, "a man stood at the door and said: 'I'm Jay Caldwell.' His daughter was at North Carolina State, and he and his wife had brought her down to start the senior year."

Mary Maner remembered that her Aunt Caroline was quite ill during the Caldwells' time in Prosperity, South Carolina, but it was years later that she learned that Carrie had had a hysterectomy. "That was when she said an angel appeared and came for her. She said: 'I can't go with you for I have a child to rear.'

"My father died in 1970," recalled Mary Maner, "and I believe Carrie passed away a couple of years earlier, roughly 1968. She was very strict and demanding as a teacher, but a lot of her students gave her credit for what they eventually became in life." It was here in the interview that this author interrupted to confirm Caroline Caldwell's habit of laundering money. "You sometimes get those dollar bills all wadded up and sticky," she explained. "I've had to do that myself at times, and whenever I do wash them, I am reminded of her."

Wrens, Georgia had its centennial in 1984. It was a weeklong celebration with each day dedicated to an occupational pursuit, such as farming, business, transportation, and the last day was set aside to honor education. Erskine and Virginia were asked to attend this final ceremony—the high school library was named the Caroline Bell Caldwell Library. The visiting author spoke briefly and noted the fact that he once attended high school in Wrens but failed to get a diploma.

As previously noted, the University of Georgia Press has brought out some of Caldwell's major works. Their reprint series of handsome trade paperback and hardcover editions, including *You Have Seen Their Faces* and *Deep South*, are *Tobacco Road*, *God's Little Acre*, *Journeyman*, *The Sacrilege of Alan Kent*, *Georgia Boy*, *In Search of Bisco*, *The Stories of Erskine Caldwell*, and a recently issued edition of *Trouble in July*. Other publishers are Da Capo with *North of the Danube* and *Say, Is This the U.S.A.?* in 1977, and Louisiana State University Press with *Poor Fool* in 1994.

Over the years, June Johnson Martin of Tucson, Arizona has been helpful in providing scholars with explanations concerning those difficult middle years of Caldwell's life and career, from 1942 to 1956. Her son, Dr. Jay Caldwell, is also supportive—he is quick to react when his father's name falls into neglect. Erskine Caldwell's omission from *The Literature of the American South* (an anthology, 1998)—as briefly mentioned in the "Openings" chapter of this book—prompted Dr. Caldwell to join a chorus of disapproval, along with The Raven Society, a book-film club, and the Erskine Caldwell Birthplace and Museum in Moreland, Georgia. "We felt that this issue could not go unaddressed," said W. Winston Skinner, Chairman of the Museum Committee. "The short stories represent some of Mr. Caldwell's best work, and to publish an anthology of Southern literature without including him is unthinkable." Another defender is Drew Fletcher. His "The Erskine Caldwell Website" is carefully updated with a listing of recent books, articles, and new developments.

Caldwell's birthplace had been a storage building or tenant house before additional rooms were added. When the A.R.P. Church of White Oak established another manse, the structure was sold to a family, and over the years this home became dilapidated in a setting of new houses that once was open farmland. When it was up for sale, in 1990, the Town of Moreland and the Moreland Historical Society combined their resources, moved the house to the town's square, and began restoration.

The museum is open to the public on weekends and is sometimes used to host teas and receptions. There are six on the board of directors with a membership of about fifty. The group's objective is the telling of Caldwell's life story while exhibiting some of his personal belongings and his books, including a variety of translated editions. Virginia Caldwell Hibbs has added substantially to the collection: a ring Helen Caldwell gave her husband, teacups and a vase belonging to Carrie, the author's wristwatch, pocket dictionary, passport documents, briefcase, hat, and a jacket with "Erskine Caldwell" lettered on the front and a bold "Write On" at the back. In 1987, Mrs. Hibbs had contacted Winston Skinner in response to an article he had written about her husband: "I'm sure you heard that Erskine passed away; if anyone ever decides to do anything about the Little Manse, please let me know." Museum organizers found her "Little Manse" description irresistible, and it was adopted as a fitting addition to the museum sign outside on the lawn.

A major controversy exists in Moreland whenever the question is raised whether Caldwell's birth was in 1902 or 1903. "I know it was in 1902," recalled one resident, "because he was born the same year as my older brother and my mother looked after them at the same time." Then another disputes the claim: "No, no, that can't be; he was born in 1903 because my mama and papa went to the manse and got married the night before he was born."

This author found his interview with Winston Skinner memorable—this museum member possesses a biographer's knowledge of Caldwell. "I have been interested in him just about my whole life," he admitted. "My grandmother lived within walking distance of where the manse was originally—I will say the older people in my family referred to Caldwell with the word 'that' in front of his name. I grew up with the knowledge that he was in the encyclopedia and I knew just where he was born." Skinner, who is the Assistant News Editor of *The Times-Herald* in Newnan and Pastor of the Mt. Zion Baptist Church in Alvaton, Georgia, has a "sense of loyalty to Virginia Caldwell—she has been such a wonderful friend to us and so supportive."

Has the older generation forgiven Caldwell for writing *Tobacco Road*? Skinner was asked. "It isn't entirely an age thing," he replied. "Certainly way back, there were people who felt very negatively. There are those who say that he was a traitor to the South, a pornographer, a Communist, and those are not popular things to be in a small town. One must remember that in some houses his work isn't welcomed warmly, but many are aware that at one time Erskine Caldwell was the Stephen King of his day."

## SOURCES AND ACKNOWLEDGMENTS

I am grateful to Helen Caldwell Cushman for giving me the beginnings of this book. She generously shared family photographs and there were three taped interviews. Her knowledge of Caldwell's parents, his childhood, and reminiscences of events before and after the move to Mount Vernon, Maine were most helpful.

I thank Phillip Cronenwett and his staff at Dartmouth College. The collection of Caldwell books, manuscripts, and miscellaneous papers at the Baker Library shaped this biography.

A microfilm edition of 38 personal scrapbooks available at University Microfilm, Inc. in Ann Arbor, Michigan, provided a wealth of research materials.

Virginia Caldwell Hibbs has been most generous in giving me permission to use quotes and photographs.

I thank W. Winston Skinner for sharing his knowledge. A visit to the Erskine Caldwell Birthplace and Museum in Moreland, Georgia is highly recommended.

I am grateful to McIntosh and Otis, Inc. for permission to use excerpts from the works of Erskine Caldwell and family papers.

Professor William A. Sutton donated his manuscript on Erskine Caldwell to the University of Illinois at Urbana. Located in the Special Collection Library, this work and assorted research papers are a treasure trove for scholars.

Acknowledgments are made to the University of Mississippi and Edwin T. Arnold, editor, for permission to use responses from *Conversations With Erskine Caldwell*, 1988, and *Erskine Caldwell Reconsidered*, 1990.

I thank the Estate Of Margaret Bourke-White for permission to quote from *Portrait of Myself* and to Harper & Row, Publishers, Inc. for Vicki Goldberg's *Margaret Bourke-White: A Biography*.

*Erskine Caldwell: The Journey from Tobacco Road* by Dan B. Miller (New York: Alfred A. Knopf, 1995) provides a well-rounded gathering of new material.

The autobiographies *Call It Experience* (New York: Duel, Sloan & Pearce, 1951) and *With All My Might* (Atlanta: Peachtree Publishers, 1987) frame a chronology of Caldwell's life, and I am grateful for permission to quote passages.

For an accountable rendering of the author's childhood see the tribute to his father, Ira Sylvester Caldwell, in *Deep South* (New York: Weybright & Talley, 1968.)

Other invaluable sources are *Erskine Caldwell* by James Korges, a pamphlet on American writers—Number 78 (Minneapolis: University of Minnesota, 1969); *Black Like It Is/Was* by William A. Sutton (Metuchen, NJ: The Scarecrow Press, 1974); *Critical Essays on Erskine Caldwell* by Scott MacDonald (Boston: G. K. Hall & Co., 1981); *Erskine Caldwell* by James E. Devlin (Boston: Twayne Publishers, 1984); *The Early Thirties Novels of Erskine Caldwell* by William Leland Howard, a thesis (Urbana: University of Illinois, 1986); *Erskine Caldwell and the Fiction of Poverty* by Sylvia Jenkins Cook (Baton Rouge: Louisiana State University Press, 1991); and *Erskine Caldwell: A Biography* by Harvey Klevar (Knoxville: University of Tennessee Press, 1993).

I am grateful to the following for permission to use brief quotes and material: Ira Sylvester Caldwell Papers, Hargrett Rare Books and Manuscript Library, The University of Georgia Libraries, Athens, Georgia; The Alfred Morang Papers, Houghton Library, Harvard University, Cambridge, Massachusetts; The New American Library Papers, Elmer Holmes Bobst Library, New York, New York; I. L. Salomon Papers, Collection of the Manuscript Division, Library of Congress, Washington, D.C.; and The Margaret Bourke-White Papers, Department of Special Collections, Syracuse University Library, Syracuse, New York.

I thank the following for providing information: Jack Barnes, Richard Childs, Althea Dolloff, Clayton Dolloff, Mary Maner, Ray Neal, Francis O'Brien, Raymond Skolfield, and Gladys Taylor.

These magazines, newspapers, and presses proved indispensable sources for review commentary: *Advocate* (Mullins, West Virginia), *The American Spectator*, *Amsterdam Star News*, *Argus* (Montpelier, Vermont), *Atlanta Constitution*, *Atlanta Journal*, *Augusta Chronicle*, *Beaumont Enterprise* (Beaumont, Kansas), *Boston Evening Transcript*, *Boston Herald*, *The Boston Post*, *Brooklyn Citizen*, *Brooklyn Daily Eagle*, *Buenos Aires Herald*, *Charlotte Observer*, *Chicago Herald-American*, *Chicago News*, *Chicago Sunday Tribune*, *Chicago Sun & Times*, *Cincinnati Enquirer*, *Columbia Missourian*, *The Commonweal*, *Courier-Journal* (Louisville, Kentucky), *Daily Mirror*, *Daily Worker*, *Dallas Morning News*, *Dalton North Georgian*, *Darien Review*, *Delta Democrat Times*, *Eugenics: A Journal of Race Betterment*, *Evening Star* (Baltimore), *Evening Times* (Glasgow, Scotland), *The Haldeman-Julius Monthly*, *The Hartford Courant*, *Hartford Times*, *Houston Post*, *Il Populo* (Rome), *The Jefferson County Reporter*, *Journal Amer-*

*ican*, *Leader* (Lexington, Kentucky), *Ledger Review* (Lakeland, Florida), *Life*, *Los Angeles Times*, *Lynchburg Advance* (Lynchburg, Virginia), *The Macon Telegraph*, *The Magazine Tucson*, *Manchester Evening Chronicle* (Manchester, England), *Messaggero* (Rome), *Miami Daily News*, *Miami Herald*, *The Minneapolis Tribune*, *Minnesota News*, *Montreal Gazette*, *Montreal Star*, *The Nation*, *The New Leader*, *New Masses*, *The New Republic*, *News* (Dayton, Ohio), *News* (Whittier, California), *News* (Wilmington, Delaware), *News & Courier* (Charleston, South Carolina), *Newsweek*, *New York American*, *New York Herald Tribune*, *New York Journal American*, *New York News*, *New York Post*, *New York Sun*, *The New York Times*, *The New York Times Book Review*, *The New York Times Magazine*, *New York World Telegram*, *Northern Echo* (Durham, England), *Norwalk Hour Newspaper* (Norwalk, Connecticut), *Oakland Tribune*, *Philadelphia Evening Bulletin*, *Philadelphia News*, *Philadelphia Public Ledger*, *Pittsburgh Press*, *PM*, *Post-Gazette* (Pittsburgh, Pennsylvania), *Publishers Weekly*, *Raleigh News and Observer*, *Republican Times* (Ottawa, Illinois), *Rocky Mountain Cities*, *San Francisco Chronicle*, *San Francisco Examiner*, *San Francisco News*, *Saturday Review of Literature*, *Sheffield Telegram* (Sheffield, England), *Southern Review*, *Star News* (Pasadena, California), *St. Louis Globe-Democrat*, *St. Paul Dispatch*, *Survey Graphic*, *Time*, *Times Herald* (Dallas, Texas), *Times Herald* (Waco, Texas), *Times-Picayune*, *Tomorrow*, *Tribune* (Tampa, Florida), *The Washington Post*, *The Washington Evening Star*, and *The Yale Review*.

Above all, I owe so much to my wife, Stella Stevens. Without her editorial assistance, love, and encouragement, this book never would have been a reality. In fact, her name also should be on the cover.

## BY ERSKINE CALDWELL

*All Night Long.* New York: Duell, Sloan & Pearce, 1942.
*All Out on the Road to Smolensk.* New York: Duell, Sloan & Pearce, 1942.
*American Earth.* New York: Scribner's Sons, 1931.
*Annette.* New York: New American Library, 1973.
*The Bastard.* New York: Heron Press, 1929.
*Call It Experience.* New York: Duell, Sloan & Pearce, 1951.
*Certain Women.* Boston: Little, Brown, 1957.
*Claudelle Inglish.* Boston: Little, Brown, 1958.
*Close to Home.* New York: Farrar, Straus & Cudahy, 1962.
*The Courting of Susie Brown.* New York: Duell, Sloan & Pearce, 1952.
*Deep South.* New York: Weybright & Talley, 1968.
*The Earnshaw Neighborhood.* New York: World Publishing Co., 1971.
*Episode in Palmetto.* New York: Duell, Sloan & Pearce, 1950.
*Georgia Boy.* New York: Duell, Sloan & Pearce, 1943.
*God's Little Acre.* New York: Viking, 1933.
*Gretta.* Boston: Little, Brown, 1955.
*Gulf Coast Stories.* Boston: Little, Brown, 1956.
*A House in the Uplands.* New York: Duell, Sloan & Pearce, 1946.
*In Search of Bisco.* New York: Farrar, Straus & Giroux, 1965.
*Jackpot.* New York: Duell, Sloan & Pearce, 1940.
*Jenny by Nature.* New York: Farrar, Straus & Cudahy, 1961.
*Journeyman.* New York: Viking, 1935.
*Kneel to the Rising Sun.* New York: Viking, 1935.
*A Lamp for Nightfall.* Boston: Little, Brown, 1952.
*The Last Night of Summer.* New York: Farrar, Straus and Giroux, 1963.
*Love and Money.* Boston: Little, Brown, 1954.
*Miss Mamma Aimee.* New York: New American Library, 1967.
*Moscow Under Fire.* London: Hutchinson, 1942.
*Place Called Estherville.* New York: Duell, Sloan & Pearce, 1949.
*Poor Fool.* New York: Rariora Press, 1930.
*The Sacrilege of Alan Kent.* Portland, Maine: Falmouth Book House, 1936.
*Some American People.* New York: R. M. MacBride, 1935.
*Southways.* New York: Viking, 1938.
*Summertime Island.* New York: World Publishing Co., 1968.
*The Sure Hand of God.* New York: Duell, Sloan & Pearce, 1947.
*Tenant Farmer.* New York: Phalanx Press, 1935.
*This Very Earth.* New York: Duell, Sloan & Pearce, 1948.
*Tobacco Road.* New York: Scribner's Sons, 1932.
*Tragic Ground.* New York: Duell, Sloan & Pearce, 1944.

*Trouble in July*. New York: Duell, Sloan & Pearce, 1940.
*We Are the Living*. New York: Viking, 1933.
*The Weather Shelter*. New York: World Publishing Co., 1969.
*When You Think of Me*. Boston: Little, Brown, 1959.
*With All My Might*. Atlanta: Peachtree Publishers, 1987.
*Writing in America*. New York: Phaedra, 1967.


## ANTHOLOGIES OF ERSKINE CALDWELL

*The Black and White Stories of Erskine Caldwell*. Selected by Ray McIver.
   Atlanta: Peachtree Publishers, 1984.
*The Caldwell Caravan: Novels and Stories*. Edited by Erskine Caldwell. Cleve-
   land and New York: World Publishing Co., 1946.
*The Humorous Side of Erskine Caldwell*. Edited by Robert Cantwell. New York:
   Duel, Sloan & Pearce, 1951.
*Men and Women*. Introduction by Carvel Collins. Boston: Little, Brown, 1961.
*Stories by Erskine Caldwell*. Introduction by Henry Seidel Canby. New York:
   Duel, Sloan & Pearce, 1944.


## FOR YOUNG READERS

*The Deer at Our House*. New York: Collier Books, 1966.
*Molly Cottontail*. Boston: Little, Brown, 1966.


## BY ERSKINE CALDWELL AND MARGARET BOURKE-WHITE

*North of the Danube*. New York: Viking, 1939.
*Russia at War*. London and New York: Hutchinson, 1942.
*Say, Is This the U.S.A.?* New York: Duell, Sloan & Pearce, 1941.
*You Have Seen Their Faces*. New York: Viking, 1937.


## BY ERSKINE CALDWELL WITH VIRGINIA M. CALDWELL

*Afternoons in Mid-America*. New York: Dodd, Mead & Co., 1976.
*Around About America*. New York: Farrar, Straus & Giroux, 1965.

# About the Author

C. J. Stevens is a native of Maine. His poems, stories, articles, Dutch and Flemish translations, and interviews have appeared in approximately five hundred publications worldwide and more than sixty anthologies and textbooks. He has taught at writers' conferences and seminars and has lectured widely. *Storyteller* is his third biography and fourteenth book. Stevens has traveled extensively and has lived in England, Ireland, Holland, Malta, and Portugal.